D1452591

American Silversmiths
and Their Marks
IV

American Silversmiths and Their Marks IV

W.CARMINE.DEL.SCULP

BY

STEPHEN GUERNSEY COOK ENSKO

A revised and enlarged edition
compiled by

DOROTHEA ENSKO WYLE

DAVID R. GODINE

Publisher

Boston

First edition published in 1989 by
David R. Godine, Publisher, Inc.
Horticultural Hall
300 Massachusetts Avenue
Boston, Massachusetts 02115

Library of Congress Catalog Card Number: 88–82003

ISBN: 0–87923–778–3

First Edition
Printed in the United States of America

This final, revised edition is a compilation of the 1915 book written by my grandfather, Robert Ensko, and the 1927, 1937, 1948 books written by my father, Stephen Guernsey Cook Ensko. This book is a tribute to the appreciation, interest and wisdom of all patrons and scholars of Robert Ensko, Inc., to the dedication and excellence of all workers at Robert Ensko, Inc., and to the integrity, enduring love and ceaseless efforts of those who created and continued Robert Ensko, Inc. as a family organization from 1878 to 1970, namely,

ROBERT ENSKO

STEPHEN GUERNSEY COOK ENSKO

DOROTHEA JOHANNA WINTERHOFF ENSKO

CHARLES E. ENSKO

LAMONT N. ENSKO

VERNON CHARLES WYLE

Dorothea Ensko Wyle
1988

CONTENTS

FOREWORD

*T*HE FIRST BOOK to record American silversmiths working between 1650 and 1850 was *Makers of Early American Silver and Their Marks*, compiled and published in 1915 by Robert Ensko (1852–1934). In New York City Directories from 1878 to 1934 Robert Ensko was listed as a dealer in furniture and antiques, and in the 1882 Directory of New Haven, Connecticut, as an auctioneer. His son Stephen shared his interest in antiques, especially American silver, and began working with him about the time that first book came out. The business was located at 598 Madison Avenue, New York, in 1915. In 1920 Robert Ensko purchased the four-story building at 682 Lexington Avenue just south of 57th Street, where the business was carried on in a ground-floor shop and the owner lived upstairs.

In 1927 Stephen Ensko published *American Silversmiths and Their Marks*, enlarging on his father's book, and ten years later he produced a further enlargement titled *American Silversmiths and Their Marks II*. A review of that volume in *The Magazine Antiques* for May 1937 concludes: "The work is quite indispensable and should be acquired without delay not only by every library in the country but by every person who has the least interest in early American silver." In 1948 Ensko *III* appeared, with many additional names and marks, and for years that book has been the invaluable standby of students of early American silver. Now this latest volume, Ensko *IV*, concludes a list of early American craftsmen which has been growing for more than sixty years.

This list is far more than a series of names. It is a record of real people who lived and practiced their craft in colonial America and the early United States. With a little interpretation the brief biographical notes reveal a great deal about who these people were and how they lived and worked.

When, for example, a smith states in his newspaper advertisement that he is "lately arrived from London", we know that he is a recent immigrant who learned his craft in England. Many of the proper names suggest other countries of origin: Dutch and French names are numerous, especially in New York. From addresses in directories and advertisements we learn that the smiths often lived near each other, or under the same roof, and customarily a craftsman's shop was in his house.

Many silversmiths held responsible offices in the local government, such as justice of the peace. Some were vestrymen or deacons of the church. Boston men were members of the Ancient and Honorable Artillery Company, and served in colonial expeditions or the Revolutionary army. Silversmiths were active in craftsmen's organizations: the Charitable Mechanics Association in

Massachusetts, the Gold and Silver Smiths' Company in New York, the Mechanics Society in Philadelphia. At least one woman carried on her husband's business after his death.

Interrelationships of various sorts were frequent. John Coney and Jeremiah Dummer married sisters; Peter Van Dyke married the daughter of his master, Bartholomew Le Roux. Often a lad was apprenticed to his father or uncle or brother-in-law, then in time became the master of his own son or nephew.

There is a pretty parallel between the way the silversmith's craft was perpetuated within a family from one generation to the next, and the way knowledge of early American silver has been pursued and disseminated by successive generations of the Ensko family. The antique silver shop and the book-publishing venture, both launched by Robert Ensko, were continued by his son Stephen, who became a highly respected authority in the field. Consulted by collectors and curators and connoisseurs, he was instrumental in forming many outstanding collections, both public and private. He transformed the dark Lexington Avenue shop into an elegant setting for shining tankards and teapots and all the other beautiful forms in early silver. During my years as editor of *Antiques* I enjoyed dropping in to look and to learn, and I always found Stephen Ensko hospitable and more than generous with helpful information. He pursued his quest for facts about early American silversmiths, devoting hours to research in old records, town and city directories, early newspapers, local histories, and every other possible source of pertinent data. He was always assisted by his wife, Dorothea. In time their daughter Dorothea took part in the research during her college vacations, and later her husband, Vernon Charles Wyle, joined the staff. They all contributed to Ensko *III*.

Now, forty years later, Ensko *IV* appears, concluding the series of related volumes by members of one family. Its publication is a labor of love on the part of Dorothea Ensko Wyle. After her father's death in 1969 she and her husband preserved all his notes and records in order to bring to completion the final book that he had planned to publish. When she had finished her teaching career she undertook the exacting task of collating and editing this material and seeing it through the press.

Ensko *IV* is not offered as the ultimate and definitive work on early American silversmiths and their marks. Perhaps, indeed, a totally complete and accurate reference on the subject can never be achieved. But this book, the mature product of years of research, is comprehensive and highly useful and it contains previously unpublished material not accessible elsewhere. It also includes facsimile pages from each of the previous Ensko books, so that it is a composite of the entire series. As each of its predecessors has been in its turn, this volume is sure to be indispensable to everyone with an interest in early American silver.

Alice Winchester

NEWTOWN, CONNECTICUT
1988

PREFACE

$\mathcal{M}$ Y FATHER, Stephen Guernsey Cook Ensko, began this book immediately upon the publication of his *American Silversmiths and Their Marks III* by writing *Errata* inside the front cover of a copy and listing the names of silversmiths, dates and locations to be corrected or added. He was continuing a procedure started in 1927 and one that he followed as long as he lived. The study of silver dominated his life and he wished everyone to understand and appreciate it. He constantly monitored the sales of the New York auction houses; read and clipped articles in the bulletins and journals of museums and historical societies and periodicals such as *Antiques, American Collector* and *Connoisseur*; traveled to view silver here and abroad; and always my mother was at his side to assist in any way. He recorded his observations in relevant parts of his books to be used at a future date. He updated most of his bibliography and assembled a file of negatives for photographic illustrations but did not complete it before he died. Although he became ill in 1966, he would not retire from Robert Ensko, Inc. In fact, he went to Washington, D.C., in October, 1968, when requested to appraise and inventory the silver in Blair House. His research ended with his death on December 16, 1969. His request that Robert Ensko, Inc. be dissolved upon his death was respected and the doors of 682 Lexington Avenue were closed June 1, 1970.

As my husband and I had worked with my father on *American Silversmiths and Their Marks III*, we appreciated his desire to revise it. The result is this book. Included in it are the marks assembled by my husband when he was on the staff of Robert Ensko, Inc., 1944–1949. He took an active interest in this publication; to my great regret he did not live to see it reach completion.

Dorothea Ensko Wyle

RANDOLPH CENTER, VERMONT
KERRVILLE, TEXAS
1988

xi

ACKNOWLEDGEMENTS

J WISH to express my sincere appreciation to my three sons, Stephen Charles, Bruce Charles and Christopher Charles Wyle, for their support and interest in the development and completion of this book; my special thanks to Christopher for his energy, moral support and knowledgeable contributions in the areas of business, computers and silver.

I am indebted to Kathryn C. Buhler for her gracious, untiring assistance in checking my notes, providing constructive criticism, imparting treasured information and supervising the contents of this presentation until her death in November, 1986.

I desire to thank Alice Winchester for her continued interest and support in the preparation, progress, and culmination of this work.

I appreciate the messages of encouragement provided by Louise Conway Belden, Frances Gruber Safford, Jonathan Fairbanks, Wendell Garrett, and Lilian Carlisle. To family and friends who have provided words of encouragement, I express my thanks. To C. Freeman Keith and Tony Pizzo whose understanding and professional advice guided this effort through the press, thank you.

I am grateful for the cooperation and efforts of the archive, reference and research departments of the following historical societies and libraries: Boston Public Library, Boston, Massachusetts; Butt-Holdsworth Memorial Library, Kerrville, Texas; Dickinson Memorial Library, Northfield, Massachusetts; Greenwich Library, Greenwich, Connecticut; Lebanon Historical Society, Lebanon, New Hampshire; Manchester Historical Society, Manchester-by-the-Sea, Massachusetts; Northampton Historical Society, Northampton, Massachusetts; Rosenberg Library, Galveston, Texas.

I am indebted to my husband, Vernon Charles Wyle, who was enthusiastic about the publication of this book. He consistently monitored its progress and degree of excellence. In his engineering capacity, he programmed the format for the Names and Marks sections. His knowledge and patience during my moments of despair and confusion were invaluable in the completion of this work.

Dorothea Ensko Wyle

Names of Early American Silversmiths
1650–1850

This section presents the names of the silversmiths in alphabetical order. Each silversmith is given the earliest known working date and location, available biographical data, a typed mark or marks which may be referred to in the hand-drawn listing of marks which follows this section.

[A]

JOHN W. ABBOTT (ABBOT) 1790–1850   1817
Portsmouth. N.H. In 1839, at 10 Market Square.
J.ABBOT – J.W.ABBOTT

FRANCIS M. ACKLEY   1797
New York, at 95 Warren Street; Bowery Lane; Henry Street;
1 New Street until 1800.
F.ACKLEY – FMA

GEORGE ACTON   1795
New York at 303 Water Street; Rose Street in 1797.
GA

JOHN ADAM, JR. 1780–1843   1800
Alexandria, Va. Advertised in 1803 as a Goldsmith and
Silversmith on King Street near Royal Street. Was also noted
Musician and Artist.
IA – I.ADAM – JA – J.ADAM

H. ADAMS   1825
Springfield, Mass.
H.ADAMS

NATHAN ADAMS 1755–1825   1785
Wiscasset, Me. Born in Newbury, Mass. Died in Boston.
ADAMS

PYGAN ADAMS 1712–1776   1735
New London, Conn. Son of Rev. Eliphalet Adams. Married Ann
Richards, May 5, 1744. Capt. Adams held prominent public
offices. General Assembly, 1753–1765. Died in New London.
PA

WILLIAM L. ADAMS   1831
New York, at 620 Greenwich Street; 10 Elm Street in 1835.
Noted politician. President of the Board of Aldermen, 1842–3.
In Troy, N.Y., 1844–1850.
W.ADAMS

CHARLES PLATT ADRIANCE 1790–1874   1816
Richmond, Va. Born in Hopewell, N.J. Learned his trade in
Poughkeepsie, N.Y. Married Sarah Camp in 1813. In
Richmond, Va., 1816–1832, when he sold his store to Charles
Gennet, Jr. Returned to Poughkeepsie where he died November
25, 1874.
CPA – C.P.ADRIANCE

3

EDWIN ADRIANCE 1809–1852   1835
St. Louis, Mo. Born in Hopewell, N.Y. Son of Abraham
Adriance and his wife, Anna Storm. Married Elizabeth
O'Connor. Firm of Mead, Adriance & Co.; Mead & Adriance,
1831.
E. ADRIANCE

GEORGE AIKEN 1765–1832   1787
Baltimore, Md., in Calvert Street. Born in Philadelphia. Married
Sarah Leret McConnell, 1803. At 118 Baltimore Street in 1815.
AITKEN – G. AIKEN

JOHN AITKEN   1785
Philadelphia, Pa., at 607 Second Street; 48 Chestnut Street in
1791. No record after 1814. Advertised as, "Gold and Sil-
versmith, Clockmaker, Musical Instrument Manufacturer and
Copper-Plate Engraver".
J. AITKEN

AKERLY & BRIGGS   1845
New York, N.Y.
AKERLY & BRIGGS

JOHN B. AKIN 1820–1860   1850
Danville, Ky.
JOHN B. AKIN

CHARLES ALDIS   1814
New York, at 399 Broadway; 23 Elm Street in 1815.
C. ALDIS

ISAAC ALEXANDER   1850
New York, at 422 Grand Street.
I. ALEXANDER

SAMUEL ALEXANDER   1797
Philadelphia, Pa., at South Second Street until 1808. Firm of
Wiltberger & Alexander, 1797.
SA – S. ALEXANDER

ALEXANDER & RIKER   1797
New York, at 350 Pearl Street until 1798. George Alexander and
Henry Riker dissolved firm, March 15, 1800. "George Alexander
died 29 years of age, Silversmith and Jeweller", *New York Gazette
and General Advertiser*, April 20, 1801.
A & RIKER

ISAAC ALLARD, JR.   1799–1864   1825
Belfast, Me.
I.ALLARD JR

ALLCOCK & ALLEN   1820
New York.
ALLCOCK & ALLEN

CHARLES ALLEN   1760
Boston, Mass.
C.ALLEN

JOHN ALLEN   1671–1760   1695
Boston, Mass. Son of Rev. James Allen. Married Elizabeth
Edwards, sister of John Edwards. Partner of John Edwards,
1700.
IA

ALLEN & EDWARDS   1700
Boston, Mass. John Allen and John Edwards in partnership.
IA IE — IE IA

JONATHAN ALLMY (ALMY)   1746–1821   1770
Newport, R.I. Also worked in New Bedford, Mass.
J.ALLMY

JERONIMUS ALSTYNE   1787
New York. At Maiden Lane until 1797. Married Eyda Beekman.
I.ALSTYNE — JA

WILLIAM ANDERSON   1746
New York. Apprenticed February 17, 1717 to noted Simeon
Soumaine. Freeman of July 1, 1746.
WA

WILLIAM ANDRAS   1795
New York, at 40 William Street. Partner of Samuel Richard,
1797.
ANDRAS

ANDRAS & RICHARD   1797
New York, at 166 Broadway. William Andras and Samuel
Richard. Firm dissolved 1799.
A & R

ANDRAS & CO.   1800
New York
ANDRAS & CO

JOHN ANDREW 1747–1791 1769
Salem, Mass., at "Sign of Golden Cup". Married Elizabeth
Watson in 1769. In Cambridge, 1775, at "Sign of the Anchor".
In Windham, Me., 1789.
I.ANDREW

HENRY ANDREWS 1795
Philadelphia, Pa., at 65 South Second Street. In Boston, 1830.
HA

JEREMIAH ANDREWS 1774
New York. Advertised as "Jeweller from London". In Philadel-
phia, 1776–1780, at Second Street between Chestnut and
Walnut Streets. In Cincinnati, Ohio, 1784–1788; Savannah,
Ga., 1789–1790; Norfolk, Va., 1791, where he died in 1817.
I.ANDREWS – J.ANDREWS

N. ANDRUS & CO. 1834
New York.
N.ANDRUS & CO

ISAAC ANTHONY 1690–1733 1715
Newport, R.I., Born April 10, 1690, son of Abraham and Alice
Wodell Anthony. Advertised as a Goldsmith in the *Boston
Gazette*, March 21, 1737. Died in Newport.
IA – I.ANTHONY

JOSEPH ANTHONY, JR. 1762–1814 1783
Philadelphia, Pa. Born in Newport, R.I., January 15, 1762, son
of Joseph and Elizabeth Sheffield Anthony. Married Henrietta
Hillegas, December 29, 1785. Advertised, *Pennsylvania Journal*,
October 4, 1783: "Joseph Anthony, Junior, In Market Street,
two doors east of the Indian King, begs leave to inform the
Public in general and his friends in particular, that he carries on
the Gold and Silver Smith Business in all its various branches,
where he makes all kinds of work in the most elegant manner."
Shop located at 45 Market Street in 1785; at 74 Market Street in
1796; at 94 High Street from 1798 to 1809 where he admitted
his sons, Michael and Thomas, to the business in 1810. Died in
Harrisburg, Pa.
IA – I.ANTHONY – JA – J.ANTHONY

JOSEPH ANTHONY & SONS 1810
Philadelphia, Pa., at 94 High Street. Firm continued until 1816
with Joseph Anthony, Jr. and sons, Michael and Thomas.
JA & IA

LORENZO D. ANTHONY
Providence, R.I.
ANTHONY

1830

GEORGE B. APPLETON
Salem, Mass.
APPLETON

1850

JAMES APPLETON 1785–1862
Marblehead, Mass. Born in Ipswich, Mass. Married Sarah Fuller
in 1807. In Portland, Me. in 1833. Died in Ipswich.
APPLETON

1823

ALLEN ARMSTRONG
Philadelphia, Pa., 4 North Second Street; 225 Arch Street,
1817.
A.ARMSTRONG

1806

GEORGE ARNOLD
Uxbridge, Mass.
G.ARNOLD

1809

THOMAS ARNOLD 1739–1828
Newport, R.I. Born in Newport. Prominent citizen. Master of
William S. Nichols. Continued in trade until 1796.
ARNOLD – TA – T.ARNOLD

1760

EBENEZER J. AUSTIN 1733–1818
Charlestown, Mass. Born in Charlestown. In Hartford, Conn.
after 1764; New York, 1788. Listed as a Revolutionary Pensioner
in 1818.
AUSTIN – EA – E.J.AUSTIN

1760

JOHN AUSTIN 1751–1825
Hartford, Conn. Born in England. In Philadelphia Directory of
1802 at 33 South Second Street; 69 South Second Street in 1806.
In Charleston, S.C., 1809–1820, at 112 Broad Street.
I.AUSTIN

1770

JOSIAH AUSTIN 1718–1780
Charlestown, Mass. Married Mary Phillips in 1743. Landowner
in 1765. Worked with Samuel Minott in 1768.
IA – I.AUSTIN – J.AUSTIN

1745

NATHANIEL AUSTIN 1743–1818
Boston, Mass. Shop in Fourth Ward. Born in Charlestown,
Mass. Married Ann Kent in 1759. In Directory, 1796–1816.
Died in Boston, October 18, 1818.
AUSTIN – NA

1760

AUSTIN & BOYER
Boston, Mass. Josiah Austin and Daniel Boyer.
IA BOYER — I.AUSTIN BOYER

1770

JOHN AVERY   1732–1794
Preston, Conn. Selftaught silversmith, opened shop in 1760.
Appointed Justice of the Peace. His four sons, John, Robert,
Samuel and William, were silversmiths.
IA — I.AVERY — JA

1760

JOHN AVERY, JR.   1755–1815
Preston, Conn. Son of John Avery. Married Lucy Ayer in 1779.
IA

1780

ROBERT STAUNTON AVERY   1771–1846
Preston, Conn. Son of John Avery. Served in the War of 1812
and became a Captain.
RA

1807

SAMUEL AVERY   1760–1836
Preston, Conn. Son of John Avery. Continued his father's busi-
ness with his brothers.
SA — S.AVERY

1786

SAMUEL AYERS   1767–1824
Lexington, Ky. Advertised, *Kentucky Gazette*, 1790, "In Shop on
Main Street, nearly opposite Mr. Collins Tavern". Offers shop for
sale in 1819. Died in September, 1824.
S.AYERS

1805

[B]

CHARLES BABBITT
Taunton, Mass.
C.BABBITT

1815

SAMUEL BABCOCK   1788–1857
Middletown, Conn. Shop located North of Episcopal Church.
Born in Saybrook where he was Collector of Customs.
BABCOCK

1812

A. BACHMAN
New York.
BACHMAN

1848

DELUCINE BACKUS   1792
New York, at 12 Crown Street. Firm of Cady and Backus.
Samuel Cady and Delucine Backus at 219 Queen Street until
1793.
D.BACKUS

H. B. & H. M. BACON   1845
Lowell, Mass.
H.B & H.M.BACON

SILAS D. BACON   1830
Boston, Mass.
S.D.BACON

BACON & SMITH   1840
Boston, Mass.
BACON & SMITH

BRADBURY M. BAILEY   1824–1913   1848
Ludlow, Vt. Apprenticed to Rosewell H. Bailey in Woodstock,
Vt. In Rutland, 1854. Died in Brooklyn, N.Y.
B.M.BAILEY

EBENEZER EATON BAILEY   1825
Portland, Me. In West Unity and Claremont, N.H., 1835. Firm
of E. E. & S. C. BAILEY.
E.E.BAILEY

E. E. & S. C. BAILEY   1830
Portland, Me. Later in West Unity and Claremont, N.H.
E.E. & S.C.BAILEY

E. L. BAILEY & CO.   1835
Claremont, N.H.
E.L.BAILEY & CO

HENRY BAILEY   1800
Boston, Mass., Directory, 1803.
HB

JOHN BAILEY   −1785   1762
New York. Silversmith and swordmaker. Advertised in Dela-
ware.
I.BAILEY

JOHN BAILEY, III   1787–1883   1810
Portland, Me. Born in Hanover, Mass. where he returned in
1811. In New Bedford, Mass., 1824.
J.BAILEY

LORING BAILEY 1740–1814   1801
Hingham, Mass. Born in Hull, Mass. Married, 1807. Caleb
Gill, Levitt Gill and Samuel Norton served apprenticeships.
Nicknamed "Thankful Loring" by townspeople.
L B

ROSWELL H. BAILEY 1804–1886   1840
Woodstock, Vt. B. M. Bailey, cousin and brother-in-law, was an
apprentice.
R. H. BAILEY

WILLIAM BAILEY   1816
Philadelphia, Pa.
W. BAILEY

BAILEY & CO.   1848
Philadelphia, Pa., at 136 Chestnut Street.
BAILEY & CO

BAILEY & KITCHEN   1833
Philadelphia, Pa., until 1846.
BAILEY & KITCHEN – B & K

ELEAZER BAKER 1764–1849   1785
Ashford, Conn. Advertised as clock and watchmaker and gold
and silversmith.
E. BAKER

GEORGE BAKER   1811
Providence, R.I., from Salem, Mass. In Providence Directory in
1825.
G. BAKER – GEORGE BAKER

STEPHEN BAKER 1787–1856   1830
New York.
S. BAKER

THOMAS BAKER 1793–1820   1819
Concord, Mass.
T. BAKER

EBENEZER BALCH 1723–1808   1750
Hartford, Conn. Born in Boston. In Wethersfield, Conn. in
1756.
E. BALCH

EBENEZER BALDWIN   1810
Hartford, Conn., until 1819.
BALDWIN

H. E. BALDWIN & CO.   1825
New Orleans, La.
H.E.BALDWIN & CO

JABEZ C. BALDWIN 1777–1819   1800
Boston, Mass. Married Ann Briggs, 1804. Brother of Jedediah.
Partner of John B. Jones in 1813.
BALDWIN – J.BALDWIN – J.C.BALDWIN

JEDEDIAH BALDWIN 1769–1849   1791
Northampton, Mass. Born in Norwich, Conn. Apprenticed to
Thomas Harland. Married Abigail Jones, April 18, 1791.
Advertised in Northampton, Mass. in 1791. In Hanover, N.H.,
he advertised in *Spooner's Journal*, October 7, 1793: "Clocks and
watches made and repaired together with plate and jewelry in
their various branches. The subscriber most respectfully informs
the inhabitants of the town of Hanover, and the towns adjacent
and the public at large, that having served a regular apprenticeship at the above branches of the business, he now proposes
carrying them on in the town of Hanover, in the vicinity of
Dartmouth College, a few rods south of the printing office. He
hopes for the patronage and employment of those who have
occasion for his labor in any of the above branches, but expects
no further than he may be found by his fidelity, punctuality and
moderate charges to merit them. N.B. The highest price given
for old Gold, Silver, Brass, Copper and Pewter. A load of coal is
wanted." In Fairfield, N.Y., 1811; Morrisville, N.Y., 1818;
Rochester, N.Y., 1834, where he died.
I.BALDWIN

S. BALDWIN   1810
Boston, Mass.
S.BALDWIN

STANLEY S. BALDWIN   1820
New York, at Franklin Square.
STANLEY S.BALDWIN

BALDWIN & CO.   1830
Newark, N.J.
BALDWIN & CO

BALDWIN & JONES   1813
Boston, Mass. Jabez Baldwin and John Jones. Directory, 1816–
20.
BALDWIN & JONES

JEDEDIAH & STORRS BALDWIN   1800
Rochester, N.Y.
J & S.BALDWIN

BALL, BLACK & CO.   1850
New York.
BALL BLACK & CO

BALL & HEALD   1812
Baltimore, Md. Later in York, Pa.
BALL & HEALD

JOHN BALL   1763
Concord, Mass., advertised in *Boston News Letter*, March 17, as
goldsmith, until 1767.
I.BALL – J.BALL – JOHN BALL

SHELDON BALL   1821
Buffalo, N.Y., until 1836.
S.BALL

BALL, TOMPKINS & BLACK   1839
New York. Successors to Marquand & Co. In 1851, Ball, Black
& Co.; 1876, Black, Starr & Frost.
BALL TOMPKINS & BLACK – B.T & B

WILLIAM BALL   1729–1810   1759
Philadelphia, Pa. Said to have learned trade in London and was a
member of The Guild. Advertised in the *Pennsylvania Gazette*,
August 30, 1795, the *Pennsylvania Journal*, November, 1759, as
Silversmith. Notice in May, 1761, "going to England". Returned
in 1765 and located on Front Street, corner of Market, until
1771. A Mason in Lodge #2 Moderns in 1750; with the #2
Ancients in 1760 to become First Grandmaster of Ancients for
twenty years. The press called him the "Venerable Patriarch of
Masonry". Buried in First Baptist Church.
BALL – WB

WILLIAM BALL, JR.   1763–1825   1789
Baltimore, Md. Son of William Ball of Philadelphia. Married
Elizabeth Dukehart in 1790. Advertised dissolution of the
partnership of Johnson & Ball in 1790. Located at the "Sign of
the Golden Urn" in 1793. Listed in Directory at Market Street,
1796–1815. Firm of Ball & Heald. First to use term, Sterling.
WB – W.BALL

ADRIAN BANCKER   1703–1772   1725
New York. Born October 10, son of Everett, Mayor of Albany,
and Elizabeth Abeel. Married in New York, January 31, 1728,
Gertrude E. Van Taerling. Served apprenticeship with Hendrick
Boelen. Freeman, 1731. Advertised at Bridge Street in 1766.
Appointed Collector of South Ward, 1733–6. Died August 21,
1772.
A B

I. L. BANGS & CO.   1810
Woonsocket, R.I.
I.L.BANGS & CO

JOHN J. BANGS   1825
Cincinnati, Ohio., until 1829.
J.J.BANGS

CONRAD BARD   1825
Philadelphia, Pa., at Chestnut Street until 1850. Firms of Bard
& Hoffman, 1837; Bard & Lamont, 1841.
C.BARD

J. BARD   1800
Philadelphia, Pa.
J.BARD

BARD & LAMONT   1841
Philadelphia, Pa., at 205 Mulberry Street until 1845.
BARD & LAMONT

GEORGE BARDICK   1790
Philadelphia, Pa., Census List of 1790. Located at Wagner's
Alley, next to shop of brother, John.
G B

BARKER & MUMFORD   1817
Newport, R.I.
BARKER & MUMFORD — B & M

JAMES BARRETT   1805
New York.
I B

JOSEPH BARRETT   1753
Nantucket, Mass.
I B

SAMUEL BARRETT 1775
Nantucket, Mass., until 1800.
S. BARRETT

DAVID BARRIERE 1806
Baltimore, Md. Son of Anthony Barriere. Apprenticed to Louis
Buichle and Simon Wedge, 1799.
D. BARRIERE

BARRINGTON & DAVENPORT 1806
Philadelphia, Pa., at 112 South Second Street.
B & D

JAMES MADISON BARROWS 1809– 1828
Tolland, Conn. Born in Mansfield, Conn.
J. M. BARROWS

STANDISH BARRY 1763–1844 1784
Baltimore, Md. Born, November 4, son of Lavallin Barry, Irish.
Apprenticed to David Evans. Married Agnes Thompson in
1788. Advertised at Market Street in 1784. Dissolved partner-
ship with Joseph Rice, 1787. Listed at Baltimore Street and later
North Gay Street, 1796–1808, when he became a merchant.
Was prominent in public affairs. Colonel of First Rifle Regiment.
Portrait was painted by Rembrandt Peale.
BARRY – SB – STANDISH

ROSWELL BARTHOLOMEW 1781–1830 1805
Hartford, Conn. Born in Harwinton. Apprenticed to Beach &
Ward. Partner of James Ward, 1804. Firm of Ward, Bar-
tholomew & Brainard, 1809.
RB

ISRAEL BARTLET 1748–1838 1800
Newbury, Mass. Later in Haverhill, Mass. Elected State Senator.
I. BARTLET

EDWARD M. BARTLETT 1836
Westchester, Pa. In Philadelphia Directory, 1843.
E. M. BARTLETT

NATHANIEL BARTLETT 1760
Concord, Mass.
NB – N. BARTLETT

SAMUEL BARTLETT 1752–1821 1775
Boston, Mass. Born in Concord, Mass. Married Mary Barrett,
1775. Elected Register of Deeds in Cambridge in 1795 which
office he held until he died, September 21.
SB – S. BARTLETT

BENJAMIN BARTON   –1816   1801
Alexandria, Va. In 1816, business continued by son, Thomas,
who died in 1821; then by his son, Benjamin Barton, 2nd.
B.BARTON

ERASTUS BARTON & CO.   1822
New York, at 166 Broadway.
E.B & CO

JOSEPH BARTON   1764–1832   1790
Stockbridge, Mass. In Utica, N.Y., 1804.
J.BARTON

WILLIAM BARTRAM   1769
Philadelphia, Pa. Advertised in the *Pennsylvania Chronicle*, June
1769, on Front Street, at the "Sign of the Golden Cup and
Crown".
WB

FRANCIS BASSETT   1774
New York.
BASSETT

BASSETT & WARFORD   1800
Albany, N.Y. Nehemiah Bassett, 1770–1844, and Joseph
Warford, 1779–1847, in partnership until 1805.
BASSETT & WARFORD

ALBERT T. BATTEL   1795–   1840
Utica, N.Y. Firm of Davies & Battel, 1844–1850.
A.T.BATTEL

HENRY BAYEUX   –1839   1801
Troy, N.Y., until 1812.
BAYEUX

BAYLEY & DOUGLAS   1798
New York, at 136 Broadway. Simeon A. Bayley and James
Douglas. Dissolved notices, January 25, 1800, *General
Advertiser*, and, October 22, 1801, *American Citizen*.
DB & AD

SIMEON A. BAYLEY   1789
New York, at Old Slip; 94 Market Street in 1794. Firm of
Bayley & Douglas, 1798.
BAYLEY

JOHN BAYLY   −1789   1755
Philadelphia, Pa. In 1755, at the "Sign of the Tea Pot" on the
lower end of Front Street, near the Drawbridge. Removed to
Front and Chestnut Streets in 1756. Advertised there in 1767.
Took a trip to England in the fall of 1771 and advertised a
settlement of all debts. Notice appeared November 5, 1783,
Pennsylvania Gazette: "At the Tea Pot in Fetter-Lane, he carries on
his business in all its branches as formerly, at the Corner of Front
and Chestnut Streets, and will be obliged to his old customers
for the continuance of their favors." Located at Cherry Alley in
1785.
IB − I. BAYLY

A. BEACH   1823
Hartford, Conn.
A. BEACH

MILES BEACH   1742−1828   1771
Litchfield, Conn., until 1785. Born in Goshen. Moved to
Hartford and formed partnership with Isaac Sanford. Dissolved
by mutual agreement, June 28, 1788. Worked with James
Ward, a former apprentice, 1789, at ten rods south of the
Bridge. Served in the Revolutionary War as Colonel. Chief of
Hartford Fire Department, 1789−1805. Died in Hartford.
BEACH − MB

BEACH & SANFORD   1785
Hartford, Conn. Col. Miles Beach and Isaac Sanford in partner-
ship until 1788.
B & S

BEACH & WARD   1789
Hartford, Conn. Miles Beach and James Ward. Advertised,
American Mercury, May 24, 1790; "Continued to carry on the
Silver and Gold Smith's Business, Brass Founding, Clock and
Watchmaking, and etc. at their shop south of the Bridge." Last
Notice, January 17, 1795. Dissolution of firm, 1797.
B & W

CALEB BEAL   1746−1801   1796
Hingham, Mass. Boston, 1796−1800.
BEAL − CB − C. BEAL

DUNCAN BEARD   −1797   1765
Appoquinimink Hundred, Del. Charter member of Masonic
Lodge #5. Noted Mason, twice Grand Master.
DB

W. D. BEASOM & CO.   1840
Nashua, N.H.
W.D.BEASOM & CO

E. A. BEAUVAIS   1840
St. Louis, Mo.
E.A.BEAUVAIS

RENE BEAUVAIS   1838
St. Louis, Mo.
R.BEAUVAIS

PHILLIP BECKER   1764
Lancaster, Pa.
PB

JOHN BEDFORD   1757–1834   1782
Fishkill, N.Y., advertised on Main Street.
I.BEDFORD – JB – J.BEDFORD

JAMES W. BEEBE   1835
New York, at 89 Reade Street.
J.W.BEEBE

JAMES W. BEEBE & CO.   1844
New York.
J.W.BEEBE & CO

WILLIAM BEEBE   1850
New York, at 102 Reade Street.
BEEBE

CLEMENT BEECHER   1778–1869   1801
Berlin, Conn., advertised in 1801. Born in Cheshire where he
returned in 1818.
CB – C.BEECHER

JOSEPH BELL   1817
New York, until 1824.
I.BELL – J.BELL

S. W. BELL   1837
Philadelphia, Pa.
S.BELL

THOMAS W. BELL   1837
Petersburg, Va. From Philadelphia, Pa. Advertised watches,
jewelry and silverware until 1848 when he sold his business to
Thomas Nowlan.
T.W.BELL

BUTLER BEMENT   1784–1869   1810
Pittsfield, Mass.
B.BEMENT – BEMENT

ANDREW C. BENEDICT   1840
New York, at 28 Bowery Lane.
A.C.BENEDICT

BENEDICT & SCUDDER   1827
New York.
BENEDICT & SCUDDER

BENEDICT & SQUIRE   1839
New York.
BENEDICT & SQUIRE

BARZILLAI BENJAMIN   1774–1844   1815
Bridgeport, Conn., worked with George Kippen. Born in
Milford, Conn. In New Haven at Chapel and Church Streets in
shop formerly occupied by Robert Fairchild, 1825–1827. Son,
Everard, took over business as Everard Benjamin & Co. in 1829.
BB – B.BENJAMIN

EVERARD BENJAMIN   1807–1874   1830
New Haven, Conn. Son of Barzillai, whose business he continued
after 1829. Partner of George H. Ford.
E.BENJAMIN

EVERARD BENJAMIN & CO.   1830
New Haven, Conn.
E.B & CO – E.BENJAMIN & CO

JOHN BENJAMIN   1731–1796   1752
Stratford, Conn. Born in Stratford. Apprenticed to Robert
Fairchild. Served as an organist in the Episcopal Church when
sixteen years of age. Married Lucretia Backus of Windham.
Town Treasurer in 1777. Took part in the Battle of Ridgefield.
Promoted from Captain to Major in 1782 and, later, to Colonel.
Died, September 14, 1796.
IB

BENNETT & THOMAS   1812
Petersburg, Va., until 1819. John Bennett and Ebenezer
Thomas.
BENNETT & THOMAS

THOMAS BENTLEY   1764–1804   1786
Boston, Mass., at Distill House Lane, 1789–1798. Apprenticed
to Stephen Emery. In Directory, 1796–1803, at Salvation Alley.
BENTLEY – TB

E. BERARD   1800
Philadelphia, Pa. Brother of Andrew.
E.BERARD

THAUVET BESLEY   –1757   1727
New York. Freeman, December 17, 1727. Advertised, *New York
Post Boy*, November, 1746, "House on Golden Hill". Also
mentioned in 1749.
TB

FRANCIS BICKNELL   1818
Rome, N.Y., until 1831.
F.BICKNELL

HENRY BIERSHING   1790–1843   1815
Hagerstown, Md., until 1843.
HB

BIGELOW BROS & KENNARD   1845
Boston, Mass.
BIGELOW BROS & KENNARD

BIGELOW & BROTHERS   1840
Boston, Mass. John Alanson and Abram O. in business in Wash-
ington Street.
BIGELOW & BROTHERS

JOHN BIGELOW   1830
Boston, Mass. Advertised on Washington Street next to Old
State House.
JOHN BIGELOW

GILBERT BIGGER   1751–1816   1783
Baltimore, Md. Watchmaker, clockmaker, silversmith from
Dublin, Ireland. Firm of Bigger & Clarke, 1783.
BIGGER

ANDREW BILLINGS   (BILLING)   1743–1808   1773
Poughkeepsie, N.Y. Born in Stonington, Conn. Property owner
in 1788. Listed with wife and nine children in First Federal
Census. President of Village in 1803.
AB – A.BILLINGS

DANIEL BILLINGS   1795
Preston, Conn. Shop located at Poquettannock Village.
D.BILLINGS

CHARLES BILLON   1821
St. Louis, Mo.
C.BILLON

JOHN STILES BIRD   1794–1887   1825
Charleston, S.C.
J.S.BIRD

JOHN BIRGE   1780–1859   1805
Brattleboro, Vt. Advertised until 1842.
J.BIRGE

BIRGE, BRACKETT & CO.   1840
Brattleboro, Vt. John Birge and Horace D. Brackett.
BIRGE BRACKETT & CO

JAMES BLACK   1795
Philadelphia, Pa., until 1819 at Second and Chestnut Streets.
I.BLACK – JB

FREDERICK STARR BLACKMAN   1810–1898   1830
Danbury, Conn. Son of John Starr Blackman and brother of John
Clark.
F.S.BLACKMAN

FREDERICK S. BLACKMAN & CO.   1840
Danbury, Conn.
F.S.B & CO

JOHN CLARK BLACKMAN   1808–1872   1827
Bridgeport, Conn. Son of John Starr Blackman.
BLACKMAN

JOHN CLARK BLACKMAN & CO.   1835
Bridgeport, Conn.
J.C.B & CO

JOHN STARR BLACKMAN   1775–1851   1805
Danbury, Conn. Shop located south of the Court House. Son,
Frederick, continued the business.
J.BLACKMAN – J.S.B

ASA BLANCHARD   –1838   1808
Lexington, Ky., at Mill and Short Streets.
A.BLANCHARD

JURIAN BLANCK, JR. 1645–1714 1666

New York. Baptised, April 9, 1645. Son of Jeuriaen Blanck,
Goutsmidt, Freeman, N.Y.C., 1657, died ca. 1673, and Tryntse
Claes, married before 1643. Admitted to Membership of the
Dutch Reformed Church in 1668. Appointed City Censor of
Weights and Measures in 1672. Married Hester Vanderbeek,
October 25, 1673. Taxed for property in New York and Brooklyn
in 1679. Freeman, December 18, 1695. Beaker, 1684, in Yale
Gallery. Witness to Baptism of Grandson, December, 1699.
I B

BLEASOM & REED 1830

Portsmouth, N.H.
BLEASOM & REED

JONATHAN BLISS 1800

Middletown, Conn.
I. BLISS

JOHN M. BLONDEL (BLONDELL) 1814

Baltimore, Md., until 1824.
J.M.BLONDEL

JOHN BLOWERS 1710–1748 1731

Boston, Mass. Born in Beverly, son of Rev. Thomas Blowers.
Married Sarah Slater, 1735. Advertised 1738, 1746, *Boston
Gazette*.
BLOWERS

CHARLES LOUIS BOEHME 1774–1868 1799

Baltimore, Md., advertised at 15 Market Street. Directory,
1801–1812. Ad, "Continues to manufacture goods of Sterling
Silver at nearly one third less price than that which is imported."
Later, became a wine merchant.
C.BOEHME – CLB – C.L.BOEHME

HENDRICK BOELEN (HENRICUS BOELEN, I) 1685
1661–1691

New York. Baptised, Dutch Church, N.Y., February 6, 1661.
Son of Boelen Roelofssen and Bayken Arents. Married Anna
Barents Court, 1686. She married, secondly, in 1692, Abraham
Keteltas whose son, baptised in 1688, became a prominent
merchant. Brother of Jacob Boelen.
H B

HENRICUS BOELEN, II   1697–1755   1718

New York. Baptised May 5, 1697, son of Jacob and Catharina
Clock. Married Jannette Waldron, baptised September 7, 1698,
on June 19, 1718. Member of Dutch Church, 1725. Was willed
father's business in 1729. His will: G.S. Sick. Dated August 11,
1755. Witnessed Jacob Goelet. Proved September 22, 1755.
Confirmed by Sir Chas. Hardy Knight, Governor. Estate to
Jannette, after her death, to Children, Joseph, Anna, wife of
Christian Frederick Arter, and Catharine, all Executors.
H B

JACOB BOELEN   1654–1729   1680

New York. Born in Amsterdam and emigrated with parents in
1659. Admitted as a member of the Dutch Church, 1676.
Married Katharina Klock, baptised N.Y. 1654, daughter of
Abraham Clock and Tryntse Alberts, May 21, 1679. Appointed
Alderman of North Ward, 1695–7–1701, and held other impor-
tant offices. Admitted Freeman, July 19, 1689. Made Gold Box
for New York City, 1702. His shop, near Hanover Square, willed
to his son, Henricus. His will, dated July 31, 1725, was proved
March 23, 1729/30.
I B

JACOB BOELEN, II   1733–1786   1755

New York. Son of Henricus, baptised September 12, 1733.
Married, April 4, 1764, (1) Magdalena Blauw, (2) Mary
Ryckman, August 31, 1773. Headed a List of Petition to
Governor of New York, dated November 27, 1783.
I B

JACOB BOELEN, III   1785

New York.
I B

EVERARDUS BOGARDUS   1675–1739   1698

New York. Baptised December 4, 1675, son of Wilhemus
Bogardus and second wife, Walburg De Silla, widow of Fras
Keiger. Freeman of July 5, 1698. Married Ann Dally, June 3,
1704. Died November 8, 1739. Buried in Montrepose Ceme-
tery, Rondout, Ulster County, N.Y.
E B

NICHOLAS J. BOGERT   1801

New York, at 10 Lombard Street.
N.BOGERT — N.J.BOGERT

WILLIAM BOGERT   1839
Albany, N.Y., until 1847.
W. BOGERT

BOLLES & DAY   1825
Hartford, Conn.
BOLLES & DAY

CHARLES BOND   1840
Boston, Mass.
C. BOND

WILLIAM BONING   1845
Philadelphia, Pa.
W. BONING

TIMOTHY BONTECOU   1693–1784   1725
New Haven, Conn. Born June 7, 1693, of Huguenot descent,
son of Pierre and Marguerite Bontecou. Baptised in the French
Church, N.Y., July 2, 1693. Learned his trade in France. Assessed £10 North Ward, N.Y.C., 1730. In Stratford, Conn.,
1735, became a member of the Church of England. Married
second wife in 1736. Contributed £15 to a new church built in
Stratford in 1743. In New Haven, 1748, on the west side of
Fleet Street. Was first Warden of Trinity Church in 1765. Advertised shop for sale in 1775. Died as a result of injuries received
during the British invasion in 1784.
TB

TIMOTHY BONTECOU, JR.   1723–1789   1747
New Haven, Conn. Born in Stratford, Conn., where he learned
the silversmith trade from his father. Married Susanna Prout,
November 5, 1747.
TB

EZRA B. BOOTH   1805–1888   1829
Middlebury, Vt. Married Desire Miller, 1832. In Rochester,
N.Y., 1838–1850, in partnership with Erastus Cook.
E. B. BOOTH

E. B. BOOTH & SON   1850
Rochester, N.Y. Ezra B. Booth and son.
E. B. BOOTH & SON

E. BORHEK   1835
Philadelphia, Pa.
E. BORHEK

ZALMON BOSTWICK   1846
New York, at 128 William Street.
Z.BOSTWICK

SAMUEL BOSWORTH   1816
Buffalo, N.Y., until 1837.
BOSWORTH

GIDEON B. BOTSFORD   1776–1856   1797
Woodbury, Conn. His shop and home now owned by the
Episcopal Diocese of Connecticut.
G.B.BOTSFORD

ELIAS BOUDINOT   1706–1770   1740
Philadelphia, Pa. Born in New York, July 8, 1706, son of Elias
and Marie Catharine Carre Boudinot. Baptised in the French
Church, July 19, 1706. Apprenticed to Simeon Soumaine for
seven years, June 6, 1721, age fifteen. Removed to Antigua
where he was married, August 8, 1729, to Susannah LeRoux; in
1733, to Catherine Williams. Removed to Philadelphia where
he advertised until 1752. In Princeton, N.J., 1753–1760. After
1761, in Elizabethtown, N.J., where he died, July 4, 1770.
Father of the Hon. Elias Boudinot, President of the Continental
Congress.
EB

HELOISE BOUDO   1827
Charleston, S.C. Continued the business of her husband, Louis,
until 1837, when her daughter, Erma Leroy, advertised for trade.
H.BOUDO

LOUIS BOUDO   1786–1827   1810
Charleston, S.C. Born in St. Domingo. Partnership with Manuel
Boudo dissolved in 1810. Advertised at Queen and King Streets,
1809–1827. His widow, Heloise, continued the business.
BOUDO – LS.BOUDO

STEPHEN BOURDETT   1730
New York. Married Hannah Earle, daughter of English Earle of
Bergen and Else Vreedlant, widow of Peter Stoutenburgh,
brother of Tobias, in 1720, in Reformed Church, Hackensack,
N.J. Admitted to Freedom of New York City, August 4, 1730,
as a Silversmith. Witness to Indenture signed by Goldsmith,
Peter Van Inburgh, 1739.
SB

JOHN BOUTIER   1805
New York, Directory until 1824. His widow continued until
1826.
J.BOUTIER

C. BOWER   1828
Philadelphia, Pa., Directory until 1833.
BOWER

ELIAS BOWMAN   1834
Rochester, N.Y.
E.BOWMAN

SAMUEL BOWNE   −1819   1780
New York, at 81 John Street. Married Mary Steeker, November
7, 1778. Bankrupt notices: *New York Evening Post*, July 19,
1802; *Commercial Advertiser*, July 21, 1802; *New York Herald*,
August 25, 1802, "House sold, June 21, 1802, to pay mortgage
on 81 John Street."
S.BOWNE

GERARDUS BOYCE   1795–1880   1814
New York, at 101 Spring Street until 1830. Firm of Boyce &
Jones, 1825.
GB−G.BOYCE

JOHN BOYCE   1801
New York, at Bowery Lane.
JB

BOYCE & JONES   1825
New York. Gerardus Boyce and Elisha Jones advertised at 101
Spring Street.
G.BOYCE E.JONES

JOSEPH W. BOYD   1820
New York.
JWB

BOYD & MULFORD   1832
Albany, New York. William Boyd and John H. Mulford dis-
solved partnership in 1842.
BOYD & MULFORD

JOSEPH BOYDEN   1801–1887   1825
Worcester, Mass. Born in Auburn, Mass. Partner of William D.
Fenno, 1825. Died in Worcester.
J.BOYDEN

BOYDEN & FENNO   1825
Worcester, Mass. Joseph Boyden and William D. Fenno.
BOYDEN & FENNO

DANIEL BOYER   1726–1779   1750
Boston, Mass. Married Elizabeth Bulfinch in 1749. Served as
Court Clerk, 1754–8. Sergeant of the Artillery Company, 1762.
Advertised, *Massachusetts Gazette*, October 30, 1766, "Opposite
the Governor's." Located near the Province House in 1773.
BOYER – DB

BOYER & AUSTIN   1770
Boston, Mass. Daniel Boyer and Josiah Austin in partnership.
IA BOYER

HORACE D. BRACKETT   1842
Brattleboro, Vt., until 1856.
H.D.BRACKETT

JEFFREY R. BRACKETT   1840
Boston, Mass.
JEFFREY R.BRACKETT

THEOPHILUS BRADBURY   1763–1803   1792
Newburyport, Mass. Married Lois Pillsbury, October 3, 1792.
TB

THEOPHILUS BRADBURY, II   1793–1848   1815
Newburyport, Mass. In Boston Directory, 1821.
B – BRADBURY

THEOPHILUS BRADBURY & SON   1815
Newburyport, Mass. Theophilus Bradbury and son, Theophilus
Bradbury, II.
BRADBURY

ABNER BRADLEY   1753–1824   1778
Watertown, Conn. Born in New Haven, Conn., where he learned
his trade. Brother of Phineas. Revolutionary hero, retiring as
Colonel of Militia, after serving at Crown Point, Ticonderoga
and in the Danbury Raid of 1778.
A.BRADLEY

LUTHER BRADLEY   1772–1830   1798
New Haven, Conn. Son of Phineas and Hannah Buel Bradley.
LB

PHINEAS BRADLEY 1745–1797   1770
New Haven, Conn. Born in Litchfield, Conn. Brother of Abner.
House and shop on Crown Street. Was Captain in Revolutionary
War.
P B

ZEBUL BRADLEY 1780–1859   1810
New Haven, Conn. Born in Guilford, Conn. Apprenticed to
Marcus Merriman. In Hiram Lodge, # 1, Mason, March 15,
1804. In partnership with Marcus Merriman in 1806. Worked
with Merriman, Jr., 1826–1848.
Z. BRADLEY

BRADLEY & MERRIMAN   1826
New Haven, Conn., until 1847, listed in New Haven Directory.
Zebul Bradley and Marcus Merriman, Jr.
B & M

E. BRADY   1825
New York.
BRADY – E. BRADY

F. BRADY   1800
Norwalk, Conn.
F. BRADY

SYLVANUS BRAMHALL   1800
Plymouth, Mass.
S. BRAMHALL

CHARLES BRANDA   1818
Norfolk, Va., until 1829.
C. BRANDA

AIME & CHARLES BRANDT   1800
Philadelphia, Pa., until 1814.
A & C. BRANDT

A. BRASHER   1790
New York. Worked at 79 Queen Street.
A. BRASHER

EPHRAIM BRASHER 1744–1810   1766
New York. Son of Ephraim and Catharina Van Keuren Brasher.
Baptised in the Dutch Church, N.Y., April 18, 1744. Married
Ann Gilbert, sister of William Gilbert, silversmith, in the

Dutch Church, November 8, 1766. Member of the Gold and
Silversmiths Society, 1786. Minted the famous "Brasher
Doubloon". Advertised at 5 Cherry Street. Firm of Brasher &
Alexander. *American Citizen and General Advertiser*, February 21,
1801, "Dissolved partnership of Ephraim Brasher and George
Alexander at 350 Pearl Street".
BRASHER—EB

AMABLE BRASIER   1794
Philadelphia, Pa., at 12 South Third Street until 1828.
A.BRASIER

WILLIAM BREED   —CA. 1761   1740
Boston, Mass. Married Susanna Barrington, October 20, 1743.
WB—W.BREED

BENJAMIN BRENTON 1695–1749   1717
Newport, R.I. Freeman, 1717. Born September 8. Married
Mary Butts, November 12, 1719. Died April 2, 1749.
BB

BENJAMIN BRENTON 1710–1766   1732
Newport, R.I. Born October 16, 1710 in Newport. Married
Alice Baker, 1732, in Trinity Church. Active in military affairs
of the Colony.
BB

JOHN BREVOORT 1715–1775   1742
New York. Freeman, October 23, 1742. Son of Elias and
Margaret Sammans Brevoort. Baptised on May 1, 1715. Married
Louisa Kockerthal in 1739. Whitehead Hicks, Mayor of New
York, son-in-law, was granted letter of administration of will,
March 3, 1775.
IBV

C. BREWER & CO.   1815
Middletown, Conn.
C.BREWER & CO

CHARLES BREWER 1778–1860   1810
Middletown, Conn. Born in Springfield, Mass. Apprenticed to
Jacob Sargeant of Hartford, Conn. Firm of Hart & Brewer,
1800–1803. Later, Brewer & Mann, 1803–1805; C. Brewer &
Co., 1815.
C.BREWER

ABEL BREWSTER   1775–1807   1797
Canterbury, Conn. Born in Preston, Conn. In Norwich, Conn.
in 1804. Due to illness, sold business to Judah Hart and Alvan
Willcox in 1805.
BREWSTER

JOHN BRIDGE   1723–1794   1751
Boston, Mass. Sergeant of Artillery Company, 1748. Constable
in 1752.
BRIDGE

TIMOTHY BRIGDEN   1774–1819   1813
Albany, N.Y., until 1816 at 106 Beaver Street. Member of the
Albany Mechanics' Society.
TB

ZACHARIAH BRIGDEN   1734–1787   1760
Boston, Mass. Born in Charlestown, Mass. First wife, daughter
of Thomas Edwards to whom he was apprenticed, died May 30,
1768. Married Elizabeth Gillem, January 2, 1774. Advertised
shop on Corn Hill. Paid $20 Assessor's Taking Tax, 1780. Died
March 11. Estate appraised by Benjamin Burt, silversmith.
ZB

ABRAHAM BRINSMAID   1770–1841   1796
Burlington, Vt. Married Elizabeth Bliss, 1807; second, Sarah
Smedley, 1836. Firm of Brinsmaid & Bliss, 1805–1809. Three
sons followed their father's trade: James, Sedgewick and
William.
A.BRINSMAID – BRINSMAID

BRINSMAID & HILDRETH   1850
Burlington, Vt.
B & H

JACOB BRITTIN   1807
Philadelphia, Pa. Worked at 46 North Second Street until 1813;
at Greene Street until 1835. In Directory until 1850.
J.BRITTIN

JOHN BROCK   1833
New York.
I.BROCK – J.BROCK

L. BROCK   1830
New York.
L.BROCK

JOHN BRONAUGH   1817
Richmond, Va., until 1827.
BRONAUGH

ROBERT BROOKHOUSE   1779–1866   1800
Salem, Mass., at Old Paved Street. Purchased the Benjamin
Pickman mansion on Washington Street, built in 1763, from
last owner, Elias Hasket Derby. Retired from silversmithing in
1819.
BROOKHOUSE – RB

SAMUEL BROOKS   1793
Philadelphia, Pa. Advertised, *Federal Gazette*, June 10, 1793,
"At 29 South Front Street, not to be excell'd by any of his profes-
sion on the Continent". In Norfolk, Va., 1794–1796. Returned
to Philadelphia, on Church Street, 1796–1802. In Richmond,
Va., 1803–1820, as Goldsmith, Seal Cutter, Engraver and
Copperplate Printer.
BROOKS

BROOKS & WARROCK   1795
Norfolk, Va., until 1796. Samuel Brooks and William Warrock
at the "Sign of the Dove and Locket", on Market Street, three
doors above Church Street.
BROOKS & WARROCK

S. & B. BROWER   1810
Albany, N.Y., until 1850.
S & B.BROWER

S. DOUGLAS BROWER   1832
Troy, N.Y., until 1836. Albany Directory, 1837–1850.
S.D.BROWER

S. D. BROWER & SON   1840
Albany, N.Y., S. Douglas and Walter S. Brower.
S.D.BROWER & SON

BROWER & RUSHER   1834
New York.
B & R

D. BROWN   1811
Philadelphia, Pa.
D.BROWN

EDWARD BROWN   1807
Baltimore, Md., Directory until 1808. In Lynchburg, Va.,
1816–1830. Advertised, *The Lynchburg Press*, June 20, July 4,
1817, "Commercial Silversmith and Jeweler Business".
BROWN – E.BROWN

ELNATHAN C. BROWN   1797–1829   1820
Westerly, R.I.
E.C.BROWN

JOHN BROWN   1785
Philadelphia, Pa., at Third Street between Spruce and Union
Streets. At 36 North Front Street, 1796. Listed until 1824.
J B

PHILIP BROWN   1789–1854   1810
Hopkinton, N.H. Died in Concord, N.H.
P B

ROBERT BROWN   1798–1882   1824
Baltimore, Md. Advertised at 168 Baltimore Street, 1830.
R.BROWN

ROBERT BROWN & SON   1849
Baltimore, Md., until 1852.
R.BROWN & SON

ROBERT JOHNSON BROWN   1790–1820   1813
Boston, Mass. Robert Brown & Son, after 1833.
ROBERT J.BROWN

SAMUEL BROWN   1791–1849   1815
New York. Born, December 1, 1791. Married Mary Crosby,
April 23, 1818. Retired from trade, 1842. Died February 10.
S.BROWN

THEODORE G. BROWN   1830
New York.
T.G.BROWN

WILLIAM BROWN   1810
Baltimore, Md.
WM.BROWN

WILLIAM BROWN   1849
Albany, N.Y.
W.BROWN

BROWN & ANDERSON   1850
Wilmington, N.C. Thomas William Brown and William S.
Anderson until Anderson's death in 1871.
BROWN & ANDERSON

BROWN & KIRBY   1850
New Haven, Conn.
BROWN & KIRBY

LIBERTY BROWNE   1801
Philadelphia, Pa., at 102 North Front Street. Listed as Collector
of Taxes at 119 Chestnut Street in 1813. Firm of Browne & Seal.
BROWNE-L.BROWNE-LIBERTY BROWNE

BROWNE & SEAL   1810
Philadelphia, Pa. Liberty Browne and William Seal dissolved
partnership the following year.
BROWNE & SEAL

CHARLES OLIVER BRUFF   1735–1787   1763
New York. January 3, 1763, advertised, *The New York Mercury*,
also in 1767, "For making silver tankard, 3 S. per ounce. For
making a silver tea-pot, £4. For making a Sugar-pot, 35 S. For
making a milk-pot, 24 S. For making a Soup-spoon 20 S. For
making six table-spoons 21 S. For making six teaspoons 10 S.
For making tea-tongs, bows or others 10 S. For making a pair of
carved silver buckles 8 S. I design to put the stamp of my name,
in full, on all my works; and will work as cheap as any in the
city." Elizabeth, N.J., 1760–1765. Continued to advertise at
"the Sign of the Tea-pot, Tankard, and Ear-ring, opposite to the
Fly-Market", until 1776. Married Mary LeTellier, October 20,
1763. Retired to Nova Scotia, 1783–1787.
CHARLES O.BRUFF – CHAS O.BRUFF – COB

JOSEPH BRUFF   1730–1785   1755
Easton.Md. Advertised at Talbot Court House, *Penna. Gazette*,
1767.
IB – I.BRUFF

JOSEPH BRUFF, JR.   1770–1803   1790
Easton, Md., until 1800 when he moved to Chestertown, Md.
Son of Joseph Bruff, younger brother of Thomas Bruff.
I.BRUFF

THOMAS BRUFF   1760–1803   1785
Easton, Md. Inherited shop from father, Joseph. Advertised in
Chestertown, 1791–1803. Advertised in *American Citizen and
General Advertiser*, October 3, 1801, of a spoon machine.
T.BRUFF

PHILLIP BRYAN   1802
Philadelphia, Pa., at 116 Plumb Street.
BRYAN

J. B. BUCKLEY   1807
Philadelphia, Pa., at 31 North Front Street. Firm of Buckley &
Anderson.
BUCKLEY

ABEL BUEL 1742–1822   1761
New Haven, Conn. Born in Clinton, Conn. Apprenticed to
Ebenezer Chittenden. Married Master's daughter in 1764; (2)
Lettice Devoe of New York in 1775. Noted engraver and
inventive genius. Convicted of counterfeiting in New London.
Pardoned, 1776. Firm of Buel & Greenleaf, 1798.
AB – BUEL

SAMUEL BUEL 1742–1819   1777
Middletown, Conn. Born in Killingsworth. Advertised in
Hartford, July 4, 1780, *Connecticut Courant*, "Removal from
Middletown . . . wanted a good journey-man, goldsmith . . .
Highest wages given, paid in gold, silver, or Continental Bills."
Died in Westfield, Mass.
SB

LEWIS (LOUIS) BUICHLE   1798
Baltimore, Md., until 1802.
LB – L. BUICHLE

G. W. BULL   1840
Farmington, Conn.
G. W. BULL

MARTIN BULL 1744–1825   1767
Farmington, Conn. Married Elizabeth Strong, November 9,
1768. Introduced music into the Congregational Church; served
as organist and Deacon. Worked on important committees
during the Revolutionary War. Held office of Town Treasurer for
eight years, Probate Court clerk for thirty-nine years.
MB

BULLES & CHILDS   1840
Hartford, Conn.
BULLES & CHILDS

BUMM & SHEPPER   1819
Philadelphia, Pa. Advertised in Directory until 1823. Peter
Bumm and John D. Shepper.
BUMM & SHEPPER

BENJAMIN BUNKER   1751–1842   1780
Nantucket, Mass. Born March 17, son of William and Mary
Bunker. Took part in Penobscot Expedition. Became Prisoner of
War during the Revolutionary War. Died April 14, 1842.
BB

A. F. BURBANK   1845
Worcester, Mass.
A.F.BURBANK

WILLIAM S. BURDICK   1812
New Haven, Conn. Firm of Ufford & Burdick dissolved in 1814
by mutual consent.
BURDICK

NICHOLAS BURDOCK   1797
Philadelphia, Pa., at Waggoner's Alley.
NB

DAVID I. BURGER   1805
New York, at 62 James Street; Mott Street, 1818–1830. Son of
John Burger.
D.I.BURGER

JOHN BURGER   1780
New York. Married Sarah Baker, January 20, 1767. Apprenticed
to Myer Myers. Advertised, *New York Packet*, January 1, 1784.
Member of the Gold and Silversmith's Society, and Geneva
Society of Mechanics and Tradesmen, 1786, working at 153
Water Street. At 207 Queen Street, 1789. Advertised at 62
James Street, 1797–1807, where his sons, David and Thomas,
joined him in business in 1805.
BURGER – IB

THOMAS & JOHN BURGER   1805
New York, at 62 James Street.
TB BURGER

THOMAS BURGER   1805
New York, at 62 James Street.
TB

ELA BURNAP   1784–1856   1810
Boston, Mass. Born in Coventry, Conn. Listed in New York
Directory, 1817. In Rochester, N.Y., 1825–1856.
E.BURNAP

SAMUEL BURNET   1795
Philadelphia, Pa. In Newark, N.J., 1796. Advertised January
2, 1798, *Centinel of Freedom*, "Watch and Clock Maker, Gold and
Silver-Smith, of Newark, respectfully informs the public that he
continues to carry on the above business at his shop, nearly
opposite Mr. Archer Gifforts' Tavren, where he has for sale and
shall continue to keep for cash or approved notes, a handsome
assortment of Gold and Silver-Smith's work." Of the firm Burnet
& Ryder, 1795.
S.BURNET

BURNET & RYDER   1795
Philadelphia, Pa.
B & R

CHARLES A. BURNETT   −1849   1793
Alexandria, Va., and Georgetown, D.C., 1806.
CAB − C.A.BURNETT

JOHN BURNHAM   1792−1870   1815
Brattleboro, Vt. Born in Hartford, Conn. Married Rachel
Rossiter. Firm of Burnham & Sons, 1835, with sons: John, Jr.,
Henry and Edward.
J.BURNHAM

ALBERT CHAPIN BURR   1806−1832   1826
Rochester, N.Y., until 1832. Apprenticed to Erastus Cook.
A.C.BURR

CHRISTOPHER A. BURR   1787−   1810
Providence, R.I., at 73 North Main Street; 42 Westminster
Road, 1824.
C.BURR

CORNELIUS A. BURR   1816−1863   1838
Rochester, N.Y., Directory until 1850, continued business of
his brother, Alexander. Son of General Timothy Burr and his
wife, Mary Chapin. Married Mary L. Lyon in 1847. Died in
Brooklyn, N.Y. Firm of C. A. Burr & Co., 1857.
C.A.BURR

EZEKIEL BURR   1765−1846   1793
Providence, R.I. Born April 14, 1765, son of Ezekiel and Elsie
Whipple Burr. Married Lydia Yates, July 9, 1786. Located with
brother William, South of the Baptist Meeting House. Advertised at 5 Benefit Street, 1822. Of the firm of Burr & Lee,
1815−19.
EB − E.BURR

E. & W. BURR   1792
Providence, R.I., Ezekiel and William Burr.
E.W.BURR

NATHANIEL BURR   1698–1784   1780
Fairfield, Conn.
NB

WILLIAM BURR   1772–1810   1793
Providence, R.I., advertised with brother Ezekiel, January 3,
1793, *United States Chronicle*, "Informs the public that they carry
on the business of gold and silversmiths in its various branches, a
few doors south of the Baptist Meeting House, and directly
opposite Capt. Richard Jackson's, where they have for sale; silver
spoons of different kinds and sizes, gold necklaces and a variety
of plated buckles."
W.BURR

SAMUEL BURRILL   1704–1740   1733
Boston, Mass. "Mr. Burrill" mentioned with Joseph
Goldthwaite, *Boston News Letter*, April 15, 22, 1731 and July
26, August 2, 1733. Advertised, *Boston Evening Post*, December
20, 1742, "A pint silver porringer made by Samuel Burrill was
stolen or lost." A flagon made by him was a gift to the Second
Christ Church, Boston, December, 1733 and Jonathan Stone,
who died July 7, 1754, age 76, gave a flagon with both Burrill
marks to the First Church of Christ in Watertown.
SB – S.BURRILL

BENJAMIN BURT   1729–1805   1750
Boston, Mass., on Fish Street. Son of John Burt. Married Joan
Hooten. Purchased silversmith's tools from widow of Zachariah
Brigden. Estate appraised at $4788.52. Tankard dated, 1769.
B.BURT – BENJAMIN BURT – BURT

JOHN BURT   1692/3–1745/6   1712
Boston, Mass. Son of William and Elizabeth Burt. Apprenticed
to John Coney. Married Abigail Cheever. Father of silversmiths:
William, Samuel and Benjamin. His estate was valued at £6460.
Made a pair of candlesticks dated 1724.
IB – I.BURT – JOHN BURT

SAMUEL BURT   1724–1754   1750
Boston, Mass. Son of John Burt. Married Elizabeth White,
1747; later, Elizabeth Kent of Newbury.
SAMUEL BURT – SB – S.BURT

WILLIAM BURT 1726–1751   1747
Boston, Mass., opened a shop. Son of John Burt. Married Mary
Glidden.
W. BURT

F. W. BURWELL   1846
Norfolk, Va.
F. W. BURWELL

PHILIP BUSH, JR. 1765–1809   1786
Winchester, Va. Son of Philip and Catherine Slough Bush from
Mannheim, Germany. Married Elizabeth Palmer. Advertised at
the Golden Urn, 1787. Died in Frankfort, Ky.
PB

PHINEAS BUSHNELL 1741–1836   1765
Saybrook, Conn. In Guilford, 1795. Died in Branford, Conn.
PB

BENJAMIN BUSSEY 1757–1842   1778
Dedham, Mass.
BB

THOMAS D. BUSSEY 1773–1804   1792
Baltimore, Md. Directory, 1796–1803.
T. D. BUSSEY

C. L. BUSWELL   1845
Lebanon, N.H.
C. L. BUSWELL

CHARLES P. BUTLER 1765–1858   1790
Charleston, S.C., at King Street, 1790–1802. Born in Boston,
Mass.
CPB

JAMES BUTLER 1713–1776   1734
Boston, Mass. Married (1) Elizabeth Davie, (2) Sarah Wakefield.
Captain of Militia, 1748.
IB – J. BUTLER

BUTLER & McCARTY   1850
Philadelphia, Pa., at 105 North Second Street.
BUTLER & M'CARTY

BUTLER, WISE & CO.   1842
Philadelphia, Pa.
BW & CO

JAMES BYRNE   1784
Philadelphia, Pa., advertised, *Cary's Penna. Herald*, January 25,
1785; "Jeweller and Silversmith, East side of Front Street, three
doors above Chestnut-street. Acknowledges with gratitude the
kind encouragement he has received since his commencement in
business; and begs leave to inform his friends and the public,
that he has now for sale the following articles, which will be
found on trial equal to any in this city." In New York at Fly
Market until 1797.
J.BYRNE

THOMAS BYRNES   1766–1798   1793
Wilmington, Del. Son of Joshua and Ruth Woodcock Byrnes.
Apprenticed to his uncle, Bancroft Woodcock, at age eleven
upon the death of his father. Married Sarah Pancoast, July 10,
1795. Advertised in *Delaware Gazette*, 1793.
T.BYRNES

[C]

J. E. CALDWELL & CO.   1848
Philadelphia, Pa.
J.E.CALDWELL & CO

JOSEPH CALLENDER   1751–1821   1774
Boston, Mass. Silversmith and excellent engraver who studied
under Paul Revere and Nathaniel Hurd.
IC

ALEXANDER CAMERON   1813
Albany, N.Y., until 1834.
AC

ELIAS CAMP   1825
Bridgeport, Conn.
EC – E.CAMP

CHRISTOPHER CAMPBELL   1808
New York, at 394 Greenwich Street; 43 Hudson and 41
Roosevelt Streets, until 1812.
CAMPBELL

JOHN CAMPBELL   1803–   1829
Fayetteville, N.C. Born in Scotland. Advertised, *Carolina
Observer*, 1831. Of firm of Selph & Campbell, 1827; Campbell &
Prior, 1834. Moved to Tennessee in 1836.
J.CAMPBELL

ROBERT CAMPBELL   1799–1872   1819
Baltimore, Md., on Market Street. Firm of Richards &
Campbell.
CAMPBELL – RC

R. & A. CAMPBELL   1835
Baltimore, Md. Robert and Andrew worked until 1854.
R & AC – R & A.CAMPBELL

THOMAS BOYCE CAMPBELL   1796–1858   1822
Winchester, Va. Born in Inverary, Scotland. Son of William L.
and Rosanna Laubinger Campbell. In Winchester, Va., 1810.
Apprenticed to his father whose tools he bought from the estate
of his father in 1816. In firm of Campbell & Meredith, 1820;
Campbell & Polk, 1850.
CAMPBELL – TBC

THOMAS CAMPBELL   1800
New York. In Philadelphia, 1828.
T.CAMPBELL

WILLIAM L. CAMPBELL   1759–1815   1810
Winchester, Va. Born in Inverary, Scotland. Father of Thomas
Boyce. He was a watchmaker, brass founder, silversmith, Clerk
of Legal Papers and large landowner.
CAMPBELL

CAMPBELL & MEREDITH   1820
Winchester, Va. Thomas Boyce and John Meredith.
CAMPBELL J.MEREDITH

CAMPBELL & POLK   1850
Winchester, Va., until 1858. Thomas B. Campbell and Robert
I. W. Polk.
CAMPBELL POLK

L. B. CANDEE & CO.   1830
Woodbury, Conn.
L.B.CANDEE & CO

CHARLES CANDELL   1795
New York, at 19 Cliff Street.
CC

SAMUEL CANFIELD   1780
Middletown, Conn., until 1801. Sheriff, 1787. Firm of Canfield
& Foot, 1795. Advertised until 1801; moved to Lansingburg,
N.Y. In Scanticoke, N.Y., 1807.
CANFIELD

CANFIELD & BROTHER   1830
Baltimore, Md. Ira C. Canfield and William B. Canfield.
CANFIELD

CANFIELD & HALL   1800
Middletown, Conn.
CANFIELD & HALL

GEORGE CANNON   1767–1835   1800
Warwick, R.I. Advertised in *The Inquirer*, 1825–1835, in
Nantucket, Mass.
GC – G.CANNON

J. CAPELLE   1850
St. Louis, Mo.
CAPELLE

WILLIAM CARIO   1712–1769   1735
Boston, Mass. Advertised in *Boston Gazette*, 1738, "Shop at
South-end of the Town, over against the White Swan." In
Portsmouth, N.H. before 1748. Father of William Cario, Jr.
WC – W.CARIO

WILLIAM CARIO, JR.   1736–1809   1760
Boston, Mass. Worked in Portsmouth and Newmarket, N.H.
Married Abigail Peavey, 1759; Lydia Coxcroft, April 16, 1768.
Died in Newmarket, N.H.
WC – W.CARIO

ABRAHAM CARLISLE (CARLILE)   1791
Philadelphia, Pa., Census List. Advertised, 1791–1794, at
Brooks Court and North Front Street.
AC – A.CARLILE – A.CARLISLE

JOHN CARMAN   1771
Philadelphia, Pa. Advertised, *Penna. Journal*, August 22, 1771;
"Goldsmith and Jeweller. At the Golden Lion, corner of Second
and Chestnut Streets." In Kingston, N.Y., 1774–1775.
IC

CHARLES CARPENTER   1790
Norwich, Conn. Son of Joseph to whom he was apprenticed.
Listed in Boston Directory, 1810.
CC

JOSEPH CARPENTER   1747–1804   1775
Norwich, Conn. Married Eunice Fitch, 1775. Advertised in
Canterbury, Conn. 1797. Returned to Norwich, 1804.
IC

JOHN & DANIEL CARRELL   1785

Philadelphia, Pa. Advertised, *Penna. Evening Herald*, February 5,
1785, "Two doors above the Old Coffee House, on Market
Street."

CARRELL

WILLIAM CARRINGTON   −1901   1830

Charleston, S.C.

W. CARRINGTON

THOMAS CARSON   1815

Albany, N.Y., until 1850. Member of the Albany Mechanic's
Society. Partner of Green Hall, 1810–1818.

TC – T. CARSON

CARSON & HALL   1810

Albany, N.Y., Directory, 1813–1818. Thomas Carson and
Green Hall dissolved partnership in 1818.

CARSON & HALL

JOSEPH SAYRE CART   1767–1822   1798

Charleston, S.C.

CART

LEWIS CARY   1798–1834   1815

Boston, Mass. Apprenticed to Churchill & Treadwell. Member
of the Massachusetts Charitable Mechanics Association, 1828.
Had many apprentices.

CARY – L. CARY

GIDEON CASEY   1726–1786   1753

South Kingstown, R.I. Born in Newport, R.I. Son of Samuel
and Dorcas Ellis Casey. In partnership with brother, Samuel,
1753–1763. Married, Jane Roberts, July 31, 1747; Elizabeth
Johnson, May 11, 1760. In Warwick, R.I., 1763.

GC – G. CASEY

SAMUEL CASEY   1723–1773   1750

South Kingstown, R.I. Born in Newport, R.I. Apprenticed to
Jacob Hurd. Made a Freeman, April, 1745. Notice in *Boston
News Letter*, October 1, 1764, "His house at South Kingstown,
R.I., was destroyed by fire, . . . occasioned by a large Fire being
kept the Day preceding in his Goldsmith's Forge." Jailed in
1770 for counterfeiting. Freed by friends; exonerated by his
wife's efforts in 1779.

SC – S. CASEY

STEPHEN CASTAN & CO. 1819
Philadelphia, Pa.
SC & CO

THOMAS CHADWICK & HEIMS 1814
Reading Pa. Advertised, April 16, 1814, *Weekly Advertiser.*
TC & H

FREDERICK CHAFFEE 1823–1891 1845
Pittsfield, Mass. Partner of Washington Root. In 1850, Rutland,
Vt., where he died.
F.CHAFFEE

JAMES CHALMERS 1749
Annapolis, Md. Advertised in *Maryland Gazette*, March 19,
1752, "Removed into South-East Street." Advertised until
1768. Was innkeeper in conjunction with goldsmith business.
IC

JOHN CHALMERS 1778
Annapolis, Md. Son of James from whom he learned his trade.
Minted the Chalmers coins, 1783.
IC

JOHN CHAMPLIN 1745–1800 1768
New London, Conn. Advertised until 1780.
IC

STEPHEN CHANDLER 1812
New York, at Chatham Square; Hester Street in 1823.
CHANDLER

MAJOR TIMOTHY CHANDLER 1762–1848 1787
Concord, N.H. Married Sarah Abbott, 1787. Advertised,
1791–1848. Worked with sons, Timothy and Abiel.
TC – T.CHANDLER

TIMOTHY JAY CHANDLER 1798– 1823
Concord, N.H. Son of Major Timothy Chandler with whom he
worked, 1820–1829, as Timothy Chandler & Son. In Belfast,
Me., 1823.
T.J.CHANDLER

OTIS CHAPIN 1791–1871 1821
Springfield, Mass., advertised shop opposite the Springfield
Hotel. Born in Bernardston, Mass.
O.CHAPIN

CHARTERS, CANN & DUNN   1850
New York, at 53 Mercer Street. James Charters, John Cann and
David Dunn.
CC & D

JOSEPH D. CHASE   1820
New York. Directory until 1839.
J.D.CHASE

SIMON CHAUDRON & CO.   1807
Philadelphia, Pa., at 12 South Third Street until 1811.
CHAUDRON – SC & CO

CHAUDRON'S & RASCH   1812
Philadelphia, Pa. Simon Chaudron and Anthony Rasch at Third
Street.
CHAUDRON'S & RASCH

JOHN HATCH CHEDELL (CHEADELL)   1806–1875   1827
Auburn, N.Y. Apprenticed to William Nichols of Cooperstown
in 1820. Advertised until 1850.
CHEADELL – CHEDELL

MARTIN CHENEY   1778–   1803
Windsor, Vt. Born in East Hartford, Conn. In Montreal,
Canada, 1809.
CHENEY

GEORGE K. CHILDS   1828
Philadelphia, Pa., at 34 Dock Street.
G.K.CHILDS

PETER CHITRY   1814
New York, at White and Elm Streets; Burrows and Henry
Streets, 1820–1825. Formerly of Philadelphia.
P.CHITRY

BERIAH CHITTENDEN   1751–1827   1787
New Haven, Conn. Son of Ebenezer. In Kinderhook, N.Y.,
1800; later, in Middlebury, Ohio.
BC

EBENEZER CHITTENDEN   1726–1812   1765
Madison, Conn. Born in Madison. In New Haven, 1770, in
partnership with son-in-law, Abel Buel. Associated with Eli
Whitney, inventor of the cotton gin. Warden of Trinity Church.
EC – E.CHITTENDEN

CHARLES CHOYSENHOLDER   1814
Philadelphia, Pa.
C.CHOYSENHOLDER

JOSEPH CHURCH   1794–1876   1815
Hartford, Conn. Apprenticed to Jacob Sargeant and Horace
Goodwin. Shop at Ferry Street in 1818. Sold business to C. C.
Strong and L. T. Welles, former apprentices. Frederick E.
Church, the landscape painter, was his son.
J.CHURCH

CHURCH & ROGERS   1825
Hartford, Conn., on Main Street, partnership of Joseph Church
and William Rogers.
CHURCH & ROGERS

JESSE CHURCHILL   1773–1819   1795
Boston, Mass., at 88 Newbury Street until 1810. Member of
Massachusetts Charitable Mechanics Association, 1810. Firm of
Churchill & Treadwell.
CHURCHILL – I.CHURCHILL

CHURCHILL & TREADWELL   1805
Boston, Mass. Partnership dissolved in 1813. Hazen and Moses
Morse, Lewis Cary and Benjamin Bailey served apprenticeships
to this firm.
CHURCHILL & TREADWELL

A. L. CLAPP   1802
New York.
A.L.CLAPP

JOSEPH CLARICO   –1828   1816
Norfolk, Va., at 54 Main Street.
I.CLARICO – J.CLARICO

F. H. CLARK & CO.   1850
Memphis, Tenn.
F.H.CLARK & CO

F. & H. CLARK   1830
Augusta, Ga., until 1840. Francis and Horace Clark.
F & H.CLARK

GABRIEL DUVALL CLARK   1813–1896   1830
Baltimore, Md., at Calvert and Water Streets.
G.D.CLARK

GEORGE C. CLARK (GEORGE G. CLARK)   1824
Providence, R.I., at Cheapside Street until 1847. In partnership
with Jabez Gorham, Christopher Burr, William Hadwen and
Henry Mumford, for five years.
G.C.CLARK – G.G.CLARK

I. CLARK (JOSEPH)   1737
Boston, Mass., until circa 1756.
CLARK – IC – I.CLARK

I. & H. CLARK   1821
Portsmouth, N.H.
I & H.CLARK

J. H. CLARK   1815
New York.
J.H.CLARK

JOSEPH CLARK   –1821   1791
Danbury, Conn., shop located near the Printing Office. Served
in Revolution in 1771. In Newburgh, N.Y., 1811. Died in
Alabama.
J.CLARK

JOSEPH CLARK   1774–1838   1803
Portsmouth, N.H. Sold business to Thomas P. Drown, 1811.
J.CLARK

LEVI CLARK   1801–1875   1825
Norwalk, Conn. Born in Danbury, Conn. Apprenticed to father-
in-law, John Starr Blackman.
CLARK

LEWIS W. CLARK   1832
Watertown, N.Y., 1832–1836; Utica, N.Y., until 1838.
L.W.CLARK

CLARK, PELLETREAU & UPSON   1823
Charleston, S.C.
CP & U

PETER G. CLARK   1793–1860   1810
New Haven, Conn. Married Lucretia Hitchcock, 1818. Died in
Cheshire, Conn.
P.CLARK

SAMUEL CLARK   1659–1705   1685
Boston, Mass. Apprenticed to John Hull in 1673.
SC

THOMAS CLARK 1725–1781   1764
Boston, Mass., advertised on South side of the Court House.
TC – T.CLARK

WILLIAM CLARK 1750–1798   1775
New Milford, Conn. Born in Colchester, Conn. One of the
founders of the Union Library, New Milford, 1796.
WC – W.CLARK

CLARK & ANTHONY   1790
New York.
CLARK & ANTHONY

CLARK & BROTHER   1825
Norwalk, Conn.
CLARK & BRO

CLARK & CO.   1830
Augusta, Ga.
CLARK & CO

CLARK & COIT   1820
Norwich, Conn.
CLARK & COIT

CLARK & PELLETREAU   1819
New York.
C & P

JONATHAN CLARKE 1706–1770   1734
Newport, R.I., later, of Providence, R.I.
IC – I.CLARKE – JC – J.CLARKE

AARON CLEVELAND 1782–1843   1820
Norwich, Conn.
AC – A.CLEVELAND

BENJAMIN CLEVELAND 1767–1837   1800
Newark, N.J.
BC – B.CLEVELAND

WILLIAM CLEVELAND 1770–1837   1791
Norwich, Conn. Born in Norwich. Apprenticed to Thomas
Harland. In New York, 1791. Partner of John P. Trott in New
London, 1792–1794. Married Margaret Falley, 1793. In Nor-
wich, Conn, 1812, as Deacon of First Congregational Church.
His son, Richard, was the father of President Grover Cleveland.
In Worthington and Salem, Mass., also, Zanesville, Ohio. Died
in Black Rock, N.Y. Firm of Cleveland & Post, 1815.
CLEVELAND – WC

CLEVELAND & POST
Norwich, Conn. William Cleveland and Samuel Post.
C & P

1815

NATHANIEL CLOUGH
Lee, N.H.
N C

1790

JOHN CLUET, JR.
Kingston, N.Y. Also near Albany, probably Fonda or Schenec-
tady, N.Y. Of the firm Van Sanford & Cluet, 1752. In *New York
Gazette*, Albany, March 9, 1758, "I:C Maker's mark on stolen
Tankard, 34 oz., engraved I.^{H}L., House of Jacob Lansing.
40 Shillings Reward."
I C

1725

MATTHEW CLUFF   −1845
Norfolk, Va. Firm of Ott & Cluff until 1806, George Ott and
Matthew Cluff. In Elizabeth City, N.C., 1816.
M.CLUFF

1802

ISAAC D. CLUSTER
St. Louis, Mo.
I.D.CLUSTER

1850

EPHRAIM COBB   1708−1777
Plymouth, Mass. Apprenticed to Moody Russell. Married
Hannah Allen.
EC − E.COBB

1735

JOHN COBURN   1725−1803
Boston, Mass., "at head of Town Dock.", *Boston News Letter*.
Married Susanna Greenleaf, 1750, (2) Catharine Vans, 1785,
daughter of first Dutch citizen of Boston. Shop in King Street.
Sergeant of Artillery in 1752. Town Warden and Census Taker.
Paid $280, Assessor's Taking Tax, 1780. Died in Boston. Made
saucepan dated 1749; plate dated 1764.
IC − JC − J.COBURN

1750

SETH STORER COBURN   1744−
Springfield, Mass. Born in Boston.
SSC

1775

JOHN CODDINGTON   1690−1743
Newport, R.I. Son of Nathaniel and Susanna Hutchinson Cod-
dington. Married, May 23, 1715. Member of the House of
Deputies, 1721−1729. Sheriff, 1733−5. Colonel of Militia.
Mentioned as goldsmith in will.
IC

1712

L. P. COE   1835
New York.
L.P.COE

COE & UPTON   1840
New York.
COE & UPTON

DANIEL BLOOM COEN   1787
New York, at 31 Maiden Lane until 1789. Married Deborah
Ogilvie, niece of John Ogilvie, silversmith. At 58 Gold Street in
1791; 95 Maiden Lane, 1797–1805. Advertised, *American
Citizen*, October 19, 1804, "Lottery, 95 Maiden Lane."
DC – D.COEN

C. COEN & CO.   1810
New York.
C.COEN & CO

HENRY COGSWELL   1760
Boston, Mass.
H.COGSWELL

HENRY COGSWELL   1846
Salem, Mass., until 1853.
H.COGSWELL

THOMAS COHEN   1808
Petersburg, Va., in the firm of Cohen & Stevens. In Lynchburg,
Va., 1809. In the Muster Rolls of the Lynchburg Rifles; "in the
service of the United States in the Fourth Regiment, July-Au-
gust, 1814, the First Sergt., Thomas Cohen." In Chillicothe,
Ohio, December, 1814.
T.COHEN

EDWARD COIT   1802–1839   1825
Norwich, Conn. Brother of Thomas Chester Coit.
E.COIT

COIT & MANSFIELD   1816
Norwich, Conn. Thomas C. Coit and Elisha H. Mansfield
dissolved partnership in 1819.
C & M

THOMAS CHESTER COIT   1791–1841   1812
Norwich, Conn. Learned trade in Canterbury, Conn. Partner of
Elisha H. Mansfield, 1816–1819. In Natchez, Miss., 1826.
Died in N.Y. Firm of Clark and Coit, 1820.
TCC

ALBERT COLE (COLES)   1844
New York, at 6 Little Green Street.
AC

EBENEZER COLE   1818
New York, at 96 Reade Street.
E.COLE

JAMES C. COLE   1791–1867   1813
Rochester, N.H. Born in Boston. Prominent silversmith and
citizen; member of Methodist Church, Masonic Lodge, State
Legislature.
J.C.COLE

JOHN A. COLE   1844
New York, worked at 4 Little Green Street.
JOHN A.COLE

SCHUBAEL B. COLE   1850
Great Falls, N.H. Trained by his father, James C. Cole.
S.B.COLE

BENJAMIN COLEMAN   1795
Burlington, N.J.
B.COLEMAN

C. C. COLEMAN   1835
Burlington, N.J.
C.C.COLEMAN

NATHANIEL COLEMAN   1765–1842   1790
Burlington, N.J. Apprenticed to James Roe of Kingston for
seven years until 1783. Member of the Society of Friends.
Married Elizabeth Lippincott, 1791.
NC – N.COLEMAN

SAMUEL COLEMAN   1761–1842   1795
Burlington, N.J. Son of Thomas and Elizabeth Coleman.
Married Elizabeth Hampton, daughter of Benjamin and Ann
Hampton of Wrightstown, Pa., June 6, 1807.
S.COLEMAN

SIMEON COLEY   1767
New York. Advertised, *New York Gazette*, March 16, 1767,
"Goldsmith from London at Shop near the Merchants Coffee
House." Dissolved partnership with William Coley, 1766. After
a public meeting charging Coley with daring infractions of the
Non-importation Agreement, Coley advertised that he intends
to leave the city in 1769.
S.COLEY

WILLIAM COLEY   1767

New York. Notice of partnership dissolved with Simeon Coley,
September 11, 1766. In partnership with Daniel Van Voorhis,
1785–1787, working on mint operations in Rubert, Vt. Listed
at 191 Washington Street, 1801; 64 Ann Street, 1804.
W. COLEY

THOMAS COLGAN   1771

New York. Apprenticed to Thomas Hammersley, 1764.
TC – T.COLGAN

ARNOLD COLLINS   –1735   1690

Newport, R.I. Married (1) in 1690, (2) Amy Ward, 1692.
Received commission to make Seal of Colony, "Anchor and
Hope," in 1702. Contributed to building the Baptist Church,
1729. Elected one of the Proprietors of the Common Council.
AC

SELDON COLLINS, JR.   1819–1885   1837

Utica, N.Y., Directory, 1837–1850.
S.COLLINS

COLLINS & J. W. FORBES   1825

New York.
C & I.W.FORBES

DEMAS COLTON, JR.   1826

New York.
D.COLTON JR

COLTON & COLLINS   1825

New York.
C & C – COLTON & COLLINS

JOHN CONEY   1655/6–1722   1676

Boston, Mass. Son of John and Elizabeth Nash Coney, born
January 5. Probably apprenticed to Hull and Sanderson from
examples of design, workmanship and engraving as of Sanderson,
Dummer and Dwight. Married three times, Sarah Blackman,
second wife, 1683; Mary Atwater Clark, widow of Captain John
Clark, November 8, 1694. Located at Court Street, 1688; near
Town Dock, 1699; at Ann Street, 1717. Died August 20, wife,
Mary, administered his estate. Notice in *Boston Gazette*,
November 5/12, 1722, "This Evening the remaining part of the
Tools of the late Mr. Coney are to be sold." Heart-shaped mark
changed to shield form, 1705, with small additional marks on
small wares and bezels.
IC

T. CONLYN   1845
Philadelphia, Pa.
T.CONLYN

JAMES CONNING   1813–1872   1825
New York. Born and worked in New York until 1840. In 1842,
at 12 Dauphin Street, Mobile, Ala. Successful silversmith and
jeweler until 1862 when he went to the aid of the South and
opened a sword factory at 41 St. Francis Street to supply swords
to the Confederacy. Returned to jewelry business after the War.
J.CONNING

JOHN H. CONNOR   1835
New York, at 6 Little Green Street. Firm of Eoff & Connor,
1833.
JHC – J.H.CONNOR

RICHARD CONYERS   –1708   1688
Boston, Mass. English trained, of Robert Sanderson's Parish of
St. Mary Woolnoth, London. Willed tools to his apprentice,
Thomas Millner, 1708.
RC

BENJAMIN E. COOK   1803–1900   1825
Northampton, Mass. Partner of Nathan Storrs, 1827–1833, as
Storrs & Cook. Later in Troy, N.Y. Died in Northampton.
B.E.COOK

ERASTUS COOK   1793–1864   1815
Rochester, N.Y., until 1864.
E.COOK

JOHN COOK   1795
New York, at 51 Ann Street. Firm of Cook & Co., 1797–1805,
at 133 William Street. At 236 Broadway, 1806. In Boston
Directory, 1813.
COOK – I.COOK – J.COOK

JOSEPH COOK (COOKE)   1785
Philadelphia, Pa. Advertised, until 1795, at his "Ware-House
on Second Street". Located on Third and Market Streets where he
offers a large and general assortment at the Federal Manufactory
and European Repository, for 15 s per ounze. In *Penna. Packet*,
July 8, 1795, "Wanted immediately, Journeymen Goldsmiths,
Small-workers, and other Mechanics. Foreman to instruct
apprentices, and do every duty incumbent, shall receive a hand
some salary for his services, with board and lodging in the
house."
JC

JOHN B. COOKE   –1852   1838
Petersburg, Va. Son of William A. Cooke. In 1838, purchased
firm of Cooke & Son, William Cooke and William A. Cooke,
1833–1838.
J.B.COOKE

WILLIAM A. COOKE   1826
Petersburg, Va. Established Cooke & White, 1829, with Andrew
White. Married Mary Wilson Sanford in Norfolk, 1831. In
1833, Andrew White died and firm became William A. Cooke
& Co. until 1834; Cooke & Son until 1838.
W.A.COOKE

COOKE & WHITE   1829
Norfolk, Va. William A. Cooke and Andrew White until
White's death, 1833.
COOKE & WHITE

OLIVER B. COOLEY   –1844   1828
Utica, N.Y. Firm of Storrs & Cooley in Directory, 1832.
COOLEY – O.B.COOLEY

JOSEPH COOLIDGE, JR.   1747–1821   1770
Boston, Mass. Advertised, "Shop located opposite Mr. William
Greenleaf, Foot of Cornhill.", *Boston News Letter*. Mentioned as
"one of the Boston Tea Party." Merchant in Directory 1789.
COOLIDGE – JC

B. & J. COOPER   1810
New York.
B & J.COOPER

FRANCIS W. COOPER   1846
New York, at 102 Reade Street.
FWC – F.W.COOPER

COOPER & FISHER   1850
New York.
COOPER & FISHER

JOSEPH COPP   1732–1813   1757
New London, Conn. Married Rachael Dennison in 1757.
Advertised shop was entered by burglars in 1776.
I.COPP – J.COPP

JOHN CORBETT   1800
Whitingham, Vt.
CORBETT – J.CORBETT

CHRISTIAN CORNELIUS   1810
Philadelphia, Pa., at 8 Pewter Platter Alley until 1819.
CC – C.CORNELIUS

WALTER CORNELL   1729–1801   1780
Providence, R.I.
CORNELL – W.CORNELL

NATHANIEL CORNWELL   1776–1837   1800
Danbury, Conn. Later, in Berlin, Conn. In Hudson, N.Y.,
1816.
N.CORNWELL

JACQUES W. CORTELYOU   1781–1822   1805
New Brunswick, N.J. Born June 16. Married Rachel Van
Harlingen. Died of typhus fever, December 8.
I.CORTELYOU – JWC – J.W.CORTELYOU

LOUIS COUVERTIE   1822
New Orleans, La., at 29 St. Peter, below Royal Street.
L.COUVERTIE

JOHN COVERLY   –1800   1766
Boston, Mass.
I.COVERLY

THOMAS COVERLY   1760
Newport, R.I. Advertised in Newburyport, Mass., 1765. In
Boston, 1789.
T.COVERLY

WILLIAM COWAN   1779–1831   1803
Fredericksburg, Va. In Richmond, Va., 1804–1830. Died in
New York, September 11.
W.COWAN

WILLIAM D. COWAN   1808
Philadelphia, Pa., at 10 German Street.
W.COWAN

JOHN COWELL   1707–   1728
Boston, Mass.
I.COWELL

WILLIAM COWELL   1682–1736   1703
Boston, Mass. Son of blacksmith, John Cowell. Probably appren-
ticed to Jeremiah Dummer. Married Elizabeth Kilby, 1706.
Advertised as a "Goldsmith.", *Boston News Letter*, August 3,

1736. Retired shortly after his son finished apprenticeship to
become an innholder, 1734. Master of Rufus Greene. Estate was
appraised by Jacob Hurd.
WC – W. COWELL

WILLIAM COWELL, JR.   1713–1761   1734
Boston, Mass. Continued father's business on his retirement.
Advertised in *Boston News Letter*, 1741; and *Boston Gazette*, 1761.
Samuel Edwards and William Simpkins, silversmiths, appraised
his estate.
WC – W. COWELL

RALPH COWLES   1840
Cleveland, Ohio.
COWLES

J. & I. COX   1817
New York. John and James Cox at 15 Maiden Lane until 1853.
J & I. COX

J. & I. COX & CLARK   1831
New York, until 1833.
J & I. C & CO

STEPHEN CRAFT   1811
New York, at Grand and Garrick Streets.
S. CRAFT

JOHN CRAWFORD   1815
New York, at 92 John Street; Bowery Lane, 1820–25. In Direc-
tory until 1836. In Philadelphia, Pa., 1837–43.
I. CRAWFORD – J. CRAWFORD

NEWTON E. CRITTENDEN   1804–1872   1824
Le Roy, N.Y. In Cleveland, Ohio, 1839, at 29 Superior Street.
N. E. CRITTENDEN

JONATHAN CROSBY   1743–1797   1764
Boston, Mass. In Directory at Fish Street, 1796.
JC

SAMUEL T. CROSBY   1849
Boston, Mass. Member of the Massachusetts Charitable
Mechanics Association, 1850. Firm of Crosby & Brown.
S. T. CROSBY

WILLIAM CROSS 1658–   1695
Boston, Mass. Born in London, son of English minister.
Apprenticed to Abraham Hind, 1673, at Sign of Golden Bell,
Fenchurch Street, London. Listed in Suffolk Probate Records,
1739.
W C

ALEXANDER CROUCKSHANKS   1768
Boston, Mass.
A C

CROWLEY & FARR   1823
Philadelphia, Pa.
CROWLEY & FARR

I. B. CURRAN   1835
Ithaca, N.Y.
I.B.CURRAN

EDMUND M. CURRIER 1793–1853   1815
Hopkinton, N.H. In Salem, Mass., 1825. Firm of Currier &
Foster, 1840.
E.CURRIER

CURRIER & TROTT   1836
Boston, Mass., at 139 Washington Street.
CURRIER & TROTT

JOHN CURRY   1831
Philadelphia, Pa., at 72 Chestnut Street. Firm of Curry &
Preston.
J.CURRY

CURRY & PRESTON   1831
Philadelphia, Pa., at 72 Chestnut Street.
C & P—CURRY & PRESTON

FREDERICK CURTIS 1786–1815   1808
Burlington. Vt. Freeman, 1808. In partnership with Lewis
Curtis as Lewis & F. Curtis, 1808–1815.
F.CURTIS

LEWIS CURTIS 1774–1845   1797
Farmington, Conn. Born in Coventry, Conn. Apprenticed to
Daniel Burnap. Advertised his shop was robbed in 1797. In
Burlington, Vt., 1806, in partnership with Frederick Curtis
until 1815. Removed to St. Charles, Mo., 1820. Died in Hazel
Green, Wis.
L.CURTIS

CURTIS & DUNNING   1821
Burlington, Vt., until 1832. Lemuel Curtis and Joseph N.
Dunning.
CURTIS & DUNNING

CURTISS, CANDEE & STILES   1831
Woodbury, Conn. Daniel Curtiss, Lewis B. Candee, Benjamin
Stiles in partnership until 1835. Successors of Curtiss & Candee,
1826–1831.
CC & S – CURTISS, CANDEE & STILES

CURTISS & STILES   1835
Woodbury, Conn. Daniel Curtiss and Benjamin Stiles until
1840 when Daniel Curtiss retired.
CURTISS & STILES

A. CUTLER   1820
Boston, Mass. In Directory, 1842.
A.CUTLER

EBEN CUTLER   1846
Boston, Mass.
E.CUTLER

RICHARD CUTLER   1736–1810   1760
New Haven, Conn. Born in Fairfield, Conn. In partnership with
H. Silliman and A. Ward, 1767; with sons, Richard and
William, as Richard Cutler & Sons, 1800–1810.
R.CUTLER

JACOB CUYLER   1741–1804   1768
Albany, N.Y. Son of Johannes and Catherine Glen Cuyler.
Witness to the will of Jacob Gerritse Lansing, probated January
23, 1768. Married Lydia van Vechten.
IC

[D]

PHILLIP DALLY   1779
New York. Son of John Dally, shipwright. Married Charity
Hunt, July 27, 1779. Partner of Jabez Halsey at 59 Queen
Street, 1787.
PD

PEYTON DANA   1803
Providence, R.I. Married Esther Sweet, 1791. Advertised,
1803, in *Providence Gazette*; 1820, in *Providence Patriot*.
P.DANA

THOMAS DANE   1726–1795   1745
Boston. Mass. Married Abigail Furnell, 1749.
T.DANE

JOHN DARBY   1801
Charleston, S.C., at 10 Beaufair Street; at 27 Archdale Street,
1831.
DARBY

WILLIAM DARBY   –1798   1790
Charleston, S.C., at No. 20 Broad Street.
DARBY

JOHN F. DARROW   1818
Catskill, N.Y.
DARROW

JONATHAN DAVENPORT   –1801   1789
Baltimore, Md., until 1793 when listed in Philadelphia.
ID – I.DAVENPORT

JOHN DAVID   1736–1798   1763
Philadelphia, Pa. Son of Peter with whom he worked. Advertised
in *Penna. Gazette*, at Second Street corner of Chestnut, near
Drawbridge, in 1772. Worked until 1794.
ID – I.DAVID

JOHN DAVID, JR.   1785
Philadelphia, Pa., at 928 South Front Street. Partner of Daniel
Dupuy, 1792–1805. Grandson of Peter David.
ID

PETER DAVID   1707–1755   1730
Philadelphia, Pa. Advertised, "Goldsmith, . . . in Front Street
. . .", *American Weekly Mercury*, April, 1739. Born in New York,
son of John, Huguenot refugee. Baptised in the Dutch Church
of N.Y., April 13, 1707. In 1722, Peter David, 15 years of age
and an orphan, was apprenticed to Peter Quintard. Married
Jeanne Dupuy, baptised, N.Y., February 15, 1715; died in
Philadelphia, October 1, 1752. Advertised in Philadelphia,
1738 and 1750, at Second Street. Married Margaret Parham,
July 28, 1753. Died October 21, 1755. Founder of three genera-
tions of Philadelphia silversmiths, son, John, and grandson,
John, Jr.
PD – P.DAVID

EDWARD DAVIS   −1781   1775
Newburyport, Mass. Left business to his fifteen-year-old appren-
tice, Jacob Perkins, who moved to Philadelphia, 1816.
ED − E.DAVIS

ELIAS DAVIS   1782–1856   1805
Boston, Mass., at 11 Union Street until 1825.
ELIAS DAVIS

JOSHUA G. DAVIS   1796
Boston, Mass., until 1840.
DAVIS − I.DAVIS − J.DAVIS

DAVIS, PALMER & CO.   1842
Boston, Mass., Directory, 1846.
DAVIS PALMER & CO

ROBERT DAVIS   1790–1861   1812
Concord, N.H. In partnership with Seth Eastman, 1826, as
Robert Davis & Co.
ROBERT DAVIS

SAMUEL DAVIS   1765–1842   1801
Plymouth, Mass. Born in Plymouth. Apprenticed to George
Tyler, Boston, 1779–1785. Member of Charitable Mechanics
Association, 1801. In Boston Directory, jeweler, at Marlboro
Street, 1807. In firms of Davis & Brown, Robert Brown, 1809;
Davis, Brown &, Co., 1816; Davis, Watson & Co., Edward
Watson and Bartlett M. Bramhill, 1825. Listed as importer of
watches and jewelry, 1830–1842.
DAVIS − S.DAVIS

THOMAS ASPINWALL DAVIS   1825
Boston, Mass., until 1830.
T.A.DAVIS

DAVIS, WATSON & CO.   1825
Boston, Mass. Partners, Samuel Davis, Edward Watson, Bartlett
M. Bramhill.
DAVIS WATSON & CO

DAVIS & BROWN   1809
Boston, Mass., until 1820. Samuel Davis, Robert Brown.
DAVIS & BROWN

DAVIS & WATSON   1815
Boston, Mass. Samuel Davis, Edward Watson.
D & W

BARZILLAI DAVISON   1740–1828   1765
Norwich, Conn. Born in Pomfret, Conn. Apprenticed to the
trade, 1754.
BD

CHARLES DAVISON   1805
Norwalk, Conn. Son of Barzillai.
CD – C.DAVISON

JOHN DAY   1820
Boston, Mass., to 1825.
J.DAY

JAMES DECKER   1833
Troy, N.Y., to 1848.
J.DECKER

DE FOREST & CO.   1827
New York.
D & CO

JABEZ DELANO   1763–1848   1784
New Bedford, Mass.
ID – I.DELANO

JOHN DE LARUE   1822
New Orleans, La.
DE LARUE

ANDREW DEMILT   1805
New York.
DEMILT

JOHN DENISE   1798
New York.
JD

JOHN & TUNIS DENISE   1798
New York.
J & TD

DENNIS & FITCH   1836
Troy, N.Y., at 197 River Street.
DENNIS & FITCH

E. W. DENNISON   1805
Bangor, Me.
E.W.DENNISON

OTTO PAUL DE PARISIEN (PARISEN)   1763
New York. Advertised, April 25, *New York Gazette*: "Goldsmith
from Berlin, makes all sorts of plate, plain and chased, in the
neatest and most expeditious manner; likewise undertakes
chasing any piece of old plate at his House, the lower end of
Batto-Street." Admitted Freeman, January 31, 1764. Notices,
1765, 1769. In 1774, "Silversmith, in the Fly, in this City, took
Fire by means of his furnace." Located in Dock Street, later at
Queen Street, 1787–1789. Son, Otto W., joined business.
Commissioned by Corporation Council of the city to make a gold
box, for which he was paid £32/18/16.
OP – PARISEN

OTTO PAUL DE PARISIEN & SON   1789
New York, at 60 Queen Street until 1791.
OPDP

WILLIAM DE PEYSTER   1732
New York. Freeman May 22, 1733. Goldsmith. Son of Johannes
De Peyster, born September 22, 1666, in New York, and his
wife, Annae Bancker, born 1670, married in Albany, October
10, 1688. William, the eleventh of twelve children, was bap-
tised May 8, 1709, the same day as his wife, Margareta
Roosevelt, married May 5, 1730, Dutch Reformed Church,
N.Y. His mark, WDP, is on a porringer made for Abraham and
Elizabeth De Peyster Boelen.
WDP

PIETER DE RIEMER 1738–1814   1763
New York. Baptised in the Dutch Reformed Church, January
28, 1739, son of Steenwyck and wife Catharine Roosevelt.
Married Elsaefje Babbington, May 10, 1763. Freeman, January
31, 1769. Probably apprenticed to his grandfather Nicholas
Roosevelt. In Poughkeepsie, 1796–1809. Died October 2, in
Hyde Park, N.Y.
PDR

DANIEL DESHON 1697–1781   1730
New London, Conn. Born in Norwich, Conn. Apprenticed to
Rene Grignon who willed him his tools. Completed his service
with John Gray. Married Ruth Christophers, 1719, in New
London.
DD

JOHN DEVERELL 1764–1813   1785
Boston, Mass.
DEVERELL

B. DEXTER   1825
New Bedford, Mass.
B.DEXTER

MICHAEL DE YOUNG   1816
Baltimore, Md., until 1836.
M.DE YOUNG

ANSON DICKINSON   1780–1852   1800
Litchfield, Conn.; in New York, 1824.
A.DICKINSON

NATHAN DICKINSON   1800–1861   1824
Amherst, Mass.
ND – N.DICKINSON

P. DICKINSON & CO.   1837
Syracuse, N.Y., until 1842. Pliny Dickinson.
P.DICKINSON & CO

AARON DIKEMAN   1824
New York.
A.DIKEMAN

JAMES DINWIDDIE   1820–1885   1840
Lynchburg, Va. Silversmith, Chief Engineer of the Lynchburg
Hose Co., active Mason affiliated with the Methodist Church.
Worked until 1868 then moved to Hale's Ford where he died.
JAMES DINWIDDIE

CHARLES E. DISBROW   1815
Norwalk, Conn. Listed in New York, 1825.
CED – C.E.DISBROW

ISAAC DIXON   1843
Philadelphia, Pa.
I.DIXON

JOHN DIXWELL   1680–1725   1710
Boston, Mass. Born in New Haven, Conn., son of Col. John (one
of the judges of Charles I of England; the regicide fled to the
Colony where he married). Married three times. One of the
founders and officers of the North Church. Son, Basil, 1711–
1746, was a silversmith. Mentioned and advertised in *Boston
News Letter*, 1713 and 1722.
ID

JOHN DOANE   1733/4–1767   1760
Boston and Cohasset, Mass. Born in Eastham, Mass. Married
Lucy Davenport. Died on island of Barbados.
J.DOANE

JOSHUA DOANE   –1753   1740
Providence, R.I. Married Mary Cooke, 1752.
DOANE – I.DOANE

EZEKIEL DODGE   1792
New York, at 31 Little Dock Street.
E.DODGE

JOHN DODGE   1800
New York. In Catskill, N.Y., 1818–1819.
J.DODGE

NEHEMIAH DODGE   1795
Providence R.I., advertised a shop near the Church, where he
makes and sells all kinds of smith's work. Located at 41 Benefit
Street in 1824.
N.DODGE

SERIL DODGE   1759–1802   1793
Providence, R.I. Born in Pomfret, Conn. Apprenticed to
Thomas Harland. February 21, 1793, advertised, *United States
Chronicle*, "At the sign of the Arm and Gold Ear-ring, at his new
shop opposite the Market. . . . offers a great variety of
goldsmith's and jewelry ware."
S.DODGE

DANIEL NOYES DOLE   1775–1841   1804
Newburyport, Mass. Married Nancy Gove, 1804. In Hallowell,
Me., 1812; later, in Wiscasset, Me. Father of Ebenezer.
D.N.DOLE

EBENEZER GOVE DOLE   1805–1885   1831
Hallowell, Me. Born in Wiscasset, Me. Married Margaret
Lennan, 1831.
E.G.DOLE

J. DOLL   1820
New York.
J.DOLL

WILLIAM DONOVAN   1784
Philadelphia, Pa., at Walnut and Chestnut Streets, goldsmith
and jeweler.
W.DONOVAN

AMOS DOOLITTLE   1754–1832   1780
New Haven, Conn. Born in Cheshire, Conn. Apprenticed to
Eliakim Hitchcock. Silversmith and engraver. The second in a
family of thirteen. At Lexington under Captain Benedict Arnold.
Fought in defense of New Haven, July, 1779. Member of Hiram
Lodge # 1 of New Haven and served as Master in 1802.
AD

SAMUEL DORRANCE   1778–1815   1803
Providence, R.I.
DORRANCE

JOSHUA DORSEY   1793
Philadelphia, Pa., at 22 North Third Street and 44 Market
Street. In Directory, 1796. At 14 Green Street until 1804.
Brother of Samuel.
I.DORSEY

ROBERT DOUGLAS   1740–1776   1766
New London, Conn., at shop next door to Capt. Hurlbuts.
Served in Revolutionary War. Died in Canterbury, Conn. Made
sugar tongs engraved 1790.
RD

JEREMOTT WILLIAM DOUGLASS   1790
Philadelphia, Pa., at 257 South Front Street until 1793.
ID – I.DOUGLASS

GEORGE CHRISTOPHER DOWIG   1724/5–1807   1765
Philadelphia, Pa., at Second Street. In Baltimore, Md., 1773.
Advertised, *Maryland Gazette*; July 7, 1789; "Having fully
determined upon quitting the Business of a Silversmith, pur-
poses to dispose of his remaining Stock in Trade by Lottery,
which will positively be the last." In Market Street, Baltimore,
until 1791.
GD

GEORGE R. DOWNING   1810
New York., working until 1844. Partner of Samuel Baldwin and
Silas Phelps of Newark, N.J. as Downing & Phelps, 1810.
GRD – DOWNING

DOWNING & BALDWIN   1836
New York, in Directory. In Newark, N.J., 1836, at 268 Broad
Street, George R. Downing and Samuel Baldwin until 1844.
D & B

DOWNING & PHELPS   1810
Newark, N.J. George Downing and Silas Phelps. Advertised,
Sentinel of Freedom, June 2, 1812. Dissolved partnership, October
5, 1824.
D & P

JOSEPH DRAPER   1800–1864   1825
Wilmington, Del., at 77 Market Street. Succeeded by Emmor
Jefferis in 1832. In Directory until 1844, Cincinnati, Ohio.
J.DRAPER

THOMAS PICKERING DROWN   1782–1849   1803
Portsmouth, N.H. Son of Samuel Drowne. Advertised until
1816.
T.P.DROWN

BENJAMIN DROWNE   1759–1793   1780
Portsmouth, N.H. Brother of Samuel. Member of St. John's
Lodge # 1, May 9, 1793.
B.DROWNE

SAMUEL DROWNE   1749–1815   1770
Portsmouth, N.H. Brother of Benjamin; father of Daniel and
Thomas Pickering Drown.
SD – S.DROWNE

ABRAHAM DUBOIS   –1807   1777
Philadelphia, Pa., advertised May 20, 1777, *Penna. Evening Post*;
"For sale at his house in Second Street, four doors below Arch
Street . . ." Listed at 65 North Second Street, 1785–1807.
Admitted sons to business in 1805.
AD – A.DUBOIS

JOSEPH DUBOIS   1790
New York, at 17 Great Dock Street and 81 John Street until
1797.
I.DUBOIS – JD – J.DUBOIS

PHILO DUBOIS   1842
Buffalo, N.Y., until 1848.
P.DUBOIS

TUNIS D. DUBOIS   1797
New York, at 90 John Street; 11 Pearl Street in 1799.
TDD – T.D.DUBOIS

JAMES DUFFEL   1761–1835   1790
Georgetown, S.C., until 1800. Born in Bucks County, Pa. In
New York at 349 Pearl Street, 1801; Fredericksburg, Va., 1802;
Lynchburg, Va. from 1810 until his death on October 21. He
made a silver tea set for each of his five daughters as a wedding
present.
I. DUFFEL – JD

DUHME & CO.   1839
Cincinnati, Ohio. Listed 1842–1896. Herman Duhme, 1819–
1888, founder.
DUHME

JEREMIAH DUMMER   1645–1718   1666
Boston, Mass. Born September 14th, son of Richard and Frances
Burr Dummer. Apprenticed to Hull & Sanderson, 1659. Married
Hannah Atwater, sister of John Coney's wife, in 1672. Was a
member of the Old South Church. Later joined the First Church
and became a Deacon. Freeman, April 21, 1679. Appointed
Captain of Artillery Company, 1697–80; Constable, 1675;
Justice of Peace, 1693–1718. Owned interests in eleven ships,
1697–1713. Died in Boston on May 24th. Success referred to by
John Hull in 1681. Made a tankard dated 1687, cup dated
1700, porringer engraved HLE, same as Grignon. Master of John
Noyes and William Cowell. In 1714, Yale University received a
collection of books from Jeremiah Dummer re: *Thomas G. Wright
Literary Culture In Early New England*, 1620–1730.
ID

JOHN BAPTISTE DUMOUTET   1761–1813   1793
Philadelphia, Pa., at 71 Elm Street; 79 North Third Street,
1796; 55–57 South Second Street, 1800. In Charleston, S.C.,
1802–1813.
DUMOUTET

RUFUS DAVENPORT DUNBAR   1807–1869   1825
Worcester, Mass.
R. D. DUNBAR

DUNBAR & BANGS   1850
Worcester, Mass.
DUNBAR & BANGS

DUNBAR & STORY   1845
Worcester, Mass.
DUNBAR & STORY

CARY DUNN   1765

New York. Freeman, October 29, 1765. Advertised, *New York Gazette*, March, 1770, "Shop, between New Dutch Church and the Fly Market." In Morristown, N.J., 1778; Newark, N.J., 1782. Returned to New York, 1784, after seven years of exile. Listed at Maiden Lane and William Street, 1786. Witness to a will, August 29, 1786. Dunn & Sons, 1787–1791. Member of the Gold and Silversmiths Society.

C . DUNN

BARNARD DUPUY   1828

Raleigh, N.C. Advertised, *The Star*, 1833–1840, as silversmith on Fayetteville Street.

B . DUPUY

DANIEL DUPUY   1719–1807   1745

Philadelphia, Pa. Born in New York, April 3, son of Dr. John and Anne Chardavoine Dupuy. Apprenticed to brother-in-law Peter David. Married Eleanor Cox, September 6, 1746. Advertised for custom until 1780, "Shop below Friends Meeting House in Second Street." Two sons, John and Daniel, in business, 1792–1805. Partner of John David, 1792–1805. A memorandum book left by him covers records of the period 1740–1807.

DD

DANIEL DUPUY, JR.   1753–1826   1785

Philadelphia, Pa. Born May 3rd. Married Mary Meredith, June 5, 1788. Advertised at 16 South Second Street, 1782–1812. Partner with brother John. Died in Daly, Pa.

D . DUPUY

DANIEL DUPUY & SONS   1784

Philadelphia, Pa., with sons, Daniel and John, at 114 Sassafras Street.

DDD

WILLIAM B. DURGIN   1850

Concord, N.H.

WM . B . DURGIN

WILLIAM C. DUSENBERRY   1819

New York, until 1835.

W . C . DUSENBERRY

DANIEL DUYCKINCK   1798

New York, at 75 Fair and 10 Dutch Streets until 1800.

D . DUYCKINCK

TIMOTHY DWIGHT   1654–1691/2   1675
Boston, Mass. Born in Dedham, Mass. Apprenticed to John
Hull. William Rouse and Thomas Savage appraised his estate.
Known by two major pieces, a salver and a tankard.
T D

JOSEPH DYAR   1795–1851   1822
Middlebury, Vt., working until 1851.
J . DYAR

DYAR & EDDY   1805
Boston, Mass.
D & E

[E]

SETH EASTMAN   1801–1885   1820
Concord, N.H.
SETH EASTMAN

JAMES EASTON, II   1807–1903   1828
Nantucket, Mass. Born in Providence, R.I. Apprenticed to
William Hadwen from whom he purchased the business. Married
Sarah C. Wyer. Delegate to the Constitutional Convention.
Died, February 20. Firm of Easton & Sanford.
J . EASTON

NATHANIEL EASTON   1815
Nantucket, Mass.
N . EASTON

EASTON & SANFORD   1830
Nantucket, Mass. James Easton, II and Frederick S. Sanford,
advertised in *The Inquirer*, April 10, 1830. Located at 62 Main
Street in 1833. Partnership dissolved, May 1, 1838.
EASTON & SANFORD

JAMES B. EATON   –1829   1805
Boston, Mass. Directory 1805–1809. In Charleston, S.C.,
1829, where he died.
J . B . EATON

TIMOTHY EATON   1793
Philadelphia, Pa., at 9 Cherry Street.
T . EATON

THOMAS STEVENS EAYRES   1760–1803   1785
Boston, Mass. Apprentice and son-in-law of Paul Revere. In
Worcester, Mass., 1791–1793, then in Boston. Declared insane,
1802.
EAYRES – TE

JOHN EDWARDS   1671–1746   1691
Boston, Mass. Born in Limehouse, England. Came to Boston
with father, a chirurgeon, in 1688. Apprenticed to Jeremiah
Dummer. Married Sybil Newmann, 1700; Abigail Fowle Smith,
1730. Partner of John Allen, 1700. Was Sergeant of the Artillery
Company, 1704. Held town offices until 1727. Notice, *Boston
Evening Post*, April 14, 1746, "John Edwards, goldsmith, 'a
Gentleman of a very fair Character and well respected by all that
knew him,' died April 8, 1746, aged 75 years." Sons, Thomas,
Samuel, and grandson, Joseph, Jr., were silversmiths. Son,
Joseph, was a stationer. Made the earliest cream jug.
IE

JOSEPH EDWARDS, JR.   1734–1783   1758
Boston, Mass. Advertised, *Boston News Letter*, March 21, 1765,
"whereas the shop of the Subscriber was last Night broken open
and the following Articles stolen, viz: . . . Whoever will make
Discovery of the Thief or Thieves, so that they may be brought
to Justice, and that I may recover my Goods again, shall receive
TWENTY DOLLARS Reward, and all necessary Charges paid
by Joseph Edwards, Jun'r."
IE – I.EDWARDS – JE

SAMUEL EDWARDS   1705–1762   1729
Boston, Mass. Son of John. Married Sarah Smith, October 4,
1733. Received commissions from General Assembly for presentation pieces. Appointed Assessor, 1760. "Esteemed as a Man of
Integrity." Sold property to R. Boyleston in 1742. Estate administered by brother Joseph, a stationer.
SE

THOMAS EDWARDS   1701–1755   1725
Boston, Mass. Son of John. Freeman of New York, May 25,
1731. Married Sarah Burr, November 20, 1723. Advertised
1747. Captain of Artillery Company. His wife, Sarah, executrix
of estate. Zachariah Brigden was his apprentice and son-in-law.
TE – T.EDWARDS

JACOB EGE (EDGE)   1754–1795   1779
Richmond, Va. Active in civic affairs until his death. His wife
was appointed administrator of his estate. *Richmond Chronicle*,
August 9, 1796, "For sale, at the house formerly occupied by
Jacob Ege, household furniture, silversmith's tools, articles of
silverwork and two cows." Died October 6, 1795.
I E

ALFRED ELDERKIN   1759–1833   1792
Windham, Conn. Born in Killingsworth, Conn. Partner of
Elderkin & Staniford, dissolved in 1792. Later, in Red Hook,
N.Y.
A E

JEREMIAH ELFRETH, JR.   1723–1765   1752
Philadelphia, Pa. Son of Jeremiah and Sarah Oldman Elfreth.
Married Hannah Trotter, August 27, 1752. Advertised at North
Second Street.
J E

GEORGE ELLIOTT   –1857   1835
Wilmington, Del. Apprenticed to Charles Canby whose business
he purchased in 1852.
G . ELLIOTT

PETER ELLISTON   1791
New York, at Vesey Street; 187 Broadway, 1795–1800.
ELLISTON

JOHN AARON ELLIOTT   1788–1864   1815
Sharon, Conn.
A E – J A E

WILLIAM ELVINS   1796
Baltimore, Md.
W . ELVINS

STEPHEN EMERY   1749–1801   1775
Boston, Mass. Born in Exeter, N.H., March 23. Married in
1777. Mentioned with Joseph Loring in Selectmen's Records in
1788. Located at 5 Union Street, 1789; Fish Street, 1796.
EMERY – SE – S . EMERY

THOMAS KNOX EMERY   1781–1815   1802
Boston, Mass. Son of Stephen. Married Mary Parker. Member of
the Massachusetts Mechanics Association, 1806. At 32 Ann
Street in 1813. Joseph Foster and Jesse Churchill appraised his
estate.
T . EMERY – TKE – T . K . EMERY

THOMAS EMOND   1802
Petersburg, Va., from Edinburgh, Scotland. In Raleigh, N.C.,
1806–1821.
T.EMOND

EDGAR M. EOFF   1785–1858   1825
New York, at 83 Duane Street until 1850.
EME

GARRET EOFF   1779–1845   1806
New York. Born, August 29, son of Garret and Sarah Heyer
Eoff. Apprenticed to Abraham G. Forbes until 1798. Advertised
at 39 Warren Street and 23 Elm Street until 1814; at 3 New
Street in 1819. Of the firms, Eoff & Howell, Eoff & Connor,
Eoff & Moore.
G.EOFF

EOFF & CONNOR   1833
New York. Garret Eoff and John H. Connor.
J.H.CONNOR – G.EOFF

EOFF & HOWELL   1805
New York, at 2 Wall Street. Garret Eoff and Paul Howell.
E & H – EOFF & HOWELL

EOFF & MOORE   1835
New York, at 51 Morton Street. Garret Eoff and John Chandler
Moore.
G.EOFF – J.C.MOORE

EOFF & PHYFE   1844
New York, at 5 Dey Street. Edgar Eoff and William Phyfe.
E & P

EOFF & SHEPHERD   1825
New York.
E & S

EOLLES & DAY   1825
Hartford, Conn.
EOLLES & DAY

HENRY ERWIN   1817
Philadelphia, Pa., at 191 South Second Street; 33 North Third
Street, 1824.
H.ERWIN

JOHN ERWIN   1809
Baltimore, Md., until 1820.
J. ERWIN

JOHN ERWIN   1815
New York, at 200 Church Street.
J. ERWIN

HENRY EVANS   1820
New York. In Newark, N.J., at 289 Broad Street, 1835. Adver-
tised in Directory, 1840–1863.
HENRY EVANS

ROBERT EVANS   1768–1812   1798
Boston, Mass. Married Mary Peabody. Died intestate. Rufus
Farnam administered estate and Hazen Morse listed as one of the
appraisers.
EVANS – RE – R. EVANS

CHARLES EDWARD EVARD   1825–1906   1848
Leesburg, Va. Born June 18. Moved to Staunton, Va., 1849.
Returned to Leesburg, 1850, where he died, November 7, 1906.
CEE

CHARLES EUGENE EVARD   –1857   1837
Philadelphia, Pa., listed in Directory. Advertised, "as a compara-
tive stranger", in Lynchburg, Va., 1840. In Winchester, Va.,
1844.
EVARD

JOHN EWAN   1786–1852   1823
Charleston, S.C.
J. EWAN

WILLIAM H. EWAN   1849
Charleston, S.C.
WM. H. EWAN

JAMES EYLAND   1795–1835   1820
Charleston, S.C. Born in England.
J. EYLAND

[F]

F. A. & CO.   1850
Galveston, Tx.
F. A & CO

ARTEMAS O. FAIRCHILD   1839
Wheeling, Va. Advertised, *Daily Wheeling Times*, August 4,
1848, "A. O. Fairchild makes sterling silver spoons and cups to
order and promptly repairs clocks and watches." Left Wheeling,
1855.
A.O.FAIRCHILD

JOSEPH FAIRCHILD   1824
New Haven, Conn., until 1837, Married Celina Amelia, 1820.
J.FAIRCHILD

ROBERT FAIRCHILD   1703–1794   1740
Durham, Conn. Born in Stratford, Conn. Moved to Durham
where he learned and practiced his trade, at the corner of Church
and Chapel Streets. Represented the Town in the General Assembly, 1739–1745. Auditor of the Colony, 1740. Appointed
Captain of Artillery Company in 1745. Returned to Stratford,
1747; in New Haven, 1772. A Mason in Hiram Lodge # 1,
April 23, 1771. Coiner of authorized Connecticut coppers. Died
in New York, November 15, 1794.
RF – R.FAIRCHILD

JAMES FALES   –1857   1805
Newport, R.I. and Bristol, R.I.
I.FALES – JAS FALES

CHARLES FARIS   1764–1800   1793
Annapolis, Md. Son of William and Priscilla Woodward Faris.
Advertised in *Maryland Gazette*, September 12, 1793, ". . . at
Church Street, where he opened a Shop." In 1799, elected
Councilman.
CHAS FARIS – CS FARIS

WILLIAM FARIS   1728–1804   1757
Annapolis, Md. Born in London, England. In *Maryland Gazette*,
March 7, 1757, advertised his shop near the Church. Father and
master of Charles. His account records and book of designs, in
care of the Maryland Historical Society, are interesting.
WF

CHARLES FARLEY   1791–1877   1812
Portland, Me. Born in Ipswich, Mass. Apprenticed to Robert
Brookhouse, Salem, Mass., 1805–1812. A Mason in Ancient
Land-Marks Lodge of Portland, Me., October 26, 1814. Partner
of Eleazer Wyer, 1828–1832.
C.FARLEY – FARLEY

HENRY FARNAM 1773–1833   1799
Boston, Mass. Born in Norwich, Conn. Apprenticed, with
brother Rufus, to Joseph Carpenter. Advertised until 1833.
HF – H.FARNAM

RUFUS FARNAM 1769–   1796
Boston, Mass. Born in Norwich, Conn. Served apprentice with
brother Henry to Joseph Carpenter. Advertised until 1833. Firm
of Farnam & Ward.
RE – R.FARNAM

RUFUS & HENRY FARNAM   1800
Boston, Mass., until 1807.
R & H.FARNAM

THOMAS FARNAM   1825
Boston, Mass., at 87 Washington Street. In Directory until
1830. Son of Rufus.
TH.FARNAM

FARNAM & WARD   1816
Boston, Mass. Rufus Farnam and Richard Ward.
FARNAM & WARD

JOHN C. FARR   1824
Philadelphia, Pa., until 1840.
J.C.FARR – JOHN C.FARR

FARRINGTON & HUNNEWELL   1837
Boston, Mass. John Farrington and George W. Hunnewell at 8
William's Court; at 4 Court Avenue in 1850.
FARRINGTON & HUNNEWELL – F & H

JOHN W. FAULKNER   1835
New York, N.Y.
JWF – J.W.FAULKNER

ABRAHAM FELLOWS 1786–1851   1809
Troy, N.Y. Born in Rhinebeck, N.Y. Son of Philip and Hannah
Milledoler Fellows. Member of Trojan Greens in War of 1812,
for which he received grant of 160 acres of land. Sold business to
Dennis & Fitch. In Albany, 1841–1844. In Buffalo, 1850.
FELLOWS

I. W. & J. K. FELLOWS   1834
Lowell, Mass. Ignatius W. and James K. Fellows.
I.W & J.K.FELLOWS

JAMES K. FELLOWS 1832
Lowell, Mass., at Merriman Street until 1834.
JAMES K.FELLOWS

FELLOWS & STORM 1839
Albany, N.Y. Abraham Fellows and Abraham G. Storm.
FELLOWS & STORM

J. S. FELT 1825
Portland, Me.
J.S.FELT

JAMES FENNO 1825
Lowell, Mass.
J.FENNO

FENNO & HALE 1840
Bangor, Me.
FENNO & HALE

WILLIAM D. FENNO 1797–1870 1822
Worcester, Mass., at 104 Main Street. Firm of Boyden & Fenno,
1825; William Fenno & Son circa 1850.
WM. D.FENNO & SON

ZIBA FERRIS 1786–1875 1810
Wilmington, Del., opened a shop at corner of Fourth and Market
Streets where he continued until 1860. Taught son, Ziba, Jr.,
and Thomas Megear.
ZIBA FERRIS

WILLIAM B. FESSENDEN 1845
Newport, R.I.
FESSENDEN

PETER FEURT 1703–1737 1732
Boston, Mass. and New York. Goldsmith from New York.
Granted liberty by Selectman of Boston, 1727, to open a shop
and exercise his calling having given, to the satisfaction for the
indemnitie, the Town £10s. Married Susannah Gray, April 23,
1728. Died insolvent. Known by three pieces: two-handled
covered cup, Yale University Art Gallery; a cann; a serving
spoon.
PF

PETER FIELD 1790
Albany, N.Y., until 1800.
FIELD

PETER FIELD, JR.   −1837   1805
New York. In Directory until 1837.
FIELD JR − P.FIELD JR

GEORGE FIELDING   1731
New York. Freeman, April 13, 1731. Married Catharina
Roseboom, daughter of Hendrick and Debora Staats Roseboom.
A child baptised, Dutch Church, N.Y., 1730. Notice appears in
New York Gazette, November 17, 1755, ". . . . Mr. Fielding,
Gold-Smith, formerly lived at corner of Broad and Princes
Streets . . ." In Albany in 1765.
GF

HIRAM FINCH   1829
Albany, N.Y. In Directory until 1839.
H.FINCH

J. P. FIRENG   1810
Burlington, N.J.
J.P.FIRENG

THOMAS FISHER   1797
Philadelphia, Pa., at German Street. In Baltimore, Md., at
Forrest Street, 1803. In Easton, Md., 1803−1807.
TF − T.FISHER

DENNIS M. FITCH   1840
Troy, N.Y.
D.M.FITCH

JAMES FITCH   1821
Auburn, N.Y., until 1826. Firm of Graves & Fitch, 1816−1821.
J.FITCH

JOHN FITCH   1743−1796   1769
Trenton, N.J. Born in Hartford, Conn. In Windsor, Conn.,
1764. Married Lucy Roberts, December, 1767. Moved to
Trenton, N.J., 1769. Account book records employment of
seven silversmiths: James Greaves, John Wilson, John Cochran,
Joseph Toy, James Wilson, Frederick Burgy and Samuel Stout.
Shop on King Street until 1776. Traveled to Northwest and
engraved a map of the territory. In New York, 1782. Moved to
Philadelphia, Pa. Died in Kentucky.
JF

JOHN FITE   1783−1818   1807
Baltimore, Md. In Directory, 1810.
I.FITE

O. M. FITON   1815
Troy, N.Y.
O.M.FITON

JOSIAH FLAGG   1765
Boston, Mass.
JF

FLAGG & CHAPIN   1825
Boston, Mass.
FLAGG & CHAPIN

THOMAS FLETCHER   1813
Philadelphia, Pa., at Chestnut and Fourth Street until 1850.
Firms of Fletcher & Gardiner; Fletcher & Bennett.
TF — T.FLETCHER

FLETCHER & GARDINER   1809
Boston, Mass., Directory until 1810; Philadelphia, Pa., 1812.
Thomas Fletcher and Sidney Gardiner at Third and Chestnut
Streets until 1822.
F & G

JOHN FOLSOM   1756–1839   1780
Albany, N.Y. Born in Stratford, Conn., May 17, son of
blacksmith Samuel Folsom and his wife, Ann Bingham Folsom.
Freeman in Albany, N.Y., 1781. Firm of Folsom & Hutton,
1790. Listed in Directory, 1813–1815.
IF

ABRAHAM GERRITZE FORBES   1769
New York, Freeman. Son of Gilbert and Philander Haylie Forbes.
Brother of William G. Forbes. Married Jane Young, May 17,
1789. Located at 75 Bowery Lane, 1790; 118 Broadway, 1795.
Marshal of the City, 1799.
AF — A.FORBES — AGF

COLIN VAN GELDER FORBES   1798
New York. Baptised in Dutch Church, N.Y., March 6, 1776,
son of William G. Forbes. Married in Dutch Church, N.Y.,
June 14, 1798, Elizabeth Bullock. At 72 Gold Street, 1816;
Collect and Pump Streets, 1823. In Directory, 1808–1839.
C.FORBES — CVGF

COLIN V. G. FORBES & SON   1826
New York. At 59 Vandam Street, 1835.
FORBES & SON

COLIN & JOHN W. FORBES 1810
New York., until 1825.
C & I.W.FORBES

GARRET FORBES 1785– 1808
New York. Born September 2, son of William G. and Catharine
Van Gelder Forbes. Baptised, Dutch Church, N.Y., September
25, 1782. At 316 Broadway, 1808; at 90 Broadway with
William G. Forbes, 1805–1809. Advertised in 1820 as a
weigher and silversmith.
G.FORBES

JOHN W. FORBES 1781– 1802
New York. Baptised, Dutch Church, N.Y., July 1, 1781, son of
William G. Forbes, brother of Colin and Garret. At 415 Pearl
Street, 1802; 421 Pearl Street, 1804; various addresses on
Broadway. Was Government measurer and weigher in 1835.
IWF – I.W.FORBES

WILLIAM FORBES 1799– 1830
New York. Born March 11, 1799. Baptised Dutch Church,
N.Y., April 14, 1799, son of Colin V. G. Forbes. At 2 Green
Street, 1830; 277 Spring Street, 1850.
FORBES – WF – W.FORBES

WILLIAM G. FORBES 1773
New York. Freeman, February 3, 1773. Married Catharine Van
Gelder, November 6, 1771, Dutch Church, N.Y. Son of Gilbert
and Philander Haylie Forbes, brother of Abraham. Member of
the Gold and Silver Smiths' Society, 1786. Listed at 88 Broadway
until 1789. Ad, *New York Gazette and General Advertiser*, September, 6, 1798, "Stolen Silver, 90 Broadway." Joined the
Mechanics' Institute in 1802. At 90 Broadway with son, Garret,
1805–1809.
W.G.FORBES

JABEZ W. FORCE 1819
New York, at 1 Staple Street.
FORCE – J.W.FORCE

JAMES M. FORD 1810
Boston, Mass., until circa 1830.
JAMES M.FORD

SAMUEL FORD 1797
Philadelphia, Pa., at 39 Arch Street. Married Eleanor Ford,
1802, in Baltimore, Md. Advertised at Green and Charles
Street, Baltimore, Md. 1802–1803.
SF

O. C. FORSYTH   1810
New York, N.Y., until circa 1845.
FORSYTH – O.C.FORSYTH

GEORGE B. FOSTER   1810–1881   1838
Salem, Mass., Boston, 1842–1854.
GEORGE B.FOSTER

JOHN FOSTER   1811
New York, at 189 William Street; 53 Pearl Street, 1815, partner
of Thomas Richards. In Directory, 1815–1817. In Winchester,
Va., 1817–1825.
IF – J.FOSTER

JOSEPH FOSTER   1760–1839   1785
Boston, Mass. Apprenticed to Benjamin Burt. Deacon of the
Old South Church. Advertised at 171 Ann Street and, later, at
Fish Street.
FOSTER – I.FOSTER

NATHANIEL & THOMAS FOSTER   1820
Newburyport, Mass., at 21 State Street, 1823–1860.
N & T.FOSTER

THOMAS FOSTER   1799–1887   1820
Newburyport, Mass., at 21 State Street, 1823–1860, working
with brother, Nathaniel.
T.FOSTER

FOSTER & RICHARDS   1815
New York. John Foster and Thomas Richards.
F & R – JF T.RICHARDS – T.RICHARDS JF

LOUIS FOURNIQUET   –1826   1795
New York, at 53 Ann Street until 1798. At 42 William Street,
20 Franklin Street, 71 Reade Street, 1800–1823. In Phoenix
Lodge, 1799. Charter member of Washington Lodge. Firm of
Fourniquet & Wheatley, 1815.
FOURNIQUET

JOHN H. FOWLE   1805
Boston, Mass. In Northampton, Mass., 1825.
J.H.FOWLE

NATHANIEL FOWLE   1748–1817   1803
Boston, Mass. In partnership with John Fowle as John &
Nathaniel Fowle, 1803–05. Died in Northampton, Mass.
FOWLE

NATHANIEL FOWLE, JR.   1815
Northampton, Mass. Son of Nathaniel. Apprentice of Nathan
Storrs. Firm of Fowle & Kirkland, 1828–1833, Nathaniel
Fowle, Jr, and Samuel W. Kirkland.
FOWLE & KIRKLAND

EDWARD FRANCIS   1828
Leesburg, Va., until 1835.
E.FRANCIS

NATHANIEL FRANCIS   1804
New York, at 55 John Street; 79 Fulton Street in 1819.
FRANCIS – N.FRANCIS

GEORGE FRANCISCUS   –1791   1776
Baltimore, Md. married Margaret Schely. Member of the
Ancient and Honorable Mechanical Society. Son, George, Jr.,
continued the business at 4 Market Place and other addresses
until 1818.
G.FRANCISCUS

GEORGE FRANCISCUS, JR.   1781–   1810
Baltimore, Md. Son of George and Margaret Schely Franciscus.
Continued his father's business in Baltimore until 1818. In
Lancaster, Pa., 1819–1840. Used his father's mark.
G.FRANCISCUS

JACOB FRANK   1793
Philadelphia, Pa., at Front Street between Market and Arch
Streets.
J.FRANK

N. FREEBORN   1810
Newport, R.I.
N.FREEBORN

JOSEPH M. FREEMAN   1806–1882   1831
Norfolk, Va. Firms of Freeman & Pollard, 1832; J. M. Freeman
& Co., 1843; J. M. Freeman & Son, 1856. Died May 26.
FREEMAN – J.M.FREEMAN

J. M. FREEMAN & CO.   1843
Norfolk, Va., until 1844. J. M. Freeman and F. Burwell.
J.M.FREEMAN & CO

FREEMAN & POLLARD   1832
Norfolk, Va., until 1834. Joseph M. Freeman and Lewis R.
Pollard.
FREEMAN & POLLARD

FREEMAN & WALLIN   1850
Philadelphia, Pa.
FREEMAN & WALLIN

BENJAMIN C. FROBISHER   1792–1862   1816
Boston, Mass., in Directory as firm of Stodder & Frobisher until
1825, then worked alone. At 69 Washington Street, 1836.
B.C.FROBISHER—FROBISHER

FROST & MUMFORD   1815
Providence, R.I.
F & M

DANIEL CHRISTIAN FUETER   1754
New York. Listed on the register at Goldsmiths' Hall, London,
England, "Dan. Christ. Fueter, Chelsea, next door to the 'Man
in the Moon'," December 8, 1753. Advertised in New York, May
27, 1754, "Near the Brew-house, facing Oswego Market." In
1763, returned to City and located in Dock Street. Took Oath of
Colonial Naturalization Act of 1740, July 31, 1765. Member of
Unitas Fratrum. In 1769, with son, Lewis Fueter, who continued
the business after father returned to his native Switzerland.
DCF

LEWIS FUETER   1770
New York. Freeman, March 28, 1775, son of Daniel C. Fueter.
Advertised in the *New York Gazette*," . . . at the Coffee-House
Bridge . . . guilding in all its branches . . . He thinks himself
obliged, in the name of his father, as well as himself, to return
thanks to the respectable public for the many favours done, and
to assure those who shall honor him with their commands, that
he will make it his utmost endeavor to deserve their Countenance
and encouragement." At Queen Street in 1774. Made salver
dated 1773.
FUETER—L.FUETER

DAVID C. FULTON   1835
Louisville, Ky.
D.C.FULTON

[G]

GREENBURY GAITHER   1822
Washington, D.C.
G.GAITHER

JOHN L. GALE   1819
New York, at 177 William Street. In Directory until 1837.
ILG – I. L. GALE – J. GALE – JLG – J. L. GALE

WILLIAM GALE   1799–1867   1820
New York, at Green Street; 29 Liberty Street until 1825. His
son, William, joined him in 1843. Firms of Gale & Stickler;
Gale, Wood & Hughes; Gale & Hughes; Gale & Willis; Gale &
Mosely.
WG – W. GALE

WILLIAM GALE, JR.   1843
New York, at 63 Liberty Street. Alderman, 1844.
WM. GALE JR

WILLIAM GALE & SON   1843
New York, at 63 Liberty Street; 116 Fulton Street, 1850.
W. GALE & SON – WM. GALE & SON

GALE & HUGHES   1846
New York, at 116 Fulton Street until 1850.
G & H

GALE & MOSELY   1830
New York, at 116 Fulton Street. William Gale and Joseph
Mosely.
G & M

GALE & STICKLER   1823
New York, at 104 Broadway. William Gale and John Stickler.
G & S

GALE & WILLIS   1840
New York, at 447 Broome Street.
GALE & WILLIS

GALE, WOOD & HUGHES   1830
New York. Founded by William Gale, Jacob Wood and Jasper
W. Hughes at 116 Fulton Street. Charles Wood and Stephen T.
Fraprie became apprentices. Dissolved in 1845 with retirement
of Gale.
GW & H

CHRISTOPHER GALLUP   1764–1849   1785
North Groton, Conn. Son of Colonel and Sarah Giddings Gal-
lup.
CG

FRANCIS GARDEN   1745
Boston, Mass., engraver from London, England.
FG

BALDWIN GARDINER   1814
Philadelphia, Pa., at Chestnut and Third Streets until 1817.
Brother of Sidney Gardiner. In New York Directory, 1827–
1847. Firms of Fletcher & Gardiner of New York; B. Gardiner &
Co.
BG – B.GARDINER

B. GARDINER & CO.   1836
New York.
B.GARDINER & CO

JOHN GARDNER   1734–1776   1760
New London, Conn. Son of Jonathan and Mary Gardner. Inven-
tory of estate lists silversmith's tools.
IG – J.GARDNER

GARNER & WINCHESTER   1840
Lexington, Ky.
GARNER & WINCHESTER

S. GARRE   1825
New York.
SG – S.GARRE

ELIAKIM GARRETSON   –1827   1785
Wilmington, Del. Married Lydia Windle, 1783. Moved to
Philadelphia, Pa., 1811.
EG – E.GARRETSON

PHILIP GARRETT   1780–1851   1811
Philadelphia, Pa., at High Street.
P.GARRETT

THOMAS C. GARRETT   1829
Philadelphia, Pa., until 1840.
T.C.GARRETT

JAMES GASKINS   1802
Portsmouth, Va., listed until 1824; Norfolk, Va., 1804–1805.
I.GASKINS – J.GASKINS

W. W. GASKINS   1806
Norfolk, Va.
WWG

JAMES GEDDY 1731–1807   1751
Williamsburg, Va. Son of James Geddy, gunsmith, whose house
he occupied after his father died in 1743. Advertised as a
Goldsmith, Silversmith and Jeweller. Notice appeared in the
Virginia Gazette, ". . . objection of his Shop's being too high up
Town . . . the Walk may be thought rather an amusement than a
Fatigue." In 1783, moved to Petersburg, Va. where he died,
May 12.
IG – JG

WILLIAM WADDILL GEDDY   1793
Petersburg, Va. Born in Williamsburg, Va., son of James and
Elizabeth Waddill Geddy. In 1790, worked in his father's firm of
James Geddy & Sons. Married Elizabeth Prentice, 1796.
WWG

JOSEPH GEE   1785
Philadelphia, Pa. Advertised in 1788.
GEE

NICHOLAS GEFFROY 1761–1839   1795
Newport, R.I. Born in France. married Sarah Shaw, September
29, 1795. Worked with her father and later joined his firm of
John Shaw & Co.
GEFFROY – N.GEFFROY

GEORGE S. GELSTON   1833
New York., at 189 Broadway until 1836. Firms of Gelston &
Co.; Gelston & Treadwell; Gelston, Ladd & Co.
GELSTON – G.S.GELSTON

HUGH GELSTON 1794–1873   1816
Baltimore, Md. Born in East Haddam, Conn. Married Rebecca
G. Durham. In partnership with James Gould, 1816–1821.
HU. GELSTON

GELSTON, LADD & CO.   1836
New York.
GELSTON LADD & CO

GELSTON & CO.   1837
New York.
GELSTON & CO

GELSTON & TREADWELL   1836
New York.
GELSTON & TREADWELL

CHARLES GENNET, JR.   1807–1887   1832
Richmond, Va. Purchased the business of C. P. Adriance, August
28, 1832. At 55 West Main Street in 1849 when firm of Gennet
& James was formed.
C. GENNET

W. GENNET   1850
Watertown, New York.
W. GENNET

GENNET & JAMES   1849
Richmond, Va. Charles Gennet, Jr. and Joseph H. James.
GENNETT & JAMES

ISAAC GERE   1771–1812   1793
Northampton, Mass., clockmaker, watchmaker, goldsmith,
silversmith until his death in Northampton. Born in Preston,
Mass.
IG

JOHN D. GERMON   1782
Philadelphia, Pa. Advertised, *Independent Gazetteer*, July 13,
1782, for a "runaway negro." Mentioned with Joseph Gee as a
standard bearer in the Federal Procession in Philadelphia in
1788. Located at 33 North Street until 1804; Quay Street until
1816.
GERMON – IG

SAMUEL A. GEROULD   1793–1887   1819
Keene, N.H., son of Theodore and Ruth Bowditch Gerould.
Firms of S. A & J. H. Gerould, 1825; S. & H. Gerould, 1830;
S. A. Gerould & Son, 1850.
S & H. GEROULD

ANDREW GERRISH   1784–1835   1814
Portsmouth, N.H. Son of Timothy.
A. GERRISH

OLIVER GERRISH   1796–1888   1825
Portland, Me. Born in Portsmouth, N.H., son of Timothy,
brother of Andrew. Apprenticed to John Gaines at fourteen years
of age. Married Sarah Little, daughter of Paul Little, goldsmith,
1825. In Directories until 1888.
O. GERRISH

TIMOTHY GERRISH   1749–1815   1775
Portsmouth, N.H. Father of Andrew and Oliver. A member of
St. John Lodge # 1 in 1804.
GERRISH – TG – T. GERRISH

GERRISH & PEARSON   1800
New York.
GERRISH & PEARSON

JOHN W. GETHEN   1811
Philadelphia, Pa., at 170 South Front Street, until 1818.
I.W.GETHEN

WILLIAM GETHEN   1797
Philadelphia, Pa., at 14 Combes Alley; 172 South Front Street,
1806–1808.
W.GETHEN

PETER GETZ   1764–1809   1782
Lancaster, Pa. Self tauught mechanic of singular ingenuity.
Mentioned for office of Chief Coiner for the Mint in 1792.
Master of lodge # 43 in 1794.
PG – P.GETZ

CAESAR GHISELIN   1670–1734   1700
Philadelphia, Pa. French Huguenot, native of Rouen,
naturalized in London, England, September 29, 1698. In Philadelphia, Pa. in 1701, from record of William Penn's account
book, until 1711. Married Catherine Reverdy in 1726. Worked
in Annapolis, Md., 1715–1726; Warden of St. Anne's Church,
April 19, 1720. John Steele, goldsmith, left him £100 in his
will, dated January 20,1721. His wife died in 1727. He returned
to Philadelphia, Pa. where he died and is buried in Christ Church
churchyard. Known pieces are a beaker and plate, porringer,
tankard, several spoons.
CG

WILLIAM GHISELIN   1751
Philadelphia, Pa. Son of Nicholas and grandson of Caesar
Ghiselin. Advertised in *Penna. Gazette*, November, 1751,
"Goldsmith, is removed from his late dwelling house in Second
Street . . . to the house a little below the Church, in second St.
where he continues Business as usual." Ad, *Penna Gazette*,
December 27, 1752. Mason in Lodge # 2 Moderns on December
27, 1752. Served as Junior Warden in 1756, then Senior and
Master. Active until 1763 and in 1770. Last record June 1785.
WG

JOHN GIBBS   1751–1797   1773
Providence, R.I. Married Elizabeth Gardiner, May 4, 1774.
Business continued by his wife, Elizabeth Gibbs, in partnership
with brother-in-law and apprentice, John C. Jenckes, 1797–
1800.
JG – J.GIBBS

JOHN FITTON GIBBS 1784–   1803
Providence, R.I. Son of John and Elizabeth Gardiner Gibbs.
Married Mary Graves, 1803.
I.F.GIBBS

MICHAEL GIBNEY   1836
New York. At 1 Trinity Place in 1844.
MG

WILLIAM GIBSON   1845
Philadelphia, Pa., at Third and Plum Streets.
GIBSON

CHRISTOPHER GIFFING   1815
New York, at 64 Partition Street; Chapel Street, 1819–1825.
CG – C.GIFFING

E. GIFFORD   1825
Fall River, Mass.
E.GIFFORD

SAMUEL GILBERT 1775–1850   1798
Hebron, Conn.
SG – S.GILBERT

WILLIAM W. GILBERT 1746–1818   1767
New York. Baptised in Dutch Church, N.Y., March 5, 1746.
Married Catharine Cosine, May 28, 1767. Notice that shop was
robbed of near £200, in plate, August 27, 1770. City Alderman
of West Ward, 1783–1788. Elected State Senator, 1809.
GILBERT – WG – W.GILBERT

CALEB GILL 1774–1855   1798
Hingham, Mass. Born August 14. Apprentice to Loring Bailey.
Married Katy Beal, 1798. Selectman for many years. Advertised
shop on South Street. Died in July.
GILL

BENJAMIN CLARK GILMAN 1763–1835   1784
Exeter, N.H., son of John and Jane Deane Gilman, brother of
John. Married Mary Thing, 1783. Elected Selectman, 1797,
1814.
BCG

JOHN WARD GILMAN 1741–1823   1767
Exeter, N.H. Born May 9, son of John and Jane Gilman, brother
of Benjamin. Married Hannah Emery, December 3, 1767.
GILMAN – IWG

JOHN B. GINOCHIO   1837
New York.
J.B.GINOCHIO

HENRY GIRAUD   1805
New York, worked at 16 Murray Street.
HG

DANIEL GODDARD   1796–1884   1817
Worcester, Mass. Born in Shrewsbury, Mass. Learned trade from
his father, Luther Goddard.
D.GODDARD

D. GODDARD & CO.   1850
Worcester, Mass.
D.GODDARD & CO

D. GODDARD & SON   1845
Worcester, Mass.
D.GODDARD & SON

NICHOLAS GODDARD   1773–1823   1797
Rutland, Vt. Born in Shrewsbury, Mass., son of Nathan. Married
Charity White, September 16, 1798. Held offices of Town Clerk
and Treasurer.
N.GODDARD

PHILIP GOELET   1708–1748   1731
New York. Freeman, May 25, 1731, Goldsmith. Baptised,
February 1, 1708, Dutch Church, New York, son of Jacobus and
Janette Cosaar Goelet. Married, March 25, 1730, Catharina
Boelen, baptised September 2, 1709, daughter of Jacob Boelen,
niece of Hendrick Boelen. Member of the Dutch Church, Feb-
ruary 17, 1730. Was Assessor, Collector and Constable of the
West Ward. Will dated February 20, 1743, proved April 4,
1748, for son, Isaac, loving Mother-in-law, Catharina Boelen,
her maintenance in my house and family, and all Estate to wife,
Catharina, wife and brothers, Jacob and John, Executors.
PG

THOMAS GOLDSMITH   1842
Troy, New York. In Directory until 1850.
T.GOLDSMITH

JOSEPH GOLDTHWAITE   1706–1780   1731
Boston, Mass., when notice of removal from "Mr. Burrill's shop
to the House adjoining the Sign of the Red Lyon." Married
February 8, 1727, Martha Lewis. In 1730, First Sergeant of

Artillery Company. In 1745, appointed Captain in siege of
Lewisburg. Constable in 1744. At meetings of St. John's Lodge,
175/–1764–1776. Died in Weston, Mass. in March.
IG

DANIEL T. GOODHUE   1824
Providence, R.I. In Directory until 1844.
DTG – D.T.GOODHUE

JOHN GOODHUE   1822
Salem, Mass., until 1855.
J.GOODHUE

HENRY GOODING   1820
Boston, Mass., until 1854.
GOODING

JOSIAH GOODING   1840
Boston, Mass. In Directory until 1859.
JOSIAH GOODING

BENJAMIN GOODWIN   1734–1792   1756
Boston, Mass. Born April 5. Referred to in Suffolk County
Records as "goldsmith" and, later, as a merchant. Died in Easton,
Bristol County, Mass.
B.GOODWIN

HORACE GOODWIN   1787–1864   1810
Hartford, Conn. Born September 11, son of Allyn and Anna
Marsh Goodwin. Married Mary Ramsey, November 29, 1812.
H.GOODWIN

H. & A. GOODWIN   1821
Hartford, Conn. Horace and brother, Allyn, dissolved firm in
1825.
GOODWIN – H & A.GOODWIN

GOODWIN & DODD   1811
Harford, Conn. Horace Goodwin and Thomas Dodd until 1821.
G & D – GOODWIN & DODD

ALEXANDER SNOW GORDON   –1813   1795
New York, at 40 William Street until 1800. Silversmith from
Great Britain. Naturalized in New York, April 23, 1790.
Master of Phoenix Lodge, later, Washington Lodge, 1800. Ad,
American Citizen & General Advertiser, April 21, 1801, "near Post
Office, offering silver polishing powder and silver for sale."
GORDON

GEORGE GORDON
Newburgh, N.Y., until 1824.
G.GORDON – GORDON

1800

JABEZ GORHAM 1792–
Providence, R.I. Apprenticed to Nehemiah Dodge, 1807.
Attaining his majority, joined in partnership with Christopher
Burr, William Hawden, George C. Clark, and Henry G. Mum-
ford for five years. Firms of Gorham & Beebe, 1825; Gorham &
Webster, 1831–1841. Located at 12 Steeple Street with son,
founding the Gorham Manufacturing Co., 1842. In 1850,
Gorham & Thurber.
J.GORHAM

1815

JABEZ GORHAM & SON
Providence, R.I., at 12 Steeple Street. Jabez and son, John.
J.GORHAM & SON

1842

MILES GORHAM 1756–1847
New Haven, Conn.
MG – M.GORHAM

1790

RICHARD GORHAM 1775–1841
New Haven, Conn., son of Miles and Abigail Morris Gorham.
In partnership with Samuel Shethar, 1806–1809.
R.GORHAM

1799

GORHAM & THURBER
Providence, R.I.
GORHAM & THURBER

1850

GORHAM & WEBSTER
Providence, R.I. Jabez Gorham and Henry L. Webster
GORHAM & WEBSTER

1831

GORHAM, WEBSTER & PRICE
Providence, R.I.
GORHAM, WEBSTER & PRICE

1835

JAMES GOUGH
New York, admitted Freeman. At 28 Beaver Street in 1795.
JG

1769

JAMES GOULD 1795–1874
Baltimore, Md., at Market Street, 1816–1821. Son of Josiah
and Abigail Williams Gould. Married Eliza Leech, 1819.
Apprenticed to Jabez Baldwin. In Baltimore, Directory in 1816;
at 189 Market Street, 1821. Firms of Geltson & Gould, 1816–

1816

1821; Gould & Ward, 1850; Gould, Stowell & Ward, 1855.
Died in Boston, Mass.

J.GOULD

GOULD & WARD   1850
Baltimore, Md. James Gould and William H. Ward.

GOULD & WARD

WILLIAM GOWDEY   −1798   1757
Charleston, S.C., advertised as a jeweler and goldsmith. In
1763, advertised "Imported English Goods". Member of South
Carolina Society, 1779.

WG

WILLIAM GOWEN   1749−1803   1777
Medford, Mass. Born in Charlestown, Mass., September 13.
Married Eleanor Cutler, April 29, 1772.

WG − W.GOWEN

THOMAS GRANT   1731−1804   1754
Marblehead, Mass. Married Margaret Burbier, July 2, 1754.

T.GRANT

WILLIAM GRANT, JR.   1785
Philadelphia, Pa., at 115 North Third Street; at Green and
Third Streets, 1798−1814. Listed in Directory, "Goldsmith,
deaf and dumb, but can read and write."

WG − W.GRANT

GEORGE GRAY   1800−1875   1826
Dover, N.H. In Directory until 1865. Married Lydia Barden,
September 16, 1827. Listed at 9 Congress Street, Portsmouth,
N.H., 1839.

GG − G.GRAY

JOHN GRAY   1692−1720   1713
Boston, Mass. Near Old South Meeting House in 1717. Ad-
vertised settlement of brother Samuel's estate. Married Mary
Christophers of New London, Conn. in 1714. Later, worked in
New London where he died.

IG

ROBERT GRAY   1792−1860   1813
Portsmouth, N.H., after completing apprenticeship in Salem,
Mass.

RG − R.GRAY − ROBT GRAY

SAMUEL GRAY 1684–1713   1710
New London, Conn. Born in Boston, Mass. Brother of John.
Married Mrs. Lucy Palmers, 1707.
SG

SAMUEL GRAY 1710–   1732
Boston, Mass. Born in Boston, Mass., nephew of Samuel Gray.
Purchased land for shop, 1732, deed witnessed by William
Simpkins and Basil Dixwell.
GRAY — S.GRAY

BARTHOLOMEW GREEN 1701–   1724
Boston, Mass., son of printer Bartholomew Green and his wife,
Mary, married 1690. Married Harriet Hanson of Newtown,
Conn. in 1724.
B.GREEN

BENJAMIN GREENE 1712–1776   1733
Boston, Mass. Worked with brother, Rufus.
BG

RUFUS GREENE 1707–1777   1730
Boston, Mass. Brother of Benjamin. Apprenticed to William
Cowell. Married Catharine Stambridge in 1728. Advertised,
Boston News Letter, 1733, "Stolen, a spoon, marked with the
Crest of Tyger's Head." Made the only New England tea caddy.
A portrait by John S. Copley in the Frick Collection.
RG — R.GREENE

DAVID GREENLEAF 1737–1800   1763
Norwich, Conn. Born in Bolton, Mass. Apprenticed to Rufus
Lathrop. Married Mary Johnson. Served in Revolutionary War.
In Coventry, Conn., 1788–1800, where he died.
D.GREENLEAF

DAVID GREENLEAF, JR. 1765–1835   1788
Hartford, Conn. Born in Norwich, Conn., son of David and
Mary Johnson Greenleaf. Married Nancy Jones, 1787. Adver-
tised, Northeast of State House. Partner of Abel Buel, 1798.
DG — GREENLEAF

GEORGE GREENLEAF 1790–1847   1812
Newburyport, Mass. Married Elizabeth Wheelwright in 1813.
G.GREENLEAF

DANIEL GREENOUGH 1685/6–1746   1708
New Castle, N.H. Born in Rowley, Mass. Married Abigail
Elliott, December 16, 1708. Will admitted to probate on May
17, 1747, in Bradford, Mass. Known for sugar box at the
Metropolitan Museum of Art, N.Y.
DG

CHARLES F. GREENWOOD   –1904   1848
Norfolk, Va. Married Mary Elizabeth Griffen, May 17, 1848.
He and his brother, Frederick, formed C. F. Greenwood & Bros.,
1851, which continued until Charles' death, July 16.
C.F.GREENWOOD

WILLIAM GREGG 1800–1867   1820
Petersburg, Va. Born February 2, in Monongahela County, West
Va. In Columbia, S.C., 1824. Married Marina Jones in 1829.
Located in Charleston, S.C. in 1838. Firm of Hayden, Gregg &
Co. until 1842; Gregg & Hayden, 1843–1846; Gregg, Hayden
& Co., 1846–1852.
W.GREGG

GREGG, HAYDEN & CO.   1846
New York, N.Y. and Charleston, S.C. until 1852.
GREGG HAYDEN & CO

MICHAEL GRETTER 1785–1868   1810
Richmond, Va. Born in Alexandria, Va., March 11. Apprenticed
to George Aiken, Baltimore, Md. Ad in *The Enquirer*, December
15, 1810, "offered to make silverware of any pattern on the
shortest notice." Prominent member of the Presbyterian Church.
Died in Richmond, Va., October 10.
ML GRETTER

PETER GRIFFEN   1815
New York, N.Y., until circa 1840.
P.GRIFFIN – P.GRIFFEN

GRIFFEN & HOYT   1819
New York. Peter Griffen and Walter A. Hoyt until 1832.
GRIFFEN & HOYT

GRIFFEN & SON   1832
New York. Peter Griffen and son, William, until 1837.
GRIFFEN & SON

DAVID GRIFFETH (GRIFFITH) 1735–1779   1757
Portsmouth, N.H. Died in Exeter, N.H.
DG – D.GRIFFETH – GRIFFETH

SAMUEL GRIFFETH (GRIFFITH) 1729–1773   1757
Portsmouth, N.H. Ad, *Gazette*, August 11, 1757, "Samuel
Griffeth, Goldsmith, . . ."; a notice in *N.H. Gazette*, September,
1770.
S.GRIFFETH – S.GRIFFITH

GREENBERRY GRIFFITH 1787–1848   1809
Alexandria, Va. Born May 30 in Maryland, son of Howard and
Jemima Jacob Griffith. Firm of Griffith & Gaither, 1809. A
Major in the War of 1812. Married Prudence Jones, February
24, 1814. Sold his business and moved to Washington, D.C.,
1820.
GG

WILLIAM GRIGG   –1797   1765
New York. Freeman, October 1, 1765. Married Helena Stout,
September 29, 1766. In Albany, N.Y., 1770–1778. Returned
to New York, 1791–1795, at Maiden Lane and William Street.
GRIGG – WG – W.GRIGG

RENE GRIGNON   –1715   1691
Oxford, Mass. Huguenot silversmith who settled in Greenwich,
Conn., 1687. In Boston, Mass., 1696, and became an Elder in
the French Church. Returned to Oxford, Mass, 1699, but left in
1704 because of the Deerfield Massacre. In Norwich, Conn.,
1708, where he died. Inventory of his estate lists silversmith's
tools which he willed to Daniel Deshon, his apprentice.
RG

GILBERT GRISWOLD 1788–   1810
Middletown, Conn. Brother of William with whom he worked.
GRISWOLD

WILLIAM GRISWOLD   1820
Middletown, Conn. Brother of Gilbert.
W.GRISWOLD

F. R. GRUMP   1825
New York.
F.R.GRUMP

FREDERICK EDWARD GUINAND   1814
Baltimore, Md., until 1827.
GUINAND

ENOS GUNN 1770–1813   1792
Waterbury, Conn. Born in Guntown, Conn., Nov. 3, son of
Enos and Abigail Candee Gunn. Firm of E. Gunn & Co.
E.GUNN – ENOS GUNN

E. GUNN & CO.   1800
Waterbury, Conn.
E.GUNN & CO

WILLIAM GURLEY   1769–1844   1804
Norwich, Conn. Born in Mansfield, Conn. Married Anna
Delpha, 1822.
WG

BENJAMIN GURNEE   1820
New York, at 98 Reade Street; at 125 Church Street, 1835. Firm
of Gurnee & Co., 1820.
GURNEE

JAMES GUTHRE   1796–1877   1822
Wilmington, Del. Advertised in *The American Watchman*, 1822,
"Gold and Silversmithing. The subscriber, James Guthre,
having purchased the stock of G. J. Wolf, continues the Gold
and Silver business at the same stand, No. 41 Market Street;
Come Friends and the Public, Come look at my Ware. Both
Silver and Gold I have plenty to spare. And such an Assortment I
constantly keep, That for Cash I can always supply you cheap."
Advertised for a runaway apprentice in 1837.
J.GUTHRE

GUTHRE & JEFFERIS   1840
Wilmington, Del. James Guthre and Emmor Jefferis.
GUTHRE & JEFFERIS

[H]

HADDOCK, LINCOLN & FOSS   1850
Boston, Mass.
HADDOCK LINCOLN & FOSS

WILLIAM HADWEN   1791–1862   1820
Nantucket, Mass. Born in Newport, R.I. Married Eunice
Starbuck, 1822. Active until 1828, when he was succeeded by
his apprentice, James Easton.
HADWEN – W.HADWEN

NELSON HAIGHT   1839
Newburgh, N.Y., until 1852. Firms of Haight & Sterling,
1841; Haight & Leonard, 1847.
HAIGHT – N.HAIGHT

HAIGHT & STERLING   1841
Newburgh, N.Y., until 1843.
H & S

CHARLES HALE   1845
Bangor, Me.
C.HALE

ABRAHAM B. HALL   1806
Geneva, N.Y., until 1839.
A.B.HALL

CHARLES HALL   1742–1783   1765
Lancaster, Pa., advertised, *Penna. Gazette*, July 4, 1765,
"Goldsmith, in Lancaster . . ." In 1777, ". . . Stolen out of a
window . . . Four Silver Tea Spoons and a Cream Jug, having no
other mark than the maker's name, C. H." In 1779, "Stolen . . .
Eight Silver table spoons stamped on the handle C. HALL . . . a
flower on the back of the bowl." Brother of David Hall.
CH – C.HALL

DAVID HALL   –1779   1765
Philadelphia, Pa., advertised in Second Street. Clerk of the
"Heart and Hand Fire Company". Continued as a silversmith
and merchant until he died.
DH – D.HALL

GREEN HALL   1782–1863   1805
Albany, N.Y. Born in Portland, Conn., son of Abijah and
Eunice Green Hall. Listed in Albany Directories in the firms of
Carson & Hall; Hall & Hewson; Hall, Hewson & Co.; Hall &
Brower; Hall, Hewson & Brower, until 1854.
G.HALL

IVORY HALL   1795–1880   1819
Concord, N.H. Married Pamela Clement, 1822; Sarah Dow,
1837.
I.HALL

JOSEPH HALL   1781
Albany, N.Y. Purchased freedom in 1781.
I.HALL

HALL & BLISS   1816
Albany, N.Y., in Directory until 1818.
HALL & BLISS

HALL & ELTON   1841
Geneva, N.Y.
HALL & ELTON

HALL & HEWSON   1828
Albany, N.Y. until 1838; 1842–1847. Green Hall and John D.
Hewson.
H & H

HALL, HEWSON & BROWER   1850
Albany, N.Y. Green Hall, John D. Hewson and S. D. Brower.
H H & B

HALL, HEWSON & MERRIFIELD   1845
Albany, N.Y. Ad, "manufacturers of Silverware, 10 Plain Street,
Albany, N.Y." Green Hall, John D. Hewson and Thomas
Merrifield.
H H & M

HALL & MERRIMAN   1825
New Haven, Conn.
H & M

JOHN HALLAM   1752–1800   1773
New London, Conn. Advertised his shop near the Sign Post. The
General Assembly commissioned him to engrave the plates for
Bills of Credit issued by the Colony, 1775.
I. HALLAM

JABEZ HALSEY   1762–1820   1789
New York, at 58 Queen Street; 105 Liberty Street, 1795. Firm
of Dally & Halsey, 1787–1789.
I. HALSEY

BENJAMIN HALSTED   1734–   1764
New York. Freeman, 1764. Son of John and Susannah Blanchard
Halsted. Married Sarah Tredwell, October 22, 1765. Advertised,
1766, in partnership with brother, Matthias, in Elizabethtown,
N.J. Notice appears in *New York Gazette*, same year. In Philadel-
phia, Pa., 1783–1785. Member of the Gold and Silversmiths'
Society, 1786. Advertised, N.Y., Maiden Lane and Nassau
Street, 1786–1789; 67 Broad Street, 1795–1805. Admitted son
to business, 1799. Worked until 1806.
HALSTED

HALSTED & MYERS   1763
New York, until 1764. Partnership of Benjamin or Matthias
Halsted and Myer Myers.
H & M

JAMES HAMILL   1816
New York, at 200 Church Street. Firm of Hamill & Co., 1817.
J.HAMILL

WILLIAM HAMLIN   1772–1869   1795
Providence, R.I. Born in Middletown, Conn. where he apprenticed and opened a shop for business. Married Eliza Bowen in
1810 in Providence, R.I. where he died.
HAMLIN – WH – W.HAMLIN

THOMAS HAMMERSLEY   1727–1781   1756
New York. Advertised in the *New York Gazette*, 1757,
". . . removed from the Change in Dock Street to Hanover
Square." Married Sarah Colgan, 1761. Last notice, ad, *New York
Mercury*, February 20, 1764, "runaway slave, 'Duke', February
13, age 35."
TH

S. HAMMOND & CO.   1810
Utica, N.Y. Seneca Hammond.
S.HAMMOND & CO

JOHN HANCOCK   1732–1784   1760
Boston, Mass. Born in Charlestown, Mass., October 10. Married
Martha Sparhawk, November 20, 1760. In 1770, in Oxford,
Md. where he died.
JH – J.HANCOCK

W. W. HANNAH   1840
Hudson, N.Y., until 1848.
W.W.HANNAH

GEORGE HANNERS   1696–1740   1720
Boston, Mass. Advertised, *Boston News Letter*, July 11, 1720,
"Goldsmith, at his House at the Dock-Head . . . " Married
Rebecca Pierson. Taught his son, George, Jr., the trade. Died in
Boston; estate appraised at £2670.
GH – G.HANNERS

GEORGE HANNERS, JR.   1721–1760   1744
Boston, Mass. Apprenticed to his father. Married Sarah Foster.
G.HANNERS

JOHN HANSELL   1825
Valley Forge, Pa.
J.HANSELL

NEWELL HARDING   1796–1862   1822
Boston, Mass. Born in Haverhill, Mass. Apprentice and brother-
in-law of Hazen Morse. Introduced power in rolling of silver.
Member of the Massachusetts Charitable Mechanics Association,
1830. Ward & Rich bought the business in 1832.
N.HARDING

N. HARDING & CO.   1842
Boston, Mass. In Directories, 1851–1862.
N.H & CO—N.HARDING & CO

STEPHEN HARDY   1781–1843   1805
Portsmouth, N.H. Apprenticed to Paul Revere. Trained with
William Simes. Married Mary B. Hill, daughter of Daniel Hill.
Sold land in Newfields to William Cario, Jr.
HARDY — SH

THOMAS HARLAND   1735–1807   1775
Norwich, Conn. Born in England where he learned his trade.
Emigrated and settled in Norwich, 1773. Married Hannah
Clark, 1779. Master of: David Greenleaf, Jr., 1788; Nathaniel
Shipman, 1790; William Cleveland, 1791; Seril Dodge, 1793.
Last advertised in 1796.
HARLAND

GEORGE HARRIS   1802
New York, at Crosbie and Park Streets. In Pittsburgh, Pa.,
1815, at Liberty and Smith Streets. Silversmith and swordmaker.
Firm of Harris & Co. in New York at 177 Broadway, 1850.
G.HARRIS

HARRIS & STANWOOD   1835
Boston, Mass.
HARRIS & STANWOOD

HARRIS & WILCOX   1844
Troy, N.Y. In Directory, 1847–1850.
HARRIS & WILCOX

ELIPHAZ HART   1789–1866   1810
Norwich, Conn. Born in New Britain, Conn. Worked with
brother, Judah, in 1810. Died in Norwich.
E.HART

JUDAH HART   1777–1824   1799
Middletown, Conn. Born in New Britain, Conn., brother of
Eliphaz. Partner of Charles Brewer, 1800–1803. Worked with
Jonathan Bliss until he removed to Norwich, Conn., 1805, and
leased a shop with Alvin Wilcox until 1807. In partnership with

brother, Eliphaz, 1810. In Griswold, Conn., 1816; Brownsville,
Ohio, 1822.
I.HART — J.HART

WILLIAM HART 1818
Philadelphia, Pa., at 19 North Third Street.
W.HART

HART & BREWER 1800
Middleton, Conn., Judah Hart and Charles Brewer, until 1803.
H & B

HART & ELIPHAZ HART 1810
Norwich, Conn., Judah Hart and brother, Eliphaz.
H & EH

HART & SMITH 1815
Baltimore, Md., at 100 Baltimore Street. William Hart and
John Smith.
HART & SMITH — H & S

HART & WILCOX 1805
Norwich, Conn. Leased shop of Abel Brewster until 1807.
Judah Hart and Alvan Wilcox.
H & W

GEORGE HARTFORD 1794
Philadelphia, Pa., at Charlotte Street.
GH

JONATHAN HARTT 1810
Canandaigua, N.Y., until 1815.
J.HARTT

ALEXANDER R. HASCY 1831
Albany, N.Y. In Directory until 1850.
HASCY

IRA HASELTON 1797–1869 1821
Portsmouth, N.H., Directory until 1827.
I.HASELTON

JOHN HASTIER 1691–1771 1726
New York. Freeman, March 29, 1726. Baptised in the French
Church, January 1, 1691. Advertised, *New York Journal*, 1735,
in Queen Street. Notice appears, 1739, of counterfeiters whom
he apprehended. Last ad, 1758, May 15, *New York Gazette*, "Run
away on Monday last from John Hastier, of this City, Goldsmith,
a lusty well-set Negro Man named Jasper . . ."
IH

MARGUETTE HASTIER   1771
New York. Carried on the business of her husband, John Hastier.
MH

B. B. HASTINGS   1835
Cleveland, Ohio, at 41 Superior Street; at 49, under Wendell
House, in 1845. Disposed of his business to John Coon in 1846.
HASTINGS

H. HASTINGS   1815
Ohio.
H.HASTINGS

SAMUEL HAUGH   1675–1717   1696
Boston, Mass. Apprenticed to Thomas Savage, October 7, 1690,
for seven years and six months, as witnessed by Samuel Sewall.
SH

WILLIAM HAVERSTICK   1781
Philadelphia, Pa., advertised in Second Street, between Arch
and Race Streets. Listed at 76 North Second Street, 1791–1793.
WH

NATHANIEL HAYDEN   1805–1875   1832
Charleston, S.C., firm of Eyland & Hayden; Hayden, Gregg &
Co. Born in Connecticut.
N.HAYDEN

HAYDEN & GREGG   1838
Charleston, S.C. Nathaniel Hayden and William Gregg dis-
solved in 1842. Firm continued until 1863.
HAYDEN & GREGG

PETER P. HAYES   1788–1842   1826
Poughkeepsie, N.Y., until 1842.
P.P.HAYES

HAYES & ADRIANCE   1816
Poughkeepsie, N.Y., until 1826. Peter P. Hayes and John
Adriance.
HAYES & ADRIANCE

ANDREW HAYS   1769
New York. Admitted Freeman, February 8, 1769. Goldsmith.
AH

N. L. HAZEN   1829
Troy, N.Y. In Cincinnati, Ohio, 1835 until 1850.
N.L.HAZEN

JOSEPH HEAD 1798
Philadelphia, Pa., at Lombard and Seventh Streets.
HEAD

J. S. HEALD 1810
Baltimore, Md. Partner of William Ball until 1812.
J.S.HEALD

JOHN HEATH 1761
New York. Freeman, March 3, 1761. Married Edith Pell,
October 18, 1760. Advertised, *The New York Mercury*, January 3,
1763, ". . . . Goldsmith, in Wall Street."
I.HEATH — JH — J.HEATH

LEWIS HECK 1755–1817 1776
Lancaster, Pa.
LH — L.HECK

DAVID HEDGES, JR. 1779–1856 1810
Easthampton, N.Y. Born June 14. Advertised, "House and
Shop next Door, South of Clinton Academy, East Hampton."
Colonel in Militia. Supervisor, 1812–1814. Represented Suffolk
County in the Assembly, 1825–1833.
HEDGES

NATHANIEL HELME 1761–1789 1782
Little Rest, R.I. Son of Judge James and Esther Powell Helme,
born December 24, in South Kingston, R.I. Died November 19.
HELME — NH

DANIEL BOOTH HEMPSTED 1784–1852 1820
New London, Conn. Born May 4, son of Captain Samuel Booth
Hempsted, Revolutionary War officer.
DBH — D.B.HEMPSTED — H

DANIEL HENCHMAN 1730–1775 1753
Boston, Mass. Son of Rev. Nathaniel Henchman. Apprenticed
to Jacob Hurd. Married Elizabeth, daughter of Jacob Hurd.
Member of St. John's Lodge, 1763–1767. Advertised June 12,
1773, *New England Chronicle*, ". . . And as his work has hitherto
met with the Approbation of the most curious, he flatters himself
that he shall have the Preference by those who are Judges of
Work, to those Strangers among us who import and sell English
Plate to the great Hurt and Prejudice of the Townsmen who have
been bred to the Business. Said Henchman will make any kind of
Plate they want equal in Goodness and Cheaper than any they
can import from London, with the greatest Dispatch." Nathaniel
Hurd, Daniel Boyer and Zachariah Brigden appraised his estate.

Brother-in-law of Nathaniel Hurd who did his engraving. Made
a tankard dated 1759 and a monteith engraved by Nathaniel
Hurd dated 1771 for presentation to the President of Dartmouth
College, now at Dartmouth College.
DH – HENCHMAN

A. A. HENDERSON   1837
Philadelphia, Pa.
A. HENDERSON – HENDERSON

ADAM HENDERSON   1794–1859   1817
Poughkeepsie, N.Y. Born in Fishkill, N.Y. Apprenticed to
George Halliwell whose business he took over in 1817 and whose
daughter, Maria, he married May 1, 1819. Firm of Henderson &
Lossing in 1833. Trustee of Village, 1847; Town Cerk, 1849.
A. HENDERSON

LOGAN HENDERSON   1767
Charleston, S.C.
LH

AHASUERUS HENDRICKS   –1727   1678
New York. Born in Albany, N.Y. Swore allegiance to the King
in 1675. Married Neeltjie Jans, widow of Adam Oncklebag,
June 11/25, 1676. Probably, Master of Gerrit Oncklebag, his
stepson. Taxed for owning property in 1677. Appointed to
report on water supply of City, 1686. Constable of the North
Ward in 1687. Freeman in 1698. Assessed £10 on the North
Ward Roll, New York City, 1730.
AH

CHARLES HEQUEMBOURG, JR.   1760–1851   1804
New Haven, Conn. Born in France, son of Charles and Mary
Cook Hequembourg. Married Mehitable Emery Fabian Morse,
October 11, 1810. Advertised on Church Street, 1809–1820.
Sergeant in War of 1812–1814. In Directory: Albany, N.Y.,
1823–1826; New York City, 1827–1829; Buffalo, N.Y.,
1835–1842.
CH – C. HEQUEMBOURG JR – HEQUEMBOURG

TIMOTHY B. HERBERT   1806
New York. At Chambers Street, 1816; 37 Jay Street, 1820; 98
Reade Street, 1823.
HERBERT

WILLIAM HEURTIN (HUERTIN)   1703–1771   1731
New York. Born in England. Freeman, April 6, 1731. Married
Susannah Sibylla, daughter of Rev. Joshua and Sibylla Carlotta
Kocherthal. Child baptised before 1729. Mentioned with John
Moulinar in Dutch Reformed Church controversy. Died intestate
in Newark, N.J. Wife appointed administrator.
W H

ABRAHAM HEWS, JR.   1797–1868   1823
Boston, Mass. In Directory, 1825.
A . HEWS JR

A. HEWS, JR. & CO.   1825
Boston, Mass.
A . HEWS JR & CO

HEYDORN & IMLAY   1810
Hartford, Conn.
H & I

WILLIAM BRAISTED HEYER   1776–1828   1798
New York. Advertised 1808, May 7, *American Citizen,* "Dissolu-
tion of Partnership with J. L. Gale, Jr." Married Sarah Hackstaff,
July 23, 1810. Served in War of 1812 to December 3, 1814 in
Capt. John V. B. Varick's Company. Listed at 47 Warren Street
until 1827. Widow continued business until 1832.
W . B . HEYER

HEYER & GALE   1807
New York, at 29 Park Street; dissolved in 1808 by William B.
Heyer and John L. Gale.
W . B . HEYER & J . GALE

HIGBIE & CROSBY   1810
Boston, Mass. Working 1820.
HIGBIE & CROSBY

SAMUEL HILDEBURN   1810
Philadelphia, Pa.
S . HILDEBURN

CHARLES HILL   1815
Canandaigua, N.Y.
C . HILL

JAMES HILL   1770
Boston, Mass. Advertised as a goldsmith. Claimed the house of
Nathaniel Austin, silversmith, for a loss in 1775. Estate sold this
house in 1798. Agreement of sale was cancelled in 1799.
J. HILL

JOSEPH HILL   1798–1859   1821
Portsmouth, N.H.
IH

WILLIAM F. HILL   1815
New York. In Directory until 1817.
W. F. HILL

BENJAMIN HILLER   1687/8–1745   1711
Boston, Mass. Apprenticed to John Coney. Married Elizabeth
Russell. Witnessed deed for John Coney, 1709. Connected with
Artillery Company, 1716. Deacon of Church in 1719.
BH

FREEMAN HINCKLEY   1757–1808   1771
Barnstable, Mass. Son of John and Bethia Freeman Hinckley.
Married Sabra Hatch, 1771.
FH

D. B. HINDMAN & CO.   1833
Philadelphia, Pa., until 1837.
DBH & CO

HORACE HINSDALE   1782–1858   1805
New York, at 146 Broadway, 1805–1807; at 144 Broadway,
1813. Branch in Newark, N.J. In partnership with John Taylor,
1805–1830. Firm of Palmer & Hinsdale, 1815–1817, Hinsdale
& Atkin, 1836.
HINSDALE

HINSDALE & ATKIN   1836
New York. Horace Hinsdale and John Atkin.
HINSDALE & ATKIN

ELIAKIM HITCHCOCK   1726–1788   1757
New Haven, Conn. Born and died in Cheshire, Conn. Advertised
in 1776. Member of the Second Company of Governor's Foot
Guard. Master of Amos Doolittle.
EH

ENOCH HOAG   1763–1817   1785
Portsmouth, Dover, Sandwich, N.H.
EH

JOSHUA HOBART (HOBARTH)   1810
New Haven, Conn., at Crown Street. Removed to Boston, Mass.
Worked with Allen Fitch as Fitch & Hobart, 1813.
J.HOBARTH

NATHAN HOBBS   1792–1868   1815
Boston, Mass., at 1 Dock Street and other addresses until 1850.
HOBBS – N.HOBBS

JOHN HODGE   1760–1840   1781
Hadley, Mass. Married Sarah Dickinson, March 19, 1789.
J.HODGE

CHRISTIAN FREDERICK HOFFMAN (HOOFMANN)   1816
1786–1886
New York. Born in Halberstadt, Prussia, where he learned his
trade. In New York, 1816, from Paris, France. In Philadelphia,
Pa., where he married Catharine Lohn, 1799–1877, in 1818.
Shop located on Chestnut Street.
F.HOFFMANN

JAMES M. HOFFMAN   1820
Philadelphia, Pa.
J.M.HOFFMAN

LITTLETON HOLLAND   1770–1847   1800
Baltimore, Md., at 217 Baltimore Street.
HOLLAND – LH – L.HOLLAND

WILLIAM HOLLINGSHEAD   1754
Philadelphia, Pa. Advertised, *Penna. Gazette*, until 1774. Listed
corner of Arch and Second Streets until 1785.
WH

JULIUS HOLLISTER   1818–1905   1846
Oswego, N.Y.
J.H.HOLLISTER – J.HOLLISTER

ROBERT HOLLOWAY   1822
Baltimore, Md., at 115 High Street.
HOLLOWAY

ADRIAN B. HOLMES   1801
New York, at Church Street until 1830. In Directory until 1850.
A.B.HOLMES – A.HOLMES

E. HOLSEY   1820
Philadelphia, Pa.
E.HOLSEY

EDWARD HOLYOKE   1817
Boston, Mass. In Directory until 1825. Mentioned in Thomas
Revere's estate.
HOLYOKE

WILLIAM HOMES   1716/7–1783   1739
Boston, Mass. Married Rebecca Dawes, July 14, 1733. Men-
tioned as Master Goldsmith, 1739. Advertised in *Boston Gazette*,
1759, ". . . near the Draw-Bridge . . ." Held public offices,
Warden, Grain Purchaser, Justice of the Town. Captain of
Artillery Company.
HOMES – WH – W. HOMES

WILLIAM HOMES, JR.   1742–1825   1783
Boston, Mass. Worked in father's shop. Married Elizabeth
Whitewell. Advertised at Ann Street, 1789–1813. Spelled
Holmes in Directory in 1796.
WH

HOOD & TOBEY   1849
Albany, N.Y.
HOOD & TOBEY

WILLIAM HOOKEY   1733–1812   1760
Newport, R.I. Listed as a silversmith, 1764, as a goldsmith,
1799.
WH

JOHN W. HOPKINS   1730–1801   1760
Waterbury, Conn. Opened shop where he also practiced law.
Appointed Judge of the Probate Court.
HOPKINS

STEPHEN HOPKINS, JR.   1721–1796   1745
Waterbury, Conn. Son of Stephen and Susannah Peck Hopkins,
brother of John W. Hopkins.
SH

HARLEY HOSFORD   1820
New York, at 103 Fulton Street.
HOSFORD

DAVID HOTCHKISS   1848
Syracuse, N.Y.
D. HOTCHKISS – HOTCHKISS

JOHN HOULTON 1797
Philadelphia, Pa. In Baltimore, Md., 1799. Firm of Houlton &
Browne.
HOULTON

HOULTON & BROWNE 1799
Baltimore, Md., at 123 Baltimore Street. John Houlton and
Liberty Browne.
HOULTON & BROWNE

HOULTON, OTTO & FALK 1797
Philadelphia, Pa.
H O & F

GEORGE C. HOWE 1825
New York. Firms of: Stebbins & Howe, 1832; G. C. Howe &
Co., 1837; Howe & Guion, 1839.
GEORGE C.HOWE

G. C. HOWE & CO. 1837
New York.
GEO C.HOWE & CO

HOWE & GUION 1839
New York.
HOWE & GUION

JAMES HOWELL 1802
Philadelphia, Pa., at 27 Key's Alley until 1804; 50 South Front
Street, 1807.
HOWELL – I.HOWELL – J.HOWELL

J. HOWELL & CO 1810
Philadelphia, Pa.
I.HOWELL & CO

PAUL HOWELL 1810
New York, at 34 George Street until 1812. Firm of Eoff &
Howell.
P.HOWELL

SILAS W. HOWELL 1770– 1798
Albany, N.Y. Advertised, *Albany Register*, December 10, "Tea
cadys, tea trays, waiters, spoons, etc. at his shop opposite City
Hall, Court Street." Firm of Howell & Arnold. Removed to New
Brunswick, N.J.
S.HOWELL – S.W.HOWELL

GEORGE A. HOYT   1822
Albany, N.Y. Firms of George A. Hoyt & Co., 1829; George A.
Hoyt & Son, 1845.
GEO A. HOYT

GEORGE B. HOYT   1830
Albany, N.Y., at 35 Market Street, 1830–1850; later, 395
Broadway. Firms of Hoyt & Kippen; Boyd & Hoyt.
GEO.B.HOYT

HENRY HOYT   1828
Albany, N.Y., until 1836.
HENRY HOYT

HENRY E. HOYT   1820
New York, at 121 Cherry Street.
H.E.HOYT

SEYMOUR HOYT   1817
New York, until circa 1850. Firm of S. Hoyt & Co.
S.HOYT

S. HOYT & CO.   1842
New York, at 266 Pearl Street.
S.HOYT & CO

CHRISTOPHER HUGHES   1744–1824   1771
Baltimore, Md. Born in Ireland. Married Peggy Sanderson,
1779. Advertised partnership with John Carnan, *Maryland
Journal*, August 30, 1773. Portrait painted by Charles Willson
Peale.
CH

EDMUND HUGHES   1781–1851   1804
Middletown, Conn. In partnership with John Ward, 1805–
1806. Firms of Hughes & Bliss, 1806; Hughes & Francis,
1807–1809.
E.HUGHES

JEREMIAH HUGHES   1783–1848   1805
Annapolis, Md. Married Priscilla Jacob, 1807. After 1820,
became editor of *Maryland Republican*.
J.HUGHES

WILLIAM HUGHES   1744–1791   1785
Baltimore, Md. In *Maryland Journal*, May 3, 1785, "From
Dublin, Ireland, after seventeen years, located at corner of
Market & Calvert Streets, Goldsmith and Jeweller." Advertised
until 1791. Probably twin or cousin of Christopher Hughes.
WH

PHILIP HULBEART   −1764   1750
Philadelphia, Pa., advertised in *Penna. Gazette*, November,
1761. Notice, 1764, "the estate of the deceased, P. Hulbeart."
PH − P.HULBEART

JOHN HULL   1624–1683   1645
Boston, Mass. Born in Market Harboro, Leicestershire, England.
In Boston, 1635. Married Judith Quincy, May 11, 1647.
Freeman, May 2, 1649. A Founder of the First Church in Boston.
In his diary he records, "After a little keeping at school I was
taken to help my father plant corn, which I attended to for
several years together; and then by God's good hand I fell to
learning by help of my brother and to practice the trade of
goldsmith. In 1652, the General Court ordered a mint to be set
up, and they made choice of me for that employment, and I
choose my friend Robert Sanderson to be my partner, to which
the Court assented. In 1659, 1st of May, I received in my house
Jeremie Dummer and Samuel Paddy, to serve me as apprentices
for eight years." Held many responsible offices, 1652–1678.
Died in Boston, October 1, 1683.
IH

HULL & SANDERSON   1652
Boston, Mass. See John Hull; Robert Sanderson.
IH − RS RS − IH

RICHARD HUMPHREYS   1772
Philadelphia, Pa., from Wilmington, Delaware, 1771. Notice
in 1772, *Penna. Packet*, (signed by Philip Syng) ". . . recommends
him as a person qualified to serve them on the best terms, and
whose fidelity in the above business will engage their future
confidence and regard." Advertised until October 31, 1781,
selections of silver and jewellery. Listed at 54 High Street,
1786–1796.
RH − R.HUMPHREYS

T. B. HUMPHREYS   −1869   1831
Louisa Court House, Va. In Richmond, Va., 1845.
T.B.HUMPHREYS

T. B. HUMPHREYS & SON   1849
Richmond, Va. Thomas B. Humphreys and son, Thomas F.
Humphreys, at 57 Main Street.
T.B.HUMPHREYS & SON

JOHN T. HUNT   1819
Lynchburg, Va., until 1840. Married Mahala Sandidge,
November 10, 1825.
JTH

HUNT & CLARK   1795
Bennington, Vt., Jonathan Hunt and Horatio Clark until 1803.
H & C

PHILIP HUNTINGTON 1770–1825   1795
Norwich, Conn. Married Theophila Grist, 1796. Held office of
Town Clerk, 1801–1823.
PH

RICHARD HUNTINGTON 1786–1855   1823
Utica, N.Y., until 1850.
HUNTINGTON

S. HUNTINGTON   1850
Portland, Me.
S.HUNTINGTON

BENJAMIN HURD 1739–1781   1760
Boston, Mass. Son of Jacob and Elizabeth Mason. Married
Priscilla Crafts, 1774. Brother-in-law of Daniel Henchman.
Received estate from brother, Nathaniel.
BH – B.HURD

JACOB HURD 1702/3–1758   1723
Boston, Mass. Son of John and Elizabeth Tufts Hurd, born in
Charlestown, Mass., February 12. Married Elizabeth Mason,
May 20, 1725. Father of Benjamin and Nathaniel; related to
William Cowell. Probably apprenticed to John Burt or John
Edwards. Constable of City in 1736. Member of the Ancient
and Honorable Artillery Company, 1743. Advertised, near the
Town House and in Pudding Lane. Died in Roxbury where he
retired in 1755. Estate was appraised by Samuel Edwards and
William Simpkins.
HURD – IH – I.HURD – JACOB HURD

NATHANIEL HURD 1729–1777   1755
Boston, Mass. Son of Jacob and Elizabeth Mason Hurd, brother
of Benjamin. Attended Latin School in 1738. Was Clerk of the
Market, 1759–1761; Scavanger in Ninth Ward, 1760–1761.
Advertised, 1765–1766. Member of Lodge # 2, May 19, 1762;
became Junior Warden. Noted engraver; engraved for his
brother-in-law, Daniel Henchman.
N.HURD

HENRY HURST 1665–1717   1690
Boston, Mass. Born in Sweden. Married Mary Billings. Master
of Bartholomew Green. Estate appraised by John Dixwell and
Thomas Millner. A tankard with New York style handle is one of
his few known pieces.
HH

STEPHEN HUSSEY   1818
Easton, Md., until 1830. Advertised, *Republican Star*, July 7,
1818, "Stephen Hussey, Gold and Silversmith, Respectfully
informs the Citizens of Easton, that he has taken the shop lately
occupied by William Needles, where he intends carrying on the
business in their various branches with punctuality, neatness and
dispatch."
S.HUSSEY

JACOB HUTCHINS   1774
New York.
HUTCHINS

NICHOLAS HUTCHINS   1777–1845   1810
Baltimore, Md., at 1 Water Street until 1829. Married Susanna
Ayres, 1816.
N H

SAMUEL HUTCHINSON   1828
Philadelphia, Pa., until 1839.
S.HUTCHINSON

ISAAC HUTTON   1767–1855   1790
Albany, N.Y. Baptised July 20, in Dutch Reformed Church of
New York, son of George and Anna Maria Viele Hutton. Probably apprenticed to John Folsom. Purchased house on Market
and Water Streets, September, 1791. Was prominent citizen,
elected to public offices, occupied important positions; Treasurer
of Albany Mechanics' Society, 1793–1802. Married Margaret
Lynott in 1797. In partnership with brother, George, 1799–
1817, at 32/33 Market Street. Died at Stuyvesant Landing.
HUTTON

JOHN STRANGEWAYS HUTTON   1720
New York. Freeman, November 8. Married Elizabeth Van Dyke,
May 25, 1729.
IH – JH

GEORGE HUYLER   1819
New York.
HUYLER

HYDE   1730
Newport, R.I.
HYDE

I. E. HYDE   1790
New York, N.Y.
I.E.HYDE

HYDE & GOODRICH   1830
New Orleans, La.
HYDE & GOODRICH

HYDE & NEVINS   1815
New York, until 1819.
H&N — HYDE & NEVINS

HENRY HYMAN   1799
Lexington, Ky., advertised in *Stewart's Kentucky Herald*. Listed in
Richmond, Va. in 1845 as watchmaker, jeweler, silversmith at
90 West Main Street.
H.HYMAN

[I]

JOHN INCH 1720–1763   1741
Annapolis, Md. Advertised, *Maryland Gazette*, "Removed from
South East St. to the House on the Point near the Guns. N.B.
The said Inch has taken out License, and keeps a good Entertainment for Man & Horse: He sells Punch every day, and also retails
rum, Wine, Cyder, etc.", December 13, 1749. "He has likewise
to sell, Ten Proved good swivel guns (planted near his House
ever since the News of the Surrender of Fort Duquesne) with a
Quantity of Shot to fit them.", March 8, 1759. ". . . a convict
servant, jeweller and motto-ring engraver by trade, age 25–30,
named Thomas Read (alias Cuthbert), runaway in June from
John Inch of Annapolis, Md.", October 1, 1759. Notice,
"Monday Morning last Died here, aged 42 years, Mr. John Inch,
Goldsmith of this City, and Yesterday his Funeral was solem-
nized in a very decent Manner being attended by a Procession of
the Brethren of the Lodge, properly Cloath'd and a great number
of others.", March 17, 1763. His widow, Jane Inch, administered estate and continued the business.
II

BARTON INGRAHAM   1801
Providence, R.I., until 1807. Firm of Ingraham & Greene,
1806.
B.INGRAHAM

[J]

JACCARD & CO.   1850
St. Louis, Mo.
JACCARD & CO

A. JACKSON 1840
Norwalk, Conn.
A.JACKSON

CLEMENT JACKSON, JR. 1741–1777 1762
Portsmouth, N.H. Born in Hampton, N.H., son of Dr. Cle-
ment and Sarah Leavitt Jackson. Advertised in *N. H. Gazette*,
August 11, 1762, "Clement Jackson, Jun., Gold and Silver
Smith from Boston, hereby informs the Public that he carries on
the Gold and Silver Smith's Business in the Shop. . . ."
CI

DANIEL JACKSON 1782
New York. On the Muster Rolls of the Fourth Regiment of the
Militia, 1775–1776.
DI – D.JACKSON

JOHN JACKSON 1731
New York. Freeman, April 6. Made a pepper box dated 1761.
IACKSON – JACKSON

JOHN JACKSON 1730–1772 1750
Nantucket, Mass. Married Abigail Coffin, 1753. Died February
26, at age 41½.
IACKSON

JOSEPH JACKSON –1831 1803
Baltimore, Md., at 13 South Street. Married Mary Robinson.
Last record on Harrison Street until 1813. Then moved outside
city limits to avoid Baltimore Assay Taxes; worked until his
death.
J.JACKSON

GEORGE JACOB 1775–1846 1802
Baltimore, Md., at 58 North Howard Street until 1845.
G.JACOB

A. JACOBS & CO. 1820
Philadelphia, Pa.
A.J & CO

ABEL JACOBS 1816
Philadelphia, Pa.
A.JACOBS

JOHN JAGGER 1713–1764 1735
Marblehead, Mass. Married Sibella Jones, widow of goldsmith
William Jones, July 22, 1735. In Boston, 1739.
J.JAGGER

MUNSON JARVIS   1742–1825   1765
Stamford, Conn. Married Mary Arnold, March 4, 1765. Advertised as silversmith and ironmonger. As a Loyalist, his shop was
confiscated in 1783; thereafter he removed to St. Johns, N.B.
MJ

HENRY J. JAVAIN   –1838   1835
Charleston, S.C., in King Street.
JAVAIN

EMMOR JEFFERIS   1804–1892   1827
Wilmington, Del. Born in Chester County, Pa. Married Ann
Robinson, 1827. Located at 77 Market Street in 1832 when he
took over Joseph Draper's business.
E.JEFFERIS

EPHRAIM JEFFERSON   1788–1844   1815
Smyrna, Del.
E.JEFFERSON

JOHN C. JENCKES   1777–1852   1798
Providence, R.I. Apprenticed to John Gibbs. Advertised, *United
States Chronicle*, May 17, 1798, "Gold and Silver Smith and
Jeweller, has taken the shop formerly occupied by Mr. John
Gibbs, in company with the widow, Elizabeth Gibbs, under the
firm of John Jenckes & Co., where he intends prosecuting busi-
ness carried on by the late John Gibbs." At Friendship Street in
1824.
I.JENCKES – J.C.JENCKES – J.JENCKES

BENJAMIN R. JENKINS   1830
Auburn, N.Y.
B.R.JENKINS

I. & H. JENKINS   1815
Albany, N.Y. In Directory until 1816. Ira and Herman Jenkins.
I & H.JENKINS

JOHN JENKINS   1777
Philadelphia, Pa., at Chestnut & Front Street. At 16 Green
Street in 1791.
IJ

JACOB JENNINGS   1729–1817   1763
Norwalk, Conn. Ad, 1763, *Boston Gazette*, "Whereas the Shop of
the Subscriber, living in Norwalk, in the Colony of Connecticut,
was broken open on the Sixth Day of April Instant at Night, and
robb'd of the following Things, viz, a Silver Cream Pot, 6 large

Spoons, 2 or 3 Dozen Tea Spoons, and other sundry articles . . .
Twenty Dollars Reward." Born in Fairfield, Conn. Married
Grace Perkins, 1762. Father of Jacob, Jr. who succeeded to the
business in 1810 when his father retired. Inventory of estate in
1817 mentions watchmaker's and goldsmith's tools.

II

JENNINGS & LANDER 1848
New York.

JENNINGS & LANDER

DAVID JESSE 1670–1705/6 1695
Boston, Mass. Born in Hartford, Conn. Married Mary Wilson,
of Hartford, Conn., in 1698. Member of the Brattle Street
Church, 1704. A Member of the Artillery Company in 1700.
Died January 3. Estate paid Rene Grignon £5.

DI

CHAUNCEY JOHNSON 1825
Albany, N.Y., until 1841.

C.JOHNSON

MAYCOCK W. JOHNSON 1815
Albany, N.Y.

M.W.JOHNSON

JOHNSON & BALL 1790
Baltimore, Md. Israel H. Johnson and William Ball.

J & B

SAMUEL JOHNSON 1726–1796 1780
New York. Assistant Alderman, 1783. Member of the Gold and
Silversmiths' Society, 1786. Shop at Crown Street, 1789; 99
Liberty Street, 1795. Commissioned by Council of the City to
do work in Gold. Will proved, February 15, 1796. Cary Dunn
mentioned as witness.

JOHNSON – SJ

JOHNSON & GODLEY 1843
Albany, N.Y., until 1850.

JOHNSON & GODLEY

JOHNSON & REAT 1804
Richmond, Va. Reuben Johnson and James Reat. Firm dissolved
upon the death of James Reat, 1815.

JOHNSON & REAT – J & R

JOHNSON & RILEY   1785
Baltimore, Md., advertised at "Sign of the Golden Coffee Pot" in
Market Street. Dissolved the following year, 1786.
I & R—J & R

A. JOHNSTON   1830
Philadelphia, Pa.
A.JOHNSTON

WILLIAM B. JOHONNOT   1766–1849   1787
Middletown, Conn., advertised "opposite Mrs. Bigelow's
Tavern." Apprenticed to Samuel Canfield, 1782–1787. In
Windsor, Vt., 1792. Firm of Johonnot & Smith, 1815. Died in
Windsor, Vt. July 3, 1849, and buried in South Congregational
Church Cemetery with his wife, Mary Branthwait Johonnot,
who died May 29, 1858.
WI – WJ

JOHONNOT & SMITH   1815
Windsor, Vt. William B. Johonnot and Richard Ransom Smith.
J & S

ALBERT JONES   1825
Greenfield, Mass.
A.JONES

JONES, BALL & CO.   1850
Boston, Mass.
JONES BALL & CO

JONES, BALL & POOR   1840
Boston, Mass.
JONES BALL & POOR

ELISHA JONES   1827
New York.
E.JONES

JOHN B. JONES   1782–1854   1813
Boston, Mass., at 10 Newbury Street; 37 Market Street, 1822.
Firms of Jones & Ward; Jones, Ball & Poor; which eventually
became Shreve, Crump & Low Co. of Boston.
J.B.JONES-J.JONES

JOHN B. JONES & CO.   1838
Boston, Mass.
J.B.JONES & CO

JONES, LOWS & BALL					1839
Boston, Mass.
JONES LOWS & BALL

PHILIP JONES					1837
Wilmington, Del. At 131 Market Street as Jones & Hutton,
1840–1843.
P.JONES

WILLIAM JONES 1694–1730					1715
Marblehead, Mass. Married Isabelle Burrington, 1720. Gave a
cup to the town's Congregational Church in 1730 which was
remade in 1772.
WI

JONES & HUTTON					1840
Wilmington, Del., at 131 Market Street until 1843. Philip
Jones and Samuel Hutton.
JONES & HUTTON

JONES & PEIRCE					1810
Boston, Mass. John B. Jones and John Peirce.
JONES & PEIRCE

JONES & WARD					1809
Boston, Mass. Listed at 15 Cornhill Street, 1815. John B. Jones
and Richard Ward.
JONES & WARD

HIRAM JUDSON					1824
Syracuse, N.Y., until 1847.
H.JUDSON

SWAN JUSTICE (JUSTIS)					1819
Richmond, Va.
S.JUSTIS

[K]

J. KEDZIE 1809–1889					1830
Rochester, N.Y. In Directory, 1838–1846.
J.KEDZIE

JOSEPH KEELER 1786–1824					1810
Norwalk, Conn.
IK – KEELER

THADDEUS KEELER   1805
New York, at 350 Pearl Street until 1813.
T.KEELER

GEORGE KEESE   1831
Richmond, Va.
G.KEESE

TIMOTHY KEITH   1774–1806   1795
Boston, Mass. Born in Bridgewater, Mass. Married Lydia Wyer,
1798. In New York, 1805. Died in Charlestown, Mass.
T.KEITH

TIMOTHY & W. KEITH   1825
Worcester, Mass. Timothy Keith, Jr. and William Keith who
continued their father's business after his death.
T & W.KEITH

CHARLES KENDALL (KINDLE, KENDAL, KENAB,
KENDLE)   1787
New York. Married Elizabeth Hallett, November 21, 1780.
Advertised at 42 Crown Street until 1792; 77 Chambers Street,
1797.
C.KENDALL

JAMES KENDALL   1768–1808   1785
Wilmington, Del., on Market Street until 1802. Son of Jesse
and Mary Marshall Kendall. His estate was appraised by John
White and Thomas McConnell. His son, Jesse, 1793–1874,
continued the business.
IK – JK

SULLIVAN KENDALL   1787–1853   1816
Hallowell, Me. Born in Athol, N.H., January 8, son of Levi and
Sally Kendall.
S.KENDALL

WILLIAM KENDRICK   1810–1880   1832
Louisville, Ky. Born in Paterson, N.J. Married Maria S.
Schwing, 1832. In partnership with James I. Lemon, 1832–
1841. Firm of William Kendrick & Son, 1878–1880.
W.KENDRICK

SAMUEL KEPLINGER   1770–1849   1812
Baltimore, Md., at 60 North Howard Street.
S.KEPLINGER

ALEXANDER KERR −1738 1730
Williamsburg, Va. Born of Scottish heritage.
A K

EDWARD KERSEY 1845
Richmond, Va. In firm of Kersey & Pearce, Edward Kersey and
Hamett A. Pearce.
E . KERSEY

JAMES KETCHAM 1807
New York, at 391 Pearl Street; 216 Water Street, 1823. In
Utica, N.Y., 1847.
I . KETCHAM

THOMAS KETTELL 1760−1850 1784
Charlestown, Mass. Born February 23. Married Mary Soley,
March 1, 1807. Was a Clerk in the Middlesex Canal Company;
an attendant at Charlestown First Church. Died September 17.
T K

ROBERT KEYWORTH 1833
Washington, D.C., at Pennsylvania Avenue between 9th and
10th Streets, West.
R . KEYWORTH

KIDNEY, CANN & JOHNSON 1850
New York.
K . C & J

KIDNEY & DUNN 1844
New York.
K & D

CORNELIUS KIERSTEDE 1674/5−1757 1696
New York. Born December 25, and baptised January 5, 1675,
son of Hans and Joanna Loockermans Kierstede. Probably
apprenticed to Jesse Kip. Freeman, July 26, 1698. Married (1)
Elizabeth Shopkreden; (2) Sarah Ellsworth, daughter of Clement
and Anna Maria Engelbrecht Ellsworth, in 1708. After 1720,
removed to New Haven, Connecticut, where he advertised at
Church Street.
C K

JOHN KIMBALL 1805
Boston, Mass.
J . KIMBALL − JOHN KIMBALL

LEWIS A. KIMBALL   1837
Buffalo, N.Y.
L. KIMBALL

WILLIAM KIMBERLY   −1821   1790
New York, at 35 Crown Street; 7 Fly Market in 1792. Advertised, October 5, 1795, *The American Mercury*, "Three journeymen that can work at different branches of the gold and
silversmith's trade." Notice of large importation in 1797. Later,
proprietor of hardware store. Probably in Baltimore, 1804–
1821, where he married Elizabeth Webb.
KIMBERLY − WK

JOSEPH W. KING   1776
Middletown, Conn., until 1807.
J. W. KING

THOMAS R. KING   1819
Baltimore, Md., until 1831.
T. R. KING

JOHN KINGSTON   1775
New York. Freeman, March 28, 1775, Goldsmith. Married
Mary Garrison, April 10, 1779. At 27 Reade Street, 1794; at
Bowery Lane, 1795. He was the last one registered as a Freeman
in New York until 1784.
KINGSTON

THOMAS KINNE (KINNEY)   1786–1824   1807
Norwich, Conn., at Shetucket Street. Thomas, Jr. in Cortlandt,
N.Y. in 1836.
TK − T. KINNE

DAVID I. KINSEY   1819–1874   1845
Cincinnati, Ohio. Firm of E. & D. Kinsey, Edward and David
Kinsey.
DAVID KINSEY − D. KINSEY

EDWARD KINSEY   1810–1865   1835
Cincinnati, Ohio. Brother of David in firm of E. & D. Kinsey.
E. KINSEY

E. & D. KINSEY   1845
Cincinnati, Ohio, at Sixth and Walnut Streets until 1861.
Edward and David Kinsey.
E & D. KINSEY

JESSE KIP 1660–1722   1682
New York. Baptised in Dutch Reformed Church, December 19,
1660, son of Jacob Hendrickson Kip and Maria de la Montague
Kip. Probably apprenticed to Jeurian Blank, Sr. or Ahasuerus
Hendricks. Married Maria Stevens, September 30, 1692. Wit-
ness to Will of Benjamin Blagge dated June 6, 1695, proved
October 2, 1702. Held public offices with other silversmiths in
the North Ward. Probably Master of Cornelius Kierstede.
Freeman, May 30, 1700. Died in Newtown, April, 1722. Made
a bowl dated 1699.
I K

GEORGE KIPPEN 1790–1845   1815
Bridgeport, Conn. Born in Middletown, Conn. Apprenticed to
Charles Brewer. In partnership with Barzillai Benjamin. In
1824, advertised at corner of Beaver and Broad Streets. Worked
with Elias Camp in 1825; with George A. Hoyt in 1830.
G. KIPPEN

SAMUEL KIRK 1793–1872   1815
Baltimore, Md. Born in Doylestown, Pa. of Quaker ancestry.
Apprenticed to James Howell, 1810. Opened shop, August 5,
1815, when he advertised for trade. At 212 Market Street in
1816. In partnership with John Smith until 1820. Petitioned for
modification of Baltimore Assay Law. In 1846, admitted son,
Henry Child Kirk, into business, founding S. Kirk, Sons, Co.,
Inc.
KIRK – SAML KIRK – SK – S. KIRK

KIRK & SMITH   1815
Baltimore, Md., until 1820. Samuel Kirk and John Smith.
KIRK & SMITH – K & S

PETER KIRKWOOD   1790
Chestertown, Md. In Annapolis, Md., 1800.
P K

JOHN KITTS   1838
Louisville, Ky. Associated with Lemon & Kendrick, 1841. In
partnership with William D. Scott, 1843. Formed John Kitts &
Company, 1859–1878.
J. KITTS

J. KNAPP   1825
Boston, Mass.
J. KNAPP

JOSEPH KNEELAND   1698/9–1740   1720
Boston, Mass.
I. KNEELAND

JOHN S. KRAUSE (KRAUS)   –1814   1805
Bethlehem, Pa.
I. S. KRAUS

PETER L. KRIDER   1850
Philadelphia, Pa. In Directory at 51 Dock Street.
PLK

KRIDER & BIDDLE   1850
Philadelphia, Pa.
KB

JACOB KUCHER   1806
Philadelphia, Pa., at 84 North Second Street; at 8th Street,
1813; 4 College Avenue, 1831.
I. KUCHER

O. KUCHLER   1850
New Orleans, La.
O. KUCHLER

[L]

WILLIAM F. LADD   1828
New York.
WM. F. LADD

JACOB LADOMUS   1843
Philadelphia, Pa., until 1850.
J. LADOMUS

JOHN JOSEPH LAFAR   1781–1849   1805
Charleston, S.C., worked with brother, Peter. Marshal in 1819.
Lieutenant in Charleston Regiment of Artillery.
LAFAR

VINCENT LAFORME   1850
Boston, Mass.
V. LAFORME

VINCENT LAFORME & BROTHER   1850
Boston, Mass.
V. L & B

EBENEZER KNOWLTON LAKEMAN 1799–1857   1819
Salem, Mass. Firm of Stevens & Lakeman, 1819–1830, with
John Stevens.
E.K.LAKEMAN

JOHN LAMOTHE   1822
New Orleans, La., at 52 Royal Street.
LAMOTHE

AARON LANE 1753–1819   1784
New Brunswick, N.J. Died in New York.
AL

EDWARD LANG 1742–1830   1763
Salem, Mass. Married Rachel Ward, 1768. Silversmith and
schoolmaster.
EL – E.LANG

JEFFREY LANG 1707–1758   1733
Salem, Mass. Married Hannah Symes, August 24, 1732. Their
three sons: Richard, Nathaniel and Edward, were silversmiths.
Advertised as a goldsmith in *Boston Evening Post*, June 10, 1745.
IL – I.LANG – LANG

NATHANIEL LANG 1736–1826   1760
Salem, Mass. Son of Jeffrey Lang. Married Priscilla Symonds,
October 11, 1778.
N.LANG

RICHARD LANG 1733–1820   1770
Salem, Mass. Son of Jeffrey Lang, brother of Nathaniel.
LANG – R.LANG

WILLIAM LANGE   1844
New York, at 6 Little Green Street.
LANGE

JACOB G. LANSING 1736–1803   1765
Albany, N.Y. Baptised April 4, son of Gerrit and Marytse
Evertsen Lansing, grandson of Jacob Gerritse Lansing,
silversmith. Married Neeltse Roseboom, 1767; (2) his second
cousin, Fenmetse Lansing, 1774. Firm of Lansing & Van
Veghten, 1774. Died November 25.
IGL – JGL

JACOB GERRITSE LANSING 1681–1767   1700
Albany, N.Y. Born June 6, son of Gerrit and Elsie Van Wythorst
Lansing. Married Helena Glen, 1710. Died December 6.
IGL

LANSING & VAN VEGHTEN   1774
Albany, N.Y. Partnership of Jacob G. Lansing and Henry Van
Veghten. A bill of sale, 1775, listed them in business together.
L & V.V

MARTIN M. LAWRENCE   1832
New York.
M.M.LAWRENCE

SAMUEL J. LEA   1815
Baltimore, Md., in Directory at 238 Baltimore Street until
1822. Lieutenant in Union Volunteers.
S.I.LEA – S.J.LEA

CHARLES LEACH   1765–1814   1789
Boston, Mass. "Shop on Ann Street, three doors below
Draw-Bridge."
CL – LEACH

NATHANIEL LEACH   1789
Boston, Mass., on Kilby Street. In Directory 1800.
NL

JOHN LEACOCK   1748
Philadelphia, Pa. Advertised, *Penna. Gazette*, "Goldsmith
Removed from Second Street to the Sign of the Cup in Water
Street where he continues." In Front Street, 1753–1759, lists a
large selection of imported goods at the sign of the "Golden
Cup." Last record, November 19, 1796.
IL – I.LEACOCK

J. LEE   1790
Middletown, Conn.
J.LEE

SAMUEL W. LEE   1785–1861   1815
Providence, R.I. Born in Connecticut. Dissolved partnership of
Burr & Lee and moved to Rochester, N.Y., 1816. Firm of
Schofield & Lee, 1822. Died in Wisconsin.
S.LEE – SWL – S.W.LEE

DANIEL LEGARE   1688–1724   1710
Boston, Mass. Married in 1723.
DL

NICHOLAS LE HURAY   1809
Philadelphia, Pa., until 1831.
N.LE HURAY

NICHOLAS Le HURAY, JR.   1821
Philadelphia, Pa., until 1846.
N.LE HURAY JR

BENJAMIN LEMAR (LAMAR, LEMAIRE)   −1785   1775
Philadelphia, Pa., at Front between Chestnut and Walnut
Streets.
BL

MATHIAS LEMAR (LAMAR, LEMAIRE)   −1809   1790
Philadelphia, Pa. Brother of Benjamin Lemar. On Census List
for 1790. Listed at 81 Market Street and other addresses until
1798. In Directory until 1803.
LAMAR − ML

G. LENHART   1845
Bowling Green, Ky.
G.LENHART

JOHN LENT   1787
New York, at 20 Beekman Street. Married Sarah Ogilvie, niece
of John Ogilvie, Silversmith. Advertised, *Impartial Gazetteer*,
August 2, 1788, "Goldsmith, silversmith and jeweller . . .
carries on the above business in all its various branches, in the
newest and most fashionable manner, 61 Beekman Street." After
1791, located at 69 Maiden Lane.
I.LENT

ALLEN LEONARD   1827
New York. At 154 Division Street, 1830. In Directory until
1840.
A.LEONARD

D. GILLIS LEONARD   1841
Newburgh, N.Y. Firm of Haight & Leonard with Nelson
Haight, 1847.
D.GILLIS LEONARD

SAMUEL T. LEONARD   1786–1848   1805
Chestertown, Md. Born November 22. Firm of Lynch &
Leonard, 1810. Died September 7.
LEONARD − S.LEONARD

LEONARD & WILSON   1847
Philadelphia, Pa., on R. Road.
L & W

PETER LERET   1779
Philadelphia, Pa. Advertised in Carlisle, Pa. until 1787. In
Baltimore, Md., 1787–1802.
PL – P. LERET

BARTHOLOMEW LE ROUX   1663–1713   1687
New York, on West Side of Broadway and Beaver Lane. Freeman,
June 6, 1687. Born in London. Married, November 2, 1688,
Geertruyd Van Rolegom, whose sister was mother of Tobias
Stoutenburgh. Assistant Alderman, 1702–1712. Witness to
brother Peter's will dated July 22, 1703. Will, dated July 10,
1713, "Sick in Body, make wife, Geertruyd, and eldest son,
Charles, Executors. Inventory of Estate as soon as possible to
permit wife to bring up children. After her decease, Estate to be
divided among His children." Codicil confirms will and mentions son, John. Proved August 28, 1713.
BR

BARTHOLOMEW LE ROUX   1717–1763   1738
New York. Son of Charles Le Roux and Catharine Beekman Le
Roux, daughter of Gerrardus and Magdalyna Abeel Beekman.
Freeman, May 15, 1739. Will, dated August 13, 1757, proved
March 30, 1763, witnessed by Frederick and Augustus Van
Cortland, "In Good Health, leave Estate to Brother Charles and
Sisters, Magdalena Cook, wife of Joseph, Catharine, wife of
Thomas Ludlow and Gertrude, wife of Thomas Doughty."
Home was on West Side of Broadway, 36 feet south of Beaver
Lane, now Morris Street.
BR

CHARLES LE ROUX   1689–1745   1710
New York. Son of Bartholomew and Geertruyd Van Rolegom Le
Roux, brother of John, baptised in Dutch Church, December
22, 1689. Freeman, February 16, 1724. Married Catharine
Beekman, daughter of Gerrardus and Magdalena Abeel Beekman. Tax Assessment Roll, February, 1730: Garden £5, House
£20. Elected Deacon of New York School. Appraised Lottery
with Peter Van Dyke in 1727. Assistant Alderman of East Ward,
1735–1738. Commissioned by Common Council for presentation pieces, one a gold box, October 11, 1720. Took Jacob Ten
Eyck as an apprentice. Listed in will of John Spratt dated September 15, 1743.
CLR

JOHN LE ROUX 1695–   1716
New York. Son of Bartholomew and Geertruyd Van Rolegom Le
Roux, brother of Charles, baptised in Dutch Church, April 19,
1695. Married Margarit Britel, Dutch Church, June 19, 1714.
Freeman, January 8, 1723. In Albany, N.Y., 1730.
IL – ILR

EDWARD P. LESCURE   1822
Philadelphia, Pa., at 75 Union Street until 1850.
E.LESCURE – EPL – E.P.LESCURE

JOHN LE TELIER (LE TELLIER) (LETELIER)   1770
Philadelphia, Pa., at Second Street between Market and Chestnut
Streets. In 1777, opposite the Coffee House. Listed in 1793 at
172 North Front Street. Same year, December 21, *Delaware
Gazette*, "John Le Telier, Gold and Silversmith, Late from Philadelphia, Hath Commenced business in Market-street, Wilmington, opposite Captain O'Flin's, the sign of the Ship, where
he intends carrying on his business in its various branches, such
as Coffee and tea urns, coffee pots, tea pots, Sugar dishes, cream
urns, Canns and tankards, spoons of all kinds, shoe and knee
buckles; likewise, makes and mends all kinds of swords and
hangers. Those who will please to favor him with Custom, may
depend upon having their work done in the neatest and most
expeditious manner, and on the most reasonable terms." In
Richmond, Va., 1810, and engraved JLT MAKER on silver cups
made for Thomas Jefferson.
ILT – I.LE TELIER – I.LE TELLIER – I.L.TELLIER – JLT –
LE TELIER

KNIGHT LEVERETT 1702/3–1753   1736
Boston, Mass. Grandson of Governor John Leverett upon whom
King Charles II conferred Knighthood. Apprenticed to Andrew
Tyler. Married Abigail Brittolph. Sergeant of Artillery Company,
1736. Served second term as Clerk of Market with Jacob Hurd
in 1728, who, in 1753, was one of the appraisers of Knight
Leverett's Estate. Held public offices, 1742–1748. Died intes-
tate, insolvent, leaving few £'s, but considerable fishing tackle.
KL – K.LEVERETT

JONAS LEVY   1835
New York.
J.LEVY

HARVEY LEWIS   1811
Philadelphia, Pa., at Second Street; at 143 Chestnut Street,
1822.
HARVEY LEWIS – HL – H.LEWIS

ISAAC LEWIS   1773–1860   1796
Huntington, Conn. Born in Monroe, Conn. Removed to
Ridgefield, Conn., 1809.
I.LEWIS

J. H. LEWIS   1810
Albany, N.Y.
J.H.LEWIS

LEWIS & SMITH   1805
Philadelphia, Pa., at 2 Second Street until 1811.
LEWIS & SMITH

GABRIEL LEWYN   1770
Baltimore, Md., in Gay Street where he leased house, May 4. In
Vestry records of St. Thomas' Parish, 1772. Last record, 1780.
GL

JACOB G. L. LIBBY   1820
Boston, Mass., until 1846.
J.G.LIBBY – LIBBY

JOHN LIDDEN   1850
St. Louis, Mo.
LIDDEN

A. L. LINCOLN   1850
St. Louis, Mo.
A.L.LINCOLN

ELIJAH LINCOLN   1794–1861   1815
Hingham, Mass.
EL – E.LINCOLN

LINCOLN & FOSS   1850
Boston, Mass.
LINCOLN & FOSS

LINCOLN & GREEN   1790
Boston, Mass., until 1810.
L & G

LINCOLN & REED   1835
Boston, Mass. until 1846.
LINCOLN & REED

BENJAMIN LINDSEY   1777–1805   1798
Providence, R.I.
B.LINDSEY

CLARK LINDSLEY   1845
Hartford, Conn. At 22 Hudson Street in 1850.
C.LINDSLEY

PAUL LITTLE   1740–1818   1760
Portland, Me. Born in Newbury, Mass. In partnership with John
Butler, September 3, 1761, in Portland, Me. Shop at the corner
of Middle and King Streets in 1771 where Capt. Daniel Tucker
was apprenticed at eleven years of age. In 1775, after the destruc-
tion of the town, Little claimed £685 property damage. In
1776, moved to Windham, Me. where he died.
PL

WILLIAM LITTLE   1775
Newburyport, Mass., where he advertised as a silversmith in
Newburyport Herald. Father of William Coffin Little.
WL

WILLIAM COFFIN LITTLE   1745–1816   1790
Amesbury, Mass. Born in Newburyport, Mass. In Salisbury,
N.H., 1801. Son of William Little.
WL

ALFRED LOCKWOOD   1817
New York, until 1831.
A.LOCKWOOD

FREDERICK LOCKWOOD   1828
New York, until 1845.
F.LOCKWOOD

JAMES LOCKWOOD   1799
New York, at 36 Lombard Street until 1801; at 53 Reed Street,
1807.
LOCKWOOD

ADAM LOGAN   1803
New York, at Cherry Street and Chatham Square until 1823.
A.LOGAN

BARTHELEMY EDWARD LOMBARD   1800–1830   1828
Charleston, S.C. Born in France.
LOMBARD

HENRY LONGLEY   1810
New York, at 178 Broadway.
H.LONGLEY – LONGLEY

LONGLEY & DODGE   1810
Charleston, S.C., at 12 Broad Street.
LONGLEY & DODGE

GUY LOOMIS   1795–1874   1820
Sheffield, Mass. Born in Windsor, Conn. Married Nancy Baker.
In Erie, Pa. in 1837, where he started G. Loomis & Co.
G.LOOMIS

G. LOOMIS & CO.   1850
Erie, Pa.
G.LOOMIS & CO

BENJAMIN LORD   1770–1843   1796
Pittsfield, Mass. Advertised, December 5, *Western Star*, "located
opposite the Meeting House on the road to Lanesborough." Born
in Norwich, Conn. In Rutland, Vt., 1797. Married Fannie
Buell, 1799. In 1831, in Athens, Ga. until his death.
B.LORD

JABEZ C. LORD   1825
New York, at 177 William Street until 1835. Firm of Lord &
Smith, with George Smith, 1825–1829.
J.LORD

ELIJAH LORING   1744–1782   1765
Barnstable, Mass.
E.LORING

HENRY LORING   1773–1818   1800
Boston, Mass. Son of Joseph and Mary Atkins Loring. Married
Sarah Stewart.
HL

JOSEPH LORING   1743–1815   1766
Boston, Mass. Born in Hull. Son of Caleb and Rebecca Lobdell
Loring. Married Mary Atkins, 1766. Advertised in Union
Street. Served in Revolution; in Artillery Company, 1791.
Mentioned as Bondsman with Stephen Emery, July 24, 1788.
Father of Henry, silversmith, who, with Jesse Churchill,
appraised estate.
I.LORING – JL – J.LORING

ROBERT LOVETT   1818
Philadelphia, Pa., until 1824, when removed to New York,
until 1839.
LOVETT

JOHN J. LOW   1800–1876   1825
Boston, Mass. Apprenticed to Jabez Baldwin. Firms of Low, Ball
& Co., 1840; Shreve, Crump & Low, 1869.
I.I.LOW – J.J.LOW

JOHN J. LOW & CO.   1830
Boston, Mass. John J. Low and his brother, Francis.
J.J.LOW & CO – LOW & CO

JOSHUA LOWE   1828
New York, until 1833.
I.LOWE – J.LOWE

ABNER LOWELL   1830
Portland, Me.
A.LOWELL

LOWELL & SENTER   1830
Portland, Me.
LOWELL & SENTER

JOSEPH LOWER   1806
Philadelphia, Pa., at Dock Street until 1820; at 44 Tammany
Street until 1831.
LOWER

EDWARD LOWNES   1792–1834   1817
Philadelphia, Pa., at 10½ South Third Street.
E.LOWNES

JOSEPH LOWNES   CA. 1754–1820   1780
Philadelphia, Pa. Son of John and Agnes Lownes. Married
Esther Middleton, daughter of Abel and Mary Middleton of
Crosswicks, N.J., January 12, 1786. Advertised, 1780, 1792,
and 1798, at Front between Walnut and Spruce Streets. Listed in
Directory in 1813 at 124 South Front Street, and other addresses
until 1816. Of firms of J. & J. H. Lownes, 1816; Lownes &
Erwin, 1816.
I.LOWNES – J.LOWNES

LOWNES & ERWIN   1816
Philadelphia, Pa. Joseph Lownes and John Erwin at 191 South
Second Street until 1817.
LOWNES & ERWIN

JOSIAH H. LOWNES   –1822   1816
Philadelphia, Pa., at 124 South Front Street with Joseph Lownes.
IHL

LOWS, BALL & CO.   1840
Boston, Mass.
LOWS BALL & CO

D. E. LUCY   1850
Waterbury, Vt.
D.E.LUCY

CHARLES LUMSDEN   1832
Petersburg, Va., from Richmond, Va. At the Sign of the Golden
Spectacles until 1863. Thomas Nowlan worked with him until
1848.
CHAS LUMSDEN

HENRY LUPP   1760–1800   1783
New Brunswick, N.J.
H.LUPP

LOUIS LUPP   1800
New Brunswick, N.J. Son of Peter Lupp.
L.LUPP

PETER LUPP   1787
New Brunswick, N.J.
PL – P.LUPP

S. V. LUPP   1815
New Brunswick, N.J.
S.V.LUPP

JOHN G. LUSCOMB   1813
Boston, Mass., located at High Street; at Harvard Place, 1823.
J.G.LUSCOMB

JOHN LYNCH   1761–1848   1786
Baltimore, Md. Census List for 1790. Located on Boundary
Street in 1796; Franklin Street, 1801–1848. Married Naomi
Willey, January 21, 1804.
I.LYNCH – JL – J.LYNCH – LYNCH

THOMAS LYNDE   1748–1812   1771
Worcester, Mass. Born in Malden, Mass., April 19. Married
Sarah Greenleafe in 1774. Died in Leicester, Mass.
T.LYNDE

JOHN BURT LYNG   –1785   1759
New York. Married Magdalane Jardine, September 11, 1759.
Freeman, March 31, 1761. Advertised, *New York Gazette*, January

5, 1764, ". . . at private Sale, the House wherein John Burt
Lyng, Silver-Smith now lives, in Broad-Way. N.B. The Gold
and Silver-Smith Business is carried on as usual, by the Public's
very humble Servant, John Burt Lyng." Notice at Great-George-
Street, May 12, 1774. Will dated, 1773, proved April 20,
1785, leaves net profits to his wife and children; settled at
auction year after death.
IBL — IL — JOHN BURT LYNG — LYNG

ADAM LYNN   1775–1836   1796
Alexandria, Va. Son of Adam and Catharine Lynn. Listed as
Silversmith, Census List for 1791. Advertised in *Alexandria
Gazette*, April 10, 1796, ". . . In King Street, makes Coffee Pots
. . . Table Crosses . . ." Firm of Coryton & Lynn, 1796. Formed
Adam Lynn & Company, 1810. Died December 6.
A.LYNN

ROBERT A. LYTLE   –1864   1825
Baltimore, Md.
R.A.LYTLE

[M]

G. MacPHERSON   1850
New York.
G.MACPHERSON

ALEXANDER MANN   1777–   1800
Middletown, Conn. Born in Hebron, Conn. Firm of Brewer &
Mann, 1805. Alexander Mann and Charles Brewer.
MANN

WILLIAM MANNERBACK   1825
Reading, Pa.
W.MANNERBACK — WMB

PINER MANSFIELD   1781–1863   1800
Smyrna, Del. Born in Charlestown, Md.
PM

SIMEON MARBLE   1777–1856   1800
New Haven, Conn., at Chapel Street; later, on State. Dissolved
partnership with Clark Sibley in 1806.
S.MARBLE

JACOB MARIUSGROEN   −1768   1701
New York. Born in Haesdrecht, Holland, son of Marius and
Margarita Groen, sister of Pieter Jacob Marius, N.Y. merchant,
who brought Jacob to New York and made him his heir. Mar-
ried, May 15, 1701, Maryhem, daughter of Capt. Sylvester and
Elizabeth Beeck Salisbury. They had six children, of whom
Sylvester, who married Femmitje Bergen, succeeded to his
father's business and changed his name to Morris. Witness to
will of Widow Barbara Stewart dated November 20, 1723,
proved January 15, 1724. Listed as Silversmith Jacob Marius
Groen when taking the 1728 Abjuration Oath in New York City
Court. Notice, *The New York Gazette* and *The Weekly Mercury*,
"Groen, Jacob Marius, Dec'd, Houses belonging to his Estate in
Pearl Street, New York City, For Sale. Apply to Sylvester Marius
Groen.", February 8, 1768.
I M

FREDERICK MARQUAND   1799–1882   1823
New York, at 166 Broadway. In partnership with brother, Isaac,
in 1825.
FM − F.MARQUAND

MARQUAND & BROTHER   1825
New York. Isaac and Frederick at 166 Broadway until 1830.
MARQUAND & BROTHER

MARQUAND & CO.   1830
New York, on Broadway until 1838. Succeeded by Ball,
Tompkins & Black, 1839; Ball, Black & Co., 1850; Black, Starr
& Frost, 1876.
MARQUAND & CO

BENJAMIN MARSH   1840
Albany, N.Y. In Directory until 1850.
B.MARSH

THOMAS K. MARSH   1804−   1830
Paris, Ky., until 1850.
T.K.MARSH

MARSHALL & TEMPEST   1813
Philadelphia, Pa., until 1830 at 87 South Second Street.
MARSHALL & TEMPEST

THOMAS H. MARSHALL   1809–1852   1832
Albany, N.Y., until 1836; Rochester, N.Y., 1838–1852
T.H.MARSHALL

PETER MARTIN   1756
New York, admitted Freeman, August 4. Received Estate of
Thomas McClean, October 30, 1756, proved March 16, 1757.
PM – P.MARTIN

PETER MARTIN, II   1825
New York.
P.MARTIN

VALENTINE MARTIN   1842
Boston, Mass., until 1846.
V.MARTIN

J. D. MASON   1830
Philadelphia, Pa.
J.D.MASON

MASTERS & MURDOCK   1800
Philadelphia, Pa.
MASTERS & MURDOCK

MATHER & NORTH   1825
New York. Thomas Mather and William B. North who retired
from the partnership in 1827. Advertised in New Britain, Conn.
MATHER & NORTH

AUGUSTUS MATHEY   1825
New York.
A.MATHEY

NEWELL MATSON   1817–1887   1845
Oswego, N.Y. Later in Ohio, Wisconsin, Illinois.
N.MATSON

GOTLIEB A. MAYER   1835
Norfolk, Va. Married Louisa J. Henry, December 10, 1835.
Firm of Minton & Mayer, 1840. In Directory, 1851–1868.
G.MAYER

R. H. MAYNARD   1825
Buffalo, N.Y., until 1840.
R.H.MAYNARD

CHARLES MAYSENHOFLDER (MAYSENHOELDER)   1810
Philadelphia, Pa. In Directory, 1810–1825. At 54 Chestnut
Street in 1824.
C.MAYSENHOFLDER

JOHN McCLYMAN   1815
New York. In Directory until 1820.
MCCLYMAN

McCLYMAN & VAN SANDFORD   1790
Albany, N.Y.
M & VS

JOHN C. McCLYMON   1805
New York, 28 and 40 Warren Street until 1808; at Rose Street,
1811. In Directory until 1840.
J.MCCLYMON

WILLIAM McCLYMON   1800
Schenectady, N.Y., until 1815.
MCCLYMON

HUGH McCONNEL   1811
Philadelphia, Pa., at Dock near Second Street. In Directory until
1813.
MCCONNEL

THOMAS McCONNELL   1768–1825   1806
Wilmington, Del., advertised removal to Market Street where
located until 1817. Held public offices. In 1818, in Richmond,
Va. where he died.
MCCONNELL – M.CONNELL – T.MCCONNELL

WILLIAM McDOUGALL   1825
Meredith, N.H.
WM, MCDOUGALL

WILLIAM HANSE McDOWELL   1795–1842   1819
Philadelphia, Pa., at 130 South Front Street. Son of George and
Susannah Hanse McDowell. Married (1) Mary Stanley; (2)
Martha Tennent Austin. Retired from business in 1840. Was
related to Elias Boudinot and Peter Vergereau.
WM.H.MCDOWELL

J. B. McFADDEN   1840
Pittsburgh, Pa.
J.B.MCFADDEN

JOHN McFARLANE   1796
Boston, Mass.
J.MCF – J.MCFARLANE

McFEE & REEDER 1793
Philadelphia, Pa., listed at 38 North Front Street. Dissolved in
1796 by John McFee and Abner Reeder.
M & R

HENRY McKEEN 1823
Philadelphia, Pa.
H.MCKEEN

HUGH A. McMASTERS 1839
Philadelphia, Pa., until 1850.
H.A.MCMASTERS

JOHN McMULLIN 1765–1843 1790
Philadelphia, Pa., 1790 Census List. Located at 120 South Front
Street, 1795. Firm of M'Mullin & Black, 1811.
IM – I.MCMULLIN – I.M.MULLIN – JM

McMULLIN & BLACK 1811
Philadelphia, Pa. John M'Mullin and John Black at 120 South
Front Street, dissolved, 1813.
MCMULLIN & BLACK

E. McNEIL 1813
Binghamton, N.Y. Listed in Directory, Troy, N.Y., 1838.
E.MCNEIL

WILLIAM McPARLIN 1780–1850 1805
Annapolis, Md. Married Cassandra Woodward, December 15,
1816. Took over shop of Charles Faris on West Street to whom
he was probably apprenticed. His account book, 1827–1850,
shows dealings with Baltimore silversmiths: Kirk, Gelston,
Campbell, Webb and others.
W.MCP

ALMON AINSWORTH MEAD 1823–1887 1846
Montpelier, Vt. Apprenticed to Ira S. Town.
A.A.MEAD

MEAD & ADRIANCE 1831
Ithaca, N.Y. Edward Mead and Edwin Adriance until 1834.
Advertised in St. Louis, Mo, 1835.
MEAD & ADRIANCE

BENJAMIN MEAD 1804
Wiscasset, Me.
B.MEAD

EDMUND MEAD   1850
St. Louis, Mo.
E.MEAD

MEADOWS & CO.   1831
Philadelphia, Pa.
MEADOWS & CO

GEORGE MECUM   1825
Boston, Mass., at South Russell Street, until 1846.
G.MECUM

THOMAS J. MEGEAR   1809–   1830
Wilmington, Del., until 1832. Apprenticed to Ziba Ferris. In
Philadelphia, Pa., 1833; listed as silversmith and watchmaker
until 1850.
T.J.MEGEAR

J. MERCHANT   1795
New York.
JM – J.MERCHANT

JAMES MEREDITH   –1860   1820
Winchester, Va. Firm of Campbell & Meredith, 1820; Meredith
& Johnston, dissolved March 16, 1827; J. Meredith & Son,
1855.
J.MEREDITH

JOSEPH P. MEREDITH   1790–   1824
Baltimore, Md., until 1851.
J.MEREDITH

JOHN H. MERKLER   –1791   1780
New York, at 93 Broadway. Died intestate. Wife, Elizabeth, was
granted letter of administration, June 24, 1791.
IHM

MARCUS MERRIMAN   1762–1850   1787
New Haven, Conn. Born in Wallingford, Conn., son of Silas,
brother of Samuel. Partner of Bethuel Tuttle, later Zebul Bradley, 1802.
MERRIMAN – MM

MARCUS MERRIMAN & CO.   1802
New Haven, Conn. Marcus Merriman, Zebul Bradley and
Bethuel Tuttle until 1817 when firm became Merriman &
Bradley.
M.M & CO

REUBEN MERRIMAN   1783–1866   1810
Cheshire, Conn. Located in Litchfield, Conn. in 1827 where he
built shop.
RM – R. MERRIMAN

SAMUEL MERRIMAN   1769–1805   1795
New Haven, Conn. Born in Cheshire, Conn., son of Silas, where
he learned trade. Removed to New Haven, Conn. and advertised
on Chapel Street. Notice, June 1, 1796, *Connecticut Journal*,
"Gold and Silversmithing. Having workmen from Europe, last
from New York, whose work will recommend itself in all
branches of this line. Shop near the College." *The Spectator*,
March 5, 1800, "Fire . . . 11:00 P.M. Destroyed shop."
SM – S. MERRIMAN

SILAS MERRIMAN   1734–1805   1760
Cheshire, Conn. Born in Wallingford, Conn. In New Haven,
Conn., 1766, at State Street. Father of Marcus and Samuel.
SM

MERRIMAN & BRADLEY   1817
New Haven, Conn. Marcus Merriman and Zebul Bradley until
1826.
M & B

JOHN MATHEW MIKSCH   1775
Bethlehem, Pa.
I. M. MIKSCH

D. B. MILLER   1850
Boston, Mass.
D. B. MILLER

EDWARD F. MILLER   1810
Providence, R.I. In Directory, 1824–1849.
E. F. MILLER

JOHN DAVID MILLER   1780
Charleston, S.C.
IDM – I. D. MILLER

I. R. MILLER   1810
Philadelphia, Pa.
I. R. MILLER

L. H. MILLER & CO.   1840
Baltimore, Md.
L. H. MILLER & CO

MATTHEW MILLER   1780–1840   1807
Charleston, S.C. Married Rose Ann, May, 1805. Adevertised as
goldsmith at 40 Queen Street in 1807; 326 King Street, 1816.
Continued work until 1840.
M.MILLER

PARDON MILLER   1797–1852   1821
Providence, R.I. Married Anna Elizabeth Martin, 1821.
P.MILLER

WILLIAM MILLER   1810
Philadelphia, Pa., at 85 Callowhill Street until 1847. Firm of
Ward & Miller in 1822.
MILLER – W.MILLER

THOMAS MILLNER   1690–1745   1715
Boston, Mass. Married Mary Reed. Received silversmith's tools
in will of Richard Conyers in 1708.
TM

GEORGE F. MILLS   1825
New York. In Directory, 1834–1847.
G.F.MILLS

MILLS & FORRISTALL   1845
Boston, Mass.
MILLS & FORRISTALL

EDMUND MILNE   1724–1822   1757
Philadelphia, Pa. Advertised, December 29, 1757, *Pennsylvania
Gazette*, "Above named who has for these two years last past
worked and carried on business for Mr. Charles Dutens, now
begs leave to inform the public, that as Dutens has gone to the
West Indies to reside, he has set up business for himself next
door to the Indian King in Market Street with Mr. David Barnes,
where all ladies and gentlemen who will honor him with their
custom, may depend upon being faithfully served in all
branches." In 1761, at Crown and Pearl Streets; at Second Street
in 1767. Advertised, in *Staatsbote, Penna. Gazette, Pennsylvania
Journal*, 1757–1773. Lost indentured servant in 1771. Made
twelve silver cups for General Washington in 1777. Retired circa
1800; lived to be ninety-eight; a "G'lmen of Northern Liberties".
Died February 4, 1822. Will dated 1818, proved February,
1822. Estate left to wife, Amelia, buried in Second Baptist
Church churchyard. His daughter, Elizabeth, married in 1793.
His son, Edmund, Jr., died in 1799.
EM – E.MILNE

THOMAS MILNE 1795
New York, at 170 Fly Market until 1797. In Directory until
1815.
T.MILNE

SAMUEL MINOTT 1732–1803 1764
Boston. Mass. Born in Concord, Mass. Married Elizabeth Davis,
1762. Partner of Josiah Austin, 1765–1769. Later, worked with
William Simpkins. Advertised his shop opposite Williams
Court, Cornhill, and, also, a shop North of the Draw-Bridge, in
1772. He was arrested as a Tory in 1776 by order of the Common
Council. Last address at Ann Street in 1789. Paid $150.00
Assessor's Taxing Book Tax, 1780.
MINOTT – SM

MINOTT & AUSTIN 1765
Boston, Mass. Samuel Minott and Josiah Austin, dissolved in
1769.
IA MINOTT – MINOTT IA

MINOTT & SIMPKINS 1769
Boston, Mass. Samuel Minott and William Simpkins.
MINOTT WS – WS MINOTT

JOSEPH B. MINTON 1840
Norfolk, Va. In partnership with Gotlieb A. Mayer until 1847.
MINTON

MINTON & MAYER 1842
Norfolk, Va., until 1847.
MINTON & MAYER

HENRY MITCHELL 1844
Philadelphia, Pa., until 1850.
MITCHELL

PHINEAS MITCHELL 1809
Boston, Mass. In Directory until 1830.
P.MITCHELL

WILLIAM MITCHELL, JR. 1795–1852 1820
Richmond, Va. Born in Boston, Mass., son of William and
Sarah Corliss Mitchell. In 1845, sold business to brother, Samuel
P. Mitchell, and John H. Tyler to start firm of Mitchell & Tyler.
WM JR – W.MITCHELL – W.MITCHELL JR

MITCHELL & TYLER   1845
Richmond, Va. Samuel Phillips Mitchell and John Henry Tyler
dissolved in 1866 due to ill health of S. P. Mitchell.
MITCHELL & TYLER

JAMES MIX   1793–1859   1817
Albany, N.Y., at 100 Hudson Street. In Directory until 1850.
JAMES MIX

JAMES MIX JR.   1846
Albany, N.Y. Probably son of silversmith James Mix. In Direc-
tory until 1880.
JAMES MIX JR

JOHN L. MOFFAT   1815
New York, at 203 Broadway. In Directory until 1835.
J.L.MOFFAT

J. & W. MOIR   1845
New York, N.Y.
J & W.MOIR

MONELL & WILLIAMS   1825
New York. John J. Monell and Charles M. Williams at 25
Rhynder Street.
I.I.MONELL & C.M.WILLIAMS – J.J.MONELL & C.M.WIL-
LIAMS

JAMES MONK   1800
Charleston, S.C., at 20 Broad Street. Married Jane Campbell,
1805. Last in Manchester, Vt.
MONK

JOHN & ROBERT MONTEITH   1814
Baltimore, Md., at 144 Baltimore Street until 1847.
MONTEITH

ROBERT MONTEITH   –1849   1814
Baltimore, Md., worked with brother, John.
RM

JOHN MOOD   1792–1864   1816
Charleston, S.C. Son of Peter Mood. Married Catharine McFar-
lane. Was Methodist preacher. Firm of J. & P. Mood, 1834.
I.MOOD – J.MOOD

J. & P. MOOD 1834
Charleston, S.C. John and Peter, Jr., brothers, advertised, "At the Sign of the Cross Spoons." Wholesale and retail dealers until 1841.
J & P.MOOD

PETER MOOD 1766–1821 1790
Charleston, S.C., from Philadelphia, Pa. Married Dorothy Sigwald. Became member of the German Friendly Society in 1789. Continued in business with sons, John and Peter, Jr., until he died.
MOOD – P.MOOD

MOOD AND EWAN 1824
Charleston, S.C. Peter Mood, Jr. and John Ewan.
MOOD & EWAN

CHARLES MOORE 1803
Philadelphia, Pa., at Combes' Alley; North Front Street, 1806–1807. Firm of Moore & Ferguson.
C.MOORE

JARED L. MOORE 1825
New York. At 294 Washington Street, 1835. In Brooklyn, N.Y., at Nassau and Stanton Streets in 1843. Listed in Directories until 1852. Firm of Moore & Brewer, 1835.
J.L.MOORE – MOORE

JOHN CHANDLER MOORE 1835
New York, at 51 Morton Street; 164 Broadway in 1844.
JCM

MOORE & BREWER 1835
New York. Jared L. Moore and Charles Brewer.
MOORE & BREWER

MOORE & FERGUSON 1801
Philadelphia, Pa., at 42 North Front Street. Charles Moore and John Ferguson dissolved partnership in 1804.
MOORE & FERGUSON

ELIJAH MORGAN 1783–1857 1807
Poughkeepsie, N.Y. Son of Elijah and Lavinia Morgan. Apprenticed to Andrew Billings. Married Nancy Smith, November 2, 1806. Of the firms: Sadd & Morgan, 1806; Morgan & Cook, 1807.
E.MORGAN – MORGAN

WILLIAM S. MORGAN 1807–1886   1837
Poughkeepsie, N.Y. Son of Elijah and Nancy Smith Morgan. In
partnership with his father as E. Morgan & Son, 1832–1837.
Worked independently, 1837–1881.
W.S.MORGAN

WILLIAM M. MORRELL   1828
New York.
W.MORRELL

SYLVESTER MORRIS 1709–1783   1745
New York. Married Maria Tevauw, October 25, 1741. Freeman,
September 29, 1759. Grandson of Jacob Mariusgroen, sil-
versmith.
SM

OBADIAH MORS   1733
Boston, Mass. Son of Nathaniel Morse.
MORS

HAZEN MORSE 1790–1874   1815
Boston, Mass. Silversmith and engraver. Born in Haverhill,
Mass. Married Lucy Carey in Milton, Mass., 1814. Member of
Massachusetts Charitable Mechanic's Association, 1833–1874.
Master and brother-in-law of Newell Harding. Brother of Moses
Morse.
H.MORSE

J. H. MORSE   1795
Boston, Mass.
J.H.MORSE

MOSES MORSE   1816
Boston, Mass. Brother of Hazen Morse. Apprenticed to Chur-
chill & Treadwell. Apprentices: Obadiah Rich, H. Haddock,
Charles West and J. Millar. Retired in 1830.
M.MORSE

NATHANIEL MORSE (MORS) 1685–1748   1709
Boston, Mass. Noted engraver and silversmith. Apprenticed to
John Coney. Married Sarah Draper, 1710. Father of Obadiah.
Estate appraised by Samuel Edwards.
NM–N.MORS

STEPHEN MORSE 1743–   1771
Portsmouth, N.H. Born in Newbury, Mass. In Boston, Mass.,
1796.
MORSE

DAVID MOSELEY   1753–1812   1775
Boston, Mass. In Directory, 1796–1810.
DM – MOSELEY

JACOB MOSES   1768
Birmingham, Ala. Advertised partnership with William Sime,
May 4, 1768, *Georgia Gazette*, "Goldsmiths and Jewellers from
London, England . . .". In Baltimore, Md., 1817–1822.
MOSES

MARTIN MOSES   1793–1893   1819
Lenox, Mass. Born in Windsor, Conn. Apprenticed to Moses
Wing in Springfield, Mass. Later, in Peekskill, N.Y. where he
died.
M.MOSES

BARNET MOSS   1840
Warrenton, Va. Silversmith and watchmaker.
B.MOSS

J. S. MOTT   1790
New York.
J.S.MOTT

JAMES S. MOTT   1830
New York.
J.MOTT

W. & J. MOTT   1789
New York, at 240 Water Street. This firm issued the first trades-
man's tokens in the United States.
MOTTS

JOHN MOULINAR   1722–   1744
New York. Son of Rev. Jean Joseph Brumauld de Moulinars.
Married to Elizabeth Bisset in 1743. Freeman in 1744. Lieuten-
ant in expedition to Canada in 1746. Last record in Albany,
N.Y.
IM

ABEL MOULTON   1784–1850   1815
Newburyport, Mass., on State Street. Brother of William.
Partner of John D. Davis in 1824.
A.MOULTON – M

EBENEZER MOULTON   1768–1824   1795
Boston, Mass. Son of Joseph. Married Abigail Bourne, 1794.
Located at 3 South Row, 1813.
MOULTON

EDWARD SHERBURNE MOULTON   1778–1855   1800
Rochester, N.H. Born in Portsmouth, N.H., son of Joseph and
Lydia Bickford Moulton. Married, 1803. In Saco, Me., 1814,
where he died.
ESM – E.S.MOULTON

ENOCH MOULTON   1780–CA. 1820   1805
Portland, Me. Born in Newburyport, Mass., brother of William,
Ebenezer and Abel.
E.MOULTON

JOSEPH MOULTON   1724–1795   1745
Newburyport, Mass. Son of Joseph Moulton, 1694–1756.,
brother of William, 1720–1793. Married Anne Boardman.
I.MOULTON – JM

JOSEPH MOULTON   1744–1816   1765
Newburyport, Mass. Son of William, 1720–1793. Married
Abigail Noyes.
IM – I.MOULTON – JM

JOSEPH MOULTON   1814–1903   1835
Newburyport, Mass. Son of William, 1772–1861. Sold business
in 1860 to predecessors of Towle Silversmiths.
J.MOULTON

WILLIAM MOULTON   1720–1793   1750
Newburyport, Mass. Married Lydia Greenleaf in 1742. Father of
Joseph, 1744–1816. Advertised in Marietta, Ohio, in 1788.
WM – W.MOULTON

WILLIAM MOULTON   1772–1861   1796
Newburyport, Mass. Son of Joseph, 1744–1816, brother of
Ebenezer, Enoch and Abel. Shop on Merrimack Street. Married
Judith Noyes, 1801.
WM – W.MOULTON

MOULTON & DAVIS   1824
Newburyport, Mass. Abel Moulton and John W. Davis dissolved
partnership in 1830.
M & D

MOULTON & WOOD   1818
Newburyport, Mass., until 1820. Abel Moulton and Davis
Wood.
M & W

JOHN H. MULFORD 1835
Albany, N.Y., at 480 Broadway and 44 State Street. Firms of
Boyd & Mulford, 1832; Mulford & Wendell, 1842.
J.H.MULFORD

MULFORD & WENDELL 1842
Albany, N.Y., at 480 Broadway until 1850. John H. Mulford
and William Wendell. Successors of Boyd & Mulford.
MULFORD & WENDELL

H. MULLIGAN 1840
Philadelphia, Pa., at 414 Second Street.
H.MULLIGAN

HENRY G. MUMFORD 1792–1859 1813
Providence, R.I. Born in Newport, R.I.
MUMFORD

ASA MUNGER 1778–1851 1810
Herkimer, N.Y. Born in Granby, Mass., son of Joseph and
Hannah Fiske Munger. Married Polly Chapin, 1801. In Auburn,
N.Y., 1818. Firm of Munger & Benedict, advertising 1826–
1828.
A.MUNGER

A. MUNGER & SON 1840
Auburn, N.Y.
A.MUNGER & SON

MUNN & JONES 1824
Greenfield, Mass. Elisha Munn and Albert Jones.
MUNN & JONES

JAMES MUNROE 1784–1879 1806
Barnstable and New Bedford, Mass.
I.MUNROE–JAMES MUNROE

NATHANIEL MUNROE 1777–1861 1815
Baltimore, Md., at 222 East Baltimore Street until 1840.
N.MUNROE

CORNELIUS MUNSON 1742– 1763
Wallingford, Conn. Born April 16, son of Caleb, Jr. and Abigail
Brockett Munson. Freeman, April, 1770. Worked in Walling-
ford until 1776. Died while in the British Army.
CM

JOHN MURDOCK   1748–1786   1779
Philadelphia, Pa. Listed at Front between Walnut and Spruce
Streets in 1785.
IM – I. MURDOCK – J. MURDOCK – MURDOCK

JAMES MURDOCK & CO.   1826
Utica, N.Y., until 1838.
JAMES MURDOCK & CO

MURDOCK & ANDREWS   1822
Utica, N.Y. James Murdock and Elon Andrews advertised until
1826. In Directory, 1838–1849.
M & A

JAMES MURPHY   1803
Boston, Mass., in Directory until 1816. Listed in Philadelphia,
Pa., 1828–1846.
J. MURPHY

JOHN B. MURPHY   1830
Norfolk, Va. In Augusta, Ga., 1834, where he married Eliza C.
Byrd. Advertised at lower corner of Broad and McIntosh Streets,
Augusta, Ga., 1845.
J. B. MURPHY

JOHN MURPHY   1798
Norfolk, Va., until 1826.
J. MURPHY

AARON MUSGRAVE, JR.   1794
West Chester, Pa.
AM

JAMES MUSGRAVE   1795
Philadelphia, Pa., at Chestnut and Third Streets. Advertised,
November 19, 1796, *The Federal Gazette*: "Goldsmith and
Jeweler, No. 42 South Second Street, all kinds of work in gold
and silver line, miniatures set, repair work executed as usual."
Listed in directory at 31 Cable Lane, 1796: at 44 South Second
Street, 1804–07. Mentioned as "The late Goldsmith" of 74
Spruce Street in 1813. Firm of Parry & Musgrave, 1793.
MUSGRAVE

HENRY BEEKMAN MYER   1818
Newburgh, N.Y., until 1835. In Directory, Buffalo, N.Y.,
1836–1848.
H. B. MYER

JOHN MYERS 1785
Philadelphia, Pa., at North Second Street until 1804. Apprenticed to Richard Humphreys.
I.MYERS

MYER MYERS 1723–1795 1745
New York. Freeman, April 29, 1746. Married Joyce Mears, March 18, 1767. Advertised, *New York Gazette*, 1753–4, 1767, 1771–3, "Removal of Shop from King Street to the Meal-Market . . ." In 1776, President of New York Silversmiths Society. Worked in Norwalk, Conn., 1776–1780; in Philadelphia, Pa. 1780–1782. Returned to New York in 1783. Chairman of the New York Gold and Silver Smiths' Society, 1786. Located at Greenwich Street in 1786; at 29 Princess Street in 1788; at 17 Pearl Street when he died. Prominent Master Mason. Firm of Myers & Halsted; Halsted & Myers.
MM – MYERS

MYERS & HALSTED 1763
New York. Ad, *New York Gazette* and *The Weekly Post Boy*, November 10, 1763 to July 5, 1764, ". . . moved to lower end of King Street." Myer Myers and Benjamin or Mathias Halsted.
M & H

COMFORT STARR MYGATT 1763–1823 1785
Danbury, Conn. Apprenticed to father, Eli Mygatt. In September, 1804, succeeded to father's business with brother, David. In 1807, in Canfield, Ohio where he died.
C.MYGATT

DAVID MYGATT 1777–1822 1800
Danbury, Conn. Son of Eli from whom he learned his trade. Worked with brother, Comfort Starr Mygatt, 1804. In Southeast, N.Y. in 1811.
DM – D.MYGATT

JACOB MYTINGER 1825
Newtown, Va. Married Evelina Watson, February 9, 1834. Later, in Warrenton, Va.
J.MYTINGER

[N]

DANIEL NEALL 1784–1846 1810
Milford, Del. In Philadelphia, Pa. in 1828.
DN – D.NEALL

WILLIAM NEEDLES (NEEDELS)   1798

Easton, Md. Firm of Bowdle & Needles until 1807. Advertised
in *Republic Star*, July 28, 1807, "Opened Silver-Smith's Shop
near the Market-House." No record after 1818 when Stephen
Hussey took over the shop of William Needles, Second Door
above the Post-Office.

W. NEEDELS

JOHN NELSON 1735–1789   1757

Portsmouth, N.H. Son of Mark and Elizabeth Mann Nelson,
brother of Mark. Died in Gilmanton, N.H.

IN

MARK NELSON 1733–1787   1754

Portsmouth, N.H. Brother of John.

MN

H. K. NEWCOMB   1821

Watertown, N.Y., until 1850.

H.K.NEWCOMB

JAN VAN NIEU KIRKE 1690–1735   1711

New York. Mentioned in 1716.

INK – IVK

TIMOTHY HARRINGTON NEWMAN 1778–1812   1800

Groton, Mass. Born in Lancaster, Mass., son of John and Sarah
Flagg Newman. Married Nancy Turner, 1800.

NEWMAN – THN

BASSET NICHOLS   1815

Providence, R.I.

NICHOLS

NATHANIEL B. NICHOLS –1831   1817

Petersburg, Va. In 1831, wife, Susanna E. Nichols, continued
business with Charles Lumsden as C. Lumsden & Co. until 1834.

N.B.NICHOLS

WILLIAM STODDARD NICHOLS 1785–1871   1808

Newport, R.I. Born in Providence, R.I. Apprenticed to Thomas
Arnold. Advertised at 155 Thames Street in 1842.

NICHOLS – WSN

RICHARD NIXON   1820

Philadelphia, Pa., at 240 South Seventh Street until 1831.

R.NIXON

NEHEMIAH NORCROSS   1765–1804   1796
Boston, Mass. In Directory until 1800.
NN

CHARLES NORDMEYER   1845
Richmond, Va.
CHAS.NORDMEYER

WILLIAM B. NORTH   1787–1838   1810
New Haven, Conn., until 1818. Born in New Haven. Advertised
in New York at 217 Broadway, 1823. Firm of Mather & North,
1825.
WBN

W. B. NORTH & CO.   1823
New York. William B. North formed company succeeded by
Mather & North, 1825.
W.B.NORTH & CO

ABIJAH NORTHEY   1741–1816   1765
Salem, Mass.
AN

DAVID I. NORTHEY (NORTHEE)   1709–1778   1732
Salem, Mass.
DN — D.I.NORTHEE — D.NORTHEE

WILLIAM NORTHEY   CA. 1734–1804   1764
Salem, Mass. Married Rebecca Collins, 1764. Son of David.
WN

ANDREW NORTON   1765–1838   1787
Goshen, Conn., at his Inn House.
A.NORTON

BENJAMIN R. NORTON   1845
Syracuse, N.Y.
B.R.NORTON

C. C. NORTON   1820
Hartford, Conn. Partner of William Pitkin, 1825.
C.C.NORTON

J. H. NORTON   1820
Hartford, Conn.
J.H.NORTON

THOMAS NORTON   1773–1834   1796
Farmington, Conn., advertised until 1806. Died in Albion,
N.Y.
TN

NORTON & PITKIN   1825
Hartford, Conn. C. C. Norton and William Pitkin.
C.C.NORTON & W.PITKIN

NORTON & SEYMOUR   1850
Syracuse, N.Y.
NORTON & SEYMOUR

THOMAS NOWLAN & CO.   1848
Petersburg, Va. In Richmond, Va., 1866, in partnership with
Robert E. Macomber. Listed in Richmond Directory in 1906.
NOWLAN & CO

MARTIN NOXON   1780–1814   1800
Edenton, N.C. Son of Pasco and Anna Harris Noxon of Oswego,
N.Y. Married Hannah Carpenter, 1804.
NOXON

JOHN NOYES   1674–1749   1699
Boston, Mass. Apprentice of Jeremiah Dummer. Advertised,
"Tankard Stolen.", 1699. Notices dated February 10, 1706;
March 15, 1707. Married Susanna Edwards, sister of John
Edwards. Member of the Artillery Company, 1699–1707. Died
in Boston, Mass. Made a dram cup, 1697; a flagon dated 1711,
in Museum of Fine Arts, Boston.
IN

FREDERICK NUSZ   –1842   1819
Frederick, Md., until 1842.
F.NUSZ

ENOCH HOYT NUTTER   1800–1880   1826
Dover, N.H. Born in Rochester, N.Y.
E.H.NUTTER

JOHANNIS NYS   1671–1734   1695
Philadelphia, Pa. Probably apprenticed to Jacobus VanDer
Spiegel, New York, using New York style base band and thumb
piece on tankards. Married Grietse Ketteltas, who was related to
Henricus Boelen. After serving apprenticeship in New York, he
removed to Bohemia Manor for religious reasons. "Jan Neuss,
Menonite and Silversmith", received the "Right of Citizenship

of Germantown" in 1698. Served in Albany Militia, 1689–
1690, for which he received a reward in 1717. William Penn
purchased six silver teaspoons from him in 1704 which he
presented to the children of Isaac Norris. Moved to Delaware in
1723. Died in Kent County, Delaware.

IN

[O]

FREDERICK OAKES 1782–1855   1810
Hartford, Conn., advertised North of Marshall's Tavern. In
1811, firm of Oakes & Spencer until 1820. Listed in Directory in
1825.

F.OAKES–OAKES

OAKES & SPENCER   1811
Hartford, Conn. Frederick Oakes and Nathaniel Spencer dissolved partnership in 1820.

O & S

JOHN OGILVIE CA. 1732–   1764
New York. Son of Alexander and Jannette Schuyler Ogilvie.
Married Anna Atkins, June 13, 1764, in Trinity Church.

I.OGILVIE

ANDREW OLIVER 1724–1776   1750
Boston, Mass. Clerk of the Market in 1753.

AO

DANIEL OLIVER   1805
Philadelphia, Pa.

D.OLIVER

PETER OLIVER 1682–1712   1705
Boston, Mass. Probably apprenticed to Edward Winslow.
Married (1) Jerusha Mather, 1709; (2) Hopestill Wensley in
Charlestown, Mass., 1711. Made a flagon dated 1711 presented
to the Second Church of Christ in Boston.

PO

PETER OLIVIER –1798   1790
Philadelphia, Pa., at 6 Strawberry Street until 1797. Died
intestate when notice appears in *Aurora*, April 30, 1798, by
order of French Consulate, advertising for settlement of estate
claims.

PO

NATHANIEL OLMSTED   1785–1860   1808
Farmington, Conn. Born in East Hartford, Conn. Apprenticed
to Daniel Burnap of East Windsor, Conn. Married Phidelia
Burnap. Advertised in New Haven, Conn. on Chapel Street in
1826. Located at 37 Olive Street, 1847, with son as N. Olmsted
& Son.
N.OLMSTED

GERRIT ONCKELBAG   1670–1732   1691
New York. Baptised in Dutch Church, April 17, 1670, son of
Adam Onckelbag and wife, Neeltse Jans, who married again in
1676, Ahasuerus Hendricks. (Daughter Neeltse, baptised July
7, 1691, married Johannes Van Gelder, January 3, 1713;
youngest son, Gerritt, was willed his grandfather's tankard and
tools as stepson of Ahasuerus Hendricks to whom he was probably apprenticed.) Freeman, September 6, 1698. Married
Elizabeth Van Schaick, daughter of Adion Cornelissen Van
Schaick and Rebecca Idens Van Voorst, first cousin of Johannis
Nys. Elected Assistant Alderman, 1700–1703. Located in New
Jersey, 1713, to escape accusations of counterfeiting of which he
was convicted, but, later, returned to N.Y. Witnessed baptisms
of grandchildren, 1713, 1728. Recorded in England, 1724–
1725. Was a "Distiller" in 1732. Will, dated July 10, 1732,
leaves Estate of Distiller to Daughters, Nelly, wife of John Van
Gelder, and Rebecca, wife of Broghter Sipkins. Will proved May
21, 1733. House and Estate assessed at £50 in 1730, North
Ward Tax List. Made a caudle cup dated 1696 in the Mabel
Brady Garvan Collection, Yale University Art Gallery.
GBO–GOB

CHARLES O'NEIL   1802
New Haven, Conn. In firm of Merriman & Bradley, 1823.
C.O'NEIL

WILLIAM OSBORN   1840
Providence, R.I.
WILLIAM OSBORN

JOHN OSGOOD   1770–1840   1795
Haverhill, Mass. Born in Andover, Mass. His son, John, Jr.,
followed in his trade.
IO–JO–J.OSGOOD

JOHN OSGOOD, JR.   1817
Boston, Mass. In Directory and Almanac, 1850. Son of John
Osgood.
J.OSGOOD

ANDREW OSTHOFF   1810
Baltimore, Md., at Pearl Street; 27 Lexington Street in 1812.
Advertised in Pittsburgh, Pa. in 1815.
A.OSTHOFF

JONATHAN OTIS   1723–1791   1750
Newport, R.I. Born in Sandwich, Mass., son of Nathaniel and
Abigail Russell Otis. Apprenticed to his uncle, Moody Russell,
in Barnstable, Mass. Major in Militia in 1778. Removed to
Middletown, Conn., during the British invasion, where he died.
IO – JO – J.OTIS – OTIS

GEORGE OTT   –1831   1801
Norfolk, Va., until 1830.
G.OTT – OTT

JESSE OWEN   1794
Philadelphia, Pa., at Priest's Alley, Silversmith, Turner and
Refiner until 1848.
JSE OWEN – OWEN

JOHN OWEN   1804
Philadelphia, Pa., at 11 North Second Street and other addresses
until 1831.
I.OWEN

[P]

JONATHAN PACKARD   1789–1854   1811
Northampton, Mass. In Albany, N.Y., 1815; in Rochester,
N.Y., 1819–1850. Died in Rochester.
PACKARD

PALMER & BACHELDERS   1850
Boston, Mass.
PALMER & BACHELDERS

SAMUEL PANCOAST   1785
Philadelphia, Pa., at Front Street between Walnut and Spruce
Streets until 1794. Advertised, 1795.
PANCOAST – SP

AMOS PANGBORN   1800–1843   1823
Burlington, Vt., at Church Street until 1843.
A.PANGBORN

PANGBORN & BRINSMAID   1833
Burlington, Vt. until 1843. Amos Pangborn and James Edgar
Brinsmaid.
PANGBORN & BRINSMAID – P & B

WILLIAM PARHAM   –1794   1785
Philadelphia, Pa., advertised as goldsmith at Front Street between Walnut and Spruce Streets; at 104 Swanson Street, 1791–
1794.
W P

OTTO PAUL De PARISEN (PARISIEN)   1763
New York, advertised, *New York Gazette*, March 14, "Goldsmith,
from Berlin, makes all Sorts of Platework, both plain and chased,
in the neatest and most expeditious Manner; likewise undertakes
chasing any piece of old Plate, at his House, the lower End of
Batto Street." Took Oath of Colonial Naturalization Act of 1740
on January 18, 1763. Admitted Freeman, January 31, 1769.
Notices, 1765, 1769. In 1774, "Silversmith in the Fly, in this
City, took Fire By Means of his Furnace," located in Dock Street.
Worked at 60 Queen Street, 1787–1789. In business with son,
Otto W., 1789–1791. Commissioned by Corporation of the City
to make a Gold Box, £32/18/16.
OP – PARISEN

OTTO W. PARISEN (PARISIEN)   1791
New York. In partnership with his father, 1789–1791. At 100
Chatham Square in 1823.
PARISEN

OTTO PAUL De PARISEN & SON   1789
New York, at 60 Queen Street until 1791.
OPDP

ALLEN PARKER   1817
New York, until 1819.
A . PARKER

CALEB PARKER, JR.   1731/2–   1758
Boston, Mass. Married Mary Mellens, November 2, 1758.
C . PARKER

DANIEL PARKER   1726–1785   1750
Boston, Mass. Advertised in *Boston Post*, December, 1750. Born
November 20. Married Margaret Jarvis, September 1, 1760. In
Union Street, near "The Golden Ball" in 1758. Continued until
1775 when he advertised in Salem, Mass. Died December 31.
DP – D.PARKER

GEORGE PARKER   1804
Baltimore, Md., at Ross Street until 1823; Biddle Street until
1831.
G.PARKER

ISAAC PARKER   1749–1805   1780
Deerfield, Mass. Merchant in Boston Directory, 1789. Died in
Boston.
IP – I.PARKER

CHARLES PARKMAN   1790
Boston, Mass. Advertised English Imported Goods in Boston
Directory, 1821.
C.PARKMAN – PARKMAN

JOHN PARKMAN   1716–1748   1738
Boston, Mass.
PARKMAN

THOMAS PARKMAN   1793
Boston, Mass.
PARKMAN – TP – T.PARKMAN

JAMES PARMELE   1763–1828   1785
Durham, Conn.
T.PARMELE

SAMUEL PARMELEE   1737–1807   1760
Guilford, Conn., until Revolutionary War, serving as Captain,
1775.
SP – S.PARMELE

T. PARROTT   1775
Boston, Mass.
TP – T.PARROTT

MARTIN PARRY   1756–1802   1780
Portsmouth, N.H. Also in Kittery, Me.
PARRY

PARRY & MUSGRAVE   1793
Philadelphia, Pa., at 42 South Second Street, advertised until
1795, "elegant assortment". In *Federal Gazette*, November 10,
1795, "Jewellers, The Partnership of Parry & Musgrave is this
day dissolved; all persons indebted to, or to whom have any
demands on said firm, will please apply to James Musgrave, at
the old stand, 42 South Second Street, or to Rowland Parry, 36
Chestnut Street."
P & M

ROWLAND PARRY   −1796   1790
Philadelphia, Pa., at 42 South Second Street. Advertised after
the dissolution of Parry & Musgrove, 1795, at South Chestnut
Street. Notice of death, November 15.
R.PARRY

JOHN PARSONS   1780
Boston, Mass.
I.PARSONS

JOHN PATTERSON   1751
Annapolis, Md.
IP

JOHN TYING PEABODY   1756−1822   1778
Enfield, Conn. Born in Norwich, Conn. In 1787, in
Wilmington, N.C. where he died.
J.PEABODY

EDWARD PEAR   1830
Boston, Mass. Apprenticed to Lewis Cary. Advertised at 15
Pleasant Street. In partnership with Thomas Bacall in 1850.
EP

PEAR & BACALL   1850
Boston, Mass. Edward Pear and Thomas Bacall at 5 Avery Street.
PEAR & BACALL

WALTER PEARCE   1830
Norfolk, Va. Married Sara Ann Slack Clarico, widow of
goldsmith, Joseph Clarico, June 4, 1831. In partnership with
James A. Sprately as Pearce & Sprately, 1831−1834.
W.PEARCE

JOHN PEARSON   1791
New York, at 13 Crown Street; Pearl Street, 1805.
IP−J.PEARSON

EMMET T. PELL   1825
New York. In Directory until 1841.
E.T.PELL

PELLETREAU, BENNETT & COOKE   1815
New York. Advertised in Directory, 1826−1828. Maltby Pelletreau, John Bennett, Jr., D. C. Cooke. Also advertised as Bennett, Cooke & Co., 1823−1828, in Charleston, S.C.
P.B & C

ELIAS PELLETREAU 1726–1810   1750

Southampton, N.Y. Born in Southampton, May 31, son of
Francis and Jane Osborn Pelletreau. His father left him, in his
will dated March 11, 1736, all of his houses and lands, his gold
watch, sword, gun and one half of his personal estate. At the age
of thirteen, he was sent to the boarding school of Mr. John
Proctor, a noted school master of New York, for one year. On
November 19, 1741, he was duly apprenticed to Simeon
Soumaine, goldsmith of New York, for a term of seven years,
"To be taught the Art and Mystery of a Goldsmith." Admitted a
freeman of the City of New York, August 31, 1750. Removed to
Southampton, where he established himself as a silversmith and
conducted a large farm. Married Sarah Gelston, December 29,
1748; (2) Sarah Conkling, June 28, 1786. Commissioned as
Lieutenant in the Southampton Company, 1761, and as Captain,
May 22, 1765. Witness to the Will of Sarah White, October 1,
1756; the Will of John Foster, Southampton, dated February 2,
1761. Moved to Simsbury, Conn., during the War years. Returned to Southampton where he died on November 2.
E P

MALTBY PELLETREAU   1813

New York, at 12 Rose Street; at 170 Broadway, 1825; at 26
Franklin Street in 1835. Firms of Pelletreau, Bennett & Cooke,
1815; Pelletreau & Upson, 1818.
M P

WILLIAM SMITH PELLETREAU 1786–1842   1810

Southampton, N.Y. Son of John and Mary Smith Pelletreau,
born June 8. Continued in the trade of his father and grandfather, Elias. Married (1) Nancy Mackie, May 23, 1810; (2)
Elizabeth Welles, June 26, 1834. Appointed Purchasing Agent
in the War of 1812. Firms of Pelletreau & Van Wyck, 1815;
Pelletreau & Richards, 1825. Died March 15.
WSP – W.S.PELLETREAU

PELLETREAU & RICHARDS   1825

New York. William Smith Pelletreau and Thomas Richards.
WSP TR

PELLETREAU & UPSON   1818

New York. Imported wares from Sheffield, England, 1818–
1824, amounted to £2,568/10/3.
P & U

PELLETREAU & VAN WYCK   1815
New York. Partnership of William S. Pelletreau and Stephen
Van Wyck.

W.S.PELLETREAU   S.VAN WYCK

JOSIAH PENFIELD & CO.   1822
Savannah, Ga., in Directory at corner of Whitaker and Bryan
Streets.

PENFIELD & CO

HENRY J. PEPPER   1814
Wilmington, Del., at 60 Market Street. Born in Wilmington,
Del. Married Keziah Moore, June 7, 1817. After selling stock to
Joseph Draper in 1825, removed to Philadelphia, Pa. Listed at
46 Kuncle Street, 1828–1850.

H.I.PEPPER – H.J.PEPPER

HENRY J. PEPPER & SON   1846
Philadelphia, Pa., until 1850.

H.J.PEPPER & SON

HOUGHTON PERKINS   1735/6–1778   1756
Boston, Mass. Son of Isaac Perkins who died in 1737, goldsmith,
and his wife, Sarah Hurd Perkins. Apprenticed to Jacob Hurd.
Later, in Taunton, Mass.

HP – H.PERKINS

ISAAC PERKINS   1676–1737   1707
Boston, Mass. Married Sarah Hurd, October 12, 1732. Father of
Houghton Perkins who was three years of age when his father
died.

IP

JACOB PERKINS   1766–1849   1787
Newburyport, Mass., engaged to make dies for Massachusetts
Mint. Born July 9. When fifteen years old, his master, Edward
Davis, died, willing him the business. Married Hannah Greenleaf, November 11, 1790. An inventive genius, he was honored
in London, England, by Society of Liberal Arts. Invented
machine to manufacture wire into nails. During the War of
1812, he supervised the restoring of old guns for the Government. Invented steam-gun to fire 100 balls a minute. Moved to
Philadelphia, Pa. in 1816. In London, England, in 1819 where
he died, July 13.

IP – PERKINS

JOSEPH PERKINS   1749–1789   1770
Little Rest, R.I. Son of Edward and Elizabeth Brenton Perkins,
born September 24. Puchased land for house in 1774. Married
Mary Gardiner, 1776. Active in Revolution as Town Agent.
Died, September 6.
JP – J.PERKINS

T. PERKINS   1810
Boston, Mass.
T.PERKINS

PETER PERREAU   1797
Philadelphia, Pa., at 220 North Front Street.
PP

JAMES PETERS   1821
Philadelphia, Pa., at 90 South Second Street. In Directory until
1850.
J.PETERS

J. PETERS & CO.   1830
Philadelphia, Pa.
J.PETERS & CO

HENRY PETERSON   1783
Philadelphia, Pa.
HP

MATTHEW PETIT   1811
New York, at Provost Street.
MP

ALEXANDER PETRIE   –1768   1748
Charleston, S.C. Advertised, *South Carolina Gazette*, August 30,
as Goldsmith. Married Elizabeth Holland. Offers imported
goods in 1756. Located "at his shop on the Bay," in 1761.
AP

CHARLES H. PHELPS   1825
Bainbridge, N.Y.
C.H.PHELPS

EBENEZER S. PHELPS   1766–   1812
Northampton, Mass. Working until 1830.
PHELPS

JAMES D. PHILIPS   1829
Cincinnati, Ohio. In Directory as boarding at David Ross'.
JAS.D.PHILIPS

JOSEPH PHILLIPPE   1791
Baltimore, Md. Advertised, *Maryland Journal*, November 4,
1791, "on Charles Street, jeweller, silversmith, and engraver,
late from Paris."
JP

SAMUEL PHILLIPS   1658–1721   1680
Salem, Mass. Born March 23. Married Mary Emerson of
Gloucester.
SP

THOMAS PHILLIPS   1799
Paris, Ky.
TP

JOHN PIERCE (PEIRCE)   1810
Boston, Mass.
PEIRCE

O. PIERCE   1824
Boston, Mass.
O.PIERCE

BENJAMIN PIERPONT   1730–1797   1756
Boston, Mass. Married Elizabeth Shepard, 1758, Shop at Newbury Street, 1760–1790. Advertised, *Boston News Letter*, October
31, 1771, "Lost four silver spoons, two London made, marked
crest, a Spread Eagle; two no mark, Maker's Name, B. PIERPONT.
If offered for sale, it is desired they may be stopped."
BP – B.PIERPONT – PIERPONT

A. PIERSON   1800
New York.
A.PIERSON

HENRY PITKIN   1834
East Hartford, Conn. Brother of three silversmiths working
there: James F., John Owen, Walter. Taught business to Nelson
P. Stratten of Waltham Watch Company. Later, in Troy, N.Y.
HP

JOHN OWEN PITKIN   1803–1891   1826
East Hartford, Conn. Worked with brother, Walter, 1830;
opened a branch in Vicksburg, Tenn, 1834–1837. James and
Henry joined John and Walter in business in Hartford to work
together until John retired in 1840.
J.O.PITKIN – PITKIN

J. O. & W. PITKIN · 1830
East Hartford, Conn. Brothers, John Owen and Walter, dissolved
partnership in 1840 when John retired. Walter continued the
business.
J.O & W.PITKIN

WALTER PITKIN · 1808–1885 · 1830
East Hartford, Conn. Employed as many as forty workmen. In
partnership with brother, John Owen, until 1840. Worked with
J. H. Norton, 1843. Fire destroyed factory in 1880.
W.PITKIN

WILLIAM J. PITKIN · 1820
East Hartford, Conn.
WM.J.PITKIN

WILLIAM L. PITKIN · 1825
East Hartford, Conn.
WM.L.PITKIN

PITKIN & NORTON · 1825
Hartford, Conn. William Pitkin and C. C. Norton.
W.PITKIN C.C.NORTON

PITKIN & NORTON · 1843
Hartford, Conn. Walter Pitkin and J. H. Norton.
W.PITKIN J.H.NORTON

BENJAMIN PITMAN · 1728–1814 · 1810
Providence, R.I.
B.PITMAN

I. PITMAN · 1785
Baltimore, Md.
I.PITTMAN

SAUNDERS PITMAN · 1732–1808 · 1775
Providence, R.I., at North corner of Main and Otis Streets.
Married Mary Kinnicutt, June 29, 1760. Advertised in *Providence Gazette*, April 2, 1796, "Takes this Method to acquaint his
old Customers and the Public, that he makes and sells, at his
Shop, a few Doors North of the State-House, Gold and Silver-
smith's Ware. . Wanted, as an Apprentice to the above Business,
an honest industrious Lad, about 14 Years of age." Firms of
Pitman & Dodge, 1790–1795; Pitman & Dorrance, 1795–
1800.
PITMAN – SP

WILLIAM R. PITMAN   1835
New Bedford, Mass.
WRP

JOHN PITTMAN   1792
Falmouth, Va. Advertised in Fredericksburg, Va., 1796. In
Alexandria, Va., 1797–1801.
J.PITTMAN

JOHN PITTS   1730
Boston, Mass.
IP

RICHARD PITTS   1742
Philadelphia, Pa. Advertised as a silversmith on Front Street
until 1745. In Charleston, S.C. in 1746.
PITTS – RP

DANIEL PLACE   1827
Rochester, N.Y. In Ithaca, N.Y., 1839–1845.
D.PLACE

PLATT & BROTHER   1825
New York. Partnership of George W. and N. C. Platt. In Direc-
tory until 1834.
PLATT & BROTHER

G. W. & N. C. PLATT   1820
New York. In Directory, 1828–1834.
G.W & N.C.PLATT

ROBERT ISAAC WATTS POLK   1818–1861   1840
Winchester, Va. Born in Washington, D.C., March 28, son of
Robert and Penelope Johnstone Fontaine Maury Polk. Married
Sarah Jane Somerville, May 10, 1838. Advertised, 1844. In
partnership with Thomas B. Campbell, 1850–1858, which
ended with Campbell's death.
POLK

WILLIAM POLLARD   1690–1740   1715
Boston, Mass. Stepson of Thomas Powell, goldsmith. Died in
Charleston, S.C.
WP

LEWIS JOSEPH PONCET   1800
Baltimore, Md., until 1822.
L.PONCET

THOMAS PONS   1757–1817   1789
Boston, Mass., at Newbury Street. In Directory until 1805.
PONS – T. PONS

WILLIAM POOLE   1764–1846   1790
Wilmington, Del. Son of William and Elizabeth Canby Poole.
Apprenticed to Bancroft Woodcock. Married Sarah Sharpless,
May 5, 1791.
W P

F. W. PORTER   1820
New York.
F. W. PORTER

HENRY C. PORTER & CO.   1830
New York, at 183 Division Street.
H. PORTER & CO

JOSEPH S. PORTER   1783–1862   1805
Utica, N.Y. Advertised in Canandaigua, N.Y., 1809–1811. In
Utica, N.Y., 1816–1850.
I. S. PORTER

FREDERICK J. POSEY   1815–1881   1839
Hagerstown, Md. Married Elizabeth McCardle, December 18,
1839.
F. J. POSEY – POSEY

JOHN POTTER   1815
Alexandria, Va. Apprenticed to John Adam. In Norfolk, Va., in
1816. Formed partnership with Henry H. Redman as Redman &
Potter, 1819–1821.
J. POTTER

J. O. & J. R. POTTER   1810
Providence, R.I. Located at 15 North Main Street in 1824. In
Directory until 1850.
J. O & J. R. POTTER

JOHN POTWINE   1698–1792   1721
Boston, Mass., on Newbury Street until 1737. Born in England,
son of John and Sarah Hill Potwine. Mentioned in his father's
will, 1700, when he was left, "my silver-headed cane, one gold
ring, and my Chirurgeon's Chest." Joined Brattle Street Church,
1715. Married (1) Sarah Jackson, 1721. Appointed Clerk of the
Market, 1734. Removed to Hartford, Conn., 1737–1753. Later
advertised in Coventry and East Windsor, Conn. Married (2)

Elizabeth Mosely, widow of Capt. Abner Mosely, 1771. His
account book, 1752–3, records transactions. Partner of Charles
Whiting, 1761–2, Hartford, Conn. Died in Scantic (East
Windsor), Conn., May 16, 1792, where for many years he was a
pastor of the Congregational Church.
IP – I. POTWINE – POTWINE

ABRAHAM POUTREAU   1701–   1726
New York. Born March 25. Baptised in French Church, April 5,
1701, son of Daniel and Martha Couson Poutreau. Married
Maria Vreeland, October 23, 1726. Robert Lyell, son of David
Lyell, silversmith, was apprenticed to him in 1726.
AP

HENRY POWER   1797–1867   1822
Poughkeepsie, N.Y., until 1850.
H. POWER

HENRY PRATT   1708–1749   1730
Philadelphia, Pa. Born April 30, son of Henry and . . . Hobart
Pratt. Apprenticed to Philip Syng. Married Rebecca Claypool,
May 1, 1729, in Christ Church. Advertised shop at corner of
Taylor's Alley, between Walnut and Chestnut Streets. Founding
member of St. John's Lodge, 1730. Coroner of City, 1741–1748.
Opened Royal Standard Tavern on Market Street, 1749. His son,
Matthew Pratt, was the noted painter. Died in Philadelphia,
January 31.
HP

NATHAN PRATT   1772–1842   1792
Essex, Conn. Born in Lyme, Conn., son of Phineas. Married
Elizabeth Spencer, 1796.
N. PRATT

HENRY PRESCOT   1828
Keeseville, N.Y., until 1831.
H. PRESCOT

STEPHEN L. PRESTON   1831
Philadelphia, Pa. Firm of Curry & Preston, 1831. John Curry
and Stephen L. Preston. Advertised in Newburgh, N.Y., 1849.
S. L. PRESTON

JOHN PRICE   1810
Lancaster, Pa.
JOHN PRICE

JOB PRINCE   1680–1703/4   1700
Milford, Conn. Born in Hull, Mass. Died in Milford.
IP

W. PRIOR   1775
Connecticut or Massachusetts.
WP – W. PRIOR

THOMAS PURSE   1776–1823   1801
Winchester, Va. Born in Charleston, S.C., son of Thomas and
Isabella Steele Purse. Married Mary Pilkington, 1795. In Balti-
more, Md., 1796–1812; Charleston, S.C., 1813.
TP

WILLIAM PURSE   1760–1844   1798
Charleston, S.C., at 112 Broad Street until 1803. Married
Elizabeth Hammett, May 1, 1793. Lieutenant in 1809.
PURSE

EDWARD PUTNAM   1810
Salem, Mass. Apprenticed to Jabez Baldwin. In Boston, Mass.,
in 1822 in firm of Putnam & Low until 1830.
EP

PUTNAM & LOW   1822
Boston, Mass. Edward Putnam and John J. Low.
PUTNAM & LOW

REUBEN H. PUTNEY   1816
Sackett's Harbor, N.Y. In Watertown, N.Y., 1821–1828.
R. PUTNEY

[Q]

PETER QUINTARD   1699–1762   1731
New York. Registered as Freeman, May 18, 1731. Son of Isaac
and Jeanne Fune Quintard of Bristol, England, born June 14.
Baptised in French Church of New York, 1700. Master of Peter
David, age fifteen, 1722. House and estate valued at £20, 1730.
Married (1) Jean O'Dart Ballereau, born July 3, 1708, N.Y.,
May 8, 1731; (2) Deborah Knapp, daughter of John Knapp of
Stamford. Advertised, *New York Gazette*, "Goldsmith, living
near the New Dutch Church.", 1735. Notice, *New York Mer-
cury*, September, 1764, "Stolen, out of the House of Daniel
Dunscomb, of this City, a Silver Tankard, marked on the Bottom

thus $_D M_D$ containing a Wine Quart. It had a large bruise on the side, the hinge pretty much wore, the Maker's Stamp PQ near the Handle." Removed to South Norwalk, Conn. in 1737 and made several land purchases, north of the present Marshall Street in South Norwalk, where he died.

PQ

[R]

ROBERT RAIT   1830
New York, at Ann Street. Commissioned by City Council to design badges for New York Police Department. In Directory until 1855.
R.RAIT

W. D. RAPP   1828
Philadelphia, Pa.
W.D.RAPP

ANTHONY RASCH   1807
Philadelphia, Pa., at High Street. Firms of Chaudron & Rasch, 1812; Rasch & Willig, 1819; Anthony Rasch & Co., 1820. Later, in New Orleans, La.
ANTY RASCH – AR

ANTHONY RASCH & CO.   1820
Philadelphia, Pa., on High Street; later, in New Orleans, La.
A.RASCH & CO

W. A. RASCH   1830
New Orleans, La.
W.A.RASCH

FREDERICK RATH   1830
New York.
F.RATH

JOSEPH RAYNES   1835
Lowell, Mass.
JOSEPH RAYNES

HENRY H. REDMAN   –1840   1819
Norfolk, Va. In firm of Redman & Potter, 1819–1821. Married Susan Francis Slack, 1823. Worked in Norfolk until his death.
REDMAN

REDMAN & POTTER   1819
Norfolk, Va., until 1821. Henry Redman and John Potter.
R & POTTER

CLAUDIUS REDON   1828
New York.
C.REDON

ISAAC REED   1746–   1770
Stamford, Conn. Born in New Canaan, Conn.
I.REED

ISAAC REED & SON   1830
Philadelphia, Pa.
I.REED & SON

JONATHAN REED   −1742   1724
Boston, Mass., until 1740.
IR

OSMON REED   1831
Philadelphia, Pa., at 176 North Second Street until 1841.
O.REED

O. REED & CO.   1841
Philadelphia, Pa.
O.REED & CO — OSMON REED & CO

STEPHEN REED   1805
New York, until 1835. In Philadelphia, Pa., at 147 South
Twelfth Street, 1846–1850.
S.REED

ABNER REEDER   1766–1841   1793
Philadelphia, Pa. Born in Ewing, N.J., October 10, son of John
and Hannah Mershon Reeder. Married Hannah Wilkinson, May
22, 1796. Advertised at 38 North Front Street, 1793–1800. In
partnership with John McFee, 1793–1796. Later, located in
Trenton, N.J., on State Street, where he was appointed Postmaster. Was President of State Bank. Died, October 25.
AR — A.REEDER

JOSEPH REEVE   −1828   1803
Newburgh, N.Y., until 1828.
I.REEVE — J.REEVE

ENOS REEVES 1753–1807   1784
Charleston, S.C. Served as Adjutant in Revolution. Reeves'
published Letter-Books give description of times. Member of
the South Carolina Society of Cincinnati.
ER – REEVES

JOSEPH F. REEVES   1835
Baltimore, Md., until 1850.
J.F.REEVES

STEPHEN REEVES   1767
Cohansey Bridge, Cumberland County, N.J.; later, in Burlington, N.J. In Philadelphia, Pa., 1766, at Black Horse Alley
and Second Street. Advertised in *New York Gazette*, October 7,
1776, "Gold and Silversmith, Living near the corner of Burling's
Slip, in Queen Street. Takes this method to inform his friends
and customers, and the public in general, that he now carries on
his business as usual, such as making and mending all kinds of
gold and silver ware, mounting and mending swords, and
making all sorts of jeweler's work, &c. &c. He returns his sincere
thanks for all past favors and he hopes for a continuance of the
same, as he flatters himself of giving general satisfaction to all
who may be pleased to employ him. N.B. Ready money for old
gold and silver."
S.REEVES

PAUL REVERE 1702–1754   1725
Boston, Mass. Born in Riaucaud, France, as Apollos Rivoire.
Apprenticed to John Coney. Rivoire did not serve his full appren-
ticeship, for the administrator of Coney's estate received £40,
"Cash for Paul Rivoire's time." At the age of twenty-one, 1723,
he revisited Guernsey Island in the English Channel for a short
time. On his return, 1725, he established himself as a gold and
silversmith and changed his name to Paul Revere. Married
Deborah Hitchborn, 1729. His third child and eldest son, Paul,
was born January 1, 1735. Member of the New Brick Church.
Died in Boston in July.
PR – P.REVERE

PAUL REVERE, JR. 1735–1818   1757
Boston, Mass. Born January 1, eldest son of Apollos Rivoire
(Paul Revere) and Deborah Hitchborn. Educated at Master
Tillston's School. Trained in father's shop. Participated in expedi-
tion to capture Crown Point in 1756. On his return, married (1)
Sarah Orne, 1757; (2) Rachael Walker, 1773. Opened a shop as a
goldsmith and engraver. Advertised completion of the "Re-

scinders Bowl" in *Boston Gazette*, August 8, 1768. Engraved
plates for the earliest paper money of Massachusetts. Became one
of thirty North-End Mechanics to patrol Boston Streets. He
made his famous ride, April 19, 1775. Became Lieutenant
Colonel of Artillery. In the Penobscot Expedition in 1776. After
the Revolution, continued his trade at 50 Cornhill Street. Established a large copper-rolling mill in Canton, Mass. in 1801. Was
first President of the Massachusetts Charitable Mechanics Association. The town, Revere, Mass., was named in his honor. John
Singleton Copley painted the famous portrait of him. Died in
Boston in May.
PR – P.REVERE – REVERE

THOMAS REVERE   1739–1817   1789
Boston, Mass., at Newbury Street. In Directory until 1803.
Brother of Paul, the patriot.
TR

JOHN REYNOLDS   1770–1832   1790
Hagerstown, Md., until 1832.
IR – JN.REYNOLDS

HENRY P. RICE   1815
Albany, N.Y. In Saratoga Springs, N.Y., 1827–1830.
H.P.RICE

JOSEPH RICE   1761–1808   1784
Baltimore, Md. Firm of Rice & Barry, 1785–1787, with Stan-
dish Barry. Advertised, *Maryland Gazette*, November 23, 1787,
"Gold and Silver-Smith's Business at the northwest corner of
Market and Calvert-streets, Baltimore, gratefully thanks the
public . . ." In 1801, in Savannah, Ga. where he died.
IR – I.RICE – RICE

JOSEPH T. RICE   1787–1854   1813
Albany, N.Y., at 5 Pearl Street. Master of John H. Mulford. In
Directory until 1853.
JOSEPH T.RICE – JTR – J.T.RICE

OBADIAH RICH   1830
Boston, Mass. Apprenticed to Moses Morse. Located at 69
Washington Street, 1830; 7 Chapman Place, 1850. Member of
the Massachusetts Charitable Mechanics Association, 1836.
Firm of Ward & Rich, 1830–1835, with Samuel L. Ward, which
bought the business of Newall Harding in 1832. Ward retired in
1835; Rich continued the business under his own name.
O.RICH

STEPHEN RICHARD   1801

New York. Advertised, *Daily Advertiser*, May 9, 1801; December
27, 1802, "Goldsmith and silversmith at 160 Broadway . . .".
In *New York Gazette* and *General Advertiser*, August 14, 1804,
"$10 Reward for Gold Watch Chain and Seal." In Directory at
153 Broadway, 1815–1822.
RICHARD – S. RICHARD

SAMUEL R. RICHARDS, JR.   1793

Philadelphia, Pa., at 136 South Front Street until 1818. Partner
of Samuel Williamson, 1797.
RICHARDS – S. RICHARDS

THOMAS RICHARDS   1802

New York, until 1829. Firm of Sayre & Richards, 1802–1811;
Pelletreau & Richards, 1825.
TR – T. RICHARDS

RICHARDS & PELLETREAU   1825

New York. Thomas Richards and William S. Pelletreau.
TR WSP

RICHARDS & WILLIAMSON   1797

Philadelphia, Pa. Samuel R. Richards, Jr. and Samuel Williamson until 1800.
RICHARDS & WILLIAMSON – S. RICHARDS SW

FRANCIS RICHARDSON   1681–1729   1710

Philadelphia, Pa. Born in New York, November 25. Removed to
Philadelphia, Pa. in 1690 where he married Elizabeth Growden,
daughter of Joseph Growden. Records of Minutes of City Common Council, "Goldsmith, Francis Richardson, on May 20th,
1717, was admitted Freeman of Philadelphia, Pa. and paid 5 s.,
6 d." Possible apprentice to Caesar Ghiselin. Six examples of
work known.
FR

FRANCIS RICHARDSON, JR.   1706–1782   1729

Philadelphia, Pa. Son of Francis and Elizabeth Growden
Richardson. Freeman, 1717. Married Mary Fitzwater, September
26, 1742. Advertised, *American Mercury*, February 18, 1734,
"Reward for runaway apprentice, Isaac Marceloe, formerly with
William Heurtin, Goldsmith of New York." Located in Market
Street, 1736–1737. Advertised, February 15, 1738, "Lately
imported and to be sold by Francis Richardson at the house of
Joseph Richardson, Goldsmith, in Front Street, China, Cam-
bricks, Etc." Active nine years after his father's death.
FR

JOSEPH RICHARDSON 1711–1784   1732
Philadelphia, Pa. Son of Francis and Elizabeth Growden
Richardson, brother of Francis, Jr. Married (1) Hannah Worrell,
1741; (2) Mary Allen, 1748. Advertised until 1784. Was joined
in business by sons, Joseph, Jr. and Nathaniel, in 1771 at Front
between Chestnut and Walnut Streets.
IR

JOSEPH RICHARDSON, JR. 1752–1831   1773
Philadelphia, Pa. Married Ruth Hoskins in Burlington, N.J.,
June 15, 1780. In partnership with brother, Nathaniel, continu-
ing father's business on Front Street, until 1791. Was appointed
Assayer to the Mint by George Washington in 1795. Then he
sold his business to James Howell. Continued as assayer until his
death.
IR – JR

JOSEPH, JR. & NATHANIEL RICHARDSON   1771
Philadelphia, Pa., at Front Street below Walnut Street, their
father's old address, until dissolved in 1791. Rendered Bill of
Sale for a Shaker, November 19, 1779. Nathaniel became an
ironmonger, 1793. Joseph sold business to James Howell, 1801.
INR

WILLIAM RICHARDSON 1757–1809   1778
Richmond, Va. Son of John and Abigail Richardson. Firm of
William & George Richardson, 1782–1795. Captain of
Richmond Light Infantry Blues, 1798. Retired from business,
1807.
WR

WILLIAM & GEORGE RICHARDSON   1782
Richmond, Va. Two brothers in partnership until 1795.
W & GR

FRANKLIN RICHMOND 1792–1869   1815
Providence, R.I., at 17 Market Street; 14 High Street in 1820.
F.RICHMOND – RICHMOND

JOHN RIDGEWAY 1780–1851   1805
Boston, Mass. At Cambridge Street, 1813. Listed in Directory
until 1830.
J. RIDGEWAY

JAMES RIDGWAY   1789
Boston, Mass. In Directory as Jeweller and Goldsmith at Friend
Street. In Worcester, Mass., 1793. Married Faith Stowell,
January 12, 1802.
J.RIDGWAY

GEORGE RIDOUT (RYDOUT)   1745
New York. From London, registered in Goldsmiths' Hall, "Geo.
Ridout, Lombard St., 17 Oct., 1743." Admitted Freeman in
New York, February 18, 1745. Advertised, "Goldsmith, Near
Ferry-Stairs. . . .", *New York Gazette*, June 10, 1751.
GR

BENJAMIN MCKENNY RIGGS   1799–1839   1820
Paris, Ky.
B.M.RIGGS

GEORGE WASHINGTON RIGGS   1777–1864   1805
Georgetown, D.C. Born in Montgomery County, Md. In Balti-
more, Md., 1810–1848. Firm of Riggs & Griffith, 1816.
GR – RIGGS

RICHARD RIGGS   –1819   1810
Philadelphia, Pa. Church records death in 1819.
RR

RIGGS & GRIFFITH   1816
Baltimore, Md., until 1818.
R & G

PETER RIKER   1797
New York, at 378 Pearl Street; 151 Cherry Street in 1814. Firms
of Riker & Alexander, 1797; Clapp & Riker, Riker & Clapp,
1802.
P.RIKER

RIKER & CLAPP   1802
New York, at 80 Cherry Street; 375 Pearl Street, 1804–1805.
Peter Riker and Philip Clapp until 1808.
R & C – RIKER & CLAPP

ROSWELL WALSTEIN ROATH   1805–   1826
Norwich, Conn.
R.W.ROATH

CHRISTOPHER ROBERT   1708–1793   1731
New York. Freeman, May 4, 1731. Born June 10, son of Daniel
and Suzanne Nicholas Du Cailleau, Susannah La Roche remar-
ried, Robert. Baptised in French Church, July 11, 1708. Apprenticed to John Hastier from May 8th, 1723 for seven years.
CR

ROBERTS & LEE   1772

Boston, Mass. Advertised, *Boston News Letter*, November 19,
"Jewellers, Opposite the Old Brick Meeting-house, Cornhill . . .
Town and Country may be supplied with every article usually
imported in that way, on very advantageous terms . . ."
R & L

ANTHONY W. ROBINSON   1798

Philadelphia, Pa., at 23 Strawberry Street. Advertised, *Federal
Gazette*, at 36 South Second Street, 1800–1803.
A . ROBINSON

EBENEZER ROBINSON   1813

Boston, Mass.
E . ROBINSON

HANNAH ROBINSON   1803–1878   1845

Wilmington, Del., at 91 Market Street. Born February 2, sister
of John F. Robinson with whom she worked.
H . ROBINSON

JOHN F. ROBINSON   1812–1867   1844

Wilmington, Del., at 91 Market Street. Son of Joseph and
Susannah Foulk Robinson, brother of Hannah who continued
business after John moved to Kentucky in 1849.
J . F . ROBINSON

O. ROBINSON   1800

New Haven, Conn.
O . ROBINSON

EDWARD ROCKWELL   1805

New York. Advertised, *New York Weekly Museum*, August 29,
1807, "Jewellery and Silverware of his own manufacture at the
shop at 4 Park Place." Located at 200 Broadway, 1811–1822. In
Directory until 1846.
ROCKWELL

SAMUEL D. ROCKWELL   1830

New York. In Directory until 1841.
S . D . ROCKWELL

THOMAS ROCKWELL   1764–1794   1785

Norwalk, Conn. Inventory of estate, dated 1795, lists tools for
manufacture of silverware and watches.
ROCKWELL

JAMES ROE   1770

Kingston, N.Y. Son of William and Eleanor . . . Roe, of Philipse
Patent, Dutchess County, N.Y. Officer in War of Revolution.
Engraved the Dial of a Clock of his Workmanship: "I serve Thee
here with all my Might, to tell the Hour by Day or Night.
Therefore Example take of Me and serve thy God as I serve
Thee." Clock at Clearwater College.

I.ROE

WILLIAM ROE   1795

Kingston, N.Y. Brother of James. Firm of W. Roe &
Stollenwerck.

WR — W.ROE

W. ROE & STOLLENWERCK   1800

New York.

W.ROE & STOLLENWERCK

DANIEL ROGERS   1735–1816   1760

Ipswich, Mass. Married (1) Elizabeth Simpkins; (2) Elizabeth
Rogers, a cousin; (3) Mary Appleton Leatherland. His marks
were previously attributed to Daniel Rogers of Newport, R.I.,
1753–1792, who, with his brother, Joseph, was apprenticed to
John Tanner. Reattribution of marks was based upon Ipswich,
Mass. church silver bearing his marks. A Daniel Rogers is listed
in New York City Directories, 1836–1839.

DR — D.ROGERS — ROGERS

JOSEPH ROGERS   1753–1825   1780

Newport, R.I. Apprenticed to John Tanner with brother,
Daniel. Married (1) Patty Hazard, April 21, 1781; (2) Ruth
Sears, December 21, 1797. Firm of Tanner & Rogers, circa
1775. Advertised, Hartford, Conn., 1808, at corner of Trumbull
and Pratt Streets.

IR — JR — J.ROGERS

WILLIAM ROGERS   1801–1873   1822

Hartford, Conn. Apprenticed to Joseph Church who admitted
him to business, 1825. Advertised, 1822–1843. Founded the
William Rogers Manufacturing Company of 1847, predecessors
of Meriden Britannia Co., 1862; International Silver Co., 1898.

WM.ROGERS — W.ROGERS

WILLIAM ROGERS & SON   1850

Hartford, Conn.

WM.ROGERS & SON

JOHN A. ROHR 1807
Philadelphia, Pa., until 1813.
I.ROHR

NICHOLAS ROOSEVELT 1715–1769 1739
New York. Freeman, March 20, 1739. Son of Nicholas
Roosevelt, II, 1685–1717, and Sarah Folman who married,
1718, New York, Philip Schuyler. Married (1) Catharina
Confert, June 5, 1737; (2) Elizabeth Thurman, March 2, 1754.
Received a commission from City for two gold boxes, £38/8/o.
Advertised, *New York Gazette*, January 30, 1769, "To be Let, and
enter'd the 1st of May next, The house in which Nicholas
Roosevelt now lives, at the lower end of Thames Street, on the
wharf fronting the North-River: The conveniency and commodi-
ousness of the situation excells any on the river; it fronts two
slips, one of which is near 100 feet broad, and the greatest part of
the year is fill'd with boats and crafts, from the Jersies and
North-River. Is a roomy and convenient house, with seven
fire-places; a large yard, in which is a pump and cistern, and a
garden and grass plot. Likewise a silversmith's shop to be let,
and the tools of the trade to be sold. Also to be sold by said
Roosevelt, a parcel of ready made silver, large and small, Viz.
Silver tea-pots and tea spoons, silver hilted swords, sauce-boats,
salts and shovels, soup-spoons both scollep'd and plain, table
spoons, tea-tongs, punch ladles and strainers, milk-pots, snuff-
boxes, and sundry other small articles, both gold and silver, as
buckles, clasps, buttons, broaches, rings, and lockets, both
plain and set with paste moco, &c. &c. which he will sell very
reasonable, as he intends declining business, and to move in the
Country in the Spring." Grandfather of Pieter De Riemer.
NRV

CHARLES BOUDINOT ROOT 1818–1903 1843
Raleigh, N.C. Son of Elihu and Sophia Gunn Root of Montague,
Mass. Apprenticed to Barnard Dupuy and bought his business in
1843. Prominent citisen who died in Raleigh, May 7.
C.B.ROOT

L. M. & A. C. ROOT 1830
Pittsfield, Mass.
L.M & A.C.ROOT

WASHINGTON M. ROOT 1840
Pittsfield, Mass. Firm of Root & Chaffee, 1850, Washington M.
Root and Frederick Chaffee, Pittsfield, Mass. and Rutland Vt.
W.M.ROOT

W. N. ROOT & BROTHER   1850
New Haven, Conn.
W.N.ROOT & BROTHER

JOHN ROSS   1756–1798   1790
Baltimore, Md.
I R

ROBERT ROSS   1789
Frederica, Kent County, Del. Advertised, *Delaware Gazette*,
April 2, 1791, "Gold and Silver-Smith, opposite to the store of
William Berry, Frederica, respectfully informs the public, and
his friends in particular, that he continues to carry on the gold
and silversmith business in its various branches, at the above
place. Work done in the best manner and on as reasonable terms
as in the City of Philadelphia."
RR – R.ROSS

NELSON ROTH   1837
Utica, N.Y. In Directory until 1857.
N.ROTH

WILLIAM ROUSE   1639–1705   1660
Boston, Mass. Mentioned, *Boston News Letter*, January 20, 1705,
"William Rowse, goldsmith, died in Boston." Appraisal of
estate by John Coney amounted to £575/11/6. Probably apprenticed to Hull and Sanderson with design of tankard and patch-
box. Worked in English style. Made the only pair of New England sucket forks, both in the Yale University Art Gallery. At the
funeral of Timothy Dwight, 1691/2.
W R

WILLIAM MADISON ROUSE   1812–1888   1835
Charleston, S.C., at King and Vanderhorst Streets. Apprenticed
to John Ewan for four years. Married Sarah Lord.
W.M.ROUSE

J. RUDD & CO.   1831
New York.
J.RUDD & CO

DANIEL RUSSELL   1698–1771   1721
Newport, R.I. Advertised, "Working Goldsmith." Made a
baptismal bowl, dated 1734, for Trinity Church, Newport, R.I.
D R

JOHN RUSSELL 1767–1839   1794
Greenfield, Mass. Born in Deerfield, Mass. Apprenticed to Isaac
Parker. Married Electra Edwards, 1796.
J.RUSSEL

JOHN H. RUSSELL   1792
New York, at 3 Broad Street and 1 New Street, 1794–1798.
IHR

JONATHAN RUSSELL 1770–   1804
Ashford, Conn.
RUSSEL

JOSEPH RUSSELL 1702–1780   1728
Barnstable, Mass. Born October 11, son of Rev. Jonathan and
Martha Moody Russell. Brother of Moody Russell. Apprenticed
to Edward Winslow. Married (1) Anne Vassall, 1728; (2) Mrs.
Sarah Paine of Bristol, R.I., 1733 where he continued his work.
Died in Bristol, July 31.
IR

MOODY RUSSELL 1694–1761   1715
Barnstable, Mass. Born August 30, son of Rev. Jonathan and
Martha Moody Russell. Brother of Joseph. Apprenticed to
Edward Winslow, his uncle. Another uncle, Eleaser Russell, was
also a silversmith, 1663–1691. Deacon of the East Church,
1740. His sister, Abigail, married Nathaniel Otis whose son was
Major Jonathan Otis, an apprentice and nephew. Master of
Ephraim Cobb. Died July 3.
MR

RICHARD RUTTER   1790
Baltimore, Md. At 87 Baltimore Street, 1796.
RUTTER

LUCAS RYERSON 1771–1855   1792
Manchester Township, N.J., now Hawthorne, N.J. Born
November 26, descendant of George Ryerson who purchased
land from the Indians in 1709. Died March 5 and buried in
Ryerson Cemetery, Hawthorne, N.J.
L.RYERSON

[S]

HARVEY SADD 1776–1840   1798
New Hartford, Conn. Born in New Windsor, Conn., son of Dr.
Thomas and Delight Warner Sadd. Advertised in Stockbridge,
Mass., 1817. In 1829, moved to Austinburg, Ohio, where he
died.
H.SADD

PHILIP B. SADTLER 1771–1860   1800
Baltimore, Md., at 166 Baltimore Street. Firm of Sadtler &
Pfaltz until 1803, Philip Benjamin Sadtler and John William
Pfaltz. In business until 1860.
P.B.SADTLER – PS – P.SADTLER

P. B. SADTLER & SON   1850
Baltimore, Md., until 1923.
P.B.SADTLER & SON

HENRY SAFFORD   1800
Gallipolis, Ohio. In Marietta, Ohio, 1810; Zanesville, Ohio,
1812.
H.SAFFORD

HENRY SALISBURY   1831
New York. In Directory until 1837.
SALISBURY

SALISBURY & CO.   1835
New York. The firm of Henry Salisbury, at 171 Broadway.
SALISBURY & CO

A. SANBORN   1850
Lowell, Mass.
A.SANBORN

EDWARD SANDELL   –1822   1816
Baltimore, Md., at 115 Baltimore Street until 1822.
ES

BENJAMIN SANDERSON 1649–1678   1675
Boston, Mass. Born and baptised in Watertown, Mass., son of
Robert and Mary Cross Sanderson. Learned trade from his father.
BS

ROBERT SANDERSON   1608–1693   1638
Boston, Mass. Born in England where he learned his trade,
apprenticed to William Rawlins of Parish of St. Mary Woolnoth,
London, at age fifteen. With first wife, Lydia, was among earliest
settlers in Hampton, N.H., 1638. Freeman, September 7,
1639. In Watertown, Mass., 1642, when he married (2) Mary
Cross, widow of John. Son, Joseph, was born in 1642; Benjamin,
1649; Sarah, 1651; Robert, Jr., 1652. Removed to Boston,
Mass. in 1652 and joined John Hull in minting Pine Tree Shillings. At the funeral of Timothy Dwight, 1691/2. Died October
7. Son, Robert, Jr., continued business although son, Benjamin,
is the known silversmith.
RS

WILLIAM SANDFORD   1817
New York, at 36 William Street; Water Street, 1818.
W.SANDFORD

FREDERICK S. SANFORD   1828
Nantucket, Mass. Firm of Easton & Sanford, 1830–1838, with
James Easton, II.
F.S.SANFORD

ISAAC SANFORD   –1842   1785
Hartford, Conn., until 1823. Designer, engraver and silversmith. Firm of Beach & Sanford, with Miles Beach, 1785–
1788. Later, in Philadelphia, Pa. where he died.
SANFORD

WILLIAM SANFORD   1817
Nantucket, Mass.
W.SANFORD

ENSIGN SARGEANT   1820
Boston, Mass., at May Street until 1823.
E.SARGEANT

HENRY SARGEANT   1796–1864   1825
Hartford, Conn. Born in Springfield, Mass., son of Thomas
Sargeant. Married Mary Holman.
H.SARGEANT

JACOB SARGEANT   1761–1843   1785
Hartford, Conn. "Shop 10 rods south of State House." Born in
Mansfield, Conn. Married Olive Payne. At 229 Main Street,
1796–1843.
I.SARGEANT – J.SARGEANT

SAMUEL SARGEANT 1767–1847   1797
Worcester, Mass. In Middlebury, Vt., 1799–1847. Firm of
Sargeant & Eells, 1816.
SS

THOMAS SARGEANT 1773–1834   1795
Springfield, Mass., until 1821. Father of Henry.
T.SARGEANT

MOREAU SARRAZIN 1710–1761   1734
Charleston, S.C., advertised as jeweller. Joined the South
Carolina Society, 1737. Ensign in Militia. Partner of William
Wright, 1745–46. Died February 4.
MS

JOHN Y. SAVAGE   1820
Raleigh, N.C. Of firm, Savage & Stedman, 1819–1820, with
John C. Stedman. Advertised in Richmond, Va., 1829.
I.Y.SAVAGE

THOMAS SAVAGE 1664–1749   1689
Boston, Mass. Admitted Freeman, March 22, 1689. Son of
Habbiah (Abia) and Hannah Ting Savage. Probably apprenticed
to Jeremiah Dummer, 1678, or Timothy Dwight, at whose
funeral he was 1691/2. Master of Samuel Haugh, 1675–1717,
from October 7, 1690, for seven years and six months, who
practiced his trade soon after attaining his majority. Married (1)
Mabel Harwood, February 5, 1690; (2) Elizabeth . . . , prior to
1717. Became a Captain in the army, 1705. In Bermuda, 1706,
returning to Boston, October 30, 1714. Appointed Sealer of
Weights, June 4, 1725–1736. "Lycence to sell Drink as a
Retaylor," granted by Edward Winslow, when Selectman, after
earlier refusal. Removed to Newbury, Mass. in 1737 where he
died August 23.
TS

WILLIAM M. SAVAGE   1805
Glasgow, Ky. Earliest prominent silversmith in Barren County.
W.M.SAVAGE

SILAS W. SAWIN   1825
New York, at 106 Reade Street until 1838.
SS

H. I. SAWYER   1840
New York.
H.I.SAWYER

JOEL SAWYER   1805–   1830
Bolton, Mass. Married Sarah Barrett, 1830.
J.SAWYER

JOEL SAYRE   1778–1818   1799
New York. Born in Southampton, N.Y., November 2, son of
Mathew and Mehitable Herrick Sayre. Brother of John. Married
Sarah Brown of Newark N.J., January 25, 1808. In New York,
at 437 Pearl Street, 1802; Maiden Lane, 1805–1811. Died in
Cairo, N.Y., September 28.
I.SAYRE – J.SAYRE

JOHN SAYRE   1771–1852   1792
New York. Born in Southampton, N.Y., June 13. Brother of
Joel. Married Elizabeth Downer of Westfield, N.J., April 10,
1816. In New York, 1796, at 281 Pearl Street until 1801.
Advertised, *Commercial Advertiser*, July 3, 1801, "For return of
stolen spoons and tongs, Mark, J.SAYRE. $20. Reward."
Partner of Thomas Richards, 1802–1811. He published first
Bible commentary and other religious works. Removed to
Cohoes, N.Y. to become director of cotton factory in 1824.
Died in Plainsfield, N.J., November 26.
I.SAYRE – SAYRE

PAUL SAYRE   1762–   1785
Southampton, N.Y.
P.SAYRE

SAYRE & RICHARDS   1802
New York. John Sayre and Thomas Richards dissolved partnership in 1811. Advertised, *Mercantile Advertiser*, November 23,
1803, ". . . at 240 Pearl Street."
S & R

BARTHOLOMEW SCHAATS   1670–1758   1695
New York. Freeman, May 22, 1708. Married (1) Christina
Kermer, November 28, 1706. Daughter, Antse, baptised, April
27, 1715. (2) Jacoba Kierstede, widow, April 21, 1734. In
Abstracts of New York Wills, "Bartholomew Skaats of New
York, Goldsmith, being weak in body, I leave to my son, Ryner,
my negro man Caesar. I leave to my grandson, Bartholomew
Skaats, £10. I leave to my wife, Jacoba, and to my son, all the
rest of my real and personal estate." Dated, July 14, 1758;
proved September 4, 1758.
BS

GARRET SCHANCK   1743–1795

1791

New York, at 25 Fair Street; 133 Water Street in 1795. Born
October 24. Married Sarah Covenhoven, January 5, 1762.
Partner of Daniel Van Voorhis, cousin, dissolved, 1792. His
wife, Sarah, and brother, John, were granted letters of administration of his estate, November 12, 1795.

G.SCHANCK

JOHN A. SCHANCK

1795

New York. Advertised, *The Time Piece*, March 31, 1797, at 133
Water Street, "Where he carries on business in all its branches,
with elegance and dispatch." John administered brother Garret's
estate in 1795.

I.SCHANCK – J.SCHANCK – SCHANCK

ABRAHAM SCHUYLER   1735–1812

1769

Albany, N.Y. Son of David and Maria Hansen Schuyler. Married
Eve Beekman, 1763. In the Book of Mortgages, 1769–1775, "I
promise to pay or cause to be paid unto Abraham Schuyler of the
City of Albany, Silver Smith, . . ."

AS

I. SCOT

1750

Albany, N.Y.

I.SCOT

ALEXANDER SCOTT   –1821

1800

Chambersburg, Pa.

A.SCOTT

JEHU SCOTT   –1819

1806

Raleigh, N.C. Advertised, *Raleigh Register*, until 1819.

I.SCOTT

JOHN B. SCOTT

1820

New York.

J.B.SCOTT – J.SCOTT

SCOVIL & KINSEY

1830

Cincinnati, Ohio.

SCOVIL & KINSEY

SCOVIL, WILLEY & CO.

1835

Cincinnati, Ohio.

SCOVIL WILLEY & CO

WILLIAM SEAL 1816
Philadelphia, Pa., at 118 South Front Street until 1820. Firm of
Browne & Seal, 1810–1811.
WS – W.SEAL

WILLIAM SELKIRK 1815
Albany, N.Y. New York, at 154 Reade Street, 1817–1819.
W.SELKIRK

JOSEPH SEYMOUR & CO. 1850
Syracuse, N.Y.
J.S & CO

OLIVER D. SEYMOUR 1843
Hartford, Conn., at 20 Windsor Street. Firm of Seymour &
Hollister, 1845.
O.D.SEYMOUR

SEYMOUR & HOLLISTER 1845
Hartford, Conn., at 20 Windsor Street. Oliver D. Seymour and
Julius Hollister.
SEYMOUR & HOLLISTER

GEORGE SHARP 1844
Philadelphia, Pa., at 19 North Rittenhouse Street. In Directory
until 1850.
S

W. & G. SHARP 1848
Philadelphia, Pa. Listed at 4 Merchant Street.
W & G.SHARP

JAMES S. SHARRARD 1850
Shelbyville, Ky.
J.S.SHARRARD

MICHAEL SHAVER 1775–1859 1807
Abingdon, Va. Son of Michael and Catherine Shaver. Married
Letitia Hill, 1807. Silversmith, watchmaker, portrait painter
and important Elder in the Presbyterian Church.
M.SHAVER

SHAW & DUNLEVY 1833
Philadelphia, Pa., at 7 Lodge Road.
SHAW & DUNLEVY

JOHN A. SHAW 1802
Newport, R.I., until 1819.
I.A.SHAW – J.SHAW

ROBERT SHEPHERD 1781–1853   1805
Albany, N.Y. Partner of William Boyd in 1806 as Shepherd &
Boyd.
R.SHEPHERD – SHEPHERD

SHEPHERD & BOYD   1806
Albany, N.Y., at 136 Market Street. Robert Shepherd and
William Boyd until 1830, succeeded by Boyd & Hoyt, 1830–
1832; Boyd & Mulford, 1832–1842.
S & B – SHEPHERD & BOYD

SHETHAR & THOMPSON   1801
Litchfield, Conn. Samuel Shethar and Isaac Thompson dissolved
partnership in 1805.
S & T

SAMUEL SHETHAR 1755–1815   1777
New Haven, Conn. In Litchfield, Conn., in firm of Shether &
Thompson, 1801–1805. In New Haven, Conn., 1806, in
partnership with Richard Gorman as Shether & Gorman until
1808. Died in New Haven.
SS

CALEB SHIELDS   1773
Baltimore, Md., advertised at his house in Gay Street, June 21,
1773. Notice of settlement of accounts requested, *Maryland
Journal*, July 30, 1782. Brother of Thomas Shields.
CS

THOMAS SHIELDS   1765
Philadelphia, Pa. "Opened Shop in Front Street, the Third Door
above the Drawbridge . . .", *Penna. Gazette*, July 14, 1765. "At
the sign of the Golden Cup and Crown.", 1771. Listed in Direc-
tory, 1785–1791, at 126 South Front Street. Brother of Caleb.
Master of Lodge # 5, September, 1744; listed as among past
Masters present, December 18, 1783.
TS

NATHANIEL SHIPMAN 1764–1853   1790
Norwich, Conn. Apprenticed to Thomas Harland. Represented
town in General Assembly. Appointed Judge of the County and
Probate Courts.
NS – N.SHIPMAN

SHIPP & COLLINS   1850
Cincinnati, Ohio.
SHIPP & COLLINS

GODFREY SHIVING (SCHRIVING) (SCHWING)   1779

Philadelphia, Pa. Advertised, *Penna. Packet*; "Goldsmith and
Jeweller. Takes this method to acquaint the Public, and his
Friends in Particular, that he is removed from Second Street, to
the South Side of the King of Prussia, where he carries on the
Goldsmith and Jewellery business, in its different branches as
usual."

GS

JOSEPH SHOEMAKER   1793

Philadelphia, Pa., at 12 North Front Street; 24 Pewter Platter
Alley until 1798; 38 North Front Street, 1802–1816. Listed
until 1839.

JS – J.SHOEMAKER

ASA SIBLEY   1764–1829   1785

Woodstock, Conn. Born in Sutton, Mass., son of Colonel
Timothy and Anne Waite Sibley, March 29. Apprenticed to
Peregrine White in Woodstock, Conn. In Walpole, N.H.,
1800. Died in Rochester, N.Y.

AS

CLARK SIBLEY   1778–1808   1800

New Haven, Conn. Born in New Haven. Advertised until 1806.
Partner of Simeon Marble in Sibley & Marble, 1801.

SIBLEY

JOHN SIBLEY   1810

New Haven, Conn.

J.SIBLEY

SIBLEY & MARBLE   1801

New Haven, Conn., on Church Street, next North of Trinity
Church. Clark Sibley and Simeon Marble until 1806.

S & M

H. SILL   1840

New York.

H.SILL

H. & R. W. SILL   1840

New York.

H & R.W.SILL

HEZEKIAH SILLIMAN   1738–1804   1767

New Haven, Conn. Born in Fairfield, Conn. Firm of Cutler,
Silliman, Ward & Co., 1768. Mason in Hiram Lodge # 1, July
9, 1765.

HS

HENRY SILVERTHORN 1810–1900   1832
Lynchburg, Va., with Williams & Victor. Apprenticed to A. E.
Warner of Baltimore, Md. at age fifteen. In Baltimore, Md.,
1835–1837. Advertised in Lynchburg, Va., 1837–1897, when
he retired. Firm of Silverthorn & Clift, 1857.
H. SILVERTHORN – SILVERTHORN

SILVERTHORN & CLIFT   1857
Lynchburg, Va. Henry Silverthorn and Josiah Clift.
SILVERTHORN & CLIFT

WILLIAM SIMES 1773–1824   1800
Portsmouth, N.H.
SIMES – WS – W. SIMES

ANTHONY SIMMONS   1797
Philadelphia, Pa., at 13 North Second Street; 27 Sassafras Street
until 1808. Firm of Simmons & Williamson, 1797; Simmons &
Alexander, 1800.
AS – A. SIMMONS

JAMES SIMMONS   1815
New York, at 46 Cliff Street. Firm of J. A. Simmons, 1805–
1814.
J. SIMMONS

J. & A. SIMMONS   1805
New York, at 275 Pearl Street until 1814. James and Abraham
Simmons.
J & A.S – J & A. SIMMONS

S. SIMMONS   1797
Philadelphia, Pa.
S. SIMMONS

SIMMONS & ALEXANDER   1800
Philadelphia, Pa., at 44 South High Street. Anthony Simmons
and Samuel Alexander continued at this address until 1804.
S & A – SIMMONS & ALEXANDER

SIMMONS & WILLIAMSON   1797
Philadelphia, Pa., at 13 North Second Street, dissolved follow-
ing year by Anthony Simmons and Samuel Williamson.
S & W

THOMAS BARTON SIMPKINS 1728–1804   1750
Boston, Mass., at Fish Street until 1789; Ann Street in 1796.
T. B. SIMPKINS – T. SIMPKINS

WILLIAM SIMPKINS   1704–1780   1730
Boston, Mass. Born March 20th. Married Eliza Symmes, May
14, 1726. Father of Thomas Barton. Served as Sergeant of
Artillery Company, 1743. Advertised, "Goldsmith near the
Drawbridge, the library of the late Rev. Robert Stanton of
Salem.", June 20, 1728. Notice, "Loss of a piece of silver three
inches broad, 1/4 inch thick and weighing fourteen ounces.",
Boston Evening Post, January 27, 1746. Firm of Minott &
Simpkins, 1769.
SIMPKINS – WS – W. SIMPKINS

ABRAHAM SKINNER   1756
New York. Freeman, May 18, 1756. Notice, *New York Gazette*,
June 7, 1762, "Silversmith, on the New-Dock between the Ferry
Stairs and Rotten Row." Married Catharine Foster, August 27,
1773.
AS

ELIZER SKINNER   –1858   1826
Hartford, Conn., at Ferry Street; at 80½ Main Street and 20
Elm Street, 1847.
E. SKINNER

MATT SKINNER   1752
Philadelphia, Pa.
MATT SKINNER

THOMAS SKINNER   1712/13–1761   1733
Marblehead, Mass., worked at his calling. Born in Boston, Mass.
SKINNER – TS

JOSHUA SLIDELL   1765
New York. Freeman, October 1, 1765. Married Jane Ashford,
April 30, 1764.
SLIDELL

DAVID SMITH   1751–   1787
Lansingburgh, N.Y., until 1793. Born in London, England.
Immigrated to Virginia, March 4, 1774. In Lansingburgh,
N.Y., firm of Smith & Whitney, 1787; Rockwell, Smith &
Whitney, 1788.
DS – D. SMITH

EBENEZER SMITH   1745–1830   1775
Brookfield, Conn. Shop located at Whisconier Hill.
E. SMITH

FLOYD SMITH   1815
New York. In Directory until 1836.
FLOYD SMITH

JOHN SMITH   1814
Baltimore, Md. Firm of Hart & Smith, 1814–1816, William
Hart and John Smith; Kirk & Smith, 1815–1820, Samuel Kirk
and John Smith.
I.SMITH

JOHN L. SMITH   1822
Middletown, Conn., advertised, *The Middlesex Gazette*, July 11,
1822.
J.L.SMITH

JOHN LEONARD SMITH   1850
Syracuse, N.Y., at 36 Montgomery Street.
J.L.SMITH

JOSEPH SMITH 1742–1789   1765
Boston, Mass. At 48 Newbury Street, 1789.
IS – I.SMITH

RICHARD EWING SMITH   1827
Louisville, Ky., until 1850. Firm of Smith & Grant, 1827–
1831.
R.E.SMITH

WILLIAM SMITH   1770
New York, advertised as, "Gold and Silver-smith in Chapel-
Street.", November 5, 1770, *New York Gazette*.
WM.SMITH

ZEBULON SMITH 1786–1865   1820
Bangor, Maine. In Ellsworth, Me., 1849, where he died.
Z.SMITH

SMITH & GRANT   1827
Louisville, Ky., until 1831. Robert Ewing Smith and William
Grant.
SMITH & GRANT

JEREMIAH SNOW, JR. 1764–   1808
Williamsburg, Mass. Opened shop and advertised for appren-
tice. Born in Amherst, Mass., July 17.
I.SNOW

SAMUEL SOUMAINE 1718–1765 1740

Annapolis, Md., until 1754. Born in New York of French
Huguenot origin, son of Daniel, nephew of Simeon Soumaine,
1685–1750, N.Y. Married Susanna Minskie, September 7,
1742. Advertised, *Maryland Gazette*, March 21, 1749,
"Goldsmith and Jeweller, from Philadelphia, opened Shop in
South-east Street, Near St. Ann's Church, where he makes all
sorts of Gold and Silver Work, such as Tureens, Tea Kettles,
Bread Baskets, Chaffing Dishes, Coffee Pots, Butter Boats, large
and small Waiters, holding from one glass to 18, fluted-soup
ladles, Tankards of all sizes, Sugar-dishes, Punch Bowles, Tea
Pots." Returned to Philadelphia, Pa. in 1754 where he worked
until his death, 1765.
SS

SIMEON SOUMAINE CA. 1685–1750 1706

New York. Born in London, England. Son of silversmith Simeon
and Jean Piaud Soumaine who came to New York in 1690.
Father became a Freeman, January 23, 1695/6. Uncle of Samuel
Soumaine. Married, about 1705, Mary Burt, daughter of Samuel
Burt, prominent merchant. Vestryman in Trinity Church,
1712–1750. William Anderson, February 17, 1717, Elias
Boudinot, age fifteen, June 6, 1721, and Elias Pelletreau,
November 19, 1741, served as his apprentices at his shop near
Old Slip Market. Notice, April 3, 1727, "Gold Work, wrought
by Simeon Soumaine of New York, Goldsmith, all of the newest
Fashion. The highest prize consists of an Eight square Tea-Pot,
six Tea-Spoons, Skimmer and Tongs, Valued, at £18 3 s. 6d."
In 1730, assessed Dockward, N.Y.C., £15.
SS

THOMAS SPARROW 1746–1784 1764

Annapolis, Md., "At the Sign of the Silver Coffee Pot, Silver
Smith, Engraver . . .". Advertised, *Maryland Gazette*, March 21,
1765, "Gold Smith and Jeweller from Philadelphia, near St.
Anne's Church in South-East Street . . .". Working until 1784.
TS

ISAAC SPEAR 1836

Boston, Mass., near Manchester Street. In Newark, N.J., 1837.
I.SPEAR

G. SPENCE 1830

Newark, N.J.
G.SPENCE

S. P. SQUIRE   1835
New York.

S.P.SQUIRE

SQUIRE & BROTHER   1846
New York.

SQUIRE & BROTHER

SQUIRE & LANDER   1840
New York.

SQUIRE & LANDER

PHILEMON STACY, JR.   1798–1829   1819
Boston, Mass. Born in Gloucester, Mass., March 1., son of
Philemon and Polly Bray Stacy. Apprenticed to Jesse Churchill,
88 Newbury Street. Young Stacy had a shop in rear of 26
Marlboro (Washington Street). Died July 13.

P.STACY

JOHN STANIFORD   1737–1811   1789
Windham, Conn. Firm of Elderkin & Staniford, 1790–1792,
Alfred Elderkin and John Staniford.

JS – STANIFORD

DANIEL STANTON   1755–1781   1776
Stonington, Conn. Son of Phineas and Elizabeth Stanton.
Brother of Enoch and Zebulon. Served in Revolutionary War at
Fort Griswold, Groton, Conn. where he was killed, September 6.

DS – D.STANTON

ENOCH STANTON   1745–1781.   1766
Stonington, Conn. Killed, with brother, Daniel, at Fort Griswold, Groton, Conn., September 6.

ES

WILLIAM P. & H. STANTON   1826
Rochester, N.Y., until 1841. William P. Stanton, 1794–1878,
and brother, Henry Stanton, 1803–1872.

W.P & H.STANTON

ZEBULON STANTON   1753–1828   1775
Stonington, Conn. Son of Phineas and Elizabeth Stanton.
Brother of Enoch and Daniel. Married Esther Gray, 1778. The
Stanton house and shop he erected with the help of his brothers
was on Main Street. Died July 18.

STANTON – ZS

HENRY B. STANWOOD 1818–1869 1840
Boston, Mass.
HENRY B.STANWOOD

J. E. STANWOOD 1850
Philadelphia, Pa.
J.E.STANWOOD

JOHN J. STAPLES, JR. 1788
New York.
JJS

RICHARD STARR 1785–1849 1807
Boston, Mass., at Franklin Street.
R.STARR

E. STEBBINS & CO. 1825
New York. In Directory, 1836–1856.
E.STEBBINS & CO

THOMAS E. STEBBINS 1830
New York.
STEBBINS – TES – T.STEBBINS

THOMAS E. STEBBINS & CO. 1835
New York.
STEBBINS & CO

STEBBINS & HOWE 1832
New York. Edwin Stebbins and George C. Howe.
STEBBINS & HOWE

T. S. STEELE 1800
Hartford, Conn.
T.STEELE

T. STEELE & CO. 1815
Hartford, Conn.
T.STEELE & CO

GEORGE STEPHENS 1791
New York, at White Hall Slip until 1793; 25 Rose Street in
1795. Possibly Gothelf Stephanis or Godfrey Shiving of
Philadelphia.
GS

THOMAS STEPHENSON   1835
Buffalo, N.Y., until 1848.
STEPHENSON

THOMAS STEPHENSON & CO.   1839
Buffalo, N.Y., until 1848.
T.STEPHENSON & CO

STEVENS & LAKEMAN   1819
Salem, Mass., until 1830. John Stevens and Ebenezer K. Lake-
man.
STEVENS & LAKEMAN

CHARLES STEWART   1833
New York, until 1849.
C.STEWART

C. W. STEWART   1850
Lexington, Ky.
C.W.STEWART

JOHN STEWART   1791
New York, at 32 Duke Street. In Baltimore, Md., after 1810.
STEWART

JONATHAN STICKNEY, JR.   1760–1808   1796
Newburyport, Mass. Advertised, *Newburyport Herald*, "Sil-
versmith and jeweler, has removed from Water Street to Middle
Street." Ordained Minister in 1800.
I.STICKNEY

M. P. STICKNEY   1820
Newburyport, Mass.
M.P.STICKNEY

BARTON STILLMAN   1791–   1810
Westerly, R.I. Silversmith, watchmaker, jeweler.
B.STILLMAN

E. STILLMAN   1825
Stonington, Conn.
E.STILLMAN

PAUL STILLMAN   1782–1810   1808
Westerly, R.I.
P.STILLMAN

RICHARD STILLMAN 1805
Philadelphia, Pa.
R. STILLMAN

JACOB STOCKMAN 1828
Philadelphia, Pa., at 46 Chestnut Street until 1850.
J. STOCKMAN

STOCKMAN & PEPPER 1828
Philadelphia, Pa., until 1845.
STOCKMAN & PEPPER

NOAH STODDARD 1830
New York.
N. STODDARD

JONATHAN STODDER, JR. 1825
New York.
J. STODDER

STODDER & FROBISHER 1816
Boston, Mass. At 59 Corn Hill, 1822. In Directory until 1825.
Jonathan Stodder and Benjamin Frobisher.
STODDER & FROBISHER

STOLLENWERCK & BROTHERS 1805
New York, in Directory at 137 William Street. Advertised,
Mercantile Advertiser, March 16, 1803, "Imported wares, jeweler
and watchmaker."
STOLLENWERCK & BROS

STOLLENWERCK & CO. 1800
New York, at 137 William Street; later, Stollenwerck &
Brothers.
STOLLENWERCK

ADAM STONE 1804
Baltimore, Md., at Saint's Lane; Baltimore Street, 1812. Married
Eliza Tilden, 1803.
AS

ABRAHAM G. STORM 1779–1836 1800
Poughkeepsie, N.Y. Born in Hopewell, N.Y., March 28, son of
Goris and Maria Conklin Storm. Married Mary Adriance. Firm
of Storm & Wilson, 1802–1818; Fellows & Storm, 1839. Secre-
tary of Mechanics Society. Trustee of Village.
A. G. STORM

A. G. STORM & SON   1823
Poughkeepsie, N.Y. until 1826. Abraham G. Storm and John
Adriance Storm.
STORM & SON

E. C. STORM   1815
Rochester, N.Y.
E.C.STORM

STORM & WILSON   1802
Poughkeepsie, N.Y. Abraham G. Storm and James Wilson
dissolved partnership in 1818.
S & WILSON

NATHAN STORRS   1768–1839   1792
Northampton, Mass., from New York. Born in Mansfield,
Conn., August 7, son of Amariah and Mary Gillett Storrs.
Apprenticed to Jacob Sargeant. Firm of Storrs & Cook, 1827.
NS – N.STORRS

STORRS & COOK   1827
Northampton, Mass. Partnership of Nathan Storrs and Benjamin
Cook until 1833.
STORRS & COOK

STORRS & COOLEY   1827
Utica, N.Y., until 1839. Charles Storrs and Oliver B. Cooley.
S & C – STORRS & COOLEY

S. N. STORY   1845
Worcester, Mass.
S.N.STORY

J. D. STOUT   1817
New York. In Directory until 1836.
J.D.STOUT

SAMUEL STOUT   1779
Princeton, N.J. Apprenticed to Thomas Shields. Worked for
John Fitch, Trenton, N.J. and Stephen Reeves, N.Y. Last
record, 1796.
SS

LUCAS STOUTENBURGH   1691–1743   1718
Charleston, S.C. Born in New York, son of Tobias and Anna Van
Roologom Stoutenburgh. Lucas and brother, Tobias, were
nephews-in-law of Bartholomew Le Roux who married Gertrud
Van Roologom, November 2, 1688, sister of Anna Van

Roologom, mother of Lucas and Tobias. Probably apprenticed to
Peter Van Dyke. Captain of Militia in 1721 and in "Command of
the Watch." Married Sarah Beating. Will, recorded, October
25, 1743, mentioned brother, Tobias, silversmith.
LSB

TOBIAS STOUTENBURGH   1700–1759   1731
New York. Brother of Lucas. Baptised in Dutch Church, N.Y.,
December 22, 1700. Freeman, May 25, 1731. Married Maria
Ten Brock, April 29, 1733. Petitioned against the election of
Adolph Philipse in 1737, with fellow silversmiths, Peter Van
Dyke, Charles Le Roux and Philip Goelet. Advertised, "Houses
for sale, all belonging to the Estate of Tobias Stoutenburgh
(father of the goldsmith), late deceased. Inquire of Tobias
Stoutenburgh, Gold-Smith, near the Spring Garden.", *New York
Weekly Post Boy*, October 22, 1744.
TSB

JOHN STOW   1748–1802   1772
Wilmington, Del. Son of Charles and Lydia Stow. Born March
18. Married, (1), June 26, 1777; (2) Mrs. Sarah Smith, 1784.
Contributed to organization of First Baptist Church in Wilmington, 1785. Advertised, *Penna. Packet*, November 30, 1772,
"Begs leave to inform the public, that he has opened a shop in
Market-Street, next door below Mr. Gabriel Springer where he
intends to carry on his business in all its branches; having had
peculiar advantages in the large way, such as making coffee-pots,
tea-pots, tankards, canns &c., he will undertake any piece of
plate that may be wanted." Died April 9.
I.STOW – J.STOW

GEORGE W. STRIKER   1825
New York. In Directory until 1835.
G.W.STRIKER

JOHN STUART   –1737   1720
Providence, R.I. Died December 11. Mentioned as jeweller in
will.
IS – STUART

C. D. SULLIVAN   1850
St. Louis, Mo.
C.D.SULLIVAN

D. SULLIVAN & CO.   1820
New York.
D.SULLIVAN & CO

ENOCH SULLIVAN   1800
Richmond, Va., until 1816.
E.SULLIVAN

GEORGE SULLIVAN   1805
Lynchburg, Va.
G.SULLIVAN

GEORGE SUTHERLAND   −1845   1796
Boston, Mass. In Directory until 1830.
GS

ROBERT SUTTON   1800
New Haven, Conn., until 1825.
RS

BENJAMIN SWAN   1792–1867   1815
Augusta, Me. Born in Haverhill, Mass. Married Hannah Smith,
1812. Father of Moody Moses Swan, 1818–1885.
B.SWAN

B. & M. M. SWAN   1846
Augusta, Me. Benjamin Swan and son, Moody Moses Swan.
B & M.M.SWAN

CALEB SWAN   1754–1816   1775
Boston, Mass. Born in Charlestown, Mass.
CS

ROBERT SWAN (SWAINE)   −1832   1795
Andover, Mass. In Philadelphia, Pa., at 77 South Second Street,
1799–1831. Spelled Swaine, 1802.
R.SWAN

WILLIAM SWAN   1715/6–1774   1740
Boston, Mass. Married Levinah Keyes, January 15, 1743 in
King's Chapel. Three children were born in Boston in 1745,
1749, 1751. Their fourth child was born, 1754, in Worcester,
Mass. where Swan worked until he died. He served in many
town offices and introduced singing into the Old South Church
where he was a member. Advertised in *Boston News-Letter*, May
27, 1773. On May 5, 1774, *Boston News-Letter* noted the death,
April 18, 1774, of "Mr. William Swan, goldsmith, formerly of
Boston, a Man of a very reputable Character." His best-known
piece is the two-handled covered cup engraved with the Pickman
arms on one side and on the other, in a matching cartouche: "The
Gift of the Province of Massachusetts Bay to Benjamin Pickman,
Esq^R., 1749."
SWAN – W.SWAN

JOHN SWEENEY
1816

Geneva, N.Y., until 1827.
I.SWEENEY – J.SWEENEY

JOHN SYMMES
1767

Boston, Mass. Advertised, "Goldsmith, near the Golden
Ball . . .", *Boston Gazette*, May 4, 1767.
I.SYMMES

DANIEL SYNG 1713–1745
1734

Lancaster, Pa. Born in Ireland, brother of Philip and John.
Married Mary Gray, August 10, 1733, Christ Church, Philadel-
phia, Pa. One of the original vestrymen of St. James Church of
Lancaster. Will was dated 1745 and proved 1746.
DS – D.SYNG

JOHN SYNG   –1738/9
1734

Philadelphia, Pa. Apprentice of Caesar Ghiselin when he died in
1734 and Ghiselin's estate paid £100 for uncompleted term.
Advertised in *Penna. Gazette*, June 27, 1734, "All sorts of Gold
and Silver Work made and mended, also Gold and Silver bought
by John Syng, Goldsmith, in Market Street over against the
Market House, next Door but one to the Crown."
IS

PHILIP SYNG 1676–1739
1714/5

Philadelphia, Pa. Born and trained in Cork, Ireland, one of nine
sons of Richard and Alicia Syng. From Bristol, England, arrived
in Philadelphia, July 14, 1714, with his first wife, Abigail
Murdock, and their three sons, Philip, Daniel and John. Mentioned as a Gentleman and Goldsmith. Philip Syng & Co.
acquired land in Maryland, May, 1722, which was later taken
away by court order. Married, second wife, Hannah Leaming,
May 24, 1724; third, Susannah Price, February 26, 1733.
Advertised, *American Mercury*, May 19, 1720; "Goldsmith, near
the Market Place." Removed to Annapolis, Md. where he died,
May 18. His eldest son, Philip, received one half of his estate,
second son, Daniel, one quarter, and his grandson, Philip Syng,
the remaining quarter.
PS

PHILIP SYNG, JR.   1703–1789
1726

Philadelphia, Pa. Born in Ireland, September 29, eldest son of
Philip and Abigail Murdock Syng. Came to America with
parents in 1714. Returned to Philadelphia after a trip to England
in 1726. Married Elizabeth Warner, February 5, 1729. Became
acquainted with Benjamin Franklin about this time. Grand

Master, Masonic Grand Lodge (Modern) in 1741; Director of the
Library Company, 1731. Advertised, *Penna. Gazette*, September
14, 1738; "Silversmith, on Front Street." The electrical machine
used by Franklin in 1747 was a contrivance of Syng's. An original
trustee of Academy of Philadelphia, later to become the University of Pennsylvania. He made the inkstand, purchased for the
Provincial Assembly for £25/16/0. in 1752, used at the signing
of the Declaration of Independence and the Constitution of the
United States, and now on exhibition in Independence Hall.
Elected Manager of the House of Employment of the Poor, May
15, 1766. Announced retirement from business in notice which
appeared, September 23, 1772, appointing Richard Humphreys,
a former apprentice, his successor to his goldsmith's business.
Died May 8. Buried in Christ Church Burying Ground, Philadelphia. Estate was shared by his eighteen children.
PHILIP SYNG – PS

[T]

SAMUEL M. TABER   1822
Providence, R.I.
S.M.TABER

JOHN TANGUY   1801
Philadelphia, Pa., at 33 North Third Street until 1818. Brother
of Peter Tanguy.
I.TANGUY – J.TANGUY

JAMES TANNER   –1782   1753
Newport, R.I. Brother of John. Married Mercy Wilcox, De-
cember 24, 1753.
JAMES TANNER

JOHN TANNER   1713–1785   1740
Newport, R.I. Born in Westerly, R.I. Married (1) Mary Col-
grove, August 4, 1736; (2) Freelove Saunders, April 5, 1779.
Taught trade to Joseph and Daniel Rogers; later, in partnership
as Tanner & Rogers circa 1775.
IT

PERRY G. TANNER   1842
Utica, N.Y., until 1844. In Cooperstown, N.Y., until 1850.
P.G.TANNER

TANNER & ROGERS   CA. 1775
Newport, R.I. John Tanner in partnership with apprentices,
Joseph and Daniel Rogers.
T & R

BENJAMIN TAPPAN   1747–1831   1768
Northampton, Mass. Apprenticed to William Homes whose
daughter, Sarah, he married, October 22, 1770.
BT

ISRAEL FOSTER TAPPAN   1797–   1820
Manchester, Mass. Born November 28 in Manchester, son of
Ebenezer Tappan, 1751/2–1849, and Betsy Forster, 1768–1845,
married March 5, 1791. Held rank of Lieutenant Colonel.
Married Deborah Forster, July 17, 1822.
I.F.TAPPAN

JOHN TARGEE   CA. 1772–1850   1797
New York, at 24 Gold Street; 192 Water Street, 1805–1815.
From Washington County, R.I., of French descent, from 17th
century Huguenot émigrés to Narragansett from Port des
Barques, opposite Ile d'Oléron, west coast of France. In Directory
until 1840.
IT

JOHN & PETER TARGEE   1811
New York, at 192 Water Street.
I & PT

WILLIAM TAYLOR   1775
Philadelphia, Pa. Advertised, *Penna. Evening Post*, October 23,
1777; "Goldsmith, In Front Street, near the Drawbridge. Makes
and Repairs all kinds of Swords and Hangers, and has for sale a
variety of Jewellery, gold, and silver articles."
WT

N. TAYLOR & CO.   1825
New York.
N.TAYLOR & CO

TAYLOR & HINSDALE   1807
New York, from Newark, N.J., located at 146 Broadway. In
Directory until 1830. John Taylor and Horace Hinsdale. Suc-
ceeded by Taylor & Baldwin.
T & H

TAYLOR & LAWRIE   1837
Philadelphia, Pa., at 114 Arch Street.
TAYLOR & LAWRIE – T & L

BARENT TEN EYCK 1714–1795   1735
Albany, N.Y. Son of Koenraet. Brother of Jacob. Baptised,
October 3, 1714. Married Effie . . . who died, 1791. Elected
Assistant Alderman in the Second Ward, 1746. In 1794, he
subscribed £40 toward establishment of Union College. Died
February 27.
BTE

JACOB C. TEN EYCK 1704/5–1793   1725
Albany, N.Y. Baptised, April 29, 1705. Son of Koenraet and
Geertje Van Schaick Ten Eyck. Brother of Barent. Apprenticed
to Cornelius Kierstede, August 10, 1718, for seven years of
which he served nine months, until July 15, 1719, to complete
term with Charles Le Roux. Married Catharyna Cuyler, August
17, 1736. On July 28, 1743, listed as a sponsor for person
taking the oath for the Colonial Naturalization Act of 1740.
Worked until 1770. Held important public offices becoming
Mayor of Albany. Died September 9.
ITE

KOENRAET TEN EYCK 1678–1753   1703
Albany, N.Y. Baptised April 9. Married Geertje Van Schaick,
October 15, 1704, in New York, where he became a Freeman,
May 8, 1716. Father of Jacob and Barent. Returned to Albany.
Held numerous appointed offices. Representative to Colonial
Assembly, 1747–1750. On January 18, 1748, listed as a sponsor
for persons taking oath to the Colonial Naturalization Act of
1740. His uncle, Dirck Ten Eyck, married the sister of Hendrick
and Jacob Boelen. Died January 23, 1753 in Albany.
KTE

WILLIAM I. TENNEY   1840
New York.
TENNEY – W.I.TENNEY

GEER TERRY 1775–1858   1800
Enfield, Conn. In Worcester, Mass., 1801–1814. Returned to
Enfield. Appointed Postmaster and held various public offices
until his death.
G.TERRY – TERRY

WILBERT TERRY   1785
Enfield, Conn.
W.TERRY

JOSEPH BLAKE THAXTER   1791–1863   1815
Hingham, Mass. Born October 15. Married Sally Gill,
November 12, 1815. Died May 8.
J.B.THAXTER

FRANCIS & FELIX THIBAULT   1807
Philadelphia, Pa., at 172 South Second Street.
F & F.THIBAULT–THIBAULT

THIBAULT & BROTHERS   1810
Philadelphia, Pa., at 66 South Second Street until 1835.
THIBAULT BROTHERS–THIBAULT & BROTHERS

EBENEZER THOMAS   1802
Petersburg, Va., advertised on Bollingbrook Street, May 10.
Firm of Bennett & Thomas, 1812–1819, John Bennett and
Ebenezer Thomas.
E.THOMAS

WALTER THOMAS   1769
New York. Registered Freeman, February 10, and March 21.
WT

DANIEL B. THOMPSON   1800–1876   1817
Brattleboro, Vt. Born in Litchfield, Conn. Son of Isaac. In
business with his father and succeeded him.
D.B.THOMPSON

WILLIAM THOMPSON   1795
Baltimore, Md., advertised at Gay Street; Market Street, 1814;
Pratt Street in 1824.
WT

ISAAC THOMSON (THOMPSON)   1801
Litchfield, Conn. until 1810. Firm of Shether & Thompson. In
Brattleboro, Vt., 1811.
I.THOMSON

JAMES THOMSON   1834
New York, at 129 William Street. In Directory until 1841.
IAS.THOMSON–JAS.THOMSON

WILLIAM THOMSON   1810
New York, at 399 Broadway; William Street, 1811–1825.
Commissioned to make silver service by the City for Captain
Samuel Reid for gallant bravery at the Battle of Fayal. In Direc-
tory until 1845.
WM.THOMSON–W.THOMSON

WILLIAM R. TICE   1850
New York.
WM.R.TICE

TIFFANY, YOUNG & ELLIS   1841
New York. Tiffany & Co., 1853.
TIFFANY YOUNG & ELLIS

JAMES TILEY 1740–1792   1765
Hartford, Conn. Member of St. John's Lodge of Free Masons,
1763. Advertised, 1765–1784, at King Street and later on
Front Street where he was injured in a gunpowder explosion.
Notice, May 11, 1784; "Offers articles in the silversmith's and
Jeweller's line in exchange for white pine boards, shingles, and
window sash stuffs." Tiley received enough building material to
erect a house suitable for entertainment, which he opened in
1786. Member of the Governor's Guard in 1771. Served as
Captain in the Revolutionary War. In the South after 1790.
I.TILEY – TILEY

SAMUEL TINGLEY   1754
New York. "Removed from his Shop in the Fly, to the Rotten-
Row, where he continues his Business. The Shop he left is to
Let.", *New York Mercury*, May 11, 1767. Married Susannah
Clem, November 6, 1767. Made Van Alstyne–Sarah Roosevelt
round tray, marked ST twice, engraved on back, Presentation
Date, 1792, with Roosevelt crest of a rose and initials SA in
script, establishing that Tingley was in N.Y. in 1792; at the
Museum of the City of New York. Removed to Philadelphia, Pa.
in 1796.
ST – S.TINGLEY

F. TINKHAM & CO.   1840
New York. In Directory until 1850.
F.TINKHAM & CO

BENJAMIN H. TISDALE   1812
Newport, R.I. Married Abigail Cary, December 28, 1816. In
Providence, R.I., at 148 North Main Street in 1824.
B.H.TISDALE

ALBERT TITCOMB 1802–   1823
Portland, Me. Born in Newburyport, Mass. In Bangor, Me.,
1832.
TITCOMB

FRANCIS TITCOMB 1790–1832   1813
Newburyport, Mass., on Merrimack Street, May 11, advertisement.
F. TITCOMB

JAMES TITUS   1833
Philadelphia, Pa.
I. TITUS

JOHN TOUZELL (TOWZELL) 1726/7–1785   1756
Salem, Mass. Grandson of Philip English. Advertised, *Boston News-Letter*, November 5, 1767; "The Subscriber's Shop in Salem was Broke Open the first of this Instant, in the Night, and the following Articles were Stolen from him, viz: 1½ Dozen Tea-Spoons marked I:T, one large Spoon, Maker's Name J. TOWZELL. Any Person that will discover the Thief or the Goods, that the Owner may recover them again, shall have Ten Dollars Reward and all necessary Charges paid by me. John Towzell, Goldsmith." Died August 14.
IT – J. TOUZELL

IRA STRONG TOWN 1809–1902   1825
Montpelier, Vt. Married Frances Marietta Witherall, 1834. Firms of I. S. & J. Town, 1825–1838; Town & Witherall, 1839–1845; Town & Hall, 1848–1851.
IRA S. TOWN – I. S. TOWN

I. S. & J. TOWN   1825
Montpelier, Vt., until 1838. Ira S. Town and brother, Josiah, Jr.
I.S & J. TOWN

THOMAS TOWNSEND 1701–1777   1725
Boston, Mass.
TT

OBADIAH W. TOWSON   1813
Baltimore, Md., 1813–1819; Philadelphia, Pa., at 73 St. John Street, 1819–1824. Apprenticed to Charles L. Boehme, April 30, 1806.
O. W. TOWSON

ISAAC N. TOY 1771–1834   1790
Abingdon, Md. Eldest son of Joseph Toy.
I. N. TOY

JOSEPH TOY   1748–1826   1776
Abingdon, Md. Married Frances Dallam, May 20, 1770. Was
Professor of Mathematics and English in Cokesbury College in
1788, as well as a silversmith. Firm of Toy & Wilson, 1790. In
Baltimore, Md. after 1796.
IT

TOY & WILSON   1790
Abingdon, Md. Joseph Toy and William Wilson.
IT WW

GORDON TRACY (GURDON TRACY)   1767–1792   1787
Norwich, Conn. Brother of Erastus. Advetised in New London,
Conn. 1791.
G.TRACY

JOHN PROCTOR TROTT   1769–1852   1792
New London, Conn. Born in Boston, Mass., son of Jonathan
from whom he learned trade. Brother of Jonathan, Jr. On State
Street in 1799. Firms of Trott & Cleveland, 1792; Trott &
Brooks, 1798; J. P. Trott & Son, 1820. Advertised, *Mercantile
Advertiser*, December 16, 1800, Hartford, Conn. "Stolen, set of
Tea Spoons, initialed, $_B$W$_E$, Maker's Name, I.J.P.T."
IPT – JPT

JONATHAN TROTT   1730–1815   1758
Boston, Mass., until 1771. Advertised, "At his Shop between
the White Horse and Lamb Tavern, South End." Married Lydia
Proctor, 1756. Father of John Proctor and Jonathan, Jr. Re-
moved to Norwich, Conn., 1772 and New London, Conn.,
1784, where he became an innkeeper of Peck's Tavern. Died in
New London.
I.TROTT – JT – J.TROTT

JONATHAN TROTT, JR.   1771–1813   1795
New London, Conn. Born in Boston, son of Jonathan and Lydia
Proctor Trott. Brother of John Proctor. Learned trade from his
father. Advertised on Beach Street in 1800.
IT

J. P. TROTT & SON   1820
New London, Conn.
I.P.T & SON – J.P.T & SON

TROTT & BROOKS   1798
New London, Conn., on State Street for one year.
T & B

TROTT & CLEVELAND 1792
New London, Conn. John Proctor Trott and William Cleveland
dissolved partnership in 1794.
T & C

HENRY R. TRAUX 1760–1834 1815
Albany, N.Y., at Steuben Street. In Directory until 1819.
HRT

ARMISTEAD TRUSLOW 1813
Lynchburg, Va., until 1820. Advertised, *The Lynchburg Press*,
July 7, 1814, "For an apprentice to the silversmith and jewelry
business . . ."
AT

GEORGE WASHINGTON TUCKERMAN 1810
Portsmouth, N.H., until 1819.
G.W.TUCKERMAN

JAMES TURNER –1759 1744
Boston, Mass. Advertised in Cornhill, 1748. Died in Philadel-
phia, Pa.
JT – J.TURNER

ANDREW TYLER 1692–1741 1715
Boston, Mass. Married Miriam Pepperell, 1714. Master of
Knight Leverett. Served on Town Board, 1720–1732. Listed as
subscriber to *Prince's Chronicle*, 1728–1736. Died August 12.
AT – A.TYLER

DAVID TYLER 1760–1804 1781
Boston, Mass. Listed in Boston Directory, 1789–1803, as
goldsmith, silversmith, jeweler.
DT

D. M. TYLER 1810
Boston, Mass.
D.M.TYLER

GEORGE TYLER 1740–1785 1765
Boston, Mass., at No. 15, now 78, Washington Street, Cornhill,
Boston.
GT

I. TYLER CA. 1778
New England.
I.TYLER

JOHN HENRY TYLER   −1883   1835
Richmond, Va. Son of Col. Samuel and Emma Rogers Tyler.
Married Elizabeth Slater Evans, 1835. Firm of Mitchell & Tyler,
1845−1866. Partnership of John Henry Tyler and son, John,
formed August 6, 1867.
JOHN H.TYLER & CO

[U]

UFFORD & BURDICK   1812
New Haven, Conn. Thomas Ufford and William S. Burdick
advertised dissolution in 1814.
U & B

ANDREW UNDERHILL   1780
New York. Brother of Thomas.
AU − A.UNDERHILL

THOMAS UNDERHILL   1779
New York. Married Elizabeth Thorne, November 25, 1779.
Admitted as Freeman, August 20, 1787. Firm of Underhill &
Vernon, 1787. Witness to will with John Vernon, dated March
16, 1787.
TU

UNDERHILL & VERNON   1787
New York. Thomas Underhill and John Vernon advertised at 41
Water Street. Witnesses to will, dated March 16, 1787.
TU IV

[V]

BENJAMIN F. VALLET   1820
Kingston, N.Y. Advertised, 1833−1850.
VALLET

JOHN VANDALL   1752
Charleston, S.C. Married Elizabeth Bonneau, June 26, 1747.
Advertised in *South Carolina Gazette* until 1767.
I.VANDALL

PETER VAN BEUREN   1795
New York, at 52 Maiden Lane; 272 Pearl Street in 1798.
PVB − P.V.BEUREN

WILLIAM VAN BEUREN

1790

New York, at Courtlandt Street; 22 Maiden Lane in 1794. In
Directory, 1796.

WVB

CORNELIUS VANDER BURGH 1652–1699

1675

New York. Son of Lucas and Annetse Cornelius Vander Burgh,
baptised May 11, 1653. Married Levyntie Leumen, baptised
1656, daughter of Jacob and Margaret Jacobs Leuman, on
January 7, 1673. On Tax List in 1677 as owner of two houses,
one on High Street, the other in the Fort, "where ye Silversmith
liv'd." Appointed High Constable in 1689. "Recommended
with Jacob Boelen for Office for Regulation of Weights and
Scales, Curr'y, Gold, and Silver." in 1694. Made the gold cup
presented to Governor Fletcher in 1693. New York's first native
silversmith.

CVB

JACOBUS VANDER SPIEGEL 1668–1708

1689

New York. Son of Laurens Vander Spiegel. Married Ann Sanders,
September 20, 1692. Daughter, Sarah, baptised, February 7,
1694. Captain in the Army, 1691. Constable in 1698. Freeman,
February 24, 1701. Witness to will of Christina Cappeons,
January 5, 1693/4 and of Robert Sinclair, August 4, 1704.
Will, dated November 29, 1708, proved, March 29, 1716.
Widow Vander Spiegel, Assessment Roll, February, 1730, £30.

ISV – IVS

PETER VAN DYKE 1684–1751

1705

New York. Baptised, August 17, 1684. Married Rachael Le
Roux, October 27, 1711, daughter of Bartholomew LeRoux, to
whom he was apprenticed. Later, married Cornelia Van Varick.
Appointed Constable of the East Ward in 1708. Mentioned as
appraiser of lottery in 1727. Assessor of City, 1730. Will, dated
August 1st, 1750, proved January 5. Will, "Peter Van Dyke,
being very sick, leave to my son, Richard £5, in lieu of all
pretence as heir-at-law, grandchildren, Daniel and Richard
Shotford, £40 each at interest till of age. Daughters, Hannah
and Cornelia, each a silver mugg, to Lena, my silver teapot,
Sarah, my smallest silver tankard, Mary, my largest silver tankard, each by weight, as part of share in Estate. All rest of Estate
to children, Richard, Rodolphus, Hannah, Cornelia, Lena,
Sarah and Mary, Executors." As a boy, lived in Broadway, next
door to Jacob Boelen. Probably master of Tobias and Lucas
Stoutenburgh, wife's nephews. Assessment Roll, February,
1730, two houses, £65.

PVD

RICHARD VAN DYKE   1717–1770   1750
New York. Son of Peter and Rachael Le Roux Van Dyke. Married
Elizabeth Strange of Rye, N.Y. Advertised at Hanover Square,
1750–1756.
RD – RVD

PETER VAN INBURGH   1689–1740   1710
New York. Signed indenture, dated 1739, as Goldsmith, wit-
nessed by Stephen Bourdett.
PIVB

JAN VAN NIEU KIRKE   1690–1735   1711
New York. Mentioned in 1716.
INK – IVNK

VAN NESS & WATERMAN   1835
New York, at 9 City Hall Place. Peter Van Ness and James
Waterman.
V & W

VAN NESS & E. S. BURSTRAND   1830
New York.
VAN NESS & E.S.BURSTRAND

NICHOLAS VAN RENSSELAER   1765
New York and Albany, N.Y.
NV

TUNIS VAN RIPER   1813
New York, at 69 Division Street until 1816. In Directory until
1829.
TVR

VANSANT & CO.   1850
Philadelphia, Pa.
V & CO

G. VAN SCHAICK   1800
Albany, N.Y.
G.VN SCHAICK

JOHN VAN STEENBERG, JR.   1775
Kingston, N.Y.
IVS

HENRY VAN VEGHTEN   –1786/7   1760
Albany, N.Y. Youngest child of Johannes Van Veghten, 1709–
1746, and Neeltje Beekman, 1710–1762, married in 1734.

Baptised in Dutch Church, Albany, March 29, 1747. In 1767,
Fire Master for the First Ward. Later, Member of the Common
Council of the City of Albany. Served as Adjutant of the First
Regiment of the Albany County Militia during the Revolu-
tionary War. Bill of Sale, 1774, shows partnership of Jacob
Gerritse Lansing and Henry Van Veghten as Lansing & Van
Veghten, 1774–1775. Died intestate April 10.

HVV

DANIEL VAN VOORHIS 1751–1824   1782

Philadelphia, Pa. Born in Oyster Bay, N.Y., August 30, son of
Cornelius and Neeltje Hoagland Van Voorhis. Married Catherine
Richards in 1775. Advertised, *Penna. Gazette*, May 6, 1782,
"Front Street, Philadelphia." In *New Jersey Gazette*, February 5,
1783, "Removal to Princeton." Located in New York, 1785, and
in partnership with William Coley working at 72 Hanover
Square until 1787; in Rupert, Vt., working in mint operations,
1788. In Queen Street in 1789. Firm of Van Voorhis & Schanck,
1791–2. At various addresses until 1798, when he admitted his
son into business. Advertised, *Mercantile Advertiser*, "At 145
Water Street.", November 2, 1802. In *New York Evening Post*,
February 11, 1803, "as Weight Master of New York appointed
by Common Council." Appointed as Weigher in Custom House
in 1805 after the death of his son. Died in Brooklyn, N.Y., June
10.

DVV – D.V.VOORHIS

VAN VOORHIS, SCHANCK & McCALL   1800

Albany, N.Y.

V.V.SCHANCK & McCALL

VAN VOORHIS & COLEY   1785

New York, at 27 Hanover Square until 1786/7. In Rupert, Vt.,
1788, to coin coppers in the mint. Minted copper coins for states
of Vermont, Connecticut and New York. Reuben Harmon and
William Coley, coiners; Daniel Van Voorhis, cashier.

V & C

VAN VOORHIS & SCHANCK   1791

New York, at Queen Street. Daniel Van Voorhis and his cousin,
Garret Schanck, dissolved partnership in 1793.

VV & S

STEPHEN VAN WYCK   1805

New York.

S.VAN WYCK

JOHN FREDERICK VENT   1783
Boston, Mass., until 1793. In Keene, N.H. until 1810.
J.F.VENT – VENT

PETER VERGEREAU   1700–1755   1720
New York. Freeman, July 11. Advertised on Queen Street,
commonly known as Smith's Valley. Married Susanna Boudinot,
sister of Elias Boudinot, silversmith, October 24, 1737. Listed
as a sponsor for persons taking the Colonial Naturalization Act of
1740 Oath in October, 1740. Will, dated November 29, 1753,
"indisposed and weak." His wife, daughter and son, Peter,
shared his estate, proved, January 23, 1756.
PV

JOHN VERNON   1787
New York. Advertised at 41 Water Street, 1793; 93 John Street,
1794–5; 75 Gold Street, 1815. Firm of Underhill & Vernon,
1787.
IV

NATHANIEL VERNON   1777–1843   1802
Charleston, S.C., at 136 Broad Street. Married Ann Eliza Russel,
1814. Continued in business until 1835. Died October 4,
buried in Christ Church Parish.
N.VERNON – VERNON

N. VERNON & CO.   1803
Charleston, S.C., at 140 Broad Street. Vernon & Co., until
1808.
N.VERNON & CO

SAMUEL VERNON   1683–1737   1705
Newport, R.I. Son of Daniel and Ann Dyer Vernon, born in
Newport, December 6. Married Elizabeth Fleet, April 10,
1707; Elizabeth Paine, January 12, 1725. Registered as Freeman
in 1714. Appointed by Assembly to settle land controversy,
1726, when he also assisted Governor in investigating health
conditions of the Colony. New York influence in style of design.
SV

WILLIAM VILANT   1725
Philadelphia, Pa. Advertised in *American Mercury*, August 12–
19, as "Goldsmith."
WV

R. H. L. VILLARD   1833
Georgetown, D.C., at Bridge Street.
VILLARD

RICHARD VINCENT (VANSANT) 1799
Baltimore, Md.
RV

DAVID VINTON 1790
Providence, R.I., until 1796. Advertised, *United States Chronicle*,
January 24, 1793, "Goldsmith and Jeweller from Boston,
Informs the Ladies and Gentlemen of Providence and its Vicinity,
that he has for sale at his Shop, the North End Corner of Market
Parade and nearly opposite, His Excellency, Governor Fenner, a
complete assortment of gold and silversmith's wares. N.B. All
kinds of Gold and Silverware made and repaired in the neatest
manner and on the shortest notice."
DV

JOHN VOGLER 1783–1881 1802
Salem, N.C. Son of George and Anna Kunzel Vogler. Married
Christina Spach in 1820. Was active in the Moravian Church.
Died in Salem, June 15.
I. VOGLER

[W]

ISAIAH WAGSTER 1780
Baltimore, Md., until 1793. Advertised as goldsmith in *Mary-
land Journal*, 1780, "at Market, near Calvert Street."
IW

JOHN WAITE 1742–1817 1763
South Kingstown, R.I. Born July 4, son of Benjamin and
Abigail Waite. Brother of William. Married Margaret Sheffield,
1767. Apprenticed to Samuel Casey. Colonel in Revolutionary
War. Held public offices. Died October 19.
I. WAITE – JW – J. WAITE

WILLIAM WAITE 1730–1826 1760
Wickford, R.I. Born January 10. Brother of John. Purchased
land in Little Rest, R.I. Removed to Cambridge, N.Y.
W. WAITE

D. WALDRON 1789
New York, at Greenwich Road.
D. WALDRON

JOHN WAKEFIELD   1797–1863   1820
East Thomaston, Me. Born in Bath, Me. Married Anna Prior,
1821.
J.WAKEFIELD

GEORGE WALKER   1797
Philadelphia, Pa., at 19 North Third Street until 1814. Brother
of Hannah.
G.WALKER

HANNAH WALKER   1816
Philadelphia, Pa., at 19 North Third Street where she worked
with brother, George.
H.WALKER

JOHN WALKER, JR.   1798
Philadelphia, Pa., at 1 North Third Street; at 12 North Second
Street, 1806; at 55 Mead Alley in 1824.
J.WALKER

L. WALKER (I.WALKER)   1825
Boston, Mass.
L.WALKER

WILLIAM WALKER   1793
Philadelphia, Pa., at 2 Quarry Street; at 4 North Second Street,
1802; 381 South Second Street, 1813–1816. Member of Lodge
5, A.Y.M.
W.WALKER

JOHN WALLEN   1763
Philadelphia, Pa.
J.WALLEN

JOHN WALRAVEN   1771–1814   1792
Baltimore, Md., at 4 Bridge Street; Baltimore Street, 1796–
1814.
I.WALRAVEN – JW – WALRAVEN

JACOB WALTER   1782–1865   1815
Baltimore, Md., until 1860. Apprenticed to Philip B. Sadtler.
J.WALTER

JOSEPH M. WALTER   1835
Baltimore, Md., until 1890.
JOS.M.WALTER

AMBROSE WARD   1735–1808   1767

New Haven, Conn. Born August 24. Brother of William. Firm
of Cutler, Silliman, Ward & Co., 1767: Richard Cutler,
Hezekiah Silliman and Ambrose Ward. Died June 10.

A W

A. M. WARD   1845

Hartford, Conn.

A.M.WARD

BILIOUS WARD   1729–1777   1750

Middletown, Conn. Born in Guilford, Conn., July 10, son of
William, Jr. First Master of Lodge at Guilford. Died in
Wallingford, Conn., March 24.

B W

JAMES WARD   1768–1856   1798

Hartford, Conn. Born in Guilford, Conn., February 2, son of
Bilious and Beulah Hall Ward. Apprenticed to Col. Miles
Beach, with whom he joined in partnership, 1790–1798.
Advertised shop located, "North of the Bridge, at the Sign of the
Golden Tea Kettle." Firms of Ward & Bartholomew, 1804;
Ward, Bartholomew & Brainard, 1809–1830.

JW – J.WARD – WARD

JEHU & W. L. WARD   1837

Philadelphia, Pa. In Directory until 1850.

JEHU & W.L.WARD

JOHN WARD   1805

Middletown, Conn. Leased the shop formerly occupied by Judah
Hart whom he succeeded. Firm of Ward & Hughes, 1805.

WARD

WILLIAM WARD   1678–1768   1700

Wallingford, Conn. Born in Killingworth, Conn., October 18.
Father of William Ward, Jr. and grandfather of Bilious Ward.

W W

WILLIAM WARD, JR.   1705–1761   1726

Guilford, Conn. Father of Bilious Ward. Silversmith and ironmonger.

W W

WILLIAM WARD   1736–1829   1757

Litchfield, Conn. Born in New Haven, Conn. Brother of Ambrose.

W.WARD

WARD & BARTHOLOMEW   1804

Hartford, Conn., at Front Street until 1809. James Ward and
Roswell Bartholomew. Later, Charles Brainard, an apprentice,
became a partner as Ward, Bartholomew & Brainard, 1809–
1830.

WARD & BARTHOLOMEW

WARD & COX   1811

Philadelphia, Pa., until 1818. John Ward and John Cox.

WARD & COX

WARD & HUGHES   1805

Middletown, Conn. John Ward and Edmund Hughes dissolved
partnership in 1806.

W & H

ABIJAH B. WARDEN   1842

Philadelphia, Pa., until 1845.

WARDEN

JOSEPH WARFORD   1779–1847   1800

Albany, N.Y. Firm of Bassett & Warford, 1800–1806.
Advertised in 1810.

WARFORD

ANDREW ELLICOTT WARNER   1786–1870   1805

Baltimore, Md. In partnership with eldest brother, Thomas,
until 1812. Captain in the War of 1812. Advertised at 5 North
Gay Street until 1870. His son, Andrew Ellicott Warner, Jr.,
1813–1896, continued the business.

AEW – A.E.WARNER – ANDW.E.WARNER

CALEB WARNER   1784–1861   1805

Salem, Mass. Born in Ipswich, Mass. Married (1) Mary Pearson,
August 8, 1807, (2) Mrs. Mary Porter, July 4, 1819; (3) Sarah
Gould, January 28, 1830. Firms of C. & J. Warner, 1820;
Warner & Lord, 1830; Warner & Fellows, 1837.

C.WARNER

C. & J. WARNER   1820

Salem, Mass., until 1822. Caleb and John Warner.

C & J.WARNER

DANIEL WARNER   1795–1820   1816

Salem, Mass. Born in Ipswich, Mass.

D.WARNER

JOSEPH WARNER 1742–1800   1775

Wilmington, Del. Son of William and Mary Warner. Advertised
as gold and silversmith at the Sign of the Golden Cann at Market
Street. *Delaware Gazette*, October 13, 1792, "Who carries on
Gold and Silver Smith Business, in its various branches, as usual:
and gives the highest price for old silver."

IW – I.WARNER – JW – J.WARNER

JOSEPH P. WARNER 1811–1862   1830

Baltimore, Md. Eldest son of Thomas and Mary Ann Meigs
Warner. Colonel of the Fourth Maryland Regiment. Appointed
City Assayer, 1844–1852. Working until 1862. Died September
30.

JPW

SAMUEL WARNER   1797

Philadelphia, Pa., at Pewter Platter Alley. Advertised in Baltimore, Md. in 1812.

SW – S.WARNER

THOMAS H. WARNER 1780–1828   1805

Baltimore, Md. Brother and partner of Andrew. Appointed
Assayer for the City of Baltimore, 1814. Advertised shop at 9
East Street in 1819.

TW – T.WARNER

THOMAS & A. E. WARNER   1805

Baltimore, Md., at 5 North Gay Street until partnership was
dissolved in 1812.

T & A.E.WARNER

WILLIAM WARROCK   1795

Norfolk, Va. Silversmith from England. Firm of Brooks &
Warrock dissolved in 1796. Robbed of $1,200. worth of goods
in July, 1800. Moved to Richmond, Va., 1802. Returned to
Norfolk, 1804.

WARROCK

SAMUEL WATERS   1803

Boston, Mass. Inherited Benjamin Burt's tools.

SW – S.WATERS

EDWARD E. WATSON   –1839   1821

Boston, Mass.

E.WATSON

JAMES WATSON   1830

Philadelphia, Pa., at 72 High Street.

J.WATSON

JOSEPH H. WATSON   1844
Warrenton, Va. Advertised until 1878.
WATSON

WATSON & BROWN   1830
Philadelphia, Pa.
WATSON & BROWN

EMMOR T. WEAVER   1808
Philadelphia, Pa., at 17 Elfreth's Alley; Lox Legs Court in 1820.
In Directory until 1833.
ETW – E.T.WEAVER – WEAVER

JOSHUA WEAVER   –1827   1794
West Chester, Pa. Working in 1815.
IW

NICHOLAS N. WEAVER   1791–1853   1815
Utica, N.Y., until 1846.
N.N.WEAVER

BARNABAS WEBB   1729–1795   1756
Boston, Mass. Advertised, *Boston Gazette*, January 19,
"Goldsmith, near the Market." Married Mary Homes in 1759.
Notice that he was burnt out and has opened a shop in Back
Street, 1761. In Ann Street, 1762–1789.
BW

EDWARD WEBB   –1718   1705
Boston, Mass. Notice appears, *Boston News-Letter*, November 24,
1718, "Goldsmith of Boston, died October 21, 1718, and
'having no poor friends in England that wanted, and getting his
money here, he bequeathed Two Hundred Pounds . . . for the use
of the poor of Boston.'" "Silver spoons with maker's marks WEBB
and COWELL were advertised as stolen", 1739, *Boston News-Letter*.
Estate inventoried by John Edwards and John Dixwell.
EW – WEBB

GEORGE W. WEBB   1812–1890   1835
Baltimore, Md., until 1890. Son and partner of James Webb.
GEO.W.WEBB – G.W.WEBB

JAMES WEBB   1788–1844   1810
Baltimore, Md., at 13 Chatham Street. Father of George W.
Webb. Firms of Webb & Johannes, 1827; Jas Webb & Son,
1850.
J.WEBB

HENRY L. WEBSTER   1831
    Providence, R.I., firm of Gorham & Webster, 1831, with Jabez
    Gorham.
    H.L.WEBSTER

HENRY L. WEBSTER & CO.   1842
    Providence, R.I.
    HLW & CO

SIMON WEDGE   1774–1823   1798
    Baltimore, Md. Married Anna Steine. Advertised shop at 13
    Light Street, 1800; at Baltimore Street until 1823.
    SW – S.WEDGE

ALFRED WELLES   1783–1860   1804
    Hebron, Conn. Worked with brother, George, in Boston, 1807.
    Served as General in War of 1812.
    A.WELLES

ALFRED & GEORGE WELLES   1807
    Boston, Mass. In Directory until 1810 at 55 Cornhill.
    A & GW – A & G.WELLES

GEORGE WELLES   1784–1823   1805
    Boston, Mass. Member of the Charitable Mechanics Association,
    1822. Brother of Alfred.
    WELLES

L. T. WELLES & CO.   1810
    Hartford, Conn.
    L.T.WELLES & CO

WELLES & CO.   1816
    Boston, Mass. George Welles and Hugh Gelston in Directory
    until 1821.
    WELLES & CO

WELLES & GELSTON   1816
    Boston, Mass. George Welles and Hugh Gelston until 1821.
    WELLES & GELSTON

LEMUEL WELLS   1790
    New York, on Broadway; at 2 Queen Street, 1791–2. Firm of
    Wells & Co., Lemuel & Horace Wells at 158 Pearl Street. Notice,
    July 29, 1795. "Horace Wells, silversmith, died of yellow fever
    at 158 Pearl Street."
    LW

LEMUEL WELLS & CO.   1794
New York. Lemuel and Horace Wells until 1795.
LW & CO

JOHN WENDOVER (WINDOVER)   −1726/7   1690
New York. Probably son of John Wendover, Goldsmith, of
Foster Lane, buried 1679. Assistant Alderman, 1692−1697,
West Ward. Active in Leister Rebellion, 1691−1694. Will
dated, July 21, 1716, "Being sick, leaves eldest son, Thomas,
£10, wife, Engeltie, all my real and personal Estate, Executor."
Witnesses to will were Abraham Van Gelder, Antonas Kaac,
Johanes Jansen, Hercules Wendover, administrator, son,
Thomas, having renounced right. Wills of John and Engeltie
proved February 23, 1726/7. Children were Thomas, Hercules,
Samuel, Nanny.
IW − JW

BARNARD WENMAN   1789
New York, at Fly Market; at Partition and William Streets until
1805. In Directory, 1796−1834.
BW − B.WENMAN

JOSHUA L. WENTWORTH (JASON)   1834
Lowell, Mass., until 1837. In Boston, 1846.
J.WENTWORTH

WENTWORTH & CO.   1850
New York.
WENTWORTH & CO

BENJAMIN WEST   1830
Boston, Mass. Advertised, "1½ metres from South Bridge."
B.WEST

JOHN L. WESTERVELT   1826−   1845
Newburgh, N.Y.
JLW

CHARLES WILLIAM WESTPHAL   1802
Philadelphia, Pa., at 118 Sassafras Street; 209 Callow Hill in
1811.
C.WESTPHAL

THOMAS WHARTENBY   1811
Philadelphia, Pa., at 47 Shippen Street. Firm of Whartenby &
Bumm, 1816−1818.
TW − WHARTENBY

WHARTENBY & BUMM   1816
Philadelphia, Pa. Thomas Whartenby and Peter Bumm at 196
South Third Street until 1818.
WHARTENBY & BUMM

CALVIN WHEATON   1764–   1790
Providence, R.I. Advertised, *United States Chronicle*, "At the Sign
of the Clock, opposite Friends Meeting House." Located on
Main Street, 1798.
C. WHEATON

WHEELER & BROOKS   1830
Livonia, N.Y.
WHEELER & BROOKS

SAMUEL H. WHERITT   1830
Richmond, Va.
S. WHERITT

WILLIAM WHETCROFT   1735–1799   1766
Annapolis, Md., "near the Town-gate." In Baltimore at Gay
Street, 1767. Returned to Annapolis where he married Frances
Cudmore Knapp, 1769. Charles Willson Peale painted his
portrait.
WW

AMOS WHITE   1745–1825   1766
East Haddam, Conn. Known as Silversmith and Sea Captain.
Served in Revolution. Later, located in Meriden, Conn. and
Maryland.
A. WHITE – WHITE

C. WHITE   1830
Mobile, Ala.
C. WHITE

EDWARD WHITE   1757
Ulster County, N.Y. Will dated, 1767.
E. WHITE

HENRY WHITE   CA. 1762–1827   1790
Fredericksburg, Va. In partnership with son, William H. White,
as H. White & Son, 1818–1822. Died May 10.
HW – H. WHITE

PEREGRINE WHITE   1747–1834   1774
Woodstock, Conn.
P. WHITE

SILAS WHITE 1754–1798   1791
New York, at Great Dock Street; 43 Roosevelt Street, 1792–
1794. Died September 23.
SW – S.WHITE

WILLIAM H. WHITE CA. 1800–1859   1822
Fredericksburg, Va., at the Sign of the Gold Watch. Son of
Henry White. Firm of Wm. H. White & Co., 1834–1836,
with Benjamin Smith.
W.H.WHITE

WILLIAM WILSON WHITE   1805
Philadelphia, Pa., at 111 North Second Street until 1806. In
New York, at 70½ Bowery Lane, 1835–1841.
WM.W.WHITE – W.W.WHITE

BRADFORD WHITING 1751–   1775
Norwich, Conn. In Great Barrington, Mass., 1787, where he
died.
B.WHITING

CHARLES WHITING 1725–1765   1750
Norwich, Conn. Married Honor Goodrich of Wethersfield in
1749. Land purchased in 1755 sold to Jacob Perkins in 1760.
CW – WHITING

EBENEZER WHITING 1735–1794   1760
Norwich, Conn. Born in Hartford, Conn. Brother of Charles
and William Bradford. Married Anne Fitch, November 29,
1767. In Savannah, Ga., 1768–1788. Married Betsy Turner,
1787. Died in Westfield, Mass.
E.WHITING

WILLIAM BRADFORD WHITING 1731–1796   1752
Norwich, Conn. Brother of Ebenezer and Charles. Died in
Canaan, N.Y.
WW – W.WHITING

THOMAS B. WHITLOCK   1805
New York, at 102 Pearl Street.
WHITLOCK

WILLIAM H. WHITLOCK   1805
New York, at 32 Ross Street. In Directory until 1827.
WM.H.WHITLOCK

AMOS WHITNEY   1800
New York, until 1805.
A.WHITNEY

EBEN WHITNEY   1805
New York, at 20 Chambers Street; 3 Franklin Square, 1822. In
Directory until 1828. Firm of Whitney & Hoyt, 1828.
E.WHITNEY—WHITNEY

M. F. WHITNEY   1823
New York and Schenectady, N.Y.
M.WHITNEY

WHITNEY & HOYT   1828
New York. Eben Whitney and Seymour Hoyt. In Directory until
1841.
WHITNEY & HOYT

EZRA WHITON 1797–1858   1819
Boston, Mass. In Directory, 1821–1825. At 87 Washington
Street, 1835; at 6 Court Avenue, 1850.
E.WHITON

WILLIAM WHITTEMORE 1710–1770   1735
Portsmouth, N.H. In Kittery, Me., 1755.
WHITTEMORE—WW

ALANSON D. WILCOX   1843
Troy, N.Y., until 1850.
A.D.WILCOX

ALVAN WILCOX 1783–1870   1805
Norwich, Conn., with Judah Hart as Hart & Wilcox until 1807.
Born in Berlin, Conn. Brother of Cyprian. Moved to New Jersey.
In Fayetteville, N.C., 1818–1824. In New Haven, Conn., at
corner of Church and Chapel Streets, 1824; advertised as silver
worker, 1841–1857.
A.WILCOX

CYPRIAN WILCOX 1795–1875   1816
New Haven, Conn. Born in Berlin, Conn. Younger brother of
Alvan. In Sparta, Ga., 1817. Returned to New Haven in 1827.
Was First Selectman; Judge of Probate, 1855–1857. Died in
Ithaca, N.Y.
C.WILCOX

ASA WILKINS   1810
Wiscasset, Me., until 1832.
A.WILKINS

A. WILLARD   1810
Utica, N.Y.
A.WILLARD

H. WILLARD   1818
Catskill, N.Y.
WILLARD

JAMES WILLARD   1815
East Windsor, Conn.
WILLARD

DEODAT WILLIAMS   CA. 1794–1857   1811
Boston, Mass.
D.WILLIAMS

JEHU WILLIAMS, SR.   1788–1859   1813
Lynchburg, Va. Born in Culpeper County, Va. In partnership
with John Victor as Williams & Victor, 1814–1845. In business
with his son, Jehu, Jr., as J. Williams & Son, 1856.
J.WILLIAMS – WILLIAMS

JOHN WILLIAMS   1793
Philadelphia, Pa., at 91 North Front Street.
J.WILLIAMS

STEPHEN WILLIAMS   –1811   1799
Providence, R.I. Advertised as jeweler and goldsmith. Died in
Scituate, Mass.
S.WILLIAMS

WILLIAM A. WILLIAMS   1787–1846   1809
Alexandria, Va. At Pennsylvania Avenue, Washington, D.C. in
1829. In Directory until 1843.
W.A.WILLIAMS

WILLIAMS & VICTOR   1814
Lynchburg, Va., until 1845. Jehu Williams and John Victor.
Dissolved upon the death of John Victor, October 21, 1845.
WILLIAMS & VICTOR – W & V

SAMUEL WILLIAMSON   1794
Philadelphia, Pa., advertised at 13 North Second Street; 118
South Front Street until 1813. Firms of Simmons & Williamson,
with Anthony Simmons, 1797–1798; Richards & Williamson,
with Samuel R. Richards, Jr., 1797–1800.
SW – WILLIAMSON

ANDREW WILLIS   1842
Boston, Mass.
ANDREW WILLIS

J. WILLIS   1820
Boston, Mass.
J.WILLIS

STILLMAN WILLIS   1813
Boston, Mass., at Union Street. In Directory until 1825.
S.WILLIS

WILLIAM S. WILLIS   1830
Boston, Mass.
WM.S.WILLIS

SAMUEL WILMOT   1777–1846   1800
New Haven, Conn. Firm of Wilmot & Stillman until 1808.
Member of Hiram Lodge #1, March 15, 1804. Removed to
Georgetown, S.C., 1825–1843.
S.WILMOT–WILMOT

SAMUEL & THOMAS T. WILMOT   1837
Charleston, S.C., listed on King Street after store burned in the
Great Fire of 1838.
S & T.T.WILMOT

THOMAS T. WILMOT   1840
Charleston, S.C. Firm of Samuel & Thomas T. Wilmot, 1837,
on King Street. In Directory until 1841.
T.T.WILMOT

HOSEA WILSON   –1819   1812
Philadelphia, Pa., at Second Street. In Baltimore, Md., 1814; at
126 Baltimore Street, 1817–1819.
H.WILSON

HOSEA WILSON & CO.   1814
Baltimore, Md., at 94 Baltimore Street until 1816.
H.WILSON & CO

ROBERT WILSON   1805
New York, at 25 Dey Street. Advertised, *Republican Watch-Tower*,
December 22, 1802, "Reward $10. for six teaspoons stolen from
23 Dey Street, marked R W MAKER." In Philadelphia, Pa. in
1816 at 80 North 5th Street until 1846. Firm of R. & W. Wilson, 1825.
R W

R. & W. WILSON   1825
Philadelphia, Pa., until 1846. Located at 82 North Fifth Street.
Robert and William Wilson.
R & W.W – R & W.WILSON

S. & S. WILSON   1805
Philadelphia, Pa.
S & S.WILSON

WILLIAM WILSON   1755–1829   1785
Abingdon, Md. Surveyor and Silversmith. Mentioned in land
records from 1782–1807. Firm of Wilson & Toy, 1790. Died in
Harford County, Md.
WW

WILSON & TOY   1790
Abingdon, Md. William Wilson and Joseph Toy worked in
partnership.
WW IT

CHRISTIAN WILTBERGER   1766–1851   1793
Philadelphia, Pa. Married Ann Warner, in Christ Church,
March or May 26, 1791. Bill from Wiltberger & Smith to
Jonathan Meredith for, "Brass Kettle, £3, 13 H.P., Philadelphia,
July 25, 1796." Firm of Wiltberger & Alexander, 1797. Advertised, *Federal Gazette*, April 29, 1799; as "Silversmith and Jeweller, Informs his Friends and the Public, that he has removed from
33 South-Second Street to No. 13 North Second Street, nearly
opposite Christ Church, where he continues to carry on the
business in all its branches as usual. A considerable quantity of
silver wares manufactured immediately under his own inspec-
tion, which he means to sell on most reasonable terms." Listed in
Directory until 1819. Died in October.
C.WILTBERGER

JOHN WINCKLER   1730–1803   1761
Charleston, S.C. Born in Essling, Germany, April 18. In Lon-
don, England, in 1751 to learn his trade and English. In
Raleigh, N.C. in 1763. Died in Boydton, Va.
IW

MOSES WING   1760–1809   1785
Windsor, Conn. Born in Rochester, Mass. In Worcester, Mass.,
1805–1809. Died in Windsor, October 23.
M.WING

EDWARD WINSLOW   1669–1753   1695
Boston, Mass. Born November 1. Son of Edward and Elizabeth
Hutchinson Winslow. Apprenticed to Jeremiah Dummer.
Married (1) Hannah Moody, daughter of Rev. Joshua Moody of
First Church of Boston, (2) Elizabeth Dixie. Appointed Consta-
ble in 1699. Freeman in 1702. Advertised in 1711. Captain of
Artillery in 1714. Sheriff of Suffolk County, 1728–1743.

Colonel in Boston Regiment, 1733. Judge of Inferior Court of Common Pleas. Master of Peter Oliver, William Pollard and nephew, Moody Russell. Working in 1734. Died in Boston. In the Yale University Art Gallery is a portrait of him by John Smibert. In the Garvan Collection of the Yale Gallery is a sugar box, 1702; a salver, 1711, by him.
E W

HUGH WISHART — 1784

New York, at two shops, 62 Wall Street and 98 Market Street; at 319 Pearl Street, 1797. Last at 66 Maiden Lane in 1810. Applied for Naturalization in Federal Courts of New York, January 2, 1806.
H. WISHART — WISHART

CHARLES & FREDERICK WITTICH — 1805

Charleston, S.C., at 25 Broad Street. Charles and Frederick continued until 1807.
C. F. WITTICH

WOLCOTT & GELSTON — 1820

Boston, Mass. Henry D. Wolcott and William Gelston. In Directory until 1830.
WOLCOTT & GELSTON

GENERAL JAMES WOLF 1780–1858 — 1800

Wilmington, Del., at Market and High Streets until 1814. Sold business to James Guthre, 1822. Active in Army with rank of Major, 1827. In Philadelphia, Pa. as G. James Wolf, 1830–1833.
G. J. WOLF

JAMES G. WOLF (WOLFF) — 1830

Philadelphia, Pa., at 125 North Second Street. In Directory until 1849.
I. WOLFF

FRANCIS H. WOLFE — 1829

Philadelphia, Pa., at 9 Norris Alley until 1845.
F. H. WOLFE

WOLFE & WRIGGINS — 1837

Philadelphia, Pa., at Chestnut and Fifth Streets. Francis H. Wolfe and Thomas Wriggins.
WOLFE & WRIGGINS

JOHN WOLTZ — 1811

Shepherdstown, Va., now W. Va. Advertised June 7, 1811
I. B. WOLTZ

BENJAMIN B. WOOD   1805
New York, at 47 Beaver Street until 1811; 96 Reade Street,
1815. In Directory until 1846.
B.B.WOOD – B.WOOD

J. E. WOOD   1845
New York.
J.E.WOOD

JOHN WOOD   1770
New York. Advertised, *New York Gazette*, April 30: ". . . Situated
in the lower end of Maiden-lane, near the upper end of the
Fly-Market, where he intends to carry on the gold and silver's
work, in its various branches . . ." In Schenectady, N.Y., 1780–
1792.
I.WOOD – J.WOOD

A. & W. WOOD   1850
New York, at 55 Thompson Street.
A & W.WOOD

WOOD & HUGHES   1846
New York, at 142 Fulton Street.
W & H – WOOD & HUGHES

BANCROFT WOODCOCK   1732–1817   1754
Wilmington, Del. Married Ruth Andrews, June 28, 1759.
Advertised in *Penna. Gazette*, July 4, 1754; "Goldsmith. Hereby
informs the publick, that he has set up his business in Wilmington, near the upper Market house, where all persons that
please to favor him with their custom, may be supplied with all
sorts of Gold and Silver work, after the neatest and newest
fashions. N.B. Said Woodcock gives full value for old gold and
silver." Continued at same address in 1772. Master of son, Isaac,
and nephew, Thomas Byrnes. Died, 1817, and buried in Friends
Meeting Yard. Firm of Woodcock & Byrnes, 1793.
BW – B.WOODCOCK – WOODCOCK

ISAAC WOODCOCK   1787
Wilmington, Del. Son of Bancroft whose silversmith tools he
inherited. In Hagerstown, Md., 1795.
I.WOODCOCK

WOODCOCK & BYRNES   1793
Wilmington, Del. Bancroft Woodcock and his nephew and
apprentice, Thomas Byrnes, in partnership.
W & BYRNES

FREEMAN WOODS   1766–1834   1791
New York, at 11 Smith Street until 1793. In New Bern, North
Carolina, 1794–1834.
FW – WOODS

ANTIPAS WOODWARD   1763–1812   1791
Middletown, Conn. Shop located, "Under the Printing Office."
Born in Waterbury, Conn. In 1792, advertised, North of the
Coffee-house, where he continues to carry on his business.
AW – WOODWARD

WOODWARD & GROSJEAN   1847
Boston, Mass., at 13 Court Square until dissolved in 1850. Eli
Woodward was the senior member.
W & G

JEREMIAH WARD WOOL   1769–   1791
New York. Freeman, June 24. Married Deborah Bratt, July 28,
1790. Listed as a Member of the General Society of Mechanics
and Tradesmen.
I W

THOMAS WRIGGINS   1837
Philadelphia, Pa. In Directory, 1837–1846. Firms of Wriggins
& Co., 1831; Wolfe & Wriggins, 1837; T. Wriggins & Co.,
1842.
T. WRIGGINS

WILLIAM WRIGHT   1740
Charleston, S.C. until 1751. In Petersburg, Va. in 1777.
W. WRIGHT

JOSEPH WYATT   1797
Philadelphia, Pa., at Callowhill Street and Cable Lane until
1798.
J W

ELEAZER WYER, JR.   1786–1848   1806
Portland, Me. In 1820, at 1 Prebles Road. Son of Eleazer Wyer,
silversmith of Boston, Mass. Firms of Wyer & Farley; Wyer &
Noble.
E. WYER

WYER & FARLEY   1828
Portland, Me., until 1832. Eleazer Wyer and Charles Farley.
WYER & FARLEY

BENJAMIN WYNKOOP   1675–1728   1698
New York. Son of Cornelius of Kingston, N.Y. Baptised in
Kingston, N.Y., April 18, 1675. Married Femmetji Van Der
Heul, October 20, 1692. Freeman, August 9, 1698. Collector
and Assessor of Taxes, 1703–1722. Son, Cornelius, continued
business. *New York Gazette* #229, "Dwelling House For Sale in
Bridge Street.", April 3, 1728. Assessment Roll, February,
1730, House £35.
BWK – WKB

BENJAMIN WYNKOOP, JR.   1705–1766   1730
Fairfield, Conn. Son of Benjamin, brother of Cornelius. Baptised, May 23, 1705. Married Eunice Burr, November 22,
1730, daughter of Judge Peter Burr.
BW

CORNELIUS WYNKOOP   1701–   1724
New York. Son of Benjamin. Married Elizabeth Vander Spiegel,
sister of Jacobus Vander Spiegel, silversmith, May 9, 1724.
Freeman, January 10, 1726. Continued business of father in
South Ward in 1727. House and estate assessed at £20, 1730,
North Ward. Retired in 1740.
CWK – WKC

JACOBUS WYNKOOP   1765
Kingston, N.Y.
WYNKOOP

CHRISTOPHER WYNN   1795–1883   1820
Baltimore, Md. Born in Centerville, Md. Apprenticed to Simon
Wedge. Listed at 44 South Charles Street, 1822. Working until
1883.
C.WYNN

[Y]

S. YATES   1810
Albany, N.Y.
SY – S.YATES

S. YATES & CO.   1825
Albany, N.Y.
SY & CO

ELIJAH YEOMANS   1738–1794   1771
>   Hadley, Mass., until 1783. Born in Tolland, Conn. In
>   Middletown, Conn., 1792. Advertised in Hartford, Conn.,
>   1794.
>   EY – YEOMANS

DANIEL YOU   –1750   1743
>   Charleston, S.C. Advertised, *South Carolina Gazette*, 1744, at
>   Broad Street; 1747; 1752, "Stolen, out of the Printer's House,
>   Four Silver Table Spoons, weighing about 2 Ounces and a half
>   each, one of them marked I.G, and pretty old; the other three
>   with maker's name twice stamp'd near the bowl, thus: D.YOU.
>   Who ever will discover the thief so that he may be convicted, or
>   will restore the spoons to me shall have a reward of Five Pounds."
>   Member of the South Carolina Society in 1749.
>   DY – YON – YOU

THOMAS YOU   –1786   1753
>   Charleston, S.C. Advertised, *South Carolina Gazette*, August 25,
>   1764–5, "Copper-plate view of St. Michaels Church engraved in
>   London." In *South Carolina Gazette* and *Country Journal*, De-
>   cember 17, 1765–6–8, "Plate of West Prospect of St. Philips."
>   Advertised at the sign of the Golden Cup on King Street, *South
>   Carolina Gazette*, to January 30, 1775; "Spoons of all Sorts.
>   Punch Bowls, Slop Ditto, Sugar Dishes, Pint Mugs, Strainers,
>   Ladles, Pepper Boxes, Salt Cellars, Rings, Buttons, Buckles,
>   and many other Articles. And, as his Dependence is entirely on
>   the working part, he will endeavor to merit the Favor of those
>   who will be kind enough to employ him." Son of Daniel You.
>   Member of the South Carolina Society, 1756. A land transaction,
>   1783, mentions Thomas You and wife, Elizabeth Clifford. Died
>   May 24.
>   TY

ALEXANDER YOUNG   1784–1856   1807
>   Camden, S.C., from Baltimore, Md. Born in Scotland. Firm of
>   A. Young & Co., 1845. Working until 1856.
>   YOUNG

EBENEZER YOUNG   1756–   1778
>   Hebron, Conn., until 1780.
>   YOUNG

LEVI YOUNG   1827
>   Bridgeport, Conn., opposite the shop of Peck & Porter on Water
>   Street.
>   L.YOUNG

J. T. YOUNG   1845
Petersburg, Va.
J.T.YOUNG

S. E. YOUNG   1840
Laconia, N.H.
S.E.YOUNG

WILLIAM YOUNG   1761
Philadelphia, Pa. Apprenticed to Joseph Richardson. Adver-
tised, *Penna. Gazette*, September 24; "In Second Street three
doors above Arch Street . . . makes and sells all sorts of
Goldsmith's Work; Where may be had, at most reasonable
Rates, Chased and plain Tea-pots, Sugar-dishes, Cream-pots,
Castors and Salts. Silver Handle Knives and Forks, with Cases of
different sizes, and sundry other Things too tedious to mention."
In *Penna. Gazette*, June 30, 1768, "Said, Young would take an
Apprentice of a reputable Family, and an Ingenios Turn, if any
should apply within three weeks, to serve not less than five
years." Mentioned as a witness to a will in Philadelphia County
in 1778.
WY – W.YOUNG

[Z]

GOTFRIED M. ZAHM   1840
Lancaster, Pa.
G.M.ZAHM

ZAHM & JACKSON   1830
New York.
ZAHM & JACKSON

ISAAC ZANE   1747–   1795
Zanesville, Ohio. Born in Wheeling, W. Va.
I.ZANE

JESSE SHENTON ZANE   –1852   1796
Wilmington, Del. Son of Joel and Esther Zane. Married, Sep-
tember 18, 1794, Susannah Hanson of Wilmington. Advertised,
The Delaware Gazette, July 5, 1796, "The corner of Third and
Market-street (Opposite Patrick O'Flinn's Tavern) the subscriber
carries on the silversmith's Business in its various Branches, and
gives The highest price for old silver." Moved to Philadelphia,
Pa. in 1813.
J.ZANE

Marks of Early American Silversmiths
1650–1850

P.M.–Pseudo English Hall Marks.

S.M.–Standard Marks.

B.M.–Baltimore Assay Office Marks.

ASTERISKS

An asterisk after a mark indicates that information exists about the silver upon which the mark was found. See "A List of Silver Objects upon which the Following Marks were Located," following this section.

A.A.MEAD

Almon Ainsworth Mead
Montpelier, Vt.   1846

A·ARMSTRONG

Allen Armstrong
Philadelphia   1806

AB   **AB**

Adrian Bancker
New York   1725

AB   **AB**

Andrew Billings
Poughkeepsie, N.Y.   1773

AB   *

Abner Bradley
Watertown, Conn.   1778

AB   **AB**

Abel Buel
New Haven, Conn.   1761

A·BEACH   **A·BEACH**
A·BEACH

A. Beach
Hartford, Conn.   1823

A.B.HALL

Abraham B. Hall
Geneva, N.Y.   1806

A.B.HOLMES   *

Adrian B. Holmes
New York   1801

A·BILLINGS   **A·BILLING**   *

Andrew Billings
Poughkeepsie, N.Y.   1773

ABLANCHARD
A·BLANCHARD   **⚜**   *

Asa Blanchard
Lexington, Ky.   1808

A·BRADLEY
✱   **A·BRADLEY**   **✱**

Abner Bradley
Watertown, Conn.   1778

ABRASHER

A. Brasher
New York   1790

A·BRASIER

Amable Brasier
Philadelphia   1794

⚜   **A·BRINSMAID**   **⚜**

Abraham Brinsmaid
Burlington, Vt.   1796

AC

Alexander Cameron
Albany, N.Y.   1813

AC

Abraham Carlisle
Philadelphia   1791

AC

Aaron Cleveland
Norwich, Conn.   1820

AC   **AC**   **AC**

Arnold Collins
Newport, R.I.   1690

⬥   **⬦**   **⬤**
⬤   **⬤**   **JOHN A.MILLER**   *

Albert Cole
New York   1844

AC

Alexander Crouckeshanks
Boston   1768

ACarlisle   *ACarlisle*

Abraham Carlisle
Philadelphia   1791

235

A·C·BENEDICT

A·C·BENEDICT 28 BOWERY *

Andrew C. Benedict
New York 1840

A & C·BRANDT

A. & C. Brandt
Philadelphia 1800

A·C·BURR

Albert Chapin Burr
Rochester, N.Y. 1826

A·CLEVELAND

Aaron Cleveland
Norwich, Conn. 1820

A·CUTLER

A·CUTLER Boston

A. Cutler
Boston 1820

AD **AD**

Amos Doolittle
New Haven, Conn. 1780

AD

Abraham Dubois
Philadelphia 1777

ADAMS

Nathan Adams
Wiscasset, Me. 1785

A·DICKINSON

Anson Dickinson
Litchfield, Conn. 1800

A·DIKEMAN

Aaron Dikeman
New York 1824

A·DUBOIS **A Dubois**
A·Dubois

Abraham Dubois
Philadelphia 1777

A·D·WILCOX

Alanson D. Wilcox
Troy, N.Y. 1843

AE

Alfred Elderkin
Windham, Conn. 1792

AE

John Aaron Elliott
Sharon, Conn. 1815

AEW **A·E·W**

Andrew E. Warner
Baltimore, Md. 1805

A·E·WARNER **II²**

Andrew E. Warner
Baltimore, Md. 1805

AF

Abraham G. Forbes
New York 1769

A.F.B. **BOSTON**

A. F. Burbank
Worcester, Mass. 1845

A.F.BURBANK

A.F.BURBANK *

A. F. Burbank
Worcester, Mass. 1845

A.Forbes *

Abraham G. Forbes
New York 1769

A·GERRISH

Andrew Gerrish
Portsmouth, N.H. 1814

AGF **NYORK**

Abraham G. Forbes
New York 1769

A.G.STORM

Abraham G. Storm
Poughkeepsie, N.Y.   1800

A&G.W.

A. & G. Welles
Boston   1807

A&G.WELLES

A. & G. Welles
Boston   1807

AH   *

Andrew Hays
New York   1769

Ahasuerus Hendricks
New York   1678

AHENDERSON

A. A. Henderson
Philadelphia   1837

✿✿✿ A.HENDERSON.

Adam Henderson
Poughkeepsie, N.Y.   1837

A.HEWS JR   A.Hews Jr

Abraham Hews, Jr.
Boston   1823

A.HEWS JR & CO

A. Hews, Jr. & Co.
Boston   1845

A.HOLMES

Adrian B. Holmes
New York   1801

AIKEN   *Aiken*

George Aiken
Baltimore, Md.   1787

A.JACKSON

A. Jackson
Norwalk, Conn.   1840

A.JACOBS

Abel Jacobs   S.M.
Philadelphia   1816

A.J.&Cº

A. J. Jacobs & Co.   S.M.
Philadelphia   1820

A.Jones.
A.JONES. GREENFIELD.

Albert Jones
Greenfield, Mass.   1825

A.JOHNSTON

A. Johnston
Philadelphia   1830

AK

Alexander Kerr
Williamsburg, Va.   1730

AKERLY & BRIGGS   *

Akerly & Briggs
New York   1845

AL

Aaron Lane
Elizabeth, N.J.   1784

AL

Adam Lynn
Alexandria, Va.   1796

A.L.CLAPP

A. L. Clapp
New York   1802

ALEONARD   **A.LEONARD**

Allen Leonard
New York   1827

ALLCOCK&ALLEN

Allcock & Allen
New York   1820

A.L.Lincoln

A. L. Lincoln
St. Louis, Mo.   1850

A·LOCKWOOD

Alfred Lockwood
New York   1817

A·LOGAN

Adam Logan
New York   1803

A.LOWELL

Abner Lowell
Portland, Me.   1830

A·LYNN **A·LYNN** **A·Lynn**

Adam Lynn
Alexandria, Va.   1796

AM

Aaron Musgrave, Jr.
West Chester, Pa.   1794

A MATHEY

A.MATHEY ▣ ▩ ▣ *

Augustus Mathey
New York   1825

A·MOULTON

Abel Moulton
Newburyport, Mass.   1815

A.MUNGER

Asa Munger   P.M.
Herkimer, N.Y.   1810

A.MUNGER & SON

A. Munger & Son
Auburn, N.Y.   1840

A.M.WARD   **HARTFORD** ▣ ▣ *

A. M. Ward
Hartford, Conn.   1845

AN

Abijah Northey
Salem, Mass.   1765

ANDRAS

William Andras   S.M.
New York   1795

ANDRAS & CO

Andras & Co.   S.M.
New York   1800

Andrew Willis

Andrew Willis
Boston   1842

ANDW E WARNER

Andrew E. Warner   B.M.
Baltimore, Md.   1805

A·NORTON **A·NORTON**

Andrew Norton
Goshen, Conn.   1787

ANTHONY

Lorenzo D. Anthony
Providence, R.I.   1830

ANTY RASCH

Anthony Rasch
Philadelphia   1807

AO **AO**

Andrew Oliver
Boston   1750

Artemas O. Fairchild
Wheeling, Va.   1839

A·OSTHOFF ▣

Andrew Osthoff
Baltimore, Md.   1810

AP

Alexander Petrie
Charleston, S.C.   1748

AP **AP** **AP**

Abraham Poutreau
New York   1726

A·PANGBORN A.PANGBORN

Amos Pangborn
Burlington, Vt.   1823

APARKER

Allen Parker
New York   1817

A.Pierson

A. Pierson
New York   1800

APPLETON

George B. Appleton
Salem, Mass.   1850

APPLETON

James Appleton
Marblehead, Mass.   1823

A·R   *

Abner Reeder
Philadelphia   1793

A·R   **PHIA**

Anthony Rasch
Philadelphia   1807

A&R

Andras & Richard
New York   1797

A·R & Co   *

Anthony Rasch & Co.
Philadelphia   1820

A·RASCH

Anthony Rasch
Philadelphia   1807

A·RASCH & CO

Anthony Rasch & Co.
Philadelphia   1820

A·REEDER

Abner Reeder
Philadelphia   1793

A&RIKER

Alexander & Riker
New York   1797

ARNOLD   **ARNOLD**

Thomas Arnold
Newport, R.I.   1760

A·ROBINSON

Anthony W. Robinson
Philadelphia   1798

AS   **AS**

Abraham Schuyler
Albany, N.Y.   1769

AS

Asa Sibley
Woodstock, Conn.   1785

AS

Anthony Simmons
Philadelphia   1797

AS   **AS**   **AS**   *   **AS**   *   *AS*   *

Abraham Skinner
New York   1756

AS

Adam Stone
Baltimore, Md.   1804

A·SANBORN   **LOWELL**

A·Sanborn   **LOWELL**   *

A. Sanborn   P.M.
Lowell, Mass.   1850

A·SCOTT   **A·Scott**   **A·Scott**   *

Alexander Scott
Chambersburg, Pa.   1800

A·SIMMONS

Anthony Simmons
Philadelphia   1797

A.Skinner

Abraham Skinner
New York   1756

A.T **AT** **A·T**

Armistead Truslow
Lynchburg, Va.   1813

AT **AT** **AT** **AT**

Andrew Tyler
Boston   1715

A·T·BATTEL

Albert T. Battel
Utica, N.Y.   1840

A·TYLER **A·TYLER**

Andrew Tyler
Boston   1715

AU

Andrew Underhill
New York   1780

A·UNDERHILL

Andrew Underhill
New York   1780

 Austin **Austin**

Ebenezer J. Austin
Charlestown, Mass.   1760

Austin

Nathaniel Austin
Boston   1760

AW

Antipas Woodward
Middletown, Conn.   1791

AW

Ambrose Ward
New Haven, Conn.   1767

A.Welles **A.WELLES**

Alfred Welles
Hebron, Conn.   1804

A·WHITE

Amos White
East Haddam, Conn.   1766

A·WHITNEY

Amos Whitney
New York   1800

A.WILCOX *A.WILCOX*

Alvan Wilcox
Norwich, Conn.   1805

A·WILKINS ✪ **B D**

Asa Wilkins
Wiscasset, Me.   1810

A·WILLARD

A. Willard
Utica, N.Y.   1810

A & W·WOOD

A. & W. Wood   S.M.
New York   1850

A·YOUNG

Alexander Young
Camden, S.C.   1807

🦅 **B** 🔱

Theophilus Bradbury, II
Newburyport, Mass.   1815

Babcock

Samuel Babcock
Middletown, Conn.   1812

BACHMAN

A. Bachman   S.M.
New York   1848

BACON & SMITH

Bacon & Smith
Boston   1840

BAILEY & CO
BAILEY & Cº 🔲🔲🔲 *   *
BAILEY & Co. 136 CHESTNUT ST.

Bailey & Co.
Philadelphia   1848

BAILEY & KITCHEN

Bailey & Kitchen
Philadelphia 1833

BALDWIN   **BALDWIN**

Ebenezer Baldwin
Hartford, Conn.   1810

BALDWIN   *

Jabez C. Baldwin
Boston   1800

BALDWIN & CO

Baldwin & Co.
Newark, N.J.   1830

BALDWIN & JONES

Baldwin & Jones
Boston   1813

BALL

William Ball
Philadelphia   1759

BALL BLACK & CO

BALL 950 & CO. NEW YORK

Ball, Black & Co.   S.M.
New York   1850

BALL & HEALD

Ball & Heald
Baltimore, Md.   1812

BALL TOMPKINS & BLACK

BALL, TOMPKINS & BLACK   *

Ball, Tompkins & Black   S.M.
New York   1839

BARD & LAMONT

BARD & LAMONT   **PHILADA**   *

Bard & Lamont
Philadelphia   1841

BARKER & MUMFORD

Barker & Mumford
Newport, R.I.   1817

Barry   **BARRY**   **No92**

Barry

Standish Barry   B.M.
Baltimore, Md.   1784

BASSETT

Francis Bassett
New York   1774

BASSETT &   **ALBANY**   *
WARFORD

Bassett & Warford
Albany, N.Y.   1800

BAYEUX

Henry Bayeux
Troy, N.Y.   1801

BAYLEY   **BAYLEY**   *

Simeon A. Bayley
New York   1789

BB   **BB**   **BRIDGEPORT**

Barzillai Benjamin
Bridgeport, Conn.   1815

BB   **BB**

Benjamin Brenton
Newport, R.I.   1717

BB

Benjamin Brenton
Newport, R.I.   1732

BB

Benjamin Bunker
Nantucket, Mass.   1780

BB

Benjamin Bussey
Dedham, Mass.   1778

B. BARTON

Benjamin Barton
Alexandria, Va.   1801

B. BEMENT

Butler Bement
Pittsfield, Mass.   1810

B.BENJAMIN

Barzillai Benjamin
Bridgeport, Conn.   1815

B.B.WOOD

Benjamin B. Wood
New York   1805

B·BURT   **BBURT**   **B·BURT**

Benjamin Burt
Boston   1750

BC

Benjamin Cleveland
Newark, N.J.   1800

B.C

Beriah Chittenden
New Haven, Conn.   1787

B.C.Frobisher

Benjamin C. Frobisher
Boston   1816

B.C.G

Benjamin Clark Gilman
Exeter, N.H.   1784

B·Cleveland   **B·CLEVELAND**
B.CLEVELAND

Benjamin Cleveland
Newark, N.J.   1800

B.COLEMAN

Benjamin Coleman
Burlington, N.J.   1795

B+D   *

Barzillai Davison
Norwich, Conn.   1765

B&D   **B&D**

Barrington & Davenport
Philadelphia   1806

B.Dexter   **Pure Coin**   **New Bedford**
B.DEXTER

B. DEXTER   **PURE COIN**   *

B. Dexter
New Bedford, Mass.   1825

B.DROWNE

Benjamin Drowne
Portsmouth, N.H.   1780

B.DUPUY

Barnard Dupuy
Raleigh, N.C.   1828

BEACH   **BEACH**

Miles Beach
Litchfield, Conn.   1771

BEAL   **BEAL**

Caleb Beal
Hingham, Mass.   1796

B.E.COOK
NORTHAMPTON

B. E. COOK   **B.E.COOK**
NORTHAMPTON

Benjamin E. Cook
Northampton, Mass.   1825

BEEBE

William Beebe   S.M.
New York   1850

BEMENT

Butler Bement
Pittsfield, Mass.   1810

BENEDICT & SCUDDER   *
NEW YORK

Benedict & Scudder
New York   1827

BENEDICT & SQUIRE

Benedict & Squire
New York   1839

BENJAMIN
BURT

Benjamin Burt
Boston   1750

BENNETT & THOMAS

Bennett & Thomas
Petersburg, Va.   1812

BENTLEY *Bentley*

Thomas Bentley
Boston 1786

B·G **◆☗◙** **B·G ◻☒◩** *

Baldwin Gardiner S.M.
Philadelphia 1814

BG

Benjamin Greene
Boston, Mass. 1733

B·GARDINER

Baldwin Gardiner S.M.
Philadelphia 1814

B·GARDINER **NEW YORK**

B.GARDINER **☒☞•☒☒** *

Baldwin Gardiner S.M.
New York 1827

B.GARDINER & CO

B. Gardiner & Co.
New York 1836

B G & CO

B. Gardiner & Co.
New York 1836

B.Goodwin **B GOODWIN**

Benjamin Goodwin
Boston 1756

B:GREEN

Bartholomew Green
Boston 1724

BH **BH**

Benjamin Hiller
Boston 1711

BH **B∗H**

Benjamin Hurd
Boston 1760

B.H.Tisdale **B·H·TISDALE** **Pure Coin**

B.H.Tisdale **Newport.R.I**

Benjamin H. Tisdale
Newport, R.I. 1812

B&H

Brinsmaid & Hildreth
Burlington, Vt. 1850

B∗Hurd **B·Hurd** *

Benjamin Hurd
Boston 1760

BIGELOW & BROTHERS

Bigelow & Brothers
Boston 1840

BIGELOW BROS. & KENNARD

Bigelow Bros. & Kennard
Boston 1845

☺ BIGGER ☺ *

Gilbert Bigger
Baltimore, Md. 1783

B·INGRAHAM *

Barton Ingraham
Providence, R.I. 1801

Birge Brackett & Co

Birge, Brackett & Co.
Brattleboro, Vt. 1840

B &J

Boyce & Jones
New York 1825

B&J **N·YORK**

Boyce & Jones
New York 1825

B&J. COOPER

B. & J. Cooper
New York 1810

B & K

Bailey & Kitchen S.M.
Philadelphia 1833

BL **BL** *

Benjamin Lemar
Philadelphia 1775

BLACKMAN

John Clark Blackman
Bridgeport, Conn. 1827

BLEASOM & REED

BLEASOM & REED

Bleasom & Reed
Portsmouth, N.H.   1830

* *B. LINDSEY* *

Benjamin Lindsey
Providence, R.I.   1798

B. LORD   B. LORD

Benjamin Lord
Pittsfield, Mass.   1796

Blowers   Blowers   Blowers   *

John Blowers
Boston   1731

BR

Bartholomew Le Roux
New York   1738

BR   BR   *

Bartholomew Le Roux
New York   1687

B & M

Bradley & Merriman
New Haven, Conn.   1826

B & M

Barker & Mumford
Newport, R.I.   1817

B. MARSH

Benjamin Marsh   S.M
Albany, N.Y.   1840

BMBAILEY   LUDLOW.VT.

B.M.BAILEY   RUTLAND.VT.   *

Bradbury M. Bailey
Ludlow, Vt.   1848

B. MEAD   B. MEAD   *

Benjamin Mead
Wiscasset, Me.   1804

B. MOSS

Barnet Moss
Warrenton, Va.   1840

B. M. RIGGS

Benjamin McK. Riggs
Paris, Ky.   1820

B & M.M. SWAN   *

Benjamin & Moses Moody Swan
Augusta, Me.   1846

BOLLES & DAY   HARTFORD

Bolles & Day
Hartford, Conn.   1825

BOSWORTH

Samuel Bosworth
Buffalo, N.Y.   1816

BOUDO

Louis Boudo
Charleston, S.C.   1810

BOWER

C. Bower
Philadelphia   1828

BOYCE & JONES

Boyce & Jones
New York   1825

BOYD & MULFORD

Boyd & Mulford
Albany, N.Y.   1832

Boyden & Fenno

BOYDEN & FENNO

Boyden & Fenno
Worcester, Mass.   1825

Boyer   BOYER

Daniel Boyer
Boston   1750

BP   BP

Benjamin Pierpont
Boston   1756

B*PIERPONT   B*PIERPONT

Benjamin Pierpont
Boston   1756

B.PITMAN **PureCoin**
Benjamin Pitman
Providence, R.I. 1810

B & R
Brower & Rusher
New York 1834

B & R
Burnet & Ryder
Philadelphia 1795

BRADBURY **1825**
Theophilus Bradbury, II s.m.
Newburyport, Mass. 1815

BRADBURY ✿ **B** ✿
Theophilus Bradbury & Son
Newburyport, Mass. 1815

BRADY
E. Brady
New York 1825

BRASHER **N.YORK**
Ephraim Brasher
New York 1766

BREWSTER
Abel Brewster
Canterbury, Conn. 1797

BRIDGE **BRIDGE**
John Bridge
Boston 1751

✿ **BRINSMAID** ✿
Abraham Brinsmaid
Burlington, Vt. 1796

B.R.Jenkins
Benjamin R. Jenkins
Auburn, N.Y. 1830

B.R.NORTON
Benjamin R. Norton
Syracuse, N.Y. 1845

BRONAUGH
John Bronaugh
Richmond, Va. 1817

Brookhouse
Robert Brookhouse
Salem, Mass. 1800

BROOKS **BROOKS**

BROOKS *
Samuel Brooks
Philadelphia 1793

Brooks & Warrock
Brooks & Warrock
Norfolk, Va. 1795

 *
Brower & Rusher
New York 1834

BROWN
Edward Brown
Baltimore, Md. 1807

BROWN & ANDERSON *
Brown & Anderson
Wilmington, N.C. 1850

BROWN & KIRBY
Brown & Kirby
New Haven, Conn. 1850

BROWNE
Liberty Browne
Philadelphia 1801

BROWNE & SEAL
 *
Browne & Seal
Philadelphia 1810

BRYAN
Phillip Bryan
Philadelphia 1802

Bartholomew Schaats
New York   1695

BS

Benjamin Sanderson
Boston   1675

B&S

Beach & Sanford   P.M.
Hartford, Conn.   1785

B.STILLMAN

Barton Stillman
Westerly, R.I.   1810

B.SWAN

Benjamin Swan
Augusta, Me.   1815

B·T   **B·J** *

Benjamin Tappan
Northampton, Mass.   1768

BT&B

Ball, Tompkins & Black
New York   1839

B·T   **B·T**

Barent Ten Eyck
Albany, N.Y.   1735

BUCKLEY

J. B. Buckley
Philadelphia   1807

BUEL   **BUEL**   **BUEL**

Abel Buel
New Haven, Conn.   1761

BULLES & CHILDS
HARTFORD

Bulles & Childs
Hartford, Conn.   1840

BUMM &
SHEPPER

Bumm & Shepper
Philadelphia   1819

BURDICK

William S. Burdick
New Haven, Conn.   1812

Burger   **Burger**   **I**   **I**   **NYork**

John Burger
New York   1780

BURT

Benjamin Burt
Boston   1750

BUTLER & M'CARTY

Butler & M'Carty
Philadelphia   1850

BW

Bilious Ward
Middletown, Conn.   1750

BW   **B·W**

Barnabas Webb
Boston   1756

BW   **NYORK**   **BW**

Barnard Wenman
New York   1789

B·W   **B·W**

Bancroft Woodcock
Wilmington, Del.   1754

BW

Benjamin Wynkooop, Jr.
Fairfield, Conn.   1730

BW&Cº

Butler, Wise & Co.
Philadelphia   1842

B&W

Beach & Ward   S.M.
Hartford, Conn.   1790

B.WENMAN

Barnard Wenman
New York   1789

B.WEST
Benjamin West
Boston 1830

B.WHITING
Bradford Whiting
Norwich, Conn. 1775

B.WOOD
Benjamin B. Wood
New York 1805

B.WOODCOCK
Bancroft Woodcock
Wilmington, Del. 1754

Benjamin Wynkoop
New York 1689

C.A.B
Charles A. Burnett
Alexandria, Va. 1793

C.A.BURNETT
Charles A. Burnett
Alexandria, Va. 1793

C.A.BURR
Cornelius A. Burr
Rochester, N.Y. 1838

C.ALDIS **C.ALDIS**
Charles Aldis
New York 1814

C.ALLEN
Charles Allen
Boston 1760

CAMPBELL
Christopher Campbell
New York 1808

CAMPBELL **10.15**
Robert Campbell B.M.
Baltimore, Md. 1819

CAMPBELL
Thomas Boyce Campbell
Winchester, Va. 1822

CAMPBELL
William L. Campbell
Winchester, Va. 1810

CAMPBELL **J.MEREDITH**
Campbell & Meredith
Winchester, Va. 1820

CAMPBELL & POLK
Campbell & Polk
Winchester, Va. 1850

CANFIELD **CANFIELD**
Samuel Canfield
Middletown, Conn. 1780

CANFIELD **1843** *
Canfield & Brother
Baltimore, Md. 1830

CANFIELD & HALL
Canfield & Hall
Middletown, Conn. 1800

CAPELLE **ST.LOUIS**
J. Capelle
St. Louis, Mo. 1850

CARLETON
George Carleton
New York 1810

CARRELL
John & Daniel Carrell
Philadelphia 1785

Carson & Hall
Carson & Hall
Albany, N.Y. 1810

CART
Joseph Sayre Cart
Charleston, S.C. 1798

CARY

Lewis Cary
Boston   1815

C·B   **CB**

Caleb Beal
Hingham, Mass.   1796

GB   **C·B**

Clement Beecher
Berlin, Conn.   1801

C·BABBITT

Charles Babbitt
Taunton, Mass.   1815

C.BARD 205ARCH ST

Conrad Bard
Philadelphia   1825

CBEAL

Caleb Beal
Hingham, Mass.   1796

C.BEECHER.

Clement Beecher
Berlin, Conn.   1801

C·BILLON

Charles Billon
St. Louis, Mo.   1821

C.Boehme   **W**

Charles L. Boehme
Baltimore, Md.   1799

C.BOND

Charles Bond
Boston   1840

C.BRANDA

Charles Branda
Norfolk, Va.   1818

C.BREWER *C.Brewer*
C.BREWER

Charles Brewer
Middletown, Conn.   1810

C·BREWER & C°

Charles Brewer & Co.
Middletown, Conn.   1815

C.B.ROOT

Charles Boudinot Root
Raleigh, N.C.   1843

C·BURR   **C·BURR**   *C.Burr*

Christopher A. Burr
Providence, R.I.   1810

CC

Charles Candell
New York   1795

CC

Charles Carpenter
Norwich, Conn.   1790

CC

Christian Cornelius
Philadelphia   1810

C&C ❋ ❂ ❂   *

Colton & Collins   S.M.
New York   1825

C.C.COLEMAN

C. C. Coleman
Burlington, N.J.   1835

❂ C.C.&D ❂

Charters, Cann & Dunn
New York   1850

C.CHOYSENHOLDER PHILA   *

Charles Choysenholder
Philadelphia   1814

CC.NORTON

C. C. Norton
Hartford, Conn.   1820

CC.NORTON&W.PITKIN

Norton & Pitkin
Hartford, Conn.   1825

C.COEN & CO

C. Coen & Co.
New York 1810

C.CORNELIUS **C.Cornelius**

Christian Cornelius
Philadelphia 1810

C.C.& S

Curtiss, Candee & Stiles
Woodbury, Conn. 1831

C.D

Charles Davison
Norwich, Conn. 1805

C.DAVISON **C.DAVISON**

Charles Davison
Norwich, Conn. 1805

C.D.SULLIVAN

C. D. Sullivan
St. Louis, Mo. 1850

C.DUNN **W** **N.YORK**

Cary Dunn
New York 1765

C.E.D

Charles E. Disbrow
Norwalk, Conn. 1815

C.E.DISBROW **N.W**

C.E.DISBROW
NORWALK

Charles E. Disbrow
Norwalk, Conn. 1815

C.E.E

Charles Edward Evard
Leesburg, Va. 1848

C.FARLEY

Charles Farley
Portland, Me. 1812

C.F.GREENWOOD

Charles F. Greenwood
Norfolk, Va. 1848

C.FORBES

Colin V. G. Forbes S.M.
New York 1810

C.F.WITTICH

Charles & Frederick Wittich
Charleston, S.C. 1805

CG

Christopher Gallup
North Groton, Conn. 1785

CG ★ **CG** **CG**

Caesar Ghiselin
Philadelphia 1700

CG **CG** **CG** **CG** *

Christopher Giffing
New York 1815

C.GENNET **C.GENNET JR**

Charles Gennet, Jr.
Richmond, Va. 1837

C.Giffing **NY**

Christopher Giffing
New York 1815

CH **CH**

Charles Hall
Lancaster, Pa. 1765

CH →CH←

Charles Hequembourg, Jr.
New Haven, Conn. 1804

CH

Christopher Hughes
Baltimore, Md. 1771

C.HALE.

Charles Hale
Bangor, Me. 1845

C.Hall

Charles Hall
Lancaster, Pa. 1765

CHANDLER
Stephen Chandler
New York 1812

Charles Oliver Bruff
New York 1763

Charles Faris
Annapolis, Md. 1793

CHAS LUMSDEN
Charles Lumsden
Petersburg, Va. 1832

Charles Nordmeyer
Richmond, Va. 1845

CHAUDRON
Chaudron & Co.
Philadelphia 1807

CHAUDRON'S & RASCH *
Chaudron's & Rasch
Philadelphia 1812

CHEDELL
John H. Chedell
Auburn, N.Y. 1827

CHENEY
Martin Cheney
Windsor, Vt. 1803

C. HEQUEMBOURG JR.
Charles Hequembourg, Jr.
New Haven, Conn. 1804

C. Hill
Charles Hill
Canandaigua, N.Y. 1815

CHPHELPS
Charles H. Phelps
Bainbridge, N.Y. 1825

CHURCH & ROGERS
Church & Rogers
Hartford, Conn. 1825

CHURCHILL
Jesse Churchill
Boston 1795

CHURCHILL & TREADWELL
Churchill & Treadwell
Boston 1805

CJ
Clement Jackson, Jr.
Portsmouth, N.H. 1762

C & I. W. FORBES
Colin & J. W. Forbes
New York 1810

C. JOHNSON
Chauncey Johnson
Albany, N.Y. 1825

C & J. WARNER
C. & J. Warner
Salem, Mass. 1820

C & J.W FORBES
Colin & J. W. Forbes
New York 1810

CK **CK**
Cornelius Kierstede
New York 1696

C.KENDALL
Charles Kendall
New York 1787

CL **CB**
Charles Le Roux
New York 1710

CL
Charles Leach
Boston 1789

CLARK **CLARK** *

I. Clark
Boston 1737

CLARK **NORWALK**

Levi Clark
Norwalk, Conn. 1825

CLARK & ANTHONY

Clark & Anthony
New York 1790

CLARK & BRO

Clark & Brother
Norwalk, Conn. 1825

✿ **CLARK** **& Co** ✿ *
CLARK & C° *

Clark & Co.
Augusta, Ga. 1830

CLARK & COIT

Clark & Coit
Norwich, Conn. 1820

C·L·B 🐑

Charles L. Boehme
Baltimore, Md. 1799

C.L.BOEHME *C.L.Boehme*
C.L.Boehme *Sterling*

Charles L. Boehme
Baltimore, Md. 1799

C.L. BUSWELL

C. L. Buswell
Lebanon, N.H. 1845

CLEVELAND

🐑 **CLEVELAND** 🐑

William Cleveland
Norwich, Conn. 1791

C.LINDSLEY

Clark Lindsley
Hartford, Conn. 1845

CB **CR**

Charles Le Roux
New York 1710

C M

Cornelius Munson
Wallingford, Conn. 1763

C & M

Coit & Mansfield
Norwich, Conn. 1816

C·MAYSENHOELDER **PHILADA** *

Charles Maysenhoelder
Philadelphia 1810

C.MOORE

Charles Moore
Philadelphia 1803

C.MYGATT

Comfort Starr Mygatt
Danbury, Conn. 1785

C.O.B **COB**

Charles Oliver Bruff
New York 1763

C.O.BRUFF

Charles Oliver Bruff
New York 1763

COE & UPTON

Coe & Upton
New York 1840

COLTON & COLLINS *

Colton & Collins
New York 1825

C.O'NEIL

Charles O'Neil
New Haven, Conn. 1802

COOK

John Cook
New York 1795

COOKE & WHITE
Cooke & White
Norfolk, Va. 1829

COOLEY
Oliver B. Cooley
Utica, N.Y. 1828

Coolidge
Joseph Coolidge, Jr.
Boston 1770

COOPER & FISHER
131 AMITY ST. N.Y.

COOPER & FISHER
131 AMITY ST. N.Y.
Cooper & Fisher
New York 1850

CORBETT *
John Corbett
Whitingham, Vt. 1800

CORNELL
Walter Cornell
Providence, R.I. 1780

COWLES
Ralph Cowles
Cleveland, Ohio 1840

C&P   C&P
Clark & Pelletreau
New York 1819

C&P
Cleveland & Post
Norwich, Conn. 1815

C&P
Curry & Preston
Philadelphia 1831

C.P.A   *
Charles Platt Adriance
Richmond, Va. 1816

C.P.ADRIANCE
Charles Platt Adriance
Richmond, Va. 1816

C.PARKER
Caleb Parker, Jr.
Boston 1758

C·PARKMAN
Charles Parkman
Boston 1790

CPB
Charles P. Butler
Charleston, S.C. 1790

CP&U
Clark, Pelletreau & Upson
Charleston, S.C. 1823

CR
Christopher Robert
New York 1731

C·REDON
Claudius Redon   P.M.
New York 1828

CROWLEY & FARR   *
Crowley & Farr
Philadelphia 1823

C·S
Caleb Shields
Baltimore, Md. 1773

CS
Caleb Swan
Boston 1775

C° Faris
Charles Faris
Annapolis, Md. 1793

C. STEWART ENG. STERLING   *
Charles Stewart
New York 1833

CURRIER *

Edmund M. Currier
Hopkinton, N.H. 1815

Currier & Trott

Currier & Trott
Boston 1836

CURRY&PRESTON

Curry & Preston
Philadelphia 1831

CURTISS.CANDEE& STILES

Curtiss, Candee & Stiles
Woodbury, Conn. 1831

CURTIS &DUNNING

Curtis & Dunning
Burlington, Vt. 1821

CURTISS&STILES

Curtiss & Stiles
Woodbury, Conn. 1835

Cornelius Vander Burgh
New York 1675

C·V·GF

Colin V. G. Forbes
New York 1798

CW **CW**

Charles Whiting
Norwich, Conn. 1750

CW

Christian Wiltberger
Philadelphia 1793

CWARNER *C.Warner* *

 C.WARNER ⊞ *

Caleb Warner
Salem, Mass. 1805

C.WESTPHAL

Charles William Westphal
Philadelphia 1802

CWHEATON

Calvin Wheaton
Providence, R.I. 1790

C.WHITE **MOBILE**

C. White
Mobile, Ala. 1830

C.WILCOX *C. Wilcox*

Cyprian Wilcox
New Haven, Conn. 1816

.Wiltberger

Christian Wiltberger
Philadelphia 1793

C.W.STEWART

C. W. Stewart
Lexington, Ky. 1850

WK
C

Cornelius Wynkoop
New York 1724

C.WYNN

Christopher Wynn
Baltimore, Md. 1820

DARBY

John Darby
Charleston, S.C. 1801

Darby

William Darby
Charleston, S.C. 1790

DARROW

John F. Darrow S.M.
Catskill, N.Y. 1818

DAVID KINSEY

David I. Kinsey
Cincinnati, Ohio 1845

DAVIS

Joshua George Davis
Boston 1796

DAVIS

Samuel Davis
Plymouth, Mass.   1801

DAVIS.PALMER&CO

Davis, Palmer & Co.
Boston   1842

DAVIS &BROWN

Davis & Brown
Boston   1809

DAVIS.WATSON & CO

DAVIS·WATSON & CO   *

Davis, Watson & Co.
Boston   1825

DB

Duncan Beard
Appoquinimink Hundred, Del.
1765

DB   **D·B**

Daniel Boyer
Boston   1750

D&B   D&B P.M.

Downing & Baldwin
New York   1832

DBACKUS

Delucine Backus
New York   1792

DB &AD

Bayley & Douglas
New York   1798

D.BARRIERE

David Barriere
Baltimore, Md.   1806

DBH

Daniel Booth Hempsted
New London, Conn.   1820

DBH&CO

D. B. Hindman & Co.
Philadelphia   1833

D.B.HEMPSTED   PURE COIN

Daniel Booth Hempsted
New London, Conn.   1820

D.Billings

Daniel Billings
Preston, Conn.   1795

D.B.MILLER

D. B. Miller
Boston   1850

D.BROWN

D. Brown
Philadelphia   1811

D.B.Thompson

Daniel B. Thompson
Brattleboro, Vt.   1817

D·C   **DC**   *

Daniel Bloom Coen
New York   1787

DCF   **YORK**

Daniel C. Fueter
New York   1754

D.C.FULTON   *

David C. Fulton
Louisville, Ky.   1835

D & CO

De Forest & Co.
New York   1827

D.COEN

Daniel Bloom Coen
New York   1787

D.COLTON JR

Demas Colton, Jr.
New York   1826

DD   **DD**

Daniel Deshon
New London, Conn.   1730

D:D DD DD

Daniel Dupuy
Philadelphia   1745

DDD

Dupuy & Sons
Philadelphia   1784

D:DUPUY

Daniel Dupuy, Jr.
Philadelphia   1785

D.DUYCKINCK

D. Duyckinck
New York   1798

✹ De Larue ✹

John De Larue
New Orleans, La.   1822

D.E.LUCY   ✶

D. E. Lucy
Waterbury, Vt.   1850

DEMILT   N.YORK

Andrew Demilt
New York   1805

DENNIS&FITCH

Dennis & Fitch
New York   1836

Deverell

John Deverell
Boston   1785

D&E

Dyer & Eddy
Boston   1805

DG   HARTFORD

David Greenleaf, Jr.
Hartford, Conn.   1788

DG

Daniel Greenough
New Castle, N.H.   1708

D:G

David Griffeth
Portsmouth, N.H.   1757

D.GILLIS LEONARD S.M×D   ✶

D. Gillis Leonard   S.M.
Newburgh, N.Y.   1841

D. GODDARD.

Daniel Goddard
Worcester, Mass.   1817

D.Goddard & Cº

D. Goddard & Co.
Worcester, Mass.   1850

D.GODDARD & SON

D. Goddard & Son
Worcester, Mass.   1845

D.Greenleaf   D·Green leaf

David Greenleaf
Norwich, Conn.   1763

D.Griffeth   DGriffith

David Griffeth
Portsmouth, N.H.   1757

DH DH

David Hall
Philadelphia   1765

D·H

Daniel Henchman
Boston   1753

DHall   D·HALL

David Hall
Philadelphia   1765

D.HOTCHKISS

David Hotchkiss
Syracuse, N.Y.   1848

DJ

Daniel Jackson
New York   1782

DJ
David Jesse
Boston   1695

DI·Burger
David I. Burger
New York   1805

D·I·NORTHEE
David I. Northey
Salem, Mass.   1732

DJACKSON
Daniel Jackson
New York   1782

D.KINSEY
David I. Kinsey
Cincinnati, Ohio   1845

DL
Daniel Legare
Boston   1710

DM
David Moseley
Boston   1775

DM
David Mygatt
Danbury, Conn.   1800

D.M.FITCH
Dennis M. Fitch
Troy, N.Y.   1840

D.Moseley   **DMoseley**
David Moseley
Boston   1775

D.M.TYLER
D. M. Tyler
Boston   1810

D.MYGATT   **D.MYGATT**
David Mygatt
Danbury, Conn.   1800

D·N
Daniel Neall
Milford, Del.   1810

DN
David I. Northey
Salem, Mass.   1732

D·N·DOLE
Daniel Noyes Dole
Newburyport, Mass.   1804

D.NEALL
Daniel Neall
Milford, Del.   1810

D·NORTHEE
David I. Northey
Salem, Mass.   1732

DOANE   **DOANE**
Joshua Doane
Providence, R.I.   1740

D.OLIVER
Daniel Oliver
Philadelphia   1805

DORRANCE
Samuel Dorrance
Providence, R.I.   1803

DOWNING
George R. Downing
New York   1810

DOWNING & PHELPS
Downing & Phelps
Newark, N.J.   1810

D:P
Daniel Parker
Boston   1750

D&P   **NEWARK**
Downing & Phelps
Newark, N.J.   1810

D.PARKER   **D.PARKER**

Daniel Parker
Boston   1750

D.PLACE

Daniel Place
Rochester, N.Y.   1827

DR   **DR**

Daniel Russell
Newport, R.I.   1721

DR   **DR**   **D·R**   **D·R**   *

Daniel Rogers
Ipswich, Mass.   1760

D.ROGERS   **D·ROGERS**

D·Rogers

Daniel Rogers
Ipswich, Mass   1760

DS

David Smith
Lansingburgh, N.Y.   1787

D·S

Daniel Stanton
Stonington, Conn.   1776

DS

Daniel Syng
Lancaster, Pa.   1734

D.SMITH   **D.SMITH**

David Smith
Lansingburgh, N.Y.   1787

D.Stanton

Daniel Stanton
Stonington, Conn.   1776

D.SULLIVAN & CO

D. Sullivan & Co.
New York   1820

D.SYNG

Daniel Syng
Lancaster, Pa.   1734

DT   **DT**   **DT**

David Tyler
Boston   1781

D.T.G

Daniel T. Goodhue
Providence, R.I.   1824

D.T.GOODHUE

Daniel T. Goodhue
Providence, R.I.   1824

DUHME

Duhme & Co.
Cincinnati, Ohio   1839

DUMOUTET

John Baptiste Dumoutet
Philadelphia   1793

DUNBAR&BANGS

Dunbar & Bangs
Worcester, Mass.   1850

DUNBAR & STORY   **WORCESTER**   *

Dunbar & Story
Worcester, Mass.   1845

DV   **DV**   **DV**

Daniel Van Voorhis
Philadelphia   1782

DV   **DV**   *

David Vinton
Providence, R.I.   1790

DVV   **DV·V**

Daniel Van Voorhis
Philadelphia   1782

D.V VOORHIS

D.V.VOORHIS   *

Daniel Van Voorhis
Philadelphia   1782

Davis & Watson
Boston 1815

D. Waldron
New York 1789

Daniel Warner
Salem, Mass. 1816

Deodot Williams
Boston 1811

Daniel You
Charleston, S.C. 1743

Ebenezer J. Austin
Charlestown, Mass. 1760

E. A. Beauvais
St. Louis, Mo. 1840

Edwin Adriance
St. Louis, Mo. 1835

Easton & Sanford
Nantucket, Mass. 1830

Thomas E. Eayres
Boston 1785

Eleazer Baker
Ashford, Conn. 1785

Ephraim Brasher
New York 1766

Everadus Bogardus
New York 1698

Elias Boudinot
Philadelphia 1730

Ezekiel Burr
Providence, R.I. 1793

Eleazer Baker
Ashford, Conn. 1785

Ebenezer Balch
Hartford, Conn. 1750

Ezra B. Booth
Middlebury, Vt. 1829

E. B. Booth & Son P.M.
Rochester, N.Y. 1850

E. Benjamin & Co.
New Haven, Conn. 1830

Erastus Barton & Co.
New York 1822

Everard Benjamin
New Haven, Conn. 1830

Evearad Benjamin & Co.
New Haven, Conn. 1830

E. Berard
Philadelphia 1800

E.BORHEK **STANDARD**
E. Borhek
Philadelphia 1835

E·BOWMAN
Elias Bowman
Rochester, N.Y. 1834

E·BRADY
E. Brady
New York 1825

E·BROWN
Edward Brown
Baltimore, Md. 1807

E.BURNAP
Ela Burnap
Boston 1810

EBURR **EBurr** **E*BURR**
Ezekiel Burr
Providence, R.I. 1793

EC
Elias Camp
Bridgeport, Conn. 1825

EC **EC** **EC** *
Ebenezer Chittenden
Madison, Conn. 1765

EC
Ephraim Cobb
Plymouth, Mass. 1735

E.CAMP
Elias Camp
Bridgeport, Conn. 1825

E.C.BROWN
Elnathan C. Brown
Westerly, R.I. 1820

E·CHITTENDEN **E Chittenden**
Ebenezer Chittenden
Madison, Conn. 1765

E Cobb **ECobb**
Ephraim Cobb
Plymouth, Mass. 1735

E·COIT **PURE COIN**
Edward Coit
Norwich, Conn. 1825

E.COLE
Ebenezer Cole
New York 1818

E·COOK **E.COOK** *
Erastus Cook
Rochester, N.Y. 1815

E.C.STORM
E. C. Storm
Rochester, N.Y. 1815

E.CURRIER
Edmund M. Currier
Hopkinton, N.H. 1815

E.CUTLER
Eben Cutler
Boston 1846

ED **ED**
Edward Davis
Newburyport, Mass. 1775

E·DAVIS **EDavis**
Edward Davis
Newburyport, Mass. 1775

E&D·KINSEY
E. & D. Kinsey
Cincinnati, Ohio 1845

E*DODGE **E.Dodge**
Ezekiel Dodge
New York 1792

E.E.BAILEY
Ebenezer Eaton Bailey
Portland, Me. 1825

EE & SC BAILEY

E. E. & S. C. Bailey
Portland, Me.   1830

E.F. Miller

Edward F. Miller
Providence, R.I.   1810

E·FRANCIS·

Edward Francis
Leesburg, Va.   1828

EG

Eliakim Garretson
Wilmington, Del.   1785

E.GARRETSON

Eliakim Garretson
Wilmington, Del.   1785

E.G. Dole

Ebenezer Gove Dole
Hallowell, Me.   1831

E.Gifford

E. Gifford
Fall River, Mass.   1825

E.GUNN

Enos Gunn
Waterbury, Conn.   1792

E. GUNN & Co

Edward Gunn & Co.
Waterbury, Conn.   1800

EH

Eliphaz Hart
Norwich, Conn.   1810

E·H   EH

Eliakim Hitchcock
New Haven, Conn.   1757

E·H

Enoch Hoag
Portsmouth, N.H.   1785

E HART   **E·HART**

Eliphaz Hart
Norwich, Conn.   1810

E&H

Eoff & Howell
New York   1805

E.H.NUTTER

Enoch Hoyt Nutter
Dover, N.H.   1826

E·HOLSEY

E. Holsey
Philadelphia   1820

E.HUGHES   **E.HUGHES**

Edmund Hughes
Middletown, Conn.   1804

E.J.AUSTIN

Ebenezer J. Austin
Charlestown, Mass.   1760

E.JEFFERIS

Emmor Jefferis
Wilmington, Del.   1827

E. JEFFERSON

Ephraim Jefferson
Smyra, Del.   1815

E.JONES

Elisha Jones
New York   1827

E.KERSEY

Edward Kersey
Richmond, Va.   1845

E.KINSEY   **ʘ**

Edward Kinsey
Cincinnati, Ohio   1835

E K LAKEMAN

E. K. Lakeman
Salem, Mass.   1819

Edward Lang
Salem, Mass. 1763

EL
Elijah Lincoln
Hingham, Mass. 1815

E·LANG
Edward Lang
Salem, Mass. 1763

E.L.BAILEY&CO
E. L. Bailey & Co.
Claremont, N.H. 1835

E.LESCURE 〔〕

E.LESCURE 〔〕 *
PHILADA
Edward P. Lescure
Philadelphia 1822

Elias Davis
Elias Davis
Boston 1805

E.Lincoln
Elijah Lincoln
Hingham, Mass. 1815

ELLISTON   **Elliston**
Peter Elliston
New York 1791

E·Loring   **E Loring**
Elijah Loring
Barnstable, Mass. 1765

E·LOWNES   **E.LOWNES**
Edward Lownes
Philadelphia 1817

EM **EM** **EM** *
Edmund Milne
Philadelphia 1757

E.M.BARTLETT **WESTCHESTER**
Edward M. Bartlett
Westchester, Pa. 1836

E.McNEIL
E. McNeil
Binghamton, N.Y. 1813

EME
Edgar M. Eoff
New York 1825

E.MEAD
Edmund Mead
St. Louis, Mo. 1850

Emery   **Emery**
Stephen Emery
Boston 1775

E·MILNE
Edmund Milne
Philadelphia 1757

E.MORGAN
Elijah Morgan
Poughkeepsie, N.Y. 1807

E·MOULTON
Enoch Moulton
Portland, Me. 1805

ENOS GUNN
Enos Gunn
Waterbury, Conn. 1792

E.OFF & HOWELL
Eoff & Howell
New York 1805

EOLLES&DAY
Eolles & Day
Hartford, Conn. 1825

EP
Edward Pear
Boston 1830

EP
Elias Pelletreau
Southampton, N.Y. 1750

E.P

Edward Putnam
Salem, Mass.   1810

E&P

Eoff & Phyfe
New York   1844

E.P.L   **EPL**

Edward P. Lescure
Philadelphia   1822

E.P.LESCURE **[mark]**   *

Edward P. Lescure
Philadelphia   1822

ER

Enos Reeves
Charleston, S.C.   1784

E·ROBINSON

Ebenezer Robinson
Boston   1813

E·S **[marks]**

Edward Sandell   B.M.
Baltimore, Md.   1816

E·S   **E·S**

Enoch Stanton
Stonington, Conn.   1766

E&S

Eoff & Shepherd   P.M.
New York   1825

E.SARGEANT

Ensign Sargeant
Boston   1820

E.SKINNER

Elizer Skinner
Hartford, Conn.   1826

E.SM   **E.S.M**

Edward S. Moulton
Rochester, N.H.   1800

E.SMITH   *

Ebenezer Smith
Brookfield, Conn.   1775

E.S.MOULTON

Edward S. Moulton
Rochester, N.H.   1800

E.STEBBINS·&CO

E.STEBBINS&CO **NY** **STERLING**   *

E. Stebbins & Co.
New York   1825

E.Stillman   **E·STILLMAN**

E. Stillman & Co.
Stonington, Conn.   1825

E SULLIVAN

Enoch Sullivan
Richmond, Va.   1800

E. Thomas

Ebenezer Thomas
Petersburg, Va.   1802

E.T.PELL

Emmet T. Pell
New York   1825

E·T·W   **E·T·W**   *

Emmor T. Weaver
Philadelphia   1808

E.T.WEAVER

Emmor T. Weaver
Philadelphia   1808

EVANS **EVANS**

Robert Evans
Boston   1798

EVARD   **EVARD**

Charles Eugene Evard
Philadelphia   1837

EW

Edward Webb
Boston   1705

Edward Winslow
Boston 1695

Edward E. Watson
Boston 1821

E.W. DENNISON *
E. W. Dennison
Bangor, Me. 1805

Edward White
Ulster County, N.Y. 1757

Ebenezer Whiting
Norwich, Conn. 1760

Eben Whitney
New York 1805

Ezra Whiton
Boston 1819

Eleazer Wyer, Jr.
Portland, Me. 1806

E&W.BURR *
Ezekial & William Burr
Providence, R.I. 1792

Elijah Yeomans
Hadley, Mass. 1771

F.A & CO. GAL.TX. *
F. A. & Co.
Galveston, Tx. 1850

Francis M. Ackley
New York 1797

Charles Farley
Portland, Me. 1812

Farnum & Ward
Boston 1816

Farrington & Hunnewell
Boston 1837

Francis Bicknell
Rome, N.Y. 1818

F. Brady
Norwalk, Conn. 1800

Frederick Chaffee
Pittsfield, Mass. 1845

Frederick Curtis
Burlington, Vt. 1808

Abraham Fellows S.M.
Troy, N.Y. 1809

Fellows & Storm
Albany, N.Y. 1839

FENNO & HALE
Fenno & Hale
Bangor, Me. 1840

Fessenden
Newport, R.I. 1845

Francis & Felix Thibault
Philadelphia 1807

F.G.

Francis Garden
Boston   1745

F.&G.

Fletcher & Gardiner
Boston   1809

F.&G. PHILADA

Fletcher & Gardiner   S.M.
Philadelphia   1812

F.H   *

Freeman Hinckley
Barnstable, Mass.   1771

F&H   ∴ F&H ∴

Farrington & Hunnewell
Boston   1837

F.H.CLARK & Cº

F. H. Clark & Co.
Memphis, Tenn.   1850

F & H CLARK   *

F. & H. Clark
Augusta, Ga.   1830

F.HOFFMANN

Christian Frederick Hoffmann
New York   1816

F.H.WOLFE

Francis H. Wolfe   S.M.
Philadelphia   1829

FIELD

Peter Field
Albany, N.Y.   1790

FIELD JR   *

Peter Field, Jr.
New York   1805

F.J.POSEY

Frederick J. Posey
Hagerstown, Md.   1839

FLAGG & CHAPIN

Flagg & Chapin
Boston   1825

   *

Fletcher & Gardiner
Philadelphia   1812

F.LOCKWOOD

Frederick Lockwood
New York   1828

FLOYD SMITH

Floyd Smith
New York   1815

F.M **C** **🐾** **F**   **F M ⊕ ⊕ ⊕**   *

Frederick Marquand
New York   1823

F&M

Frost & Mumford
Providence, R.I.   1815

FMA

Francis M. Ackley
New York   1797

F.MARQUAND

Frederick Marquand   S.M.
New York   1823

F.NUSZ

Frederick Nusz
Frederick, Md.   1819

F.OAKES

Frederick Oakes   S.M.
Hartford, Conn.   1810

FORBES

William Forbes
New York   1830

FORBES & SON

C. V. G. Forbes & Son
New York   1826

FORCE

Jabez W. Force
New York 1819

FORSYTH *

O. C. Forsyth
New York 1810

FOSTER **FOSTER**

Joseph Foster
Boston 1785

Fourniquet

Louis Fourniquet
New York 1795

FOWLE

Nathaniel Fowle
Boston 1803

FOWLE & KIRKLAND

Nathaniel Fowle, Jr.
Northampton, Mass. 1815

Francis Richardson
Philadelphia 1710

FR

Francis Richardson, Jr.
Philadelphia 1729

FRANCIS **FRANCIS**

Nathaniel Francis
New York 1804

F.RATH **F.RATH**

Frederick Rath
New York 1830

FREEMAN **NORFOLK**

Joseph M. Freeman
Norfolk, Va. 1831

FREEMAN & POLLARD

Freeman & Pollard
Norfolk, Va. 1832

FREEMAN & WALLIN

Freeman & Wallin
Philadelphia 1850

F.R.GRUMP NY *

F. R. Grump s.m.
New York 1825

F.RICHMOND **F. Richmond**

Franklin Richmond
Providence, R.I. 1815

F ROBISHER

Benjamin C. Frobisher
Boston 1816

F & R *

Foster & Richards
New York 1815

F.S.B & Co

Frederick S. Blackman & Co.
Danbury, Conn. 1840

F.S.BLACKMAN

Frederick Starr Blackman
Danbury, Conn. 1830

F.S.Sandford

F. S. Sanford
Nantucket, Mass. 1828

F.TINKHAM & Co

F. Tinkham & Co.
New York 1840

F.TITCOMB

Francis Titcomb
Newburyport, Mass. 1813

FUETER **FUETER**

Lewis Fueter
New York 1770

FW

Freeman Woods s.m.
New York 1791

F. W. BURWELL

F. W. Burwell
Norfolk, Va.   1846

F.W.C
NY

Francis W. Cooper   S.M.
New York   1846

F.W.COOPER

Francis W. Cooper
New York   1846

F.W.PORTER

F. W. Porter
New York   1820

GA   **N.YORK**

George Acton
New York   1795

G·A   **G·A**   **GA**   **GA**

George Aiken
Baltimore, Md.   1787

G.Aiken   **G.AIKEN**

George Aiken
Baltimore, Md.   1787

GALE & WILLIS

Gale & Willis
New York   1840

GARNER & WINCHESTER   *
LEX. KY

Garner & Winchester
Lexington, Ky.   1840

G.ARNOLD

George Arnold
Uxbridge, Mass.   1809

G.B

George Bardick
Philadelphia   1790

G.B   **N.Y.**

Geradus Boyce
New York   1814

G.BAKER   *

George Baker
Providence, R.I.   1811

G.B.BOTSFORD   **G.B.BOTSFORD**

Gideon B. Botsford
Woodbury, Conn.   1797

G·B·O

Gerrit Onckelbag
New York   1691

G.BOYCE   **N.YORK**

Geradus Boyce
New York   1814

G.BOYCE   **E.JONES**

Boyce & Jones
New York   1825

GC

George Cannon
Warwick, R.I.   1800

G.C

Gideon Casey
South Kingston, R.I.   1753

G.CANNON

George Cannon
Warwick, R.I.   1800

G·CASEY

Gideon Casey
South Kingston, R.I.   1753

G.C.CLARK

George C. Clark
Providence, R.I.   1824

GD   **GD**   **GD**   *

George Christopher Dowig
Baltimore, Md.   1763

G&D

Goodwin & Dodd
Hartford, Conn.   1811

GD.CLARK **10.15**
George Duvall Clark   B.M.
Baltimore, Md.   1830

GEE
Joseph Gee
Philadelphia   1785

GEFFROY
Nicholas Geffroy
Newport, R.I.   1795

G.ELLIOTT
George Elliott
Wilmington, Del.   1835

GELSTON
George S. Gelston   S.M.
New York   1833

GELSTON & CO
Gelston & Co.
New York   1837

GELSTON LADD & CO
Gelston, Ladd & Co.   S.M.
New York   1836

GELSTON & TREADWELL
GELSTON & TREADWELL *
Gelston & Treadwell   S.M.
New York   1836

GENNET & JAMES
Gennet & James
Richmond, Va.   1849

GEO.A.HOYT ✦ ✪ Ⓓ *
George A. Hoyt
Albany, N.Y.   1822

GEO.B.HOYT **Coin**
George B. Hoyt
Albany, N.Y.   1830

GEO.C.HOWE & CO
George C. Howe & Co.   P.M.
New York   1837

G.EOFF *
Garret Eoff
New York   1806

G.EOFF **J.C.MOORE**
Eoff & Moore
New York   1835

George Baker
George Baker
Providence, R.I.   1811

GEORGE B.FOSTER
George B. Foster
Salem, Mass.   1838

GEORGE C.HOWE
GEORGE C. HOWE
George C. Howe
New York   1825

GEO W.WEBB
George W. Webb
Baltimore, Md.   1835

Germon **Phila**
John D. Germon
Philadelphia   1782

GERRISH
Timothy Gerrish
Portsmouth, N.H.   1775

Gerrish & Pearson
Gerrish & Pearson
New York   1800

GF
George Fielding
New York   1731

G.F.MILLS *
George F. Mills
New York   1825

G.F.ORBES
Garret Forbes
New York   1808

G.FRANCISCUS

George Franciscus
Baltimore, Md.   1776

G.FRANCISCUS

George Franciscus, Jr.
Baltimore, Md.   1810

G.G.

George Gray
Dover, N.H.   1826

Greenberry Griffith
Alexandria, Va.   1814

G GAITHER

Greenberry Gaither
Washington, D.C.   1822

G.G.CLARK *

George C. Clark
Providence, R.I.   1824

G.GORDON

George Gordon
Newburgh, N.Y.   1800

G.GRAY

George Gray
Dover, N.H.   1826

G.GREENLEAF

George Greenleaf
Newburyport, Mass.   1812

   GH

George Hanners
Boston   1720

GH *

George Hartford
Philadelphia   1794

G&H

Gale & Hughes
New York   1846

G.HALL

Green Hall
Albany, N.Y.   1805

G.HANNERS **G.HANNERS**

George Hanners
Boston   1720

G·HANNERS

George Hanners, Jr.
Boston   1744

G·HARRIS *

George Harris
New York   1802

GHISELIN

William Ghiselin
Philadelphia   1751

GIBSON

William Gibson
Philadelphia   1845

Gilbert **N.York** **GILBERT**
GILBERT **NEW YORK** *

William W. Gilbert
New York   1767

GILL

Caleb Gill
Hingham, Mass.   1798

Gilman

John Ward Gilman
Exeter, N.H.   1767

G.JACOB

George Jacob
Baltimore, Md.   1802

G·J·WOLF

General James Wolf
Wilmington, Del.   1800

G.K.CHILDS **G.K.CHILDS**

George K. Childs
Philadelphia   1828

G.KEESEE

George Keese
Richmond, Va.   1831

GKippen **GKIPPEN** *G.Kippen*

George Kippen
Bridgeport, Conn.   1815

GL

Gabriel Lewyn
Baltimore, Md.   1770

GLenhart

G. Lenhart
Bowling Green, Ky.   1845

G:LOOMIS

Guy Loomis
Sheffield, Mass.   1820

G.LOOMIS & CO **ERIE**

G. Loomis & Co.
Erie, Pa.   1850

G.MACPHERSON   *

G. MacPherson
New York   1850

G.MAYER **NORFOLK**

Gotlieb A. Mayer
Norfolk, Va.   1835

G&M   ☽ ☙

Gale & Mosely
New York   1830

G.MECUM

George Mecum
Boston   1825

G.MZAHM

G. M. Zahm
Lancaster, Pa.   1840

B
G O

Gerrit Onckelbag
New York   1691

GOODING

Henry Gooding
Boston   1820

GOODWIN

H. & A. Goodwin
Hartford, Conn.   1821

Goodwin & Dodd **Hartford**

Goodwin & Dodd
Hartford, Conn.   1811

Gordon **GORDON** ☆

Alexander S. Gordon
New York   1795

GORDON   *

George Gordon
Newburgh, N.Y.   1800

Gorham & Thurber

Gorham & Thurber
Providence, R.I.   1850

Gorham & Webster

Gorham & Webster
Providence, R.I.   1831

Gorham Webster & Price

Gorham, Webster & Price
Providence, R.I.   1835

G.Ott

George Ott
Norfolk, Va.   1801

GOULD&WARD

Gould & Ward
Baltimore, Md.   1850

G.PARKER

George Parker   B.M.
Baltimore, Md.   1804

GR

George Ridout
New York   1745

GR

George W. Riggs
Baltimore, Md.   1810

GRAY   **GRAY**

Samuel Gray
Boston   1732

GR.D   **N·YORK**

George R. Downing
New York   1810

GREGG,HAYDEN&CO

Gregg, Hayden & Co.
New York   1846

GREENLEAF

David Greenleaf, Jr.
Hartford, Conn.   1788

GRIFFEN & HOYT

Griffen & Hoyt   S.M.
New York   1819

GRIFFEN & SON

Griffen & Son   S.M.
New York   1832

Griffeth

David Griffeth
Portsmouth, N.H.   1757

Grigg   **Grigg**   **Grigg**

William Grigg
New York   1765

GRISWOLD

Gilbert Griswold
Middletown, Conn.   1810

GS   **GS** *   **GS** *

Godfrey Shiving
Philadelphia   1779

GS

George Stephens   P.M.
New York   1791

GS

George Sutherland
Boston   1796

G.&S

Gale & Stickler
New York   1823

GSCHANCK

G.SCHANCK

Garret Schanck
New York   1791

G.S.GELSTON

George S. Gelston
New York   1833

**G.SPENCE
NEWARK N.J.**

G. Spence
Newark, N.J.   1830

G.Sullivan *

George Sullivan
Lynchburg, Va.   1805

G.T

George Tyler
Boston   1765

G.TERRY   **G.TERRY** *

Geer Terry
Enfield, Conn.   1800

G.TRACY

Gurdon Tracy
Norwich, Conn.   1787

GUINAND

Frederick E. Guinand   B.M.
Baltimore, Md.   1814

GURNEE

GURNEE

Benjamin Gurnee   S.M.
New York   1820

GUTHRE& JEFFERIS.

Guthre & Jefferis
Wilmington, Del. 1840

G.V.ⁿ Schaick

G. Van Schaick
Albany, N.Y. 1800

G.Walker

George Walker
Philadelphia 1797

G.W.BULL

G. W. Bull
Farmington, Conn. 1840

G.W.&H   G.W.&H ⊙⊗   *   *

Gale, Wood & Hughes   P.M.
New York 1830

G.W.&N.C.PLATT

G. W. & N. C. Platt
New York 1820

G.W.STRIKER

George W. Striker
New York 1825

G.W.TUCKERMAN

George W. Tuckerman
Portsmouth, N.H. 1810

G.W.WEBB   **10·15**

George W. Webb
Baltimore, Md. 1835

꜀Hꜜ   *

Daniel Booth Hempsted
New London, Conn. 1820

HA

Henry Andrews
Philadelphia 1795

H. ADAMS   SPRINGFIELD

H. Adams
Springfield, Mass. 1825

HADDOCK, LINCOLN &FOSS

Haddock, Lincoln & Foss
Boston 1850

H&ADRIANCE

Hayes & Adriance
Poughkeepsie, N.Y. 1816

H.&A.GOODWIN

H. & A. Goodwin
Hartford, Conn. 1821

HADWEN   ★

William Hadwen
Nantucket, Mass. 1820

HAIGHT   *

Nelson Haight
Newburgh, N.Y. 1839

Halsted   **HALSTED**

HALSTED N.Y.   *

Benjamin Halsted
New York 1764

HALL & BLISS

Hall & Bliss
Albany, N.Y. 1816

HALL&ELTON

HALL&ELTON   *

Hall & Elton
Geneva, N.Y. 1841

HAMLIN

William Hamlin
Providence, R.I. 1795

H.A.McMASTERS

Hugh A. McMasters
Philadelphia 1839

HARDY   **HARDY.**

Stephen Hardy
Portsmouth, N.H. 1805

HARLAND

Thomas Harland
Norwich, Conn.   1775

HARRIS & STANWOOD

Harris & Stanwood
Boston   1835

HARRIS & WILCOX

Harris & Wilcox
Troy, N.Y.   1844

HART & SMITH

Hart & Smith   B.M.
Baltimore, Md.   1815

HARVEY. LEWIS

Harvey Lewis
Philadelphia   1811

HASCY

Alexander R. Hascy
Albany, N.Y.   1831

HASTINGS

B. B. Hastings
Cleveland, Ohio   1835

H.A.Seymour

Holister A. Seymour
Hartford, Conn.   1843

HAYDEN & GREGG

Hayden & Gregg
Charleston, S.C.   1838

HAYES & ADRIANCE

Hayes & Adriance
Poughkeepsie, N.Y.   1816

HB

Henry Bailey   S.M.
Boston   1800

HB

Henry Biershing
Hagerstown, Md.   1815

Hendrick Boelen
New York   1685

HB   **HB**   **HB**   *

Henricus Boelen, II
New York   1718

H&B

Hart & Brewer
Middletown, Conn.   1800

H.B. & H.M.BACON. LOWELL   *

H. B. & H. M. Bacon
Lowell, Mass.   1845

HBMyer

Henry Beekman Myer
Newburgh, N.Y.   1818

H.BOUDO

Heloise Boudo   S.M.
Charleston, S.C.   1827

H&C

Hunt & Clark
Bennington, Vt.   1795

H. COGSWELL

Henry Cogswell
Boston   1760

H.COGSWELL

Henry Cogswell
Salem, Mass.   1846

H. D. BRACKETT

Horace D. Brackett
Brattleboro, Vt.   1842

HEAD   **G**   **✪**   **D**

Joseph Head
Philadelphia   1798

H.E.BALDWIN&Co.

H. E. Baldwin & Co.
New Orleans, La.   1825

HEDGES

David Hedges, Jr.
East Hampton, N.Y. 1810

H.E.HOYT

Henry E. Hoyt
New York 1820

H&EH.

Judah & Eliphaz Hart
Norwich, Conn. 1810

Helme

Nathaniel Helme
Little Rest, R.I. 1782

Henchman **Henchman** *

Daniel Henchman
Boston 1753

HENDERSON

A. A. Henderson
Philadelphia 1837

Henry B. Stanwood

Henry B. Stanwood S.M.
Boston 1840

HENRY EVANS

Henry Evans S.M.
New York 1820

HENRY HOYT

Henry Hoyt
Albany, N.Y. 1828

HEQUEMBOURG.

HEQUEMBOURG.JR

Charles Hequembourg, Jr. S.M.
New Haven, Conn. 1804

HERBERT *

Timothy B. Herbert
New York 1806

H.ERWIN **H.ERWIN**

Henry Erwin
Philadelphia 1817

HF

Henry Farnam
Boston 1799

H·FARNAM

Henry Farnam
Boston 1799

H.FINCH 🐦 ❀ ❂

Hiram Finch
Albany, N.Y. 1829

HG *

Henry Giraud
New York 1805

HG

Horace Goodwin
Hartford, Conn. 1810

H.GOODWIN **H.GOODWIN**

Horace Goodwin
Hartford, Conn. 1810

HH **HH** **HH**

Henry Hurst
Boston 1690

H&H

Hall & Hewson
Albany, N.Y. 1828

H·HASTINGS

H.HASTINGS 🐗 *

H. Hastings
Ohio 1815

HH&B

Hall, Hewson & Brower
Albany, N.Y. 1850

HH&M

Hall, Hewson & Merrifield
Albany, N.Y. 1845

HHYMAN **H.HYMAN. RHD**

Henry Hyman
Lexington, Ky. 1799

H&I **H&I**

Heydorn & Imley
Hartford, Conn.   1810

HIGBIE & CROSBY

HIGBY & CROSBY *

Higbie & Crosby
Boston   1810

HINSDALE

Horace Hinsdale
New York   1805

HINSDALE & ATKIN

Hinsdale & Atkin
New York   1836

H I PEPPER

Henry J. Pepper
Wilmington, Del.   1814

H.I. SAWYER

H. I. Sawyer
New York   1840

H.J. PEPPER

Henry J. Pepper
Wilmington, Del.   1814

H.J.PEPPER & SON

Henry J. Pepper & Son
Philadelphia   1846

H JUDSON

Hiram Judson
Syracuse, N.Y.   1824

H·K·NEWCOMB

H. K. Newcomb
Watertown, N.Y.   1821

H·L

Harvey Lewis
Philadelphia   1811

H·L

Henry Loring
Boston   1800

H·LEWIS   **H. LEWIS**

Harvey Lewis
Philadelphia   1811

H·Longley

Henry Longley
New York   1810

H·Lupp

Henry Lupp
New Brunswick, N.J.   1783

H.L.W & CO   **Providence**

Henry L. Webster & Co.
Providence, R.I.   1842

H.L.WEBSTER

Henry L. Webster
Providence, R.I.   1831

H&M   **H&M**

Hall & Merriman
New Haven, Conn.   1825

H&M

Halsted & Meyers
New York   1763

H McKEEN   **H. McKEEN**

Henry McKeen
Philadelphia   1823

H·MORSE

Hazen Morse
Boston   1815

H·MULLIGAN
414 2ND ST.PHIA

H. Mulligan
Philadelphia   1840

H&N

Hyde & Nevins   S.M.
New York   1815

H·O&F

Houlton, Otto & Folk
Philadelphia   1797

HOBBS HOBBS *

Nathan Hobbs S.M.
Boston 1815

HOLLAND

Littleton Holland B.M.
Baltimore, Md. 1800

HOLLOWAY

HOLLOWAY BALTIMORE *
Robert Holloway
Baltimore, Md. 1822

HOLYOKE

Edward Holyoke
Boston 1817

HOOD & TOBEY

Hood & Tobey
Albany, N.Y. 1849

HOMES

William Homes
Boston 1739

Hopkins **HOPKINS** *Hopkins*

Joseph W. Hopkins
Waterbury, Conn. 1760

HOSFORD

Harley Hosford
New York 1820

HOTCHKISS *

David Hotchkiss
Syracuse 1848

HOULTON

John Houlton
Philadelphia 1797

HOULTON & BROWNE

Houlton & Browne
Baltimore, Md. 1799

HOWE & GUION *

Howe & Guion S.M.
New York 1839

Howell *Howell*

James Howell
Philadelphia 1802

H.P

Houghton Perkins
Boston 1756

HP

Henry Peterson
Philadelphia 1783

HP

Henry Pitkin
East Hartford, Conn. 1834

HP

Henry Pratt
Philadelphia 1730

H • PERKINS *H•Perkins* *

Houghton Perkins
Boston 1756

H.PORTER&CO

Henry C. Porter & Co.
New York 1830

H.POWER *

Henry Power
Poughkeepsie, N.Y. 1822

H·PRESCOT

Henry Prescot
Keeseville, N.Y. 1828

H·P·RICE

Henry P. Rice P.M.
Albany, N.Y. 1815

H.ROBINSON

Hannah Robinson
Wilmington, Del. 1845

HRT

Henry R. Traux
Albany, N.Y. 1815

H&R.W.SILL

H. & R. W. Sill
New York　1840

HS　　**HS**　**HGS**　*

Hezekiah Silliman
New Haven, Conn.　1767

H&S　*

Haight & Sterling
Newburgh, N.Y.　1841

H&S

Hart & Smith　B.M.
Baltimore, Md.　1815

H.SADD

Harvey Sadd
New Haven, Conn.　1798

H.SAFFORD

Henry Safford
Gallipolis, Ohio　1800

H.Sargeant　　　　　　　*

★ **H.SARGEANT. SPRINGFIELD** ★

Henry Sargeant
Hartford, Conn.　1825

H.SILL

H. Sill
New York　1840

H.SILVERTHORN

H.SILVERTHORN COIN

Henry Silverthorn
Lynchburg, Va.　1832

HU.GELSTON

Hugh Gelston　B.M.
Baltimore, Md.　1816

Huntington　**HUNTINGTON**

Richard Huntington
Utica, N.Y.　1823

Hurd　**HURD**　**Hurd**　**Hurd**

Jacob Hurd
Boston　1723

HUTCHINS

Jacob Hutchins
New York　1774

HUTTON　　**ALBANY**

Isaac Hutton
Albany, N.Y.　1790

HUYLER

George Huyler
New York　1819

H.V.V

Henry Van Veghten
Albany, N.Y.　1760

H W　*

Hugh Wishart　S.M.
New York　1784

H·W

Henry White
Fredericksburg, Va.　1790

H&W

Hart & Wilcox
Norwich, Conn.　1805

HWALKER

Hannah Walker
Philadelphia　1816

H·WHITE

Henry White
Fredericksburg, Va.　1790

H.WILSON

Hosea Wilson
Philadelphia　1812

H.WILSON&CO

Hosea Wilson & Co.
Baltimore, Md.　1814

H.WISHART (ⓗ)

Hugh Wishart   S.M.
New York   1784

HYDE

Hyde
Newport, R.I.   1730

HYDE & GOODRICH

Hyde & Goodrich
New Orleans, La.   1830

Hyde & NEVINS

Hyde & Nevins   S.M.
New York   1815

𝓙𝓐

John Adam, Jr.
Alexandria, Va.   1800

𝓙𝓐 **IA** **𝓐** **IA**

John Allen
Boston   1695

𝓙𝓐 **IA** **IA** *

Isaac Anthony
Newport, R.I.   1715

IA **𝓙𝓐** **IA**

Joseph Anthony, Jr.
Philadelphia   1783

IA **IA**

Josiah Austin
Charlestown, Mass.   1745

IA **JA**

John Avery
Preston, Conn.   1760

JA

John Avery, Jr.
Preston, Conn.   1780

JA **JE**

Allen & Edwards
Boston   1700

IA **BOYER**

Boyer & Austin
Boston   1770

IA **Minott**

Minott & Austin
Boston   1765

JACKSON **JACKSON** *

John Jackson
New York   1731

JACKSON

John Jackson
Nantucket, Mass.   1750

I.ADAM * **J.Adam** **𝓙𝓐**

John Adams, Jr.
Alexandria, Va.   1800

J.Aitken **J.AITKEN**

John Aitken
Philadelphia   1785

I.ALEXANDER

Isaac Alexander
New York   1850

I.ALLARD.JR

Isaac Allard, Jr.
Belfast, Me.   1825

J.Alstyne **J.Alstyne** *

Jeronimus Alstyne
New York   1787

I.ANDREW

John Andrew
Salem, Mass.   1769

I.ANDREWS **NORFOLK**

Jeremiah Andrews
New York   1774

J.Anthony

Joseph Anthony, Jr.
Philadelphia   1783

Isaac Anthony
Newport, R.I.   1715

John A. Shaw
Newport, R.I.   1802

James Thomson
New York   1834

John Austin
Hartford, Conn.   1770

Josiah Austin
Charlestown, Mass.   1745

Austin & Boyer
Boston   1770

Minott & Austin
Boston   1765

John Avery
Preston, Conn.   1760

James Barrett
New York   1805

Joseph Barrett
Nantucket, Mass.   1753

John Bayly
Philadelphia   1755

John Benjamin
Stratford, Conn.   1752

Jurian Blanck, Jr.
New York   1666

Jacob Boelen, III
New York   1785

Jacob Boelen, II
New York   1755

Jacob Boelen
New York   1680

Joseph Bruff
Easton, Md.   1755

John Burger
New York   1780

John Burt
Boston   1712

James Butler
Boston   1734

John Bailey
New York   1762

Jedediah Baldwin
Northampton, Mass.   1791

John Ball
Concord, Mass.   1763

Israel Bartlet
Newbury, Mass.   1800

IBAYLY   **JBayly**

John Bayly
Philadelphia   1755

I.B.CURRAN

I. B. Curran
Ithaca, N.Y.   1835

JBedford

John Bedford
Fishkill, N.Y.   1782

IBELL

Joseph Bell
New York   1817

IBL   **NYORK**

John Burt Lyng
New York   1759

IBLACK

James Black
Philadelphia   1795

IBLISS   **I.BLISS**   *

Jonathan Bliss
Middletown, Conn.   1800

IBOONE

Jeremiah Boone
Philadelphia   1791

IBRIDGE

John Bridge
Boston   1751

IBROCK   **NEWYORK**

John Brock
New York   1833

IBRUFF

Joseph Bruff
Easton, Md.   1755

I·BRUFF

Joseph Bruff, Jr.
Easton, Md.   1790

IBURT   **IBURT**   **I·BURT**

John Burt
Boston   1712

IBV   **B**
            IV

John Brevoort
New York   1742

I.BWOLTZ

John Woltz
Sheperdstown, Va.   1811

JC

Joseph Callender
Boston   1774

IC

Joseph Carman
Philadelphia   1771

IC   **I.C**   **IC**

Joseph Carpenter
Norwich, Conn.   1775

IC   **IC**

James Chalmers
Annapolis, Md.   1749

IC   **IC**   *

John Chalmers
Annapolis, Md.   1778

I·C   **IC**

John Champlin
New London, Conn.   1768

I.C

I. Clark
Boston   1737

IC   **IC**   **IC**

Jonathan Clarke
Newport, R.I.   1734

IC   **I:C**   *

John Cluet, Jr.
Kingston, N.Y.   1725

I.C

John Coburn
Boston   1750

 *

John Coddington
Newport, R.I.   1712

John Coney
Boston   1676

I·C

Joseph Cook
Philadelphia   1785

Jacob Cuyler
Albany, N.Y.   1765

I·CHURCHILL

Jesse Churchill
Boston   1795

I·CLARICO   **I·CLARICO**

Joseph Clarico
Norfolk, Va.   1816

ICLARK   **I·CLARK**

I. Clark
Boston   1737

I.Clarke

Jonathan Clarke
Newport, R.I.   1734

I. COPP

Joseph Copp
New London, Conn.   1757

ICOOK

John Cook
New York   1795

I Cortelyou

Jacques W. Cortelyou
New Brunswick, N.J.   1805

I·COVERLY

John Coverly
Boston   1766

I Cowell

John Cowell
Boston   1728

I.CRAWFORD

John Crawford
New York   1815

I·D   **ID**

John David
Philadelphia   1763

ID

John Dixwell
Boston   1710

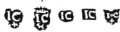 *

Jeremott W. Douglass
Philadelphia   1790

ID

Jeremiah Dummer
Boston   1666

I·D

Jonathan Davenport
Baltimore, Md.   1789

I·D·

Jabez Delano
New Bedford, Mass.   1784

I·DAVENPORT

Jonathan Davenport
Baltimore, Md.   1789

IDAVID   **IDAVID**

John David
Philadelphia   1763

IDAVIS   **I·DAVIS**

I·DAVIS *

Joshua G. Davis
Boston   1796

I.D.CLUSTER

Isaac D. Cluster
St. Louis, Mo.   1850

I.DELANO

Jabez Delano
New Bedford, Mass.   1784

I.DIXON

Isaac Dixon
Philadelphia   1843

IDM

John D. Miller
Charleston, S.C.   1780

I.B.Miller

John D. Miller
Charleston, S.C.   1780

I.DOANE

Joshua Doane
Providence, R.I.   1740

I.DORSEY

Joshua Dorsey
Philadelphia   1793

I.Douglass

Jeremott W. Douglass
Philadelphia   1790

I.DUBOIS

Joseph Dubois
New York   1790

I.DUFFEL

James Duffel
Georgetown, S.C.   1790

I.E

Jacob Ege
Richmond, Va.   1779

IE   IE   IE   IE

John Edwards
Boston   1691

IE   IE   IE

Joseph Edwards, Jr.
Boston   ·1758

IE   IA

Allen & Edwards
Boston   1700

I.Edwards   I.Edwards

Joseph Edwards, Jr.
Boston   1758

I.E.HYDE   N.YORK   *

I. E. Hyde
New York   1790

IF

John Folsom
Albany, N.Y.   1780

I.F   *

John Foster
New York   1811

I.FALES

James Fales
Newport, R.I.   1805

I.F.GIBBS

John Fitton Gibbs
Providence, R.I.   1803

I.FITE

John Fite
Baltimore, Md.   1807

I.FOSTER

John Foster
Boston   1785

I.F TAPPAN   *

Israel Foster Tappan
Manchester, Mass.   1820

IG

John Gardner
New London, Conn.   1760

James Geddy
Williamsburg, Va.   1751

John D. Germon
Philadelphia   1782

Isaac Gere
Northampton, Mass.   1793

    *

Joseph Goldthwaite
Boston   1731

John Gray
Boston   1713

Jacob Gerritse Lansing
Albany, N.Y.   1700

Jacob G. Lansing
Albany, N.Y.   1765

James Gaskins
Portsmouth, Va.   1802

John Hastier
New York   1726

*

John Heath
New York   1761

Joseph Hill
Portsmouth, N.H.   1821

John Hull
Boston   1645

Jacob Hurd
Boston   1723

John S. Hutton
New York   1720

Hull & Sanderson
Boston   1652

Joseph Hall
Albany, N.Y.   1781

Ivory Hall
Concord, N.H.   1819

John Hallam
New London, Conn.   1773

Jabez Halsey
New York   1789

Judah Hart
Middletown, Conn.   1799

Ira Haselton
Portsmouth, N.H.   1821

I. & H. Clark
Portsmouth, N.H.   1821

I. & H. Jenkins
Albany, N.Y.   1815

John Heath
New York   1761

IHL
Josiah H. Lownes
Philadelphia 1816

IHM
John H. Merkler
New York 1780

J.Howell
James Howell
Philadelphia 1802

J.Howell&Co
J. Howell & Co.
Philadelphia 1810

IHR
John H. Russell
New York 1792

I.HURD **I.Hurd**
Jacob Hurd
Boston 1725

II
John Inch
Annapolis, Md. 1741

II **II**
Jacob Jennings
Norwalk, Conn. 1763

I.I.LOW
John J. Low
Boston 1825

*J.I.Monell &
C.M.Williams*
Monell & Williams
New York 1825

IJ
John Jenkins
Philadelphia 1777

I.JENCKES
John C. Jenckes
Providence, R.I. 1798

IK **IK**
Joseph Keeler
Norwalk, Conn. 1810

I.K
James Kendall
Wilmington, Del. 1785

IK
Jesse Kip
New York 1682

I.KETCHAM
James Ketcham
New York 1807

I.Kneeland
Joseph Kneeland
Boston 1720

I.KUCHER
Jacob Kucher
Philadelphia 1806

I.L **IL**
Jeffery Lang
Salem, Mass. 1733

IL **IL** **IL**
John Leacock
Philadelphia 1748

IL * **IL** **IL** *
John Le Roux
New York 1716

IL **IL** **O**
John Lynch
Baltimore, Md. 1786

I.L **I.L** **I.L** *
John Burt Lyng
New York 1759

I.LANG **I.LANG**
Jeffery Lang
Salem, Mass. 1733

I.L.BANGS & CO

I. L. Bangs & Co.
Woonsocket, R.I.　1810

I.LEACOCK

John Leacock
Philadelphia　1748

I. Lent

John Lent
New York　1787

I.LeTelier　　**I.LeTelier**
I.LeTellier　　**I.L.TELLIER**

John Le Telier
Philadelphia　1770

I.LEWIS　**I.LEWIS**

Isaac Lewis
Huntington, Conn.　1796

I.L.G

John L. Gale
New York　1819

I.L.GALE　　**I.L.GALE.**

John L. Gale
New York　1819

I.Loring　*I.Loring*

Joseph Loring
Boston　1766

I.LOWE

Joshua Lowe　P.M.
New York　1828

I.Lownes

Joseph Lownes
Philadelphia　1780

I.R

John Le Roux
New York　1716

I.L.T

John Le Telier
Philadelphia　1770

I.LYNCH

John Lynch
Baltimore, Md.　1786

IM　**I.M**　(🌸)

John McMullin
Philadelphia　1790

IM

Jacob Mariusgroen
New York　1701

I.M　**I.M**　**I.M**　**I.M**　**I.M** *

John Moulinar
New York　1744

I.M　*I.M*

Joseph Moulton
Newburyport, Mass.　1765

I.M

John Murdock
Philadelphia　1779

I.McClymon

John C. McClymon
New York　1805

I.McMullin 🌸

John McMullin
Philadelphia　1790

I.M.MIKSCH

John M. Miksch
Bethlehem, Pa.　1775

I.M.MULLIN　🌸

John McMullin
Philadelphia　1790

I.MOOD

John Mood
Charleston, S.C.　1816

I.MOULTON

Joseph Moulton
Newburyport, Mass.　1745

Joseph Moulton
Newburyport, Mass.   1765

James Munroe
Barnstable, Mass.   1806

John Murdock
Philadelphia   1779

John Myers
Philadelphia   1785

John Nelson
Portsmouth, N.H.   1757

Jan Van Nieu Kirke
New York   1711

John Noyes
Boston   1699

Johannis Nys
Philadelphia   1695

J. & N. Richardson
Philadelphia   1771

Isaac N. Toy
Abingdon, Md.   1790

John Osgood
Haverhill, Mass.   1795

Jonathan Otis
Newburyport, R.I.   1750

John Ogilvie
New York   1764

John Burt Lyng
New York   1759

Jonathan Otis
Newport, R.I.   1750

John Owen
Philadelphia   1804

Isaac Parker
Deerfield, Mass.   1774

John Patterson
Annapolis, Md.   1751

John Pearson
New York   1791

Isaac Perkins
Boston   1707

Jacob Perkins
Newburyport, Mass.   1787

John Pitts
Boston   1730

John Potwine
Boston   1721

Job Prince
Milford, Conn.   1700

IPARKER

Isaac Parker
Deerfield, Mass.   1774

I·PARMELE

James Parmele
Durham, Conn.   1785

IPARSONS

John Parsons
Boston   1780

IPearson

John Pearson
New York   1791

IPittman

I. Pitman
Baltimore, Md.   1785

I·Potwine

John Potwine
Boston   1721

IPT

John Proctor Trott
New London, Conn.   1792

IPT&SON

John P. Trott & Son   P.M.
New London, Conn.   1820

I&PT **⚜** **🌀** **🜊** *

John & Peter Targee
New York   1811

I·PTARGEE **🌀** **⚜**

John & Peter Targee
New York   1811

IR **⚜** *

Jonathan Reed
Boston   1724

IR **IR**

John Reynolds
Hagerstown, Md.   1790

IR **IR** **IR** **🐦**

Joseph Richardson
Philadelphia   1732

IR **IR** **IR** **IR**

Joseph Richardson, Jr.
Philadelphia   1773

IR

Joseph Rice
Baltimore, Md.   1784

IR **IR** **IR**

Joseph Rogers
Newport, R.I.   1780

IR

John Ross
Baltimore, Md.   1790

I·R

Joseph Russell
Barnstable, Mass.   1728

JR

Johnson & Riley
Baltimore, Md.   1785

IRA·STOWN **⚜**

Ira S. Town
Montpelier, Vt.   1825

I.REED

Isaac Reed
Stamford, Conn.   1770

IREED & SON **I. REED & SON** *

Isaac Reed & Son
Philadelphia   1830

IReeve

Joseph Reeve
Newburgh, N.Y.   1803

I.Rice **IRICE**

Joseph Rice
Baltimore, Md.   1784

I. R. Miller
Philadelphia 1810

James Roe
Kingston, N.Y. 1770

John A. Rohr
Philadelphia 1807

Isaac Reed & Son
Philadelphia 1830

John Stuart
Providence, R.I. 1720

Joseph Smith
Boston 1765

Isaac Sanford
Hartford, Conn. 1785

John Syng
Philadelphia 1734

Isaac Sanford
Hartford, Conn. 1785

Jacob Sargeant
Hartford, Conn. 1785

Joel Sayre
New York 1799

John Sayre
New York 1792

John A. Schanck
New York 1795

I. Scot
Albany, N.Y. 1750

John Scott
Raleigh, N.C. 1806

I. S. Town & J. Town, Jr.
Montpelier, Vt. 1825

John S. Krause
Bethlehem, Pa. 1805

Joseph Smith
Boston 1765

John Smith
Baltimore, Md. 1814

Jeremiah Snow, Jr.
Williamsburg, Mass. 1808

Isaac Spear P.M.
Boston 1836

Joseph S. Porter
Utica, N.Y. 1805

Jonathan Stickney, Jr.
Newburyport, Mass. 1796

John Stow
Wilmington, Del. 1772

I.S.TOWN   *

Ira S. Town
Montpelier, Vt.   1825

Jacobus VanDer Spiegel
New York   1689

John Sweeney
Geneva, N.Y.   1816

John Symmes
Boston   1767

John Tanner
Newport, R.I.   1740

*

John Targee
New York   1797

Jacob C. Ten Eyck
Albany, N.Y.   1725

John Touzell
Salem, Mass.   1756

Joseph Toy
Abingdon, Md.   1776

Toy & Wilson
Abingdon, Md.   1790

Jonathan Trott, Jr.
New London, Conn.   1795

*

James Turner
Boston   1744

John Tanguy
Philadelphia   1801

Jacob C. Ten Eyck
Albany, N.Y.   1725

Isaac Thomson
Litchfield, Conn.   1801

James Tiley
Hartford, Conn.   1765

James Titus
Philadelphia   1833

Jonathan Trott
Boston   1758

I. Tyler
New England   1778

John Vernon
New York   1787

John Vanall
Charleston, S.C.   1752

Jan Van Nieu Kirke
New York   1711

John Vogler
Salem, N.C.   1802

Jacobus Vander Spiegel
New York   1689

IVS IVS

John Van Steenberg, Jr.
Kingston, N.Y.   1775

IW

Isaiah Wagster
Baltimore, Md.   1780

IW

Joseph Warner
Wilmington, Del.   1775

IW   IW

Joshua Weaver
West Chester, Pa.   1794

IW   *

John Wendover
New York   1690

IW

John Winckler
Charleston, S.C.   1761

IW

Jeremiah Ward Wool
New York   1791

IWAITE

John Waite
South Kingstown, R.I.   1763

I Walraven

John Walraven
Baltimore, Md.   1792

Jacques W. Cortelyou
New Brunswick, N.J.   1805

IWARNER

Joseph Warner
Wilmington, Del.   1775

IWF ✪ ✪ ✪ ✪

John W. Forbes   P.M.
New York   1802

I.W.FORBES

John W. Forbes   P.M.
New York   1802

I·W·G   IWG

John Ward Gilman
Exeter, N.H.   1767

I.W Gethen

John W. Gethen
Philadelphia   1811

I.W.&I.K.FELLOWS

I. W. & J. K. Fellows
Lowell, Mass.   1834

I.WOLFF

James G. Wolf
Philadelphia   1830

I.WOODCOCK

Isaac Woodcock
Wilmington, Del.   1787

I.Wood

John Wood
New York   1770

I.Y·SAVAGE

John Y. Savage
Raleigh, N.C.   1820

I·ZANE

Isaac Zane
Zanesfield, Ohio   1795

JA

John Adam, Jr.
Alexandria, Va.   1800

J·A   JA

Jeronimus Alstyne
New York   1787

J·A   JA *   1 **JA** *   2 **JA** *

Joseph Anthony, Jr.
Philadelphia   1783

John Avery
Preston, Conn.   1760

Joseph Anthony & Sons
Philadelphia   1810

JABBOTT   **J.ABBOT**

John W. Abbott
Portsmouth, N.H.   1817

JACCARD & CO

Jaccard & Co.
St. Louis, Mo.   1850

Jacob Hurd
Boston   1723

JACKSON *

John Jackson
New York   1731

J.ADAM

John Adam, Jr.
Alexandria, Va.   1800

JAE

John Aaron Elliott
Sharon, Conn.   1815

J.Allmy   **New Bedford**

Jonathan Allmy
Newport, R.I.   1770

JAMES DINWIDDIE   **o-i**

James Dinwiddie
Lynchburg, Va.   1840

JAMES M.FORD

James M. Ford
Boston   1810

JAMES MIX

James Mix   S.M.
Albany, N.Y.   1817

JAMES MIX JR. *

James Mix, Jr.   S.M.
Albany, N.Y.   1846

James Munroe

James Munroe
Barnstable, Mass.   1806

JAMES MURDOCK & CO

James Murdock & Co.
Utica, N.Y.   1826

JAMES TANNER

James Tanner
Newport, R.I.   1753

J.ANDREWS   **J.Andrews**
J-ANDREWS, NORFOLK

Jeremiah Andrews
New York   1774

J.Anthony

Joseph Anthony, Jr.
Philadelphia   1783

JAS.D.PHILIPS

James D. Philips
Cincinnati, Ohio   1829

J.& A.S

J. & A. Simmons
New York   1805

J.&.A.SIMMONS

J. & A. Simmons
New York   1805

Jas Fales

James Fales
Newport, R.I.   1805

Jas Thomson   **NY**   **1837**

James Thomson
New York   1834

J·AUSTIN **J·AUSTIN**

Josiah Austin
Charlestown, Mass. 1745

JAVAIN

Henry J. Javain
Charleston, S.C. 1835

JB

John Bedford
Fishkill, N.Y. 1782

JB

James Black
Philadelphia 1795

JB **N.Y.**

John Boyce
New York 1801

JB

John Brown
Philadelphia 1785

J&B

Johnson & Ball
Baltimore, Md. 1790

J.BALDWIN

Jabez C. Baldwin
Boston 1800

J.Bailey

John Bailey, III
Portland, Me. 1810

J·BALL **JOHN BALL**

John Ball
Concord, Mass. 1763

J·BARD *

J. Bard
Philadelphia 1800

J·BARTON

Joseph Barton
Stockbridge, Mass. 1790

J.B.COOKE
J.B.COOKE **STANDARD**

John B. Cooke
Petersburg, Va. 1838

J.BEATON

James B. Eaton
Boston 1805

J.Bedford

John Bedford
Fishkill, N.Y. 1782

J.BELL

Joseph Bell
New York 1817

J.B.GINOCHIO

John B. Ginochio P.M.
New York 1837

J·BIRGE·

John Birge
Brattleboro, Vt. 1805

J.B.JONES **J.B.Jones**
J·B·JONES *

John B. Jones
Boston 1813

J.B.JONES & CO

John B. Jones & Co.
Boston 1838

J.BLACKMAN

John Starr Blackman
Danbury, Conn. 1805

J.B.M'FADDEN

J. B. M'Fadden
Pittsburgh, Pa. 1840

J.B.MURPHY
J·B·Murphy **NORFOLK**

John B. Murphy
Norfolk, Va. 1830

J.BOONE

Jeremiah Boone
Philadelphia 1791

J.BOUTIER

John Boutier
New York   1805

J. Boyden   **Worcester**

Joseph Boyden
Worcester, Mass.   1825

Bridge   *

John Bridge
Boston   1751

J.BRITTIN   *

Jacob Brittin
Philadelphia   1807

J.BROCK

John Brock
New York   1833

J.B.THAXTER

Joseph B. Thaxter
Hingham, Mass.   1815

J. BURNHAM.

John Burnham
Brattleboro, Vt.   1815

JBUTLER   *J BUTLER*

James Butler
Boston   1734

J.Byrne

James Byrne
Philadelphia   1784

JC

Joseph Clark
Danbury, Conn.   1791

JC

Jonathan Clarke
Newport, R.I.   1734

JC   **J.C**

John Coburn
Boston   1750

J.C

Joseph Cook
Philadelphia   1785

JC

Joseph Coolidge, Jr.
Boston   1770

JC   **JC**

Jonathan Crosby
Boston   1764

J.CAMPBELL

John Campbell
Fayetteville, N.C.   1829

J.C.B&CO   **J.C.B&C?**   *
                BRIDGEPORT

J. C. Blackman & Co.
Bridgeport, Conn.   1835

J.C.BALDWIN

Jabez C. Baldwin
Boston   1800

J.C.COLE

James C. Cole
Rochester, N.H.   1813

J.C.FARR

John C. Farr
Philadelphia   1824

J.CHURCH   **J.CHURCH**

Joseph Church
Hartford, Conn.   1815

J.C.JENCKES

John C. Jenckes
Providence, R.I.   1798

J.CLARICO   *

Joseph Clarico
Norfolk, Va.   1816

J:CLARK

Joseph Clark
Danbury, Conn.   1791

J·Clark

Joseph Clark
Portsmouth, N.H.   1803

J·CLARKE **J·Clarke**

J:CLARK   *   **J:CLARKE**   *

Jonathan Clarke
Newport, R.I.   1734

J.C.M

John C. Moore   S.M.
New York   1835

J.COBURN

John Coburn
Boston   1750

J.CONNING MOBILE

James Conning
New York   1825

J.COOK

John Cook
New York   1795

J.COPP   **J.COPP**

Joseph Copp
New London, Conn.   1757

J.CORBETT

John Corbett
Whitingham, Vt.   1800

J.CRAWFORD

John Crawford
New York   1815

J.CURRY J PHILA

John Curry
Philadelphia   1831

J D

John David, Jr.
Philadelphia   1785

J·D **J·D**   **J·D** **J·D** **J·D**   *

John Denise
New York   1798

J·D

Joseph Dubois
New York   1790

J·D

James Duffel
Georgetown, S.C.   1790

J.DAVIS

Joshua G. Davis
Boston   1796

J·DAY·C

John Day
Boston   1820

J.D.CHASE   **J.D.CHASE**

J.D.CHASE   *

Joseph D. Chase
New York   1820

J.DECKER

James Decker   S.M.
Troy, N.Y.   1833

J.D.MASON

J. D. Mason
Philadelphia   1830

J DOANE

John Doane
Boston   1760

J.DODGE

John Dodge
New York   1800

J.DOLL

J. Doll
New York   1820

J.DRAPER

Joseph Draper
Wilmington, Del.   1825

J.D.STOUT

J. D. Stout
New York   1817

J·DUBOIS

Joseph Dubois
New York   1790

J. DUFFEL

James Duffel
Georgetown, S.C.   1790

✱J. DYAR✱

Joseph Dyar
Middlebury, Vt.   1822

J·E

Joseph Edwards, Jr.
Boston   1758

JE   **J·E**

Jeremiah Elfreth, Jr.
Philadelphia   1752

J.Easton 24   **J.EASTON**   **NANTUCKET**

James Easton, II
Nantucket, Mass.   1828

J E CALDWELL & CO *

J. E. Caldwell & Co.
Philadelphia   1848

JEFFREY R.BRACKETT

Jeffrey R. Brackett
Boston   1840

JEHU & W.L.WARD PHILA

Jehu & W. L. Ward
Philadelphia   1837

JENNINGS & LANDER

Jennings & Lander   P.M.
New York   1848

J.ERWIN

John Erwin   B.M.
Baltimore, Md.   1809

J·ERWIN

John Erwin
New York   1815

J.E.STANWOOD

J. E. Stanwood
Philadelphia   1850

J.EWAN

John Ewan   S.M.
Charleston, S.C.   1823

J.E.WOOD

J. E. Wood
New York   1845

J.EYLAND

James Eyland
Charleston, S.C.   1820

J·F   **J·F**

John Fitch
Trenton, N.J.   1769

J·F

Josiah Flagg
Boston   1765

J·F   **T.RICHARDS**

Foster & Richards
New York   1815

J FAIRCHILD

Joseph Fairchild
New Haven, Conn.   1824

J.Fenno   **LOWELL.**   *

James Fenno
Lowell, Mass.   1825

J.FITCH   **AUBURN**   **☙**

James Fitch
Auburn, N.Y.   1821

JFOSTER   **☙**   **❷**   **J. Foster**

John Foster   S.M.
New York   1811

J·FRANK

Jacob Frank
Philadelphia   1793

J·F·REEVES 1045

Joseph F. Reeves
Baltimore, Md.   1835

J.F.ROBINSON

John F. Robinson
Wilmington, Del.   1844

J·F·Vent

John F. Vent
Boston   1783

JG

John Gardner
New London, Conn.   1760

JG

James Geddy
Williamsburg, Va.   1751

J·G   JG

John Gibbs
Providence, R.I.   1773

JG

James Gough
New York   1769

J·GALE

John L. Gale
New York   1819

J·GARDNER

John Gardner
New York   1760

J·Gaskins   J.Gaskins   J·GASKINS

JGaskins   NORFOLK

J. Gaskins

James Gaskins
Portsmouth, Va.   1802

J·GIBBS   J·GIBBS

John Gibbs
Providence, R.I.   1773

JGL

Jacob G. Lansing
Albany, N.Y.   1765

J.G.Libby

Jacob G. L. Libby
Boston   1820

J. G. LUSCOMB.

John G. Luscomb
Boston   1813

J.GOODHUE

John Goodhue
Salem, Mass.   1822

J.GORHAM

Jabez Gorham
Providence, R.I.   1815

J.Gorham & Son

Jabez Gorham & Son
Providence, R.I.   1842

J.GOULD   1045

James Gould   B.M.
Baltimore, Md.   1816

J.GUTHRE

James Guthre
Wilmington, Del.   1822

JH

John Hancock
Boston   1760

J·H   *

John S. Hutton
New York   1720

JH   JH   JH   *

John Heath
New York   1761

JH   JH

Judah Hart
Middletown, Conn.   1799

J·HAMILL NY

James Hamill
New York 1816

J·HANCOCK

John Hancock
Boston 1760

J.HANSELL

J. Hansell
Valley Forge, Pa. 1825

J HART

J:HART NORWICH

Judah Hart
Middletown, Conn. 1799

J·HARTT **J HARTT**

Jonathan Hartt
Canandaigua, N.Y. 1810

JHC

John H. Connor
New York 1835

J.H.CLARK

J. H. Clark
New York 1815

J.H.CONNOR

John H. Connor
New York 1835

J.H.CONNOR G.EOFF

Eoff & Connor
New York 1833

J·HEATH

John Heath
New York 1761

J.H.FOWLE NORTHAMPTON.

John H. Fowle
Boston 1805

J.H.HOLLISTER PURE, COIN. *

Julius Hollister
Oswego, N.Y. 1846

J·HILL

James Hill
Boston 1770

J.H.LEWIS

J. H. Lewis
Albany, N.Y. 1810

J.H.MORSE

J. H. Morse
Boston 1795

J.H.MULFORD

J. H. Mulford
Albany, N.Y. 1835

J.H.NORTON

J. H. Norton
Hartford, Conn. 1820

J·HOBARTH

Joshua Hobart
New Haven, Conn. 1810

J.HODGE HADLEY

John Hodge
Hadley, Mass. 1781

J.HOLLISTER PURE COIN

Julius Hollister
Oswego, N.Y. 1846

J.Howell

James Howell
Philadelphia 1802

J·HUGHES

Jeremiah Hughes
Annapolis, Md. 1805

J&IC

John & James Cox
New York 1817

J&IC&C

J. & I. Cox & Clark
New York 1831

J.&I.COX   **N.Y.**

John & James Cox
New York   1817

J.Jackson   *J.Jackson*

Joseph Jackson
Baltimore, Md.   1803

J.JAGGER

John Jagger
Marblehead, Mass.   1735

J.J.BANGS

John J. Bangs
Cincinnati, Ohio   1825

J.JENCKES   **J.JENCKES**

John C. Jenckes
Providence, R.I.   1798

J.J.LOW

John J. Low
Boston   1825

J.J.LOW&CO

J. J. Low & Co.
Boston   1830

J.J.Monell   *C.M.Williams*

J. J. Monell & C. M. Williams
New York   1825

J.JONES

J.JONES.37MARKET.ST   *

John B. Jones
Boston   1813

J.J.S.

John J. Staples, Jr.
New York   1788

JK

James Kendall
Wilmington, Del.   1785

J.KEDZIE

J. Kedzie   S.M.
Rochester, N.Y.   1830

J.KENDALL

James Kendall
Wilmington, Del.   1785

J.K.FELLOWS

James K. Fellows
Lowell, Mass.   1832

J.KIMBALL   **BOSTON**

John Kimball
Boston, Mass.   1805

J.KITTS

John Kitts
Louisville, Ky.   1838

J.KNAPP   **BOSTON**

J. Knapp
Boston   1825

J.L   **J.L**   **J.L**   **J.L**   **JL**

Joseph Loring
Boston   1766

JL

John Lynch
Baltimore, Md.   1786

J.LADOMUS

Jacob Ladomus
Philadelphia   1843

J.Lee

J. Lee
Middletown, Conn.   1790

J.LEVY

Jonas Levy
New York   1835

J.L.G

John L. Gale
New York   1819

J.L.GALE

John L. Gale
New York   1819

J·L·MOFFAT

J. L. Moffat
New York   1815

J.L.MOORE

Jared L. Moore   P.M.
New York   1835

J.LORD

Jabez C. Lord   P.M.
New York   1825

J.Loring   **J.Loring**

Joseph Loring
Boston   1766

J.LOWE

Joshua Lowe
New York   1828

J.Lownes

Joseph Lownes
Philadelphia   1780

J.L.SMITH

John L. Smith
Middletown, Conn.   1822

J.L.SMITH

John Leonard Smith
Syracuse, N.Y.   1850

ENGRAVED J L:T MAKER

John Le Telier
Richmond, Va.   1810

J.LW

John L. Westervelt
Newburgh, N.Y.   1845

J.LYNCH

John Lynch
Baltimore, Md.   1786

J·M

J. Merchant
New York   1795

JM   *

John McMullin
Philadelphia   1790

J·M

Joseph Moulton
Newburyport, Mass.   1745

J·M   **J·M**   **JM**   **JM**

Joseph Moulton
Newburyport, Mass.   1765

J.M.BARROWS

James Madison Barrows
Tolland, Conn.   1828

J·M·BLONDEL   ☺ ☺

John M. Blondell
Baltimore, Md.   1814

J.M.F.

John McFarlane
Boston   1796

J·MᶜFARLANE   **J.MᶜFARLANE**

John McFarlane
Boston   1796

J·MERCHANT

J. Merchant
New York   1795

J·MEREDITH

James Meredith
Winchester, Va.   1820

J·MEREDITH

Joseph P. Meredith
Baltimore, Md.   1824

J.M.FREEMAN **NORFOLK**

Joseph M. Freeman
Norfolk, Va.   1831

J.M.FREEMAN & Co

J. M. Freeman & Co.
Norfolk, Va.   1843

J.M.HOFFMAN

James M. Hoffman
Philadelphia 1820

J.MOOD **J.MOOD**

John Mood
Charleston, S.C. 1816

J MOTT

James S. Mott
New York 1830

J.MOULTON **J. MOULTON**

Joseph Moulton
Newburyport, Mass. 1835

J.Murdock

John Murdock
Philadelphia 1779

J.MURPHY **J.MURPHY**

James Murphy
Boston 1803

J.MURPHY

John Murphy
Norfolk, Va. 1798

J.MYTINGER

Jacob Mytinger
Newtown, Va. 1825

Jn Reynolds

John Reynolds
Hagerstown, Md. 1790

J.O

John Osgood
Haverhill, Mass. 1795

JO *

Jonathan Otis
Newport, R.I. 1750

JOHN A. COLE

John A. Cole
New York 1844

JOHN B. AKIN

John B. Akin
Danville, Ky. 1850

JOHN BALL **JOHN BALL**

John Ball
Concord, Mass. 1763

JOHN BIGELOW **PURE COIN**

John Bigelow
Boston 1830

JOHN B. SCOTT

John B. Scott
New York 1820

JOHN BURT

John Burt
Boston 1712

JOHN C. FARR

John C. Farr
Philadelphia 1824

JOHN H. TYLER & CO

John H. Tyler & Co.
Richmond, Va. 1835

JOHN KIMBALL **BOSTON**

John Kimball
Boston, Mass. 1805

JOHN PRICE *

John Price S.M.
Lancaster, Pa. 1810

JOHNSON **Johnson**

Samuel Johnson
New York 1780

JOHNSON & GODLEY *

Johnson & Godley S.M.
Albany, N.Y. 1843

JOHNSON & REAT

Johnson & Reat
Richmond, Va. 1804

J.O.&J.R.POTTER

J. O. & J. R. Potter
Providence, R.I.   1810

JONES BALL & CO

JONES, BALL & CO *

Jones, Ball & Co.
Boston   1850

JONES.BALL & POOR

Jones, Ball & Poor
Boston   1840

JONES & HUTTON

Jones & Hutton
Wilmington, Del.   1840

JONES,LOWS & BALL

Jones, Lows & Ball
Boston   1839

JONES & PEIRCE

Jones & Peirce
Boston   1810

JONES & WARD

Jones & ward

Jones & Ward
Boston   1809

J.O.PITKIN

John O. Pitkin
East Hartford, Conn.   1826

JOSEPH RAYNES

Joseph Raynes
Lowell, Mass.   1835

Joseph T. Rice   **ALBANY**

Joseph T. Rice
Albany, N.Y.   1813

J:OSGOOD

John Osgood
Haverhill, Mass.   1795

J·OSGOOD

John Osgood, Jr.
Boston   1817

Josiah Gooding

Josiah Gooding
Boston   1840

JOS.M.WALTER

Joseph M. Walter
Baltimore, Md.   1835

J·OTIS   **J.Otis**

Jonathan Otis
Newport, R.I.   1750

J.O.& W.PITKIN

J. O. & W. Pitkin   P.M.
East Hartford, Conn.   1830

J.P

Joseph Perkins
Little Rest, R.I.   1770

J.P

Joseph Phillippe
Baltimore, Md.   1791

J.PEABODY   *

John Tyng Peabody
Enfield, Conn.   1778

J.Pearson

John Pearson
New York   1791

J.PERKINS   **J.PERKINS**

Joseph Perkins
Little Rest, R.I.   1770

J.PETERS

James Peters
Philadelphia   1821

J.PETERS & CO

J. Peters & Co.
Philadelphia   1830

J.P.FIRENG · BURLINGTON N.J.

J. P. Fireng
Burlington, N.J.   1810

J. Pittman

John Pittman
Falmouth, Va.   1792

J.&P.MOOD · PURE COIN   *

J. & P. Mood
Charleston, S.C.   1834

J. POTTER · NORFOLK

John Potter
Alexandria, Va.   1815

JPT · JPT · JPT

John Proctor Trott
New London, Conn.   1792

J.P.T & SON

J. P. Trott & Son
New London, Conn.   1820

J.P.TROTT

John Proctor Trott
New London, Conn.   1792

J.P.W.

Joseph P. Warner
Baltimore, Md.   1830

JR · JR · JR

Joseph Richardson, Jr.
Philadelphia   1773

JR

Joseph Rogers
Newport, R.I.   1780

J&R · J&R

Johnson & Reat
Richmond, Va.   1804

J&R

Johnson & Riley
Baltimore, Md.   1785

J.Reeve · J. Reeve

Joseph Reeve
Newburgh, N.Y.   1803

J·RIDGEWAY

John Ridgeway
Boston   1805

J.RIDGWAY

James Ridgway
Boston   1789

J.ROGERS

Joseph Rogers
Newport, R.I.   1780

J.RUDD&CO

J. Rudd & Co.
New York   1831

J.RUSSEL

John Russell
Greenfield, Mass.   1794

JS

Joel Sayre
New York   1799

J·S

Joseph Shoemaker
Philadelphia   1793

JS · J·S

John Staniford
Windham, Conn.   1789

J.SARGEANT · HARTFORD   *

Jacob Sargeant
Hartford, Conn.   1785

J.SAWYER

Joel Sawyer
Bolton, Mass.   1830

J Sayre · P · J Sayre

Joel Sayre
New York   1799

J.S.B **J.S.B**

John Starr Blackman
Danbury, Conn.   1805

J.S.BIRD

John S. Bird
Charleston, S.C.   1825

⚜ J&S ⚜

Johonnot & Smith
Windsor, Vt.   1815

J & S.BALDWIN

J. & S. Baldwin
Rochester, N.Y.   1800

J.SCHANK **m**

John A. Schanck
New York   1795

J.S.&Co

Joseph Seymour & Co.
Syracuse, N.Y.   1850

J.Scott **J.SCOTT**

John B. Scott
New York   1820

Jˢᵉ OWEN

Jesse Owen
Philadelphia   1794

J.S.FELT

J. S. Felt
Portland, Me.   1825

J.SHAW

John A. Shaw
Newport, R.I.   1802

J.SHEALD

J. S. Heald   B.M.
Baltimore, Md.   1810

J.SHOEMAKER *

Joseph Shoemaker
Philadelphia   1793

J.SIBLEY

John Sibley
New Haven, Conn.   1810

J.Simmons

James Simmons
New York   1815

J.S.MOTT

J. S. Mott
New York   1790

J.S.SHARRARD

James S. Sharrard
Shelbyville, Ky.   1850

J.STOCKMAN

Jacob Stockman
Philadelphia   1828

J.STODDER

Jonathan Stodder, Jr.
New York   1825

J.Stow

John Stow
Wilmington, Del.   1772

✱ J.SWEENEY ✱

John Sweeney
Geneva, N.Y.   1816

J.T

Jonathan Trott
Boston   1758

J TANGUY   **J.TANGUY**

John Tanguy
Philadelphia   1801

J.&T.D **🔔** **🔔**

John & Tunis Denise
New York   1798

J J H

John T. Hunt
Lynchburg, Va.   1819

JTOUZELL J.TOUZELL

John Touzell
Salem, Mass. 1756

J.T.R

Joseph T. Rice
Albany, N.Y. 1813

J.T.RICE **Albany**

Joseph T. Rice
Albany, N.Y. 1813

J.TROTT **JTrott** **J.TROTT**

Jonathan Trott
Boston 1758

J.TURNER

James Turner
Boston 1744

J.T.YOUNG PETERSBURGH

J. T. Young
Petersburg, Va. 1845

J.W

John Waite
South Kingston, R.I. 1763

J.W

John Walraven
Baltimore, Md. 1792

JW

James Ward
Hartford, Conn. 1798

JW **JW**

Joseph Warner
Wilmington, Del. 1775

J.W

John Wendover
New York 1690

J.W

Joseph Wyatt
Philadelphia 1797

J.W.ABBOTT

John W. Abbott
Portsmouth, N.H. 1817

J.WAKEFIELD.

John Wakefield
East Thomaston, Me. 1820

J.WAITE **J:WAITE**

John Waite
South Kingston, R.I. 1763

J•WALKER

John Walker, Jr.
Philadelphia 1798

J.WALLEN

John Wallen
Philadelphia 1763

J.WALTER

Jacob Walter B.M.
Baltimore, Md. 1815

J.WARD **HARTFORD**

James Ward
Hartford, Conn. 1798

J:WARNER

Joseph Warner
Wilmington, Del. 1775

J.WATSON

James Watson
Philadelphia 1830

J.W.B ▨ ▨▨ *

Joseph W. Boyd
New York 1820

J.W.BEEBE ✿✿✿

James W. Beebe S.M.
New York 1835

J.W.BEEBE & CO

J. W. Beebe & Co.
New York 1844

J.W.CORTELYOU.

J. W. Cortelyou
New Brunswick, N.J.   1805

J.WEBB

James Webb   B.M.
Baltimore, Md.   1810

J.WENTWORTH
J. WENTWORTH   *

Joshua L. Wentworth
Lowell, Mass.   1834

J.W.F.

John W. Faulkner
New York   1835

J.W.FAULKNER

John W. Faulkner
New York   1835

J.W.FORCE

Jabez W. Force
New York   1819

J.Williams

John Williams
Philadelphia   1793

J.WILLIAMS.   **J.WILLIAMS**

Jehu Williams, Sr.
Lynchburg, Va.   1813

J.WILLIS

J. Willis
Boston   1820

J.W.KING   **PURE COIN**

Joseph W. King
Middletown, Conn.   1776

J.WOOD

John Wood
New York   1770

J &.W.MOIR   *

J. & W. Moir
New York   1845

J.ZANE

Jesse S. Zane
Wilmington, Del.   1796

Krider & Biddle
Philadelphia   1850

K.C.&J.

Kidney, Cann & Johnson
New York   1850

K&D

Kidney & Dunn
New York   1844

KEELER

Joseph Keeler
Norwalk, Conn.   1810

Kimberly   **KIMBERLY**

William Kimberly
New York   1790

KINGSTON

John Kingston
New York   1775

Kirk   **KIRK**

Samuel Kirk   B.M.
Baltimore, Md.   1815

KIRK&SMITH

Kirk & Smith   B.M.
Baltimore, Md.   1815

KL   **KL**

Knight Leverett
Boston   1736

K.Leverett   *K.Leverett*

Knight Leverett
Boston   1736

K&S.

Kirk & Smith   B.M.
Baltimore, Md.   1815

KE   **KE**

Koenraet Ten Eyck
Albany, N.Y.   1703

LAFAR

John J. Lafar
Charleston, S.C.   1805

LAMAR   *

Mathias Lemar
Philadelphia   1790

Lamothe

John Lamothe
New Orleans, La.   1822

LANG

Richard Lang
Salem, Mass.   1770

LANG

Jeffrey Lang
Salem, Mass.   1733

LANGE

William Lange
New York   1844

L·B   **LB**   **L·B**   *

Loring Bailey
Hingham, Mass.   1801

L·B

Luther Bradley
New Haven, Conn.   1798

L·B   **✡**   **LB**

Lewis Buichle
Baltimore, Md.   1798

L.B.CANDEE & CO.

L. B. Candee & Co.
Woodbury, Conn.   1830

L.BROCK   **NEW YORK**

L. Brock
New York   1830

L·Browne   **L·BROWNE**   **L·BROWNE**

Liberty Browne
Philadelphia   1801

L.Buichle

Lewis Buichle
Baltimore, Md.   1798

L.CARY   **L·CARY**

Lewis Cary
Boston   1815

L'COUVERTIE

Louis Couvertie
New Orleans, La.   1822

L·CURTIS   **L. CURTIS.**

Lewis Curtis
Farmington, Conn.   1797

LEACH

Charles Leach
Boston   1789

LEONARD

Samuel T. Leonard
Chestertown, Md.   1805

LeTelier

John Le Telier
Philadelphia   1770

Lewis & Smith

Lewis & Smith
Philadelphia   1805

LF   **LF**

Lewis Fueter
New York   1770

L.FUETER   **N.YORK**   **L.FUETER**
L.Fueter   *

Lewis Fueter
New York   1770

L&G

Lincoln & Green
Boston 1810

LH

Lewis Heck
Lancaster, Pa. 1776

LH

Logan Henderson
Charleston, S.C. 1767

LH **LH** **STERLING**

Littleton Holland
Baltimore, Md. 1800

L.HECK

Lewis Heck
Lancaster, Pa. 1776

L.H.Miller&Co.

L. H. Miller & Co.
Baltimore, Md. 1840

L.HOLLAND **L.HOLLAND**

L.Holland *

Littleton Holland
Baltimore, Md. 1800

Libby **Boston** **Libby**

Jacob G. L. Libby
Boston 1820

LIBERTY·BROWNE

Liberty Browne
Philadelphia 1801

LIDDEN

John Lidden
St. Louis, Mo. 1850

LINCOLN &FOSS *

Lincoln & Foss
Boston 1850

LINCOLN & REED

Lincoln & Reed
Boston 1835

L.KIMBALL

Lewis A. Kimball
Buffalo, N.Y. 1837

L.Lupp **L.Lupp**

Lewis Lupp
New Brunswick, N.J. 1800

L.M.&A.C.ROOT

L. M. & A. C. Root
Pittsfield, Mass. 1830

LOCKWOOD

James Lockwood
New York 1799

LOMBARD

B. E. Lombard
Charleston, S.C. 1828

Longley **Longley**

Henry Longley
New York 1810

Longley & Dodge

Longley & Dodge
Charleston, S.C. 1810

LOVETT

Robert Lovett
Philadelphia 1818

LOW&CO

John J. Low & Co.
Boston 1830

LOWELL & SENTER
LOWELL & SENTER

Lowell & Senter
Portland, Me. 1830

LOWER

Joseph Lower
Philadelphia 1806

LOWNES & ERWIN

Lownes & Erwin
Philadelphia 1816

LOWS,BALL & CO

LOWS, BALL & Co   *

Lows, Ball & Co.
Boston   1840

L.P.COE

L. P. Coe
New York   1835

L PONCET   L.PONCET

Louis Joseph Poncet
Baltimore, Md.   1800

L.Ryerson

Lucas Ryerson
Hawthorne, N.J.   1792

L.S.B

Lucas Stoutenburgh
Charleston, S.C.   1718

L S BOUDO

Louis Boudo
Charleston, S.C.   1810

L.T.WELLES & CO

L. T. Welles & Co.
Hartford, Conn.   1810

L.&VV

Lansing & Van Veghten
Albany, N.Y.   1774

LW

Lemuel Wells
New York   1790

L&W   STANDARD

Leonard & Wilson
Philadelphia   1847

L.Walker

L. Walker
Boston   1825

L.W.CLARK

Lewis W. Clark
Watertown, N.Y.   1832

L.W.&Co

Lemuel Wells & Co.
New York   1794

LYNCH

John Lynch
Baltimore, Md.   1786

LYNG   N.YORK

John Burt Lyng
New York   1759

L.YOUNG

Levi Young
Bridgeport, Conn.   1827

*   *

Abel Moulton
Newburyport, Mass.   1815

M&A   Utica

Murdock & Andrews
Utica, N.Y.   1822

MANN

Alexander Mann
Middletown, Conn.   1800

MARQUAND & BROTHER NEW YORK

Marquand & Brother
New York   1825

MARQUAND & CO
MARQUAND & CO   *

Marquand & Co.
New York   1830

MARSHALL &
TEMPEST
Marshall & Tempest
Philadelphia   1813

    *

Masters & Murdock
Philadelphia   1800

MATHER & NORTH
Mather & North
New York   1825

MATT SKINNER
Matt Skinner
Philadelphia   1752

MB   **MB**
Miles Beach
Litchfield, Conn.   1771

M·B
Martin Bull
Farmington, Conn.   1767

M&B   **M·B**   **⚜**
Merriman & Bradley
New Haven, Conn.   1817

Mc CLYMAN
John McClyman
New York   1815

Mc Clymon
William McClymon
Schenectady, N.Y.   1800

Mc CONNEL   **◈**
Hugh McConnel
Philadelphia   1811

McCONNELL
Thomas McConnell
Wilmington, Del.   1806

M.CLUFF   **NORFOLK**
Matthew Cluff
Norfolk, Va.   1802

Mc Mullin & Black
McMullin & Black
Philadelphia   1811

M·CONNELL   *
Thomas McConnell
Wilmington, Del.   1806

M&D
Moulton & Davis
Newburyport, Mass.   1824

M·De Young   **M·DE YOUNG.**
Michael De Young
Baltimore, Md.   1816

MEAD & ADRIANCE
Mead & Adriance
Ithaca, N.Y.   1831

MEADOWS & CO
Meadows & Co.
Philadelphia   1831

MERRIMAN
Marcus Merriman
New Haven, Conn.   1787

Σ·℧   **❖**
Michael Gibney
New York   1836

M.G   **MG**   **MG**
Miles Gorham
New Haven, Conn.   1790

M.GORHAM
Miles Gorham
New Haven, Conn.   1790

MH
Marquette Hastier
New York   1771

M+H   *
Myers & Halsted
New York   1763

M·I
Munson Jarvis
Stamford, Conn.   1765

MILLER
William Miller
Philadelphia   1810

MILLS & FORRISTALL

Mills & Forristall
Boston 1845

Minott *Minott* **M**

Samuel Minott
Boston 1764

Minott **I·A**

Minott & Austin
Boston 1765

Minott **WS**

Minott & Simpkins
Boston 1769

MINTON

Joseph B. Minton
Norfolk, Va. 1840

MINTON & MAYER

Minton & Mayer
Norfolk, Va. 1842

MITCHELL

Henry Mitchell
Philadelphia 1844

MITCHELL & TYLER

Mitchell & Tyler
Richmond, Va. 1845

M·J **MJ**

Munson Jarvis
Stamford, Conn. 1765

ML

Mathias Lemar
Philadelphia 1790

M:GRETTER

Michael Gretter
Richmond, Va. 1810

MM **M.M** **MM**

Marcus Merriman S.M.
New Haven, Conn. 1787

MM **MM** **MM**

Myer Myers
New York 1745

M.M&Co **M**

Marcus Merriman & Co.
New Haven, Conn. 1802

M·MILLER

Mathew Miller P.M.
Charleston, S.C. 1807

M.M.LAWRENCE

Martin M. Lawrence
New York 1832

M.MORSE **M.MORSE**

Moses Morse
Boston 1816

M.MOSES

Martin Moses
Lenox, Mass. 1819

MN

Mark Nelson
Portsmouth, N.H. 1754

MONK

James Monk
Charleston, S.C. 1800

MONTEITH **10·15**

John & Robert Monteith B.M.
Baltimore, Md. 1814

MOOD

Peter Mood
Charleston, S.C. 1790

MOOD & EWAN *

Mood & Ewan
Charleston, S.C. 1824

MOORE

Jared L. Moore
New York 1835

MOORE & BREWER

Moore & Brewer
New York   1835

MOORE & FERGUSON

Moore & Ferguson
Philadelphia   1801

MORGAN

Elijah Morgan
Poughkeepsie, N.Y.   1807

Mors

Obadiah Mors
Boston   1733

MORSE

Stephen Morse
Portsmouth, N.H.   1771

MOSELEY

David Moseley
Boston   1775

MOSES

Jacob Moses
Birmingham, Ala.   1768

MOTTS   **MOTTS**   MOTT'S

W. & J. S. Mott
New York   1789

MOULTON

Ebenezer Moulton
Boston   1795

MOULTON

Joseph Moulton
Newburyport, Mass.   1765

M.P

Maltby Pelletreau   P.M.
New York   1813

MP   **M·P**

Matthew Petit   S.M.
New York   1811

M.P. STICKNEY

M. P. Stickney
Newburyport, Mass.   1820

MR   **MR**   **MR**   **MR**

Moody Russell
Barnstable, Mass.   1715

M&R

McFee & Reeder
Philadelphia   1793

MS

Moreau Sarrazin
Charleston, S.C.   1734

M·SHAVER

Michael Shaver
Abingdon, Va.   1807

MULFORD & WENDELL

Mulford & Wendell   P.M.
Albany, N.Y.   1842

MUMFORD

Henry G. Mumford
Providence, R.I.   1813

MUNN & JONES

Munn & Jones
Greenfield, Mass.   1824

MURDOCK

John Murdock
Philadelphia   1779

Musgrove   **Musgrave**

James Musgrave
Philadelphia   1795

M.&VS   *

McClyman & Van Sandford
Albany, N.Y.   1790

M&W *

Moulton & Wood
Newburyport, Mass.   1818

M.WHITNEY

M. F. Whitney
New York   1823

MWING

Moses Wing
Windsor, Conn.   1785

M.W.JOHNSON   **M.W.JOHNSON**

Maycock W. Johnson
Albany, N.Y.   1815

Myers   *Myers*   **MYERS** *

Myer Myers
New York   1745

N.A

Nathaniel Austin
Boston   1760

N.ANDRUS & CO

N. Andrus & Co.
New York   1834

N.B

Nathaniel Bartlett
Concord, Mass.   1760

N.B

Nicholas Burdock
Philadelphia   1797

NB

Nathaniel Burr
Fairfield, Conn.   1780

N.BARTLETT

Nathaniel Bartlett
Concord, Mass.   1760

N.B.NICHOLS

Nathaniel B. Nichols
Petersburg, Va.   1817

N.BOGERT

Nicholas J. Bogert
New York   1801

NC

Nathaniel Clough
Lee, N.H.   1790

NC   **NC**   **N·C**

Nathaniel Coleman
Burlington, N.J.   1790

N.COLEMAN   **N·COLEMAN**

Nathaniel Colman
Burlington, N.J.   1790

N.CORNWELL *

Nathaniel Cornwell
Danbury, Conn.   1800

N.D

Nathan Dickinson
Amherst, Mass.   1824

N.DICKINSON

Nathan Dickinson
Amherst, Mass.   1824

N·DODGE   **N.DODGE**

Nehemiah Dodge
Providence, R.I.   1795

N·EASTON

Nathaniel Easton
Nantucket, Mass.   1815

N·E·CRITTENDEN

Newton E. Crittenden
Le Roy, N.Y.   1824

Newman ★

Timothy H. Newman
Groton, Mass.   1800

N.FRANCIS   *NF*   **N·FRANCIS**

Nathaniel Francis
New York   1804

N⋅FREEBORN

N. Freeborn
Newport, R.I.   1810

N.GEFFROY   **N⋅GEFFROY**

N.GEFFROY

Nicholas Geffroy
Newport, R.I.   1795

N. GODDARD

Nicholas Goodard
Rutland, Vt.   1797

NH

Nathaniel Helme
Little Rest, R.I.   1782

NH   **◎**

Nicholas Hutchins
Baltimore, Md.   1810

N.H&CO

N. Harding & Co.
Boston   1842

N⋅HAIGHT

Nelson Haight
Newburgh, N.Y.   1839

NHARDING   **N.Harding**   *

N.Harding   *

N.Harding   **A.WARREN**   *

Newell Harding
Boston   1822

N. HARDING & CO ✱ COIN

N. Harding & Co.
Boston   1842

N.HAYDEN

Nathaniel Hayden
Charleston, S.C.   1832

N.Hobbs

Nathan Hobbs
Boston   1815

N⋅Hurd   **N⋅Hurd**

Nathaniel Hurd
Boston   1755

NICHOLS   **◐ ✪ ◑**

Basset Nichols
Providence, R.I.   1815

NICHOLS

William S. Nichols
Newport, R.I.   1808

N.J.BOGERT

Nichols J. Bogert
New York   1801

N⋅L   **NeL**   *

Nathaniel Leach
Boston   1789

N⋅LANG

Nathaniel Long
Salem, Mass.   1760

N.LE HURAY

Nicholas Le Huray
Philadelphia   1809

N.LE HURAY.JR

Nicholas Le Huray, Jr.
Philadelphia   1821

 *N.L.Hazen*   **CINCINNATI**   *

N. L. Hazen
Troy, N.Y.   1829

NM   **NM**   **NM**   **NM**   **NM**   *

Nathaniel Morse
Boston   1709

N.MATSON   **PURE COIN**   *

Newell Matson
Oswego, N.Y.   1845

NMORS

Nathaniel Morse
Boston   1709

N·MUNROE

Nathaniel Munroe
Baltimore, Md.   1815

N N   **N N**

Nehemiah Norcross
Boston   1796

N.N.WEAVER

Nicholas N. Weaver
Utica, N.Y.   1815

N.OLMSTED

Nathaniel Olmsted
Farmington, Conn.   1808

NORTON & SEYMOUR

Norton & Seymour
Syracuse, N.Y.   1850

NOWLAN & CO

Thomas Nowlan & Co.
Petersburg, Va.   1848

NOXON

Martin Noxon
Edenton, N.C.   1800

N.PRATT

Nathan Pratt
Essex, Conn.   1792

N.ROTH-UTICA

Nelson Roth
Utica, N.Y.   1837

NR   **N·R**

Nicholas Roosevelt
New York   1738

NS   **N·S**

Nathaniel Shipman
Norwich, Conn.   1790

N.S

Nathan Storrs
Northampton, Mass.   1792

N·SHIPMAN

Nathaniel Shipman
Norwich, Conn.   1790

N.STODDARD

Noah Stoddard
New York   1830

N.STORRS

Nathan Storrs
Northampton, Mass.   1792

N.TAYLOR & CO

N. Taylor & Co.
New York   1825

N&T.F

Nathaniel & Thomas Foster
Newburyport, Mass.   1820

N & T.FOSTER

Nathaniel & Thomas Foster
Newburyport, Mass.   1820

NV

Nathaniel Vernon
Charleston, S.C.   1802

NV

Nicholas Van Rensselaer
New York   1765

N·VERNON

Nathaniel Vernon
Charleston, S.C.   1802

N·VERNON & CO

N. Vernon & Co.
Charleston, S.C.   1803

N·R   **N·R**

Nicholas Roosevelt
New York   1738

OAKES   **K**   **OAKES**   **O**

Frederick Oakes   S.M.
Hartford, Conn.   1810

O. B. Cooley

Oliver B. Cooley
Utica, N.Y.   1828

O.C.FORSYTH

O. C. Forsyth   S.M.
New York   1810

O.CHAPIN

Otis Chapin
Springfield, Mass.   1821

O.D.Seymour

Oliver D. Seymour
Hartford, Conn.   1843

O.Gerrish.   *

Oliver Gerrish
Portland, Me.   1825

O.KUCHLER   NEW ORLEANS

O. Kuchler
New Orleans, La.   1850

O.M.FITON   TROY

O. M. Fiton   P.M.
Troy, N.Y.   1815

OP

Otto Paul De Parisen
New York   1763

OPDP

Otto Paul De Parisen & Son
New York   1789

O.PIERCE   O.PIERCE

O. Pierce
Boston   1824

OREED   PHILA   O. REED   *

Osmon Reed
Philadelphia   1831

O.REED & CO   🐾

O. Reed & Co.
Philadelphia   1841

ORICH   BOSTON

O. RICH ★ BOSTON   O.RICH   *

Obadiah Rich
Boston   1830

O·ROBINSON

O. Robinson
New Haven, Conn.   1800

O.& S.   O&S

Oakes & Spencer
Hartford, Conn.   1811

OSMON REED & CO

Osmon Reed & Co.
Philadelphia   1841

OTIS   Otis   NEWPORT   Otis   Otis

Jonathan Otis
Newport, R.I.   1750

Ott

George Ott
Norfolk, Va.   1801

OWEN

Jesse Owen
Philadelphia   1794

O.W.Towson   A

O.W.TOWSON

Obadiah W. Towson   B.M.
Baltimore, Md.   1813

PA   PA

Pygan Adams
New London, Conn.   1735

PACKARD

Jonathan Packard
Northampton, Mass.   1811

PALMER & BACHELDERS

Palmer & Bachelders
Boston   1850

PANCOAST

Samuel Pancoast
Philadelphia   1785

Ω Đ Ŋ PANGBORN & BRINSMAID

Pangborn & Brinsmaid
Burlington, Vt.   1833

PARISEN

Otto Paul De Parisen
New York   1763

PARISEN   *

Otto W. Parisen
New York   1791

PARKMAN   *

Charles Parkman
Boston   1790

PARKMAN

John Parkman
Boston   1738

Parkman   Parkman

Thomas Parkman
Boston   1793

PARRY

Martin Parry
Portsmouth, N.H.   1780

PB

Phillip Becker
Lancaster, Pa.   1764

PB

Philip Brown
Hopkinton, N.H.   1810

PB

Phineas Bradley
New Haven, Conn.   1770

PB

Philip Bush, Jr.
Winchester, Va.   1786

P.B

Phineas Bushnell
Saybrook, Conn.   1765

P.B.&C

Pelletreau, Bennett & Cooke
New York   1815

P.&B   P.&B

Pangborn & Brinsmaid
Burlington, Vt.   1833

P.B.SADTLER&SON

P. B. Sadtler & Son
Baltimore, Md.   1850

P.Chitry   N·YORK

Peter Chitry
New York   1814

P.CLARK

Peter G. Clark
New Haven, Conn.   1810

P.D

Philip Dally
New York   1779

P.D   P.D   P.D

Peter David
Philadelphia   1730

P.DANA

Peyton Dana
Providence, R.I.   1803

P.DAVID   P.DAVID

Peter David
Philadelphia   1730

P.DICKINSON & CO.   *

P. Dickinson & Co.
Syracuse, N.Y.   1837

PDR   PDR

Peter De Riemer
New York   1763

P.DUBOIS **BUFFALO**

Philo Dubois
Buffalo, N.Y.   1842

PEAR & BACALL   **BOSTON**   *

Pear & Bacall
Boston   1850

PEIRCE

John Pierce
Boston   1810

PENFIELD & CO

Josiah Penfield & Co.
Savannah, Ga.   1822

PERKINS

Jacob Perkins
Newburyport, Mass.   1787

PF   **PF**

Peter Feurt
Boston   1732

P.FIELD **JR**

Peter Field, Jr.
New York   1805

P.G   **P.G**

Peter Getz
Lancaster, Pa.   1782

PG   **PG**   **PG**

Philip Goelet
New York   1731

P.GARRETT

Philip Garret
Philadelphia   1811

P.Getz

Peter Getz
Lancaster, Pa.   1782

P.GRIFFIN   **P.GRIFFEN**

Peter Griffen
New York   1815

P.G.TANNER

Perry G. Tanner   s.m.
Utica, N.Y.   1842

PH   **PH**   **PH**   *

Philip Hulbeart
Philadelphia   1750

PH   **P.H.**

Philip Huntington
Norwich, Conn.   1795

PHELPS

Ebenezer S. Phelps
Northampton, Mass.   1812

PhilipSyng *

Philip Syng, Jr.
Philadelphia   1726

P.Howell   **P.HOWELL**

Paul Howell
New York   1810

P.Hulbeart   *

Philip Hulbeart
Philadelphia   1750

PIERPONT

Benjamin Pierpont
Boston   1756

PITKIN

John O. Pitkin
East Hartford, Conn.   1826

PITMAN   **Pitman**

Saunders Pitman
Providence, R.I.   1775

Pitts

Richard Pitts
Philadelphia   1742

PVB   **PVB**   **PVB**

Peter Van Inburgh
New York   1710

P.JONES

Philip Jones
Wilmington, Del.   1837

PK

Peter Kirkwood
Chestertown, Md.   1790

P.L   **PL**

Peter Leret
Philadelphia   1779

PL   **PL**

Paul Little
Portland, Me.   1760

PL   **PL**

Peter Lupp
New Brunswick, N.J.   1787

PLATT & BROTHER

Platt & Brother
New York   1825

P.Leret

Peter Leret
Philadelphia   1779

P.L.K

Peter L. Krider
Philadelphia   1850

P.Lupp

Peter Lupp
New Brunswick, N.J.   1787

P.M   *

Piner Mansfield
Smyrna, Del.   1800

PM

Peter Martin
New York   1756

PM

Peter Mood
Charleston, S.C.   1790

P&M   **P&M**   *

Parry & Musgrave
Philadelphia   1793

P.MARTIN

Peter Martin
New York   1756

P.MARTIN

Peter Martin , II
New York   1825

P.MILLER   **P.Miller**

Pardon Miller
Providence, R.I.   1821

P.MITCHELL

Phineas Mitchell
Boston   1809

P.MOOD

Peter Mood
Charleston, S.C.   1790

PO

Peter Oliver
Boston   1705

PO   **P.O**

Peter Olivier
Philadelphia   1790

POLK

Robert I. W. Polk
Winchester, Va.   1840

PONS   **PON**   **PONS**   **PONS**

Thomas Pons
Boston   1789

:Potwine

John Potwine
Boston   1721

PP   **PP**

Peter Perreau
Philadelphia   1797

P. P. HAYES   *
POKEEPSIE

Peter P. Hayes
Poughkeepsie, N.Y.   1826

Peter Quintard
New York   1731

Paul Revere
Boston   1725

Paul Revere, Jr.
Boston   1757

Paul Revere
Boston   1725

Paul Revere, Jr.
Boston   1757

Peter Riker
New York   1797

Philip B. Sadtler   B.M.
Baltimore, Md.   1800

Philip Syng
Philadelphia   1714

   *

Philip Syng, Jr.
Philadelphia   1726

Philip B. Sadtler   B.M.
Baltimore, Md.   1800

*

Peter Vergereau
New York   1720

Paul Sayre
Southampton, N.Y.   1785

Philemon Stacy, Jr.
Boston   1819

Paul Stillman
Westerly, R.I.   1808

Pelletreau & Upson
New York   1818

William Purse
Charleston, S.C.   1798

Putnam & Low
Boston   1822

Peter Vergereau
New York   1720

Peter Van Beuren
New York   1795

Peter Van Beuren
New York   1795

Peter Van Dyke
New York   1705

P.WHITE

Peregrine White
Woodstock, Conn. 1774

RA

Robert S. Avery
Preston, Conn. 1807

R&A.C.

R. & A. Campbell B.M.
Baltimore, Md. 1835

R&ACAMPBELL **1015** *

R. & A. Campbell B.M.
Baltimore, Md. 1835

RALYTLE **1015**

Robert A. Lytle B.M
Baltimore, Md. 1825

RB **RB**

Roswell Bartholomew
Hartford, Conn. 1805

RB **RB** **RB** *

Robert Brookhouse
Salem, Mass. 1800

R.BEAUVAIS

René Beauvais
St. Louis, Mo. 1838

RBROWN ★ **10≺15**

Robert Brown
Baltimore, Md. 1830

R.BROWN & SON

Robert Brown & Son
Baltimore, Md. 1849

RC

Robert Campbell B.M.
Baltimore, Md. 1819

RC **RC**

Richard Conyers
Boston 1688

R&C **N-YORK**

Riker & Clapp
New York 1802

R·CUTLER

Richard Cutler
New Haven, Conn. 1760

RD **RD** **N** *

Robert Douglas
New London, Conn. 1766

R.D.DUNBAR

Rufus Davenport Dunbar
Worcester, Mass. 1825

RD

Richard Van Dyke
New York 1750

RE **RE**

Robert Evans
Boston 1798

REDMAN **NORFOLK**

Henry H. Redman
Norfolk, Va. 1819

REEVES

Enos Reeves
Charleston, S.C. 1784

R.E.SMITH

Richard E. Smith
Louisville, Ky. 1827

R.EVANS

Robert Evans
Boston 1798

REVERE **REVERE** **Revere**

Paul Revere, Jr.
Boston 1757

RF

Rufus Farnam
Boston 1796

R·F **RF** **R·F**

Robert Fairchild
Durham, Conn.   1740

R·FAIRCHILD

Robert Fairchild
Durham, Conn.   1740

R·FARNAM

Rufus Farnam
Boston   1796

RG

Robert Gray
Portsmouth, N.H.   1813

R·G **RG** **RG**

Rufus Greene
Boston   1730

Rene Grignon
Oxford, Mass.   1691

R&G

Riggs & Griffith   B.M.
Baltimore, Md.   1816

R·GORHAM

Richard Gorham
New Haven, Conn.   1799

R·Gray

Robert Gray
Portsmouth, N.H.   1813

R·GREENE **RGreene**

Rufus Greene
Boston   1730

R·H **R·H** **RH**

Richard Humphreys
Philadelphia   1772

R.H.BAILEY

Roswell H. Bailey
Woodstock, Vt.   1840

R·H·MAYNARD

R. H. Maynard
Buffalo, N.Y.   1825

R·Humphreys

Richard Humphreys
Philadelphia   1772

R&H·FARNAM

R. & H. Farnam
Boston   1800

Rice

Joseph Rice
Baltimore, Md.   1784

RICHARD

Stephen Richard
New York   1801

RICHARDS

Samuel R. Richards, Jr.
Philadelphia   1793

**RICHARDS &
WILLIAMSON**

Richards & Williamson
Philadelphia   1797

RICHMOND

Franklin Richmond
Providence, R.I.   1815

RIGGS **Riggs** **RIGGS**

George W. Riggs   B.M.
Baltimore, Md.   1810

RIKER&CLAPP **N·YORK** **R&C** **R&C** *

Riker & Clapp
New York   1802

R·KEYWORTH

R·KEYWORTH *

Robert Keyworth
Washington, D.C.   1833

RL

Richard Lang
Salem, Mass.   1770

R♥L

Roberts & Lee
Boston   1772

R·LANG

Richard Lang
Salem, Mass.   1770

R·M   Pure Coin

Reuben Merriman
Cheshire, Conn.   1810

RM

Robert Monteith   B.M.
Baltimore, Md.   1814

R.MERRIMAN

Reuben Merriman
Cheshire, Conn.   1810

R.NIXON

Richard Nixon
Philadelphia   1820

Robert Davis.

Robert Davis
Concord, N.H.   1812

ROBERT J.BROWN

Robert J. Brown
Boston   1813

ROBT GRAY

Robert Gray
Portsmouth, N.H.   1813

ROCKWELL   ROCKWELL
ROCKWELL   D   R   D   *
Rockwell   R   G   *

Edward Rockwell
New York   1807

Rockwell

Thomas Rockwell
Norwalk, Conn.   1785

·ROGERS·   ROG·RS

Daniel Rogers
Ipswich, Mass.   1760

R·P

Richard Pitts
Philadelphia   1742

R.PARRY

Rowland Parry
Philadelphia   1790

R.PUTNEY   R.PUTNEY

Reueben H. Putney
Sackets Harbor, N.Y.   1816

R & POTTER   NORFOLK

Redman & Potter
Norfolk, Va.   1819

RR   RR

Richard Riggs
Philadelphia   1810

RR   R.R.

Robert Ross
Frederica, Del.   1789

R·RAIT   R·RAIT   *

Robert Rait
New York   1830

R.ROSS   R·ROSS

Robert Ross
Frederica, Del.   1789

Robert Sanderson
Boston   1638

Hull & Sanderson
Boston   1652

R.S.

Robert Sutton
New Haven, Conn   1800

R Shepherd

Robert Shepherd
Albany, N.Y.   1805

R STARR   R.STARR

Richard Starr
Boston   1807

R.STILLMAN

Richard Stillman
Philadelphia   1805

R.SWAN

Robert Swan
Andover, Mass.   1795

RUSSEL   .RUSSEL

Jonathan Russell
Ashford, Conn.   1804

Rutter

Richard Rutter
Baltimore, Md.   1790

R.V

Richard Vincent
Baltimore, Md.   1799

RD   RVD

Richard Van Dyke
New York   1750

R.W   RW   R.W

Robert Wilson
New York   1805

R.W.ROATH   PURE COIN

Roswell Walstein Roath
Norwich, Conn.   1826

R&WW

R. & W. Wilson
Philadelphia   1825

R&W WILSON

R & W. WILSON   *

R. & W. Wilson
Philadelphia   1825

G S W

George Sharp
Philadelphia   1844

SA

Samuel Alexander
Philadelphia   1797

SA   SA   SA

Samuel Avery
Preston, Conn.   1786

S&A

Simmons & Alexander
Philadelphia   1800

S.ALEXANDER

Samuel Alexander
Philadelphia   1797

SALISBURY   NY

Henry Salisbury   S.M.
New York   1831

SALISBURY & CO

Salisbury & Co.
New York   1835

SAM.KIRK   10.15

Samuel Kirk   B.M.
Baltimore, Md.   1815

SAMUEL BURT   SAMUEL BURT

Samuel Burt
Boston   1750

S.AVERY

Samuel Avery
Preston, Conn.   1786

SANFORD

Isaac Sanford
Hartford, Conn.   1785

SAYRE   🔲

John Sayre
New York   1792

SAYRES-LEX.K

Samuel Ayres
Lexington, Ky.   1805

SB   **SB**   🔲   **SB**   *   **SB**   🔲

Standish Barry
Baltimore, Md.   1784

SB   **SB**

Samuel Bartlett
Boston   1775

SB

Samuel Bourdett
New York   1730

S·B

Samuel Buel
Middletown, Conn.   1777

SB   **SB**

Samuel Burrill
Boston   1733

SB

Samuel Burt
Boston   1750

S&B

Shepherd & Boyd
Albany, N.Y.   1806

S.BAKER

Stephen Baker
New York   1830

S. BALDWIN

S. Baldwin   P.M.
Boston   1810

S.Ball

Sheldon Ball
Buffalo, N.Y.   1821

S.BARRETT   ★

Samuel Barrett
Nantucket, Mass.   1775

S.BARTLETT

Samuel Bartlett
Boston   1775

S.B. COLE

Schubael B. Cole
Great Falls, N.H.   1850

S.BELL

S. W. Bell
Philadelphia   1837

S.Bowne   **S:Bowne**

Samuel Bowne
New York   1780

S.BRAMHALL

Sylvanus Bramhall
Plymouth, Mass.   1800

S.BROWN

Samuel Brown   S.M.
New York   1815

S·BURNET   *

Samuel Burnet
Philadelphia   1795

S:Burrill   **S:Burrill**

Samuel Burrill
Boston   1733

S:BURT

Samuel Burt
Boston   1750

S&B.BROWER

S. & B. Brower
Albany, N.Y.   1810

Samuel Casey
South Kingstown, R.I.   1750

Samuel Clark
Boston   1685

S:CASEY

Samuel Casey
South Kingstown, R.I.   1750

S.C.& Co.

Simon Chaudron & Co.
Philadelphia   1807

S&C

Storrs & Cooley
Utica, N.Y.   1827

SC & CO

Stephen Castan & Co.
Philadelphia   1819

SCHANCK

John A. Schanck
New York   1795

S.COLEMAN

Samuel Coleman
Burlington, N.J.   1795

S Coley

Simeon Coley
New York   1767

S.COLLINS

Seldon Collins, Jr.
Utica, N.Y.   1837

S COVIL& KINSEY

Scovil & Kinsey
Cincinnati, Ohio   1830

SCOVIL WILLEY & CO   *

Scovil, Willey & Co.
Cincinnati, Ohio   1835

S.CRAFT   *

Stephen Craft
New York   1811

SD **SD** **SD**

Samuel Drowne
Portsmouth, N.H.   1770

S.DAVIS

Samuel Davis
Plymouth, Mass.   1801

S.D.BACON.   *

Silas D. Bacon
Boston   1830

S.D.BROWER

S. D. Brower   s.m.
Troy, N.Y.   1832   *

S.D.BROWER & SON   STERLING 925

S. D. Brower & Son
Albany, N.Y.   1850

★ **S.DODGE** ★

Seril Dodge
Providence, R.I.   1793

S.D.ROCKWELL   **NEW YORK**

S. D. Rockwell
New York   1830

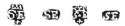

SDrowne   *

Samuel Drowne
Portsmouth, N.H.   1770

Samuel Edwards
Boston   1729

SE   **SE**

Stephen Emery
Boston   1775

S.Emery   **S.Emery**   *

Stephen Emery
Boston   1775

SETH.EASTMAN

Seth Eastman
Concord, N.H.   1820

SEYMOUR&HOLLISTER

✿ SEYMOUR & HOLLISTER ✿

Seymour & Hollister
Hartford, Conn.   1845

SE.YOUNG LACONIA

S. E. Young
Laconia, N.H.   1840

SF

Samuel Ford
Philadelphia   1797

SG

S. Garre
New York   1825

SG

Samuel Gilbert
Hebron, Conn.   1798

SG

Samuel Gray
New London, Conn.   1710

S GARRE

S. Garre
New York   1825

S.GILBERT

Samuel Gilbert
Hebron, Conn.   1798

S.GRAY

Samuel Gray
Boston   1732

S.Griffith   SGriffeth

Samuel Griffith
Portsmouth, N.H.   1757

S·H   SH   S.H

Stephen Hardy
Portsmouth, N.H.   1805

SH

Samuel Haugh
Boston   1696

S:H

Stephen Hopkins, Jr.
Waterbury, Conn.   1745

S. HAMMOND & Cº   *

S. Hammond & Co.
Utica, N.Y.   1810

SHAW & DUNLEVY

Shaw & Dunlevy
Philadelphia   1833

SHEPHERD

Robert Shepherd
Albany, N.Y.   1805

SHEPHERD & BOYD

SHEPHERD & BOYD   *

Shepherd & Boyd
Albany, N.Y.   1806

S.HILDEBURN
PHILADELPHIA   ✿   *

Samuel Hildeburn
Philadelphia   1810

SHIPP & COLLINS

Shipp & Collins
Cincinnati, Ohio   1850

S.Howell

Silas W. Howell
Albany, N.Y.   1798

S.HOYT   PEARL ST

S.HOYT.PEARL ST

Seymour Hoyt
New York   1817

S.HOYT & CO

S. Hoyt & Co.
New York   1842

S.HUNTINGTON

S. Huntington
Portland, Me.　1850

S·Hussey　S.HUSSEY

Stephen Hussey
Easton, Md.　1818

S.HUTCHINSON

Samuel Hutchinson
Philadelphia　1828

S.&H.GEROULD

Samuel A. Gerould
Keene, N.H.　1819

SIBLEY

Clark Sibley
New Haven, Conn.　1800

S·LEA

Samuel J. Lea　B.M.
Baltimore, Md.　1815

SILVERTHORN

Henry Silverthorn
Lynchburg, Va.　1832

Silverthorn & Clift
SILVERTHORN & CLIFT

Silverthorn & Clift
Lynchburg, Va.　1857

SIMMONS & ALEXANDER

Simmons & Alexander
Philadelphia　1800

Simes　Simes

William Simes
Portsmouth, N.H.　1800

Simpkins　Simpkins

William Simpkins
Boston　1730

S.J

Samuel Johnson
New York　1780

S.J.LEA

Samuel J. Lea　B.M.
Baltimore, Md.　1815

S Justis

Swan Justice
Richmond, Va.　1819

S.K　11/12　1102　SK　*

Samuel Kirk　B.M.
Baltimore, Md.　1815

S.KENDALL

Sullivan Kendall
Hallowell, Me.　1816

SKEPLINGER

Samuel Keplinger　B.M.
Baltimore, Md.　1812

Skinner　Skinner　SKINNER

Thomas Skinner
Marblehead, Mass.　1733

S.KIRK　SKirk

Samuel Kirk
Baltimore, Md.　1815

S.LEE

Samuel W. Lee
Providence, R.I.　1815

S.LEONARD

Samuel T. Leonard
Chestertown, Md.　1805

SLIDELL　N·YORK　SLIDELL　*

Joshua Slidell
New York　1765

S.L.PRESTON

Stephen L. Preston
Philadelphia　1831

SM

Samuel Merriman
New Haven, Conn.　1795

S·M
Silas Merriman
New Haven, Conn.   1760

S·M **M**
Samuel Minott
Boston   1764

SM
Sylvester Morris
New York   1745

S&M
Sibley & Marble
New Haven, Conn.   1801

S.MARBLE **S.MARBLE**
Simeon Marble
New Haven, Conn.   1800

SMERRIMAN
Samuel Merriman
New Haven, Conn.   1795

Smith & Grant
Smith & Grant
Louisville, Ky.   1827

S.M.Taber
Samuel M. Tabor
Providence, R.I.   1822

S.N.Story
S. N. Story
Worcester, Mass.   1845

SP
Samuel Pancoast
Philadelphia   1785

SP **S.P** **SP** **SP** **S.P** **S.P**   *
Samuel Parmelee
Guilford, Conn.   1760

SP
Samuel Phillips
Salem, Mass.   1680

S·Parmele **S·Parmele**
Samuel Parmelee
Guilford, Conn.   1760

SP
Saunders Pitman
Providence, R.I.   1775

S.P.SQUIRE
S. P. Squire
New York   1835

SQUIRE.&.BROTHER
Squire & Brother
New York   1846

SQUIRE.&.LANDER
Squire & Lander
New York   1840

SR   *
Stephen Reeves
Philadelphia   1766

SR **SR**   *
Samuel R. Richards, Jr.
Philadelphia   1793

S&R
Sayre & Richards
New York   1802

S.REED
Stephen Reed
New York   1805

SReeves
Stephen Reeves
Cohansey Bridge, N.J.   1767

S.RICHARD **SRICHARD**
SRichard
Stephen Richard
New York   1801

S.RICHARDS **SRICHARDS**   *
Samuel R. Richards, Jr.
Philadelphia   1793

SRICHARDS **SW**

Richards & Williamson
Philadelphia   1797

S·S·S

Samuel Sargeant
Worcester, Mass.   1797

S·S   **S·S·S**

Samuel Shethar
New Haven, Conn.   1777

S·S

Samuel Soumaine
Annapolis, Md.   1740

S·S

Samuel Stout
Princeton, N.J.   1779

S·S

Silas W. Sawin
New York   1825

SS **SS**

Simeon Soumaine
New York   1706

S·S·C

Seth Storer Coburn
Springfield, Mass.   1775

S·SIMMONS

S. Simmons
Philadelphia   1797

S & S WILSON

S. & S. Wilson
Philadelphia   1805

ST   **ST ST**   *N.York*   *

ST   *N.York*   *
Samuel Tingley
New York   1754

S.&T.

Shethar & Thompson
Litchfield, Conn.   1801

S & T.T WILMOT

Samuel & Thomas T. Wilmot
Charleston, S.C.   1837

Standish   **Barry**

Standish Barry
Baltimore, Md.   1784

STANIFORD **Staniford**

John Staniford
Windham, Conn.   1789

STANLEY S BALDWIN

Stanley S. Baldwin
New York   1820

STANTON

Zebulon Stanton
Stonington, Conn.   1775

S.T. CROSBY

Samuel T. Crosby
Boston   1849

STEBBINS

Thomas E. Stebbins
New York   1830

STEBBINS&CO   *

STEBBENS & Cº 264B.WAY NY

T. E. Stebbins & Co.
New York   1835

STEBBINS&HOWE

Stebbins & Howe
New York   1832

STEPHENSON

Thomas Stephenson
Buffalo, N.Y.   1835

STEVENS&LAKEMAN

Stevens & Lakeman
Salem, Mass.   1819

STEWART   **IOS**

John Stewart
New York   1791

Samuel Tingley
New York   1754

STOCKMAN&PEPPER

Stockman & Pepper
Philadelphia   1828

STODDER&FROBISHER

Stodder & Frobisher
Boston   1816

Stollenwerck

Stollenwerck & Co.
New York   1800

Stollenwerck&Bros

Stollenwerck & Bros.
New York   1805

Storm&Son

A. G. Storm & Son
Poughkeepsie, N.Y.   1823

Storrs & Cook

Storrs & Cook
Northampton, Mass.   1827

Storrs&Cooley. Utica

Storrs & Cooley
Utica, N.Y.   1827

Stuart   ✳   *Stuart*   ✳   *

John Stuart
Providence, R.I.   1720

SV   SV   SV

Samuel Vernon
Newport, R.I.   1705

W.S.PELLETREAU
S.VAN WYCK

W. S. Pelletreau & Van Wyck
New York   1815

S.VAN WYCK

Stephen Van Wyck
New York   1805

S.V.LUPP

S. V. Lupp
New Brunswick, N.J.   1815

SW   S

Samuel Warner
Philadelphia   1797

S.W

Samuel Waters
Boston   1803

SW   SW   S

Simon Wedge   B.M.
Baltimore, Md.   1798

SW   S   W   S

Silas White
New York   1791

SW   SW

Samuel Williamson
Philadelphia   1794

S&W

Simmons & Williamson
Philadelphia   1797

Swan   SWAN   Swan

William Swan
Boston   1740

S.Warner.

Samuel Warner
Philadelphia   1797

S.WATERS

Samuel Waters
Boston   1803

S.WEDGE   S.Wedge

Samuel Wedge   B.M.
Baltimore, Md.   1798

S.WHERITT   *

Samuel H. Wheritt
Richmond, Va.   1830

S.WHITE *SWhite*
Silas White
New York   1791

S.W.Howell *S.W.Howell*
Silas W. Howell
Albany, N.Y.   1798

S.WILLIAMS S.WILLIAMS
Stephen Williams
Providence, R.I.   1799

S.WILLIS
Stillman Willis
Boston   1813

S.WILMOT
Samuel Wilmot
New Haven, Conn.   1800

S&WILSON
Storm & Wilson
Poughkeepsie, N.Y.   1802

SWL *I* *W*
Samuel W. Lee
Providence, R.I.   1815

S.W.LEE *S.W.LEE*
Samuel W. Lee
Providence, R.I.   1815

SY
S. Yates
Albany, N.Y.   1810

S.Y & Co   *
S. Yates & Co.
Albany, N.Y.   1825

SYATES
S. Yates
Albany, N.Y.   1810

T.A *TA* *TA*
Thomas Arnold
Newport, R.I.   1760

T.A.DAVIS T.A.DAVIS
Thomas Aspinwall Davis
Boston   1825

T&A.E.WARNER
Thomas & A. E. Warner
Baltimore, Md.   1805

T.ARNOLD T.ARNOLD
Thomas Arnold
Newport, R.I.   1760

TAYLOR&LAWRIE
Taylor & Lawrie
Philadelphia   1837

TB
Thomas Bentley
Boston   1786

B B
Thauvet Besley
New York   1727

TB
Timothy Bontecou
New Haven, Conn.   1725

T.B TB *
Timothy Bontecou, Jr.
New Haven, Conn.   1747

T.B
Theophilus Bradbury
Newburyport, Mass.   1792

TB
Timothy Brigden
Albany, N.Y.   1813

TB UB
Thomas Burger
New York   1805

T&B
Trott & Brooks
New London, Conn.   1798

T·B *Burger*

Thomas & John Burger
New York 1805

T.BAKER

Thomas Baker
Concord, N.H. 1819

TBC

Thomas Boyce Campbell
Winchester, Va. 1822

T· B. HUMPHREYS.

Thomas B. Humphreys
Louisa Court House, Va. 1831

T. B. HUMPHREYS & SON

Thomas B. Humphreys & Son
Richmond, Va. 1849

T.BRUFF

Thomas Bruff
Easton, Md. 1785

TB.Simpkins

Thomas B. Simpkins
Boston 1750

T.BYRNES

Thomas Byrnes
Wilmington, Del. 1793

TC

Thomas Carson
Albany, N.Y. 1815

T.C

Major Timothy Chandler
Concord, N.H. 1787

T.C

Thomas Clark
Boston 1764

TC

Thomas Colgan
New York 1771

T&C

Trott & Cleveland
New London, Conn. 1792

T.CAMPBELL

Thomas Campbell
New York 1800

T.CARSON

Thomas Carson
Albany, N.Y. 1815

J.C.C

Thomas Chester Coit
Norwich, Conn. 1812

T.C.GARRETT

Thomas C. Garrett
Philadelphia 1829

T. CHANDLER

Major Timothy Chandler
Concord, N.H. 1787

TC&H

Thomas Chadwick & Heims
Reading, Pa. 1814

TC Clark   **T·CLARK**

Thomas Clark
Boston 1764

TCOHEN

Thomas Cohen
Petersburg, Va. 1808

TCOLGAN   **T.COLGAN** *

Thomas Colgan
New York 1771

T.CONLYN

T. Conlyn
Philadelphia 1845

T.COVERLY

Thomas Coverly
Newport, R.I. 1760

Timothy Dwight
Boston   1675

T·DANE   **T·DANE**

Thomas Dane
Boston   1745

JDBussy

Thomas D. Bussey
Baltimore, Md.   1792

TDD   ▯

Tunis D. Dubois
New York   1797

T·D·DUBOIS

Thomas D. Dubois
New York   1797

T.E   **T.E**

Thomas Stevens Eayres
Boston   1785

T.E   **T.E**   **T.E**

Thomas Edwards
Boston   1725

T.E

Thomas Knox Emery
Boston   1802

T·EATON

Timothy Eaton
Philadelphia   1793

T·Edwards   **T·EDWARDS**

Thomas Edwards
Boston   1725

T·Emery   **T·KEMERY**

Thomas Knox Edwards
Boston   1802

T·EMOND

Thomas Emond
Petersburg, Va.   1802

TENNEY 251BWAY

William I. Tenney
New York   1840

TERRY   **TERRY**   **TERRY**

Geer Terry
Enfield, Conn.   1800

T.E.S

Thomas E. Stebbins
New York   1830

T.F

Thomas Fletcher
Philadelphia   1813

T.F   *

Thomas Fisher
Philadelphia   1797

T·Fisher

Thomas Fisher
Philadelphia   1797

T·FLETCHER

Thomas Fletcher
Philadelphia   1813

T·FOSTER   **T·FOSTER**

Thomas Foster
Newburyport, Mass.   1820

TG

Timothy Gerrish
Portsmouth, N.H.   1775

TG Brown   *

Theodore G. Brown
New York   1830

T·Gerrish

Timothy Gerrish
Portsmouth, N.H.   1775

T. GOLDSMITH ◈   *

Thomas Goldsmith   S.M.
Troy, N.Y.   1842

T·GRANT
Thomas Grant
Marblehead, Mass. 1754

TH **TH** **TH**

TH * **TR** * **TH** *

Thomas Hammersley
New York 1756

T&H **C** **TH** **T**
Taylor & Hinsdale
New York 1807

Th·Farnum
Thomas Farnum
Boston 1825

THIBAULT
Francis & Felix Thibault
Philadelphia 1807

THBAULT BROTHERS **THIBAULT & BROTHERS.** *
Thibault & Brothers
Philadelphia 1810

TH.MARSHALL
Thomas H. Marshall
Albany, N.Y. 1832

THN
Timothy H. Newman
Groton, Mass. 1800

TH·Newman
Timothy H. Newman
Groton, Mass. 1800

TIFFANY, YOUNG & ELLIS *
Tiffany, Young & Ellis
New York 1841

Tiley
James Tiley
Hartford, Conn. 1765

TITCOMB
Albert Titcomb
Portland, Me. 1823

T.J. CHANDLER
Timothy Jay Chandler
Concord, N.H. 1820

T.J.MEGEAR
Thomas J. Megear
Wilmington, Del. 1830

T.K
Thaddeus Keeler
New York 1805

T.K **TK**
Thomas Kettell
Charlestown, Mass. 1784

TK **TK**
Thomas Kinne
Norwich, Conn. 1807

T·K·E
Thomas Knox Emery
Boston 1802

T.KEELER
Thaddeus Keeler
New York 1805

T·KEITH
Timothy Keith
Boston 1795

T·K·EMERY
Thomas Knox Emery
Boston 1802

T.KINNE **PURE COIN**
Thomas Kinne
Norwich, Conn. 1807

T.K.MARSH **PARIS**
Thomas K. Marsh
Paris, Ky. 1830

T&L **T** **T** **T**
Taylor & Lawrie
Philadelphia 1837

T·LYNDE

Thomas Lynde
Worcester, Mass.   1771

 *

Thomas Millner
Boston   1715

Thomas McConnell
Wilmington, Del.   1806

T MILNE

Thomas Milne
New York   1795

T·N   T·N   T·N

Thomas Norton
Farmington, Conn.   1796

TP

Thomas Parrott
Boston   1775

TP

Thomas Purse
Winchester, Va.   1801

TP

Thomas Parkman
Boston   1793

TP **PARIS** *

Thomas Phillips
Paris, Ky.   1799

T·PARKMAN

Thomas Parkman
Boston   1793

T·PARROTT

T. Parrott
Boston   1775

T·P·DROWN

Thomas Pickering Drown
Portsmouth, N.H.   1803

T·PERKINS   T·PERKINS

T. Perkins
Boston   1810

T·PONS

Thomas Pons
Boston   1789

TR

Thomas Revere
Boston   1789

T·R   TR   R *

Thomas Richards   P.M.
New York   1802

TR   W·S·P

Richards & Pelletreau
New York   1825

T&R

Tanner & Rogers
Newport, R.I.   1775

T·RICHARDS

Thomas Richards
New York   1802

T·RICHARDS   J·F   N·YORK *

Thomas Richards & John Foster
New York   1815

T·R·KING

Thomas R. King   B.M.
Baltimore, Md.   1819

TS

Thomas Savage
Boston   1689

T·S   TS

Thomas Shields
Philadelphia   1765

TS   TS

Thomas Skinner
Marblehead, Mass.   1733

Thomas Sparrow
Annapolis, Md.   1764

T.SARGEANT

Thomas Sargeant
Springfield, Mass.   1795

TSB

Tobias Stoutenburgh
New York   1731

T SIMPKINS

Thomas Barton Simpkins
Boston   1750

T.STEBBINS

Thomas E. Stebbins
New York   1830

T Steele

T. S. Steele
Hartford, Conn.   1800

T Steele & Co

T. S. Steele & Co.
Hartford, Conn.   1815

T. STEPHENSON & Cº

Thomas Stephenson & Co.
Buffalo, N.Y.   1839

T·T   **TT**   **TT**

Thomas Townsend
Boston   1725

T.T.WILMOT

Thomas T. Wilmot
Charleston, S.C.   1840

T.U   **N YORK**

Thomas Underhill
New York   1779

T.U   **TV**

Underhill & Vernon
New York   1787

T.V.R

Tunis Van Riper
New York   1813

T·W

Thomas Whartenby
Philadelphia   1811

T.W   **STERLING**   ❁

Thomas H. Warner   B.M.
Baltimore, Md.   1805

T.WARNER   **STERLING**

Thomas H. Warner   B.M.
Baltimore, Md.   1805

T.W.BELL

Thomas W. Bell
Petersburg, Va.   1837

T❖W.KEITH

T. & W. Keith
Worcester, Mass.   1825

T.WRIGGINS

Thomas Wriggins
Philadelphia   1837

TY

Thomas You
Charleston, S.C.   1753

U&B

Ufford & Burdick
New Haven, Conn.   1812

VALLET   *

Benjamin F. Vallet
Kingston, N.Y.   1820

V&C   ◆

Van Voorhis & Coley
New York   1786

❁   **V&Co**   ❧

Vansant & Co.
Philadelphia   1850

VAN NESS & E.S.BURSTRAND

Van Ness & E. S. Burstrand
New York   1830

☆ **VENT** ☆

John Frederick Vent
Boston   1783

VERNON

Nathaniel Vernon   S.M.
Charleston, S.C.   1802

VILLARD *Villard*

R. H. Villard
Georgetown, D.C.   1833

V.LAFORME

Vincent LaForme
Boston   1850

VL&B **PURE COIN**

Vincent LaForme & Bro.
Boston   1850

V.MARTIN

Valentine Martin
Boston   1842

VV&S **VV&S** ❦ **V&S**

V.V.&S. **V&S** ❦ *

Van Voorhis & Schanck
New York   1791

V.V.SCHANCK & McCALL

Van Voorhis, Schanck & McCall
Albany, N.Y.   1800

V&W

Van Ness & Waterman
New York   1835

WA   **WA**

William Anderson
New York   1746

W.A.COOKE ⊛

William A. Cooke
Petersburg, Va.   1826

W.ADAMS **NEW YORK**

William L. Adams
New York   1831

Walraven ❦ ◑

John Walraven
Baltimore, Md.   1792

WARD **HARTFORD**

James Ward
Hartford, Conn.   1798

WARD 67 MARKET ST

John Ward
Middletown, Conn.   1805

WARD & BARTHOLOMEW

Ward & Bartholomew
Hartford, Conn.   1804

Ward & Cox

Ward & Cox
Philadelphia   1811

WARDEN

Abijah B. Warden
Philadelphia   1842

W.A.RASCH

W. A. Rasch
New Orleans, La.   1830

WARFORD

Joseph Warford
Albany, N.Y.   1800

Warrock

William Warrock
Norfolk, Va.   1795

◑ **WATSON** ◑

Joseph H. Watson
Warrenton, Va.   1844

WATSON & BROWN

Watson & Brown
Philadelphia 1830

W.A.WILLIAMS

William A. Williams
Alexandria, Va. 1809

WB

William Bartram
Philadelphia 1769

WB

William Ball
Philadelphia 1759

W.B

William Ball, Jr.
Baltimore, Md. 1785

WB **WB** **WB**

William Breed
Boston 1740

W&B **W&B.** **HARTFORD**

Ward & Bartholomew
Hartford, Conn. 1804

W.BAILEY **W**

William Bailey
Philadelphia 1816

W.Ball **W.BALL** **W.BALL**

William Ball, Jr.
Baltimore, Md. 1785

W.B.HEYER *W.B.Heyer*

William B. Heyer
New York 1798

W.B.HEYER & J.GALE

Heyer & Gale
New York 1807

W.B.N

William B. North
New Haven, Conn. 1810

W.B.NORTH&CO

W. B. North & Co.
New York 1823

W.BOGERT **ALBANY** *

William Bogert S.M.
Albany, N.Y. 1839

W.BONING

William Boning
Philadelphia 1845

W.Breed **W.Breed**

William Breed
Boston 1740

W.BROWN

William Brown
Albany, N.Y. 1849

W.BURR

William Burr
Providence, R.I. 1793

W.BURT

William Burt
Boston 1747

W.&BYRNES

Woodcock & Byrnes
Wilmington, Del. 1793

W+C

William Cario
Boston 1735

W•C

William Cario, Jr.
Boston 1760

W/C **WC**

William Clark
New Milford, Conn. 1775

WC **WC** **W.C**

William Cleveland
Norwich, Conn. 1791

William Cowell
Boston   1703

William Cowell, Jr.
Boston   1734

William Cross
Boston   1695

William Cario
Boston   1735

William Cario, Jr.
Boston   1760

W. CARRINGTON

William Carrington
Charleston, S.C.   1830

W. C. DUSENBERRY

W. C. Dusenberry
New York   1819

William Clark
New Milford, Conn.   1775

William Coley
New York   1767

W. CORNELL

Walter Cornell
Providence, R.I.   1780

William Cowan
Fredericksburg, Va.   1803

William D. Cowan
Philadelphia   1808

William Cowell
Boston   1703

William Cowell, Jr.
Boston   1734

W. D. BEASOM & CO.   NASHUA   *

W. D. Beasom & Co.
Nashua, N.H.   1840

William Donovan
Philadelphia   1784

WDP   *

Willian De Peyster
New York   1732

W. D. RAPP   STANDARD

W. D. Rapp
Philadelphia   1828

Emmor T. Weaver
Philadelphia   1808

WEBB

Edward Webb
Boston   1705

WELLES   BOSTON

George Welles
Boston   1805

WELLES & CO

Welles & Co.
Boston   1816

WELLES & GELSTON

Welles & Gelston
Boston   1816

William Elvins
Baltimore, Md.   1796

WENTWORTH&CO
Wentworth & Co.
New York   1850

WF **WF**
William Faris
Annapolis, Md.   1757

WF **NEW YORK**
William Forbes   S.M.
New York   1830

W.F.Hill
William F. Hill
New York   1815

WFORBES **NY**
William Forbes   S.M.
New York   1830

W.G 🔯 ☘ **W.G** ☘ 🔯 *
William Gale   S.M.
New York   1820

WG
William Ghiselin
Philadelphia   1751

WG
William W. Gilbert
New York   1767

W.G **W.G** *
William Gowdey
Charleston, S.C.   1757

WG
William Gowen
Medford, Mass.   1777

WG
William Grant, Jr.
Philadelphia   1785

W.G
William Gurley
Norwich, Conn.   1804

WG * **WG** *
William Grigg
New York   1765

W&G **BOSTON**
Woodward & Grosjean
Boston   1847

W.GALE
William Gale   S.M.
New York   1820

W.GALE & SON
William Gale & Son
New York   1843

W.GENNET **PREMIUM** *
W. Gennet
Watertown, N.Y.   1850

W.GETHEN
William Gethen
Philadelphia   1797

W.G.Forbes **W.G.Forbes** 🔯 🔯

W.G.FORBES
William G. Forbes
New York   1773

W.Gilbert
William W. Gilbert
New York   1767

W.GOWEN **W.Gowen**
William Gowen
Medford, Mass.   1777

W&GR
William & George Richardson
Virginia   1782

W.GRANT **W.Grant**
William Grant, Jr.
Philadelphia   1785

W. GREGG

William Gregg
Petersburg, Va.   1820

W GRIGG

William Grigg
New York   1765

W.GRISWOLD

William Griswold
Middletown, Conn.   1820

W.G.&S

William Gale & Son
New York   1843

W.& G.SHARP

W. & G. Sharp
Philadelphia   1848

WH   **WH**

William Hamlin
Providence, R.I.   1795

WH

William Haverstick
Philadelphia   1781

WH

William Heurtin
New York   1731

WH   **WH**   **WH**   **WH**   *

William Hollingshead
Philadelphia   1754

WH   **WH**

William Homes
Boston   1739

WH

William Homes, Jr.
Boston   1783

WH

William Hookey
Newport, R.I.   1760

WH

William Hughes
Baltimore, Md.   1785

W&H

Ward & Hughes
Middletown, Conn.   1805

W&H   *

Wood & Hughes
New York   1846

W·HADWEN

William Hadwen
Nantucket, Mass.   1820

W·HAMLIN

William Hamlin
Providence, R.I.   1795

W·HART

William Hart
Philadelphia   1818

WHARTENBY

Thomas Whartenby
Philadelphia   1811

WHARTENBY & BUMM

Whartenby & Bumm
Philadelphia   1816

WHEELER &BROOKS

Wheeler & Brooks
Livonia, N.Y.   1830

WHITE

Amos White
East Haddam, Conn.   1766

WHITING

Charles Whiting
Norwich, Conn.   1750

Whitlock

Thomas B. Whitlock
New York   1805

Whitney
Eben Whitney
New York   1805

WHITNEY & HOYT
Whitney & Hoyt
New York   1828

Whittemore
William Whittemore
Portsmouth, N.H.   1735

W·Homes
William Homes
Boston   1739

W.H.WHITE
William H. White
Fredericksburg, Va.   1822

WB
William B. Johonnot   S.M.
Middletown, Conn.   1787

W·J   **WJ**
William Jones
Marblehead, Mass.   1715

WILLARD   *D* 🔴 Ω   *
H. Willard
Catskill, N.Y.   1818

WILLARD   **WILLARD** 🔴
James Willard
East Windsor, Conn.   1815

Williams
Jehu Williams, Sr.
Lynchburg, Va.   1813

William Osborn
William Osborn
Providence, R.I.   1840

WILLIAMS & VICTOR   **WILLIAMS & VICTOR**
Williams & Victor
Lynchburg, Va.   1814

WILLIAMSON
Samuel Williamson
Philadelphia   1794

WILMOT   **WILMOT**
Samuel Wilmot
New Haven, Conn.   1800

WISHART   🔴
Hugh Wishart   P.M.
New York   1784

W.I.TENNEY   **N.Y.**
William I. Tenney   P.M.
New York   1840

WJ   🔴 **WJ** 🔴
William B. Johonnot   S.M.
Middletown, Conn.   1787

W·K
William Kimberly
New York   1790

Benjamin Wynkoop
New York   1698

Cornelius Wynkoop
New York   1724

W KENDRICK
W.KENDRICK. LOUISVILLE
William Kendrick
Louisville, Ky.   1832

WL   **WL**
William Little
Newburyport, Mass.   1775

WCL   **WCL**
William Coffin Little
Amesbury, Mass.   1790

W·M **W·M**

William Moulton
Newburyport, Mass. 1750

W·M **W-M** **W·M** *

William Moulton
Newburyport, Mass. 1796

W.MANNERBACK *

William Mannerback
Reading, Pa. 1825

W·M·B **READING**

William Mannerback
Reading, Pa. 1825

WM.B.DURGIN

William B. Durgin
Concord, N.H. 1850

W·BROWN **IO5**

William Brown B.M.
Baltimore, Md. 1810

W.MℂP. **Q**

William McParlin B.M.
Annapolis, Md. 1805

W·D·Fenno & Son

William D. Fenno
Worcester, Mass. 1822

W·F LADD **□** *

William F. Ladd
New York 1828

WM GALE JR

William Gale, Jr.
New York 1843

WᴹGALE & SON *

William Gale & Son
New York 1843

WM.H.McDowell

William H. McDowell
Philadelphia 1819

W·HEWAN **U** **W**

William H. Ewan P.M.
Charleston, S.C. 1849

W·HWHITLOCK

William H. Whitlock
New York 1805

W.MILLER

William Miller
Philadelphia 1810

W.MITCHELL **W·MITCHELL JR**

W. MITCHELL

William Mitchel, Jr.
Richmond, Va. 1820

WM.J.PITKIN

William J. Pitkin
East Hartford, Conn. 1820

W.M.JR

William Mitchel, Jr.
Richmond, Va. 1820

WᴹL.PITKIN

William L. Pitkin
East Hartford, Conn. 1825

WM.MCDOUGALL

William McDougall
Meredith, N.H. 1825

W.MORRELL **W.MORRELL**

William M. Morrell
New York 1828

W·Moulton

William Moulton
Newburyport, Mass. 1750

W.MOULTON **W.MOULTON**

William Moulton
Newburyport, Mass. 1796

W⁼ROGERS

WM ROGERS **HARTFORD**

William Rogers
Hartford, Conn. 1822

WM.ROGERS & SON

William Rogers & Son
Hartford, Conn. 1850

W.M.ROOT

W.M.ROOT ⊕ ✪ **PITTSFIELD** *

William M. Root
Pittsfield, Mass. 1840

W.M.ROUSE **W.M.ROUSE**

William M. Rouse
Charleston, S.C. 1835

W⁼ R. TICE *

William R. Tice
New York 1850

W.M.SAVAGE

William M. Savage
Glasgow, Ky. 1805

W⁓ SMITH

William Smith
New York 1770

W⁓ S. Willis

William S. Willis
Boston 1830

W⁓ Thom-son

William Thomson
New York 1810

W⁼ W.WHITE

William W. White
Philadelphia 1805

WN

William Northey
Salem, Mass. 1764

W.NEEDELS

William Needles
Easton, Md. 1798

W.N.ROOT & BROTHER

W. N. Root & Brother
New Haven, Conn. 1850

Wolcott & Gelston

Wolcott & Gelston
Boston 1820

WOLFE & WRIGGINS

Wolfe & Wriggins
Philadelphia 1837

WOOD & HUGHES

Wood & Hughes
New York 1846

WOODCOCK

Bancroft Woodcock
Wilmington, Del. 1754

Woods **Woods**

Freeman Woods
New York 1791

Woodward

Antipas Woodward
Middletown, Conn. 1791

W·P

William Parham
Philadelphia 1785

W·P **WP**

William Pollard
Boston 1715

WP

William Poole
Wilmington, Del. 1790

W·P *

W. Prior
Connecticut or Massachusetts 1775

Walter Pearce
Norfolk, Va.　1830

W.P.&H.STANTON

W. P. & H. Stanton
Rochester, N.Y.　1826

W.PITKIN ⊛

Walter Pitkin
East Hartford, Conn.　1830

W.PITKIN C.C.NORTON

Pitkin & Norton
Hartford, Conn.　1825

W.PITKIN ⊛ **J.H.NORTON**

Pitkin & Norton
Hartford, Conn.　1843

W.PRIOR *

W. Prior
Connecticut or Massachusetts　1775

W·R **W.R**

William Richardson
Richmond, Va.　1778

W·R **WR** ▮ ⦿

William Roe
Kingston, N.Y.　1795

WR **WR** **WR** **WR**

William Rouse
Boston　1660

W·ROE ▮

William Roe
Kingston, N.Y.　1795

W.ROE & STOLLENWERCK

W. Roe & Stollenwerck
New York　1800

W·ROGERS

William Rogers
Hartford, Conn.　1822

W.R.P **WRP**

W. R. Pitman
New Bedford, Mass.　1835

W.S ▮ ⊡ ◈ *

William Seal
Philadelphia　1816

WS

William Simes
Portsmouth, N.H.　1800

WS **W.S**

William Simpkins
Boston　1730

WS

William Swan
Boston　1740

W.Sandford

William Sandford
New York　1817

W.Sanford

William Sanford
Nantucket, Mass.　1817

W.SEAL

William Seal
Philadelphia　1816

W.SELKIRK **ALBANY** *

William Selkirk
Albany, N.Y.　1815

W.SIMES **W.SIMES** **W.Simes** *

William Simes
Portsmouth, N.H.　1800

W.Simpkins **W.SIMPKINS**

William Simpkins
Boston　1730

WS **Minott**

Minott & Simpkins
Boston 1769

W.S. MORGAN *

William S. Morgan S.M.
Poughkeepsie, N.Y. 1837

W·S·N

William S. Nicholas
Newport, R.I. 1808

W.SP **W.S.P**

William S. Pelletreau
Southampton, N.Y. 1810

W.S.PELLETREAU

W.S.PELLTREAU

William S. Pelletreau
Southampton, N.Y. 1810

W.S.PELLETREAU
S.VAN WYCK

Pelletreau & Van Wyck
New York 1815

W.SP **TR**

Pelletreau & Richards
New York 1825

W SWAN

William Swan
Boston 1740

W.T **W.T** *

William Taylor
Philadelphia 1775

WT

Walter Thomas
New York 1769

WT

William Thompson
Baltimore, Md. 1795

W.TERRY **W.TERRY**

Wilbert Terry
Enfield, Conn. 1785

W.Thomson **W. Thomson** *

William Thomson
New York 1810

WV **WV** *

William Vilant
Philadelphia 1725

W.V.B

William Van Beuren
New York 1790

W&V **W&V**

Williams & Victor
Lynchburg, Va. 1814

WW

William Ward
Wallingford, Conn. 1700

W·W *

William Ward
Guilford, Conn. 1726

W.W

William Ward
Litchfield, Conn. 1757

WW

William Whetcroft
Annapolis, Conn. 1766

W.W

William Whittemore
Portsmouth, N.H. 1735

W.W

William Bradford Whiting
Norwich, Conn. 1752

W·W

William Wilson
Abingdon, Md. 1785

W.W **IT**

Wilson & Toy
Abdingdon, Md.   1790

W.WAITE

William Waite
Wickford, R.I.   1760

W.WALKER

William Walker
Philadelphia   1793

WWARD   **WWard**

William Ward
Litchfield, Conn.   1757

WWG

W. W. Gaskins
Norfolk, Va.   1806

WWG

William Waddill Geddy
Petersburg, Va.   1793

W.W.HANNAH

W. W. Hannah   P.M.
Hudson, N.Y.   1840

W·WHITING

William Bradford Whiting
Norwich, Conn.   1752

W.Wright

William Wright
Charleston, S.C.   1740

W.W.WHITE

William W. White
Philadelphia   1805

WY *

William Young
Philadelphia   1761

⊕ **WYER&FARLEY** **⊕**

Wyer & Farley
Portland, Me.   1828

WYNKOOP

Jacobus Wynkoop
Kingston, N.Y.   1765

WYoung

William Young
Philadelphia   1761

YEOMANS

Elijah Yeomans
Hadley, Mass.   1771

YOU

Daniel You
Charleston, S.C.   1743

YOU

Daniel You
Charleston, S.C.   1743

YOUNG

Ebenezer Young
Hebron, Conn.   1778

YOUNG

Alexander Young
Camden, S.C.   1807

ZAHM&JACKSON

Zahm & Jackson
New York   1830

Zalmon Bostwick
New York   1846

Z·B   **Z·B**

Zachariah Brigden
Boston   1760

Z BOSTWICK

Zalmon Bostwick
New York   1846

Z.BRADLEY   **❖**

Zebul Bradley
New Haven, Conn.   1810

Zachariah Brigden
Boston 1760

ZIBA FERRIS

Ziba Ferris
Wilmington, Del. 1810

Zebulon Stanton
Stonington, Conn. 1775

Z.SMITH Z.Smith

Zebulon Smith
Bangor, Me. 1820

A List of Silver Objects upon which
the Following Marks Were Located

An asterisk placed after a mark indicates that a reference exists in this list of silver which relates to that mark. This information was gleaned from notes written on margins and pages of Ensko editions by my father and husband as they worked with the silver in Robert Ensko, Inc. The information is sparse, undated, unformulated. However, it does provide a source of form, style, period, validity that will interest the collector and student. The marks are presented alphabetically.

AB	Fiddle tablespoon circa 1805.
AB Holmes	Fiddle thread tablespoon engraved script *LK to Sk* on front of curved down handle. L. 7 in.
A Billing	Two bright-cut tablespoons.
A Blanchard	Beaker engraved B.
AC	Fiddle fork with short midrib curved up handle. L. 7⅛ in.
AC Benedict	Fiddle thread forks.
AF Burbank	Serving spoon engraved script *HLL* on front of short midrib curved up handle. L. 8³⁄₁₆ in.
A Forbes	Strainer ladles.
AH	Serving spoon.
Akerly & Briggs	Fiddle dessert spoon circa 1810.
A Mathey	Fiddle tablespoons circa 1810.
AM Ward	Late fiddle dessert spoon engraved script *Frazierl* on front of curved up handle. L. 7½ in.
AR	Spoon circa 1805. (Houghton)
AR & Co	Spoons
AS	Tankard with mark struck twice. (Verplanck)
AS	Marrow spoon struck with no pellet in mark.
AS	Coffin-end spoon.

A Sanborn	Two violin fiddle teaspoons engraved script *NRS* on curved up handle. L. 5¾ in.
A Scott	Teaspoon
Bailey & Co	Fiddle thread fork engraved script *M* on back. L. 7⅞ in.
Bailey & Co	Four fiddle thread forks engraved script *AEBJ* on back. L. 7 in.
Baldwin	Spatulate-end spoon engraved feathered script *C* on front of handle. L. 9 in.
Ball Tompkins & Black	Fiddle thread fork. L. 6⅝ in.
Bard & Lamont	Two fiddle thread forks engraved script *AEBJ* on back. L. 7 in.
Basset & Warford	Covered creamer.
Bayley	Helmet creamer circa 1790.
BD	Spoon with scallop shell drop. L. 5¹⁄₁₆ in.
B Dexter	Spoon 1825.
Benjamin & Scudder	Tablespoon with basket of flowers.
BG	Two fiddle thread forks with crest on back of handle. L. 6¾ in.
B Gardiner	Six fiddle thread forks. L. 7½ in.
B Hurd	Tablespoon circa 1760.
Bigger	Three teaspoons engraved feathered script *G* on front of handle. L. 5⅜ in.
B Ingram	Teaspoon circa 1800.
BL	Bright-cut tablespoon with bird on bowl.
Blowers	Footed salt dishes.
BLR	Trinity Church paten. Mark has oval break.
BM Bailey	Fiddle dessert spoon.
B Mead	Coffin-end spoons.
B & M M Swan	Violin fiddle spoon with curved up handle circa 1834. L. 7⅛ in.
Brooks	Cocoanut cup.
Brower & Rusher	Silver pitcher.

Brown & Anderson	Fiddle teaspoon engraved script *Le Grand* on front of handle. L. 5¾ in.
Browne & Seal	Teaspoon circa 1805–1810.
BT	Footed creamer circa 1750–1760.
Canfield & Brother	Fiddle salt spoon with shell on bowl and curved down handle.
C & C	Tablespoon circa 1790. Mark without pseudo-marks.
C Choysenholder	Snuff box.
CG	Teaspoon with shell drop. L. 5⅞ in.
Chaudron's & Rasch	Sugar tongs of bow form. L. 6½ in.
Clark	Pepper box shaker circa 1740 formerly owned by Gov. Richard Ward.
Clark & Co	Julep cup engraved script *VLA*.
Clark & Co	Fiddle dessert spoon circa 1810.
C Maysenhoflder	Snuff box.
Colton & Collins	Teaspoon with sheaf of wheat.
Corbett	Small fiddle teaspoons circa 1805–1810.
CPA	Sugar tongs of bow form. L. 6⁵⁄₁₆ in.
Crowley & Farr	Teaspoon with sheaf of wheat.
C Stewart	Fiddle thread fork. L. 7 in.
Currier	Fiddle spoon circa 1810 engraved feathered script *JAL* on front, script *1832* on back of handle.
C Warner	Two fiddle teaspoons engraved feathered script *JAW* on front of handle. L. 6 in.
C Warner	Violin tablespoon with Indian and bow circa 1825–1840.
Davis Watson & Co	Fiddle spoon with shell on front. L. 8⅜ in.
DC	Teaspoon with featheredge engraved block VANC. (Van Cortlandt).
DC Fulton	Soup ladle with eagle incised four times circa 1835.
DE Lucy	Teaspoon.

D Gillis Leonard	Two fiddle teaspoons engraved feathered script *HY* on front of curved up handle. L. 6³⁄₁₆ in.
DR	Dessert Spoon circa 1775. (Carpenter).
D Smith	Fiddle spoon with arch drop engraved feathered script *EB* on front of handle. L. 6 in.
Dunbar & Story	Fiddle teaspoon.
DV	Round tray with riveted bead edge presented to Chief Justice John Jay.
DV Voorhis	Oval dish of Spanish style with reed ogee edge W. ³⁄₁₆ in. Top D. 12³⁄₄ in., base D. 9¼ in., H. 2³⁄₈ in., Weight 28 oz.
EB (Ephraim Brasher)	Helmet creamer engraved.
EB (Everadus Bogardus)	Gold buckle on exhibition, 1962, in the Museum of the City of New York. (Sarah Bayard)
EB (Ezekiel Burr)	Teaspoon circa 1795.
EC	Creamer. (New Haven, Conn., Historical Society)
E Cook	Teaspoon with basket of flowers.
E Lescure	Fiddle teaspoon.
EM	Teaspoon circa 1795.
EP Lescure	Fiddle teaspoons circa 1820.
E Smith	Tablespoon with spatulate handle. L. 7½ in.
E Stebbins & Co	Fiddle thread tablespoon.
ETW	Sword.
EW Dennison	Fiddle dessert spoon circa 1805.
E & W Burr	Six teaspoons with bright-cut edges.
FA & Co	Fiddle thread forks: one L. 6³⁄₄ in., three L. 7³⁄₈ in. circa 1870.
F Chaffee	Six teaspoons.
FH	Spoons circa 1790–1800.
F & H Clark	Sugar tongs with basket of fruit.
Field Jr	Coffin-end teaspoon engraved feathered script *MJ* on front of curved down handle. L. 6³⁄₈ in.
Fletcher & Gardiner	Silver cup.
FM	Dessert fork.

Forsyth	Fiddle teaspoon circa 1805.
FR Grump	Teaspoons with basket of flowers.
F & R	Knee buckle.
Garner & Winchester	Beaker circa 1850.
G Baker	Fiddle teaspoon engraved feathered script *EMD* on front of handle. L. 5⅝ in.
GD	Inverted pear-shaped chased sugar bowl with gadroon edge.
Gelston & Treadwell	Fiddle thread dinner fork.
Geo A Hoyt	Fiddle and shell teaspoon; six fiddle dessert forks.
G Eoff	King's pattern fork engraved feathered script *MRS* on front and *JER* on back of handle. L. 7¹¹⁄₁₆ in.
GF Mills	Dish with gadroon edge. D. 7 in.
GG Clark	Fiddle thread fork engraved script *MTC* on back.
GH	Teaspoons with bird on back of bowl and pointed ends engraved feathered script *EW.*
G Harris	Fiddle spoon with curved down handle.
Gilbert	Creamer.
G MacPherson	Fiddle thread butter spreader.
Gordon	Pair of beakers circa 1825.
GS	Featheredge teaspoon. Bottom marked.
GS	Sauce ladle circa 1790 engraved script *JMP.* (John M. Phillips)
G Sullivan	Coffin-end soup ladle with round bowl circa 1805.
G Terry	Teaspoons with incised V drop on pointed bowl engraved script *HME.* L. 5⅜ in.
G W & H	Fiddle fork engraved script *ECH* on back of handle. L. 7½ in.; seven fiddle thread forks engraved script *JAB* on back of handle. L. 8¼ in.
H	Tongs with sheaf of wheat circa 1820.
Haight	Spoon circa 1830–1850.
Halsted	Pair of sauce boats of 1770 style. (Stevens family of Stevens Institute Collection)
Hall & Elton	Luncheon knife.

HB	Teaspoon circa 1750.
H B & H M Bacon	Fiddle teaspoons engraved script *SL* on curved up handle. L. 5⅞ in.
Henchman	Rib-front spoon with long drop circa 1775.
Herbert	Fiddle teaspoon.
HG	Coffin-end tablespoon.
H Hastings	Fiddle spoon. L. 7⁵⁄₁₆ in.
Higbie & Crosby	Three-piece tea set circa 1825 style.
Hobbs	Fiddle spoon with broad drop engraved script *Ripley* on front of curved down shell handle. L. 8⅝ in.
Holloway	Fiddle dessert spoon engraved feathered script *GWE* on front of handle. L. 7½ in.
Hotchkiss	Fiddle thread soup ladle.
Howe & Guion	Teaspoons with basket of fruit.
H Perkins	Teaspoon. (Museum of Fine Arts, Boston)
H Power	Fiddle spoon with broad drop engraved script *JEO* on front of handle. L. 7½ in.
HS HGS	Teaspoon circa 1790.
H & S	Teaspoon circa 1830–1850.
H Sargeant	Cream ladle circa 1830.
HW	Sugar tongs circa 1790.
IA	Rattail spoon. (Carpenter)
Iackson	Dredger with handle engraved script *John Way To Anna Joy 1761*.
I Adam	Pierced oval basket with mark alongside of hall marks LONDON 1784–5 by Robert Hennell. (Stevens Institute Collection)
I Alstyne	Bright-cut teaspoon circa 1790.
I Anthony	Rattail tablespoon. (Carpenter)
IB (James Barrett)	Plain pointed-end tablespoons.
IB (John Benjamin)	Tablespoon with mark struck twice circa 1750–1760.
IB (Jurian Blanck Jr)	Spoon 1687.

IB (Jacob Boelen II)	Rattail teaspoon circa 1745–50.
IB (John Burger)	Teaspoon. (Seeler)
I Bliss	Sugar tongs.
IC (John Chalmers)	Creamer circa 1790.
IC (John Cluet Jr)	Stolen tankard with Maker's mark of I:C.
IC	Tankard with spout removed. (Ford)
ID	Tablespoon circa 1790–1800. Probably Jeremott W. Douglas.
I Davis	Tongs with basket of flowers.
IF Hyde	Sugar tongs.
IF	Knee buckle.
IF Tappan	Tablespoon circa 1830.
IG	Rib-front rattail teaspoon. (D. G. Grover, 1950)
IH	Inverted pear-shaped creamer engraved EL 1772; PL 1778; SLC 1829; CLM 1850; SFL 1880. (Martin Van Cortlandt)
IL (John Le Roux)	Rib-front tablespoon with double drop engraved Hendrick Gansevoort. obt 26 Sept A.E. 30, 1746 H x G.
IL (John Le Roux)	Three-hole New York or Albany porringer. (Mrs. Peltz)
IL (John Burt Lyng)	Inverted pear-shaped sugar bowl without cover engraved with Goelet crest. Both marks struck.
IM	Inverted pear-shaped shaker engraved block $M*D$. Three very crude marks struck. (R. S. Hutchins)
I Moulton	Tablespoon circa 1800.
I Myers	Dessert spoon.
IN (John Nelson)	Rib-front teaspoon with shell on bowl circa 1760.
IN (John Noyes)	Spoon. (Museum of Fine Arts Boston, January 3, 1963)
IN (Johannis Nys)	Brazier. (Philadelphia Museum, 1967)
I & NR	Twelve dessert spoons and twelve tablespoons bright-cut with featheredge. Early sterling mark.
John Burt Lang	Covered sugar bowl.

IP (Isaac Perkins)	Early porringer.
IP (John Potwine)	Cup with interesting geometric handle attachment. (Gray)
I & PT	Pair of sauce boats without sheaf of wheat engraved with Goelet crest. L. 6¾ in. including handle.
IR	Keyhole porringer circa 1740.
I Reed & Son	Fiddle thread teaspoon.
IS Town	Teaspoon.
IT (John Targee)	Sauce ladle with Goelet crest circa 1805–1810. L. 7¾ in. (Goelet)
IT (James Turner)	Spoon circa 1730–1740. (Museum of Fine Arts Boston, January 30, 1963)
IW	Octagonal spice box. (Goelet)
JA (1)	High pear-shaped coffee pot with gadroon mounts. Mark three times on base. (Blankarn)
JA (2)	Inverted pear-shaped sugar bowl with galley on cover and gadroon edge. Both marks struck three times.
Jackson	Dredger with handle engraved script *John Way To Anna Joy 1761*.
James Mix Jr	Fiddle teaspoons.
J Bard	Spoon circa 1800.
JB Jones	Fiddle teaspoon.
J Bridge	Rib-front tablespoon with shell heel engraved Derby crest.
J Brittin	Teaspoon with bird on bowl.
JCB & Co	Fiddle dessert spoon circa 1810.
J Clarico	Fiddle spoon with slashed drop engraved script *JAT* on back of curved up handle.
J Clark	Globular teapot engraved block $T^{H}_{*}M$.
J Clarke	Rattail tablespoon circa 1735.
JD	Spoon. (Kernan)
JD Chase	Fiddle thread teaspoon. L. 5¾ in.
JE Caldwell & Co	Repoussé child's cup.

J Fenno	Fiddle teaspoons circa 1810 engraved script *LWF.*
JH (John S. Hutton)	Porringer with New York geometric cross heart handle. (Mrs. Monica Wyatt)
JH (John Heath)	Coffee pot with mark struck twice.
JH Hollister	Violin fiddle teaspoon engraved script *LASeymour* on front of curved down handle.
J Jones	Fiddle teaspoon with round drop. L. 5⅝ in.
JM	Silver spurs circa 1825. (Mason)
Jo	Inverted pear-shaped covered sauce top sugar bowl circa 1765 engraved italics *JLP.*
John Price	Teaspoon circa 1810.
Johnson & Godley	Fiddle teaspoon.
Jones Ball & Co	Two violin fiddle dessert teaspoons engraved script *NAS* on front of curved up handle. L. 6⅞ in.
J Peabody	Fiddle dessert spoon engraved feathered script *CMA.* L. 7³⁄₁₆ in.
J & P Mood	Beaker dated 1825. (C. Foulke)
J Sargeant	Tongs circa 1790.
J Shoemaker	Tablespoon circa 1825.
JWB	Tablespoons.
J Wentworth	Violin fiddle tablespoon engraved script *CW* on front of handle. L. 8⅜ in.
JW Moir	Fiddle thread tablespoon.
Lamar	Bright-cut long tablespoon with mark struck twice.
LB	Teaspoon circa 1775–1780.
L Fueter	Tankard.
L Holland	Tablespoons.
Lincoln & Foss	Violin fiddle spoon engraved feathered script *BAS* on front of curved up handle. L. 5⅞ in.
Lows Ball & Co	Fiddle thread forks
LP Coe	Fiddle dessert spoon with pointed bowl engraved feathered script *ABS* on front of curved up handle. L. 7⅛ in.

M	Sugar tong circa 1810.
M	Fiddle thread butter spreader.
Marquand & Co	Two fiddle thread dinner forks with one engraved feathered script *JAB* on back of handle. L. 8¼ in.
Masters & Murdock	Teaspoon. L. 5⅝ in.
M Connell	Dessert spoons.
MH	Tankard. (F. P. Garvan, Jr.)
Mood & Ewan	Beaker dated 1825. (Foulke)
M & VS	Slop bowl.
M & W	Spoons.
Myers	Dessert spoon with Goelet crest; pair of dessert spoons #85–86 in exhibition February 2–March 15, 1954, at Brooklyn Museum of New York. (Mrs. J. H. Morgan)
N Cornwell	Coffin-end tablespoon.
N Harding	Violin fiddle dessert spoon engraved script *Graves* on back of curved up handle. L. 7¼ in.
N Harding	Fiddle spoon engraved feathered script *LAW* on front of curved down handle. L. 5⅞ in.
N Harding A Warren	Violin teaspoons circa 1850 engraved script *EF.*
NL	Rib-front teaspoons with shell back circa 1765.
NL Hazen	Water pitcher circa 1835.
NM	Pair of candlesticks; child's cup engraved block C^{T}F.
N Matson	Fiddle teaspoon with curved up handle. L. 6 in.
O Gerrish	Violin fiddle spoon engraved script *LAH* on back of curved up handle. L. 6⅛ in.
O Reed	Fiddle thread spoon. L. 6 in.
O Rich	Tankard dated 1836 with mark struck twice.
Parisen	Spoon with sheaf of wheat circa 1815; tablespoon with sheaf of wheat circa 1825.
Parkman (Charles)	Three teaspoons circa 1790.
P Dickinson & Co	Fiddle tablespoon.
Pear & Bacall	Engraved pie knife.

PH	Creamer. (Jeffords)
P Hulbeart	Rib-front tablespoon with shell drop engraved block E*B.
PM	Tablespoon with pointed ends.
P & M	Teaspoon circa 1795.
PP Hayes	Fiddle teaspoon circa 1810.
PS (Philip Syng Jr)	Declaration of Independence inkstand marked three times on bottom. Weight 36 ozs.
PS (P Syng Jr)	Declaration of Independence inkstand marked once in front.
P Sadtler	Sugar bowl circa 1800.
R & A Campbell	Teaspoons with sheaf of wheat.
RB	Coffin-end tablespoon with double V incised drop engraved feathered script *WEC* on front of handle.
RD	Engraved sugar tongs circa 1790.
Riker & Clapp	Three-piece oval panel tea set.
R Keyworth	Fiddle teaspoons circa 1810.
Rockwell	Fiddle tablespoon with curved down handle circa 1825.
Rockwell	Teaspoon and tablespoons with sheaf of wheat circa 1825.
R Rait	Fiddle thread tablespoon.
R & W Wilson	Three fiddle thread forks. L. 7¼ in.
SB	Round helmet-shaped creamer.
S Burnet	Two pointed antique teaspoons with panel engraving circa 1800.
Scovil Willey & Co	Beaker.
S Craft	Sugar tongs circa 1800.
SD Bacon	Two fiddle teaspoons engraved script *EF* on front of curved down handle. L. 5¹³⁄₁₆ in.
SD Brower & Son	Fiddle thread fork. L. 7⅜ in.
S Drowne	Three teaspoons circa 1760 engraved block L:B M:L.

S Emery	Tablespoon with leaf drop circa 1775.
S Hammond & Co	Fiddle thread dessert spoon.
Shepherd & Boyd	Fiddle dessert spoon with incised drop engraved feathered script *HCDB* on curved down handle. L. 7 in.
S Hildeburn	Fiddle dessert spoons circa 1810.
SK	King pattern thread spoon engraved italic *Gadsby* on back of handle. L. 7⅜ in.
Slidell	Teaspoon with peacock bird on bowl.
SP	Footed creamer marked twice. (Edison Institute)
SR (Reeves)	Coffeepot, Wilmington Museum. (Miss Jessie Harrington)
SR (S R Richards Jr)	Tablespoon with shell back and pointed-end engraved block A*W. Mark struck twice.
S Richards (SRR Jr)	Philadelphia covered urn-shaped sugar bowl circa 1790.
ST	Spoons engraved block J $\overset{V\ C}{\cdot}$ E. (Augustus Van Cortlandt)
ST	Teaspoons engraved block F. VC. (Van Cortlandt)
Stebbins & Co	Fiddle teaspoon.
Stuart	Trifid-end tablespoon with star punch marks of ten rays at each end of mark. (Hammerslough)
S Wheritt	Dessert spoon circa 1830.
SY & Co	Fiddle thread fork. L. 6½ in.
TB (T Bontecou Jr)	Rib-front teaspoon with shell back engraved block 1740 AS, 1758 R.P, script *JM*, block 1808 CAM, script *1833 CLM, 1853 LJL.*
T Colgan	Tankard exhibited at the Museum of the City of New York, 1937–1938; sold by Parke-Bernet Galleries on May 8, 1943.
TF	Tablespoon circa 1790.
TG Brown	Tablespoon with basket of fruit.
T Goldsmith	Fiddle teaspoon circa 1810.
TH	Pear-shaped teapot marked twice.
TH	Rib-front coffee spoon 1775 engraved block PB*M $\overset{L}{}$. (Mr. H. F. Keen)

TH	Saucer on covered inverted pear-shaped sugar bowl. Mark struck twice. (Netter)
Thibault & Brothers	King's pattern fork engraved italics *Gadsby*. L. 8¼ in.; King's pattern spoon engraved *Gadsby* on back. L. 8¾ in.
Tiffany Young & Ellis	Fiddle thread fork. L. 7⅛ in.
TM	Round spice box engraved block Henry Sibson To Dy Sibson on bottom. H. 3¼ in., D. base 1⅞ in.
TP Paris	Spoons with slight shoulders circa 1805.
TR	Fiddle shell teaspoons circa 1825.
T Richards JF	Fiddle teaspoon engraved script *JMF* on curved down handle.
Vallet	Teaspoon with sheaf of wheat circa 1820.
VV & S	Snuffer and tray. (De Kay)
W Bogert	Three-footed repoussé creamer circa 1835.
WD Beasom & Co	Violin fiddle tablespoon. L. 7¾ in.
WDP	Silver. (Banker)
WG	Table forks. (Van Cortlandt)
WG (William Gowdey)	Sauce boat engraved script *MM* on sides. Mark struck three times.
WG (William Grigg)	Eight dessert spoons. (Miss Anne Van Cortlandt); three-piece tea set with Goelet crest. BAYLEY mark overstamped.
WG (William Grigg)	Dessert spoon 1790 with Livingston crest for Pierre and Mary Livingston.
W Gennet	Fiddle dessert spoon engraved script *Sarah* on front of curved up handle circa 1805. L. 7⅛ in.
WH	Tablespoon circa 1760.
W & H (Wood & Hughes)	Fiddle spoon engraved feathered script *BMB to WBP* on front of curved up handle. L. 7⅛ in.
Willard	Fiddle spoon with pointed bowl engraved script *Sayre* on front of curved down handle. L. 8½ in.
WM	Teaspoon with pointed-ends engraved script *JRP* on front of handle. L. 4⅞ in.
W Mannerback	Tea set.

Wm F Ladd	Fiddle thread sugar spoon.
Wm Gale & Son	Three fiddle thread forks. L. 6⅞ in.
WM Root	Fiddle teaspoon engraved script *BAW* on front of curved up handle. L. 6⁹⁄₁₆ in.
Wm R Tice	Fiddle thread fork. L. 6⅝ in.
WP W Prior	Feathered-edge tablespoon engraved feathered script *FMB* circa 1775.
WS (William Seal)	Table fork.
W Selkirk	Beakers.
W Simes	Coffin-end teaspoon.
WS Morgan	Fiddle thread dessert fork.
WT	Flat rib-front spoon circa 1765–1775.
W Thompson	Earlier mark.
WV	Early covered tankard engraved block R*H and *Maison* script *J*A*. On bottom 30 oz. (C. P. De Vean)
WW	Engraved teaspoon 1760. (Reverend Samuel Johnson of Guilford)
WY	Cann 1765. Marked twice on bottom.

Unidentified Marks of American Silversmiths
1650–1850

A. FRANKFELD & CO (incised)	Fiddle teaspoon circa 1805
A. LAUDER	Fiddle teaspoons circa 1810; fiddle teaspoons engraved script *CW*. L. 5⅞ in.
A. WARREN	Violin fiddle spoons engraved script *EF*. L. 8¾ in.
BALDWIN & COWLES - C. RICHARDS	Spoon circa 1825.
BOURNE & LEWIS Pure Coin	Violin fiddle teaspoon engraved script *JMT*. L. 6 in.
CHAS. W. KENNARD & Co. (incised)	Fiddle thread fork engraved script *AHMcC*. L. 8⁵⁄₁₆ in.
CLARK COIT & CARGILL	Fiddle dinner fork circa 1810.
C D	Tablespoon circa 1775 engraved script *B*.
D. LOMBARD	Teaspoon with basket of fruit circa 1825.
E. GUEY	Heavy saucepan circa 1800.
F. CORDESS & CO.	Pointed teaspoon circa 1800.
GOURNEY & HITCHCOCK	Fiddle spoon.
HAM & CUSHING (incised)	Fiddle teaspoons.
H. A. OSGOOD & CO. (incised)	Spoon circa 1830.
HART & PEARCE	Spoon circa 1825.
HASKINS & MARTIN	Teaspoons with sheaf of wheat.
HENDERSON & GAINES (incised)	Fiddle thread fork. L. 7½ in.
H & G (incised)	Beaker.

363

H. SCHOONMAKER — Fiddle teaspoon with broad drop engraved script *GKC*. L. 5¹³⁄₁₆ in.

H. & W. WILSON (incised) — Fiddle thread salad forks engraved script *Miller*. L. 6½ in.

I. HIALLAM (in cartouche) — Worn rib-front tablespoon with plain drop circa 1750. Probably New England.

I. P. S. — Rattail tablespoon circa 1725 engraved block R*P.

I S or S I (serrated) — Pointed-end teaspoon circa 1790–1800. Probably New York.

J. LOCKWOOD — Four teaspoons circa 1810.

J. R. LEE — Teaspoons with basket of fruit.

J. V. D. — Tablespoon circa 1805 engraved script *WMAS*; fiddle shell teaspoons circa 1810 engraved script *TCLS*.

KINSEY & SNOW P.M. — Fiddle teaspoon circa 1810 engraved feathered script *MC*. L. 5½ in.

L & W — Teaspoon circa 1800.

M. MARTIN — Teaspoons circa 1800.

M. TUCKER — Teaspoons with sheaf of wheat.

MUNK — Tablespoon circa 1785 engraved script *BR*.

O. H. MOSES (incised) — Fiddle thread spoon engraved worn feathered script. L. 5¾ in.

RUSSELL & CLARKE — Violin fiddle spoons engraved feathered script *LBM* on front. L. 6 in.

S I — Spoon with V drop. L. 5½ in.

WM STEDMAN — Spoon and forks circa 1840.

Wm P. McKay & CO. — Violin fiddle teaspoons engraved script *EF*.

Y G — Two-handled punch strainer with bead edge circa 1775–1785.

Locations of Silversmiths' Shops

*T*HE LOCATIONS of the shops of the early American silversmiths as indicated on these maps of New York, Philadelphia,
and Boston are intended to show as nearly as possible the places
where the craftsmen made the many beautiful and valuable examples, still
extant, of their workmanship. The writer makes no claim to accuracy in these
locations for the reason that, except in very few instances, it is impossible to
denote other than an approximate site of the houses and shops—because most
of the early notices are no more explicit than: "Nigh the New Dutch Church";
"At Burling's Slip"; "In Third Street"; "At the North End," etc., and because
even the original early records, from which many of the data have been
gathered, have been found to occasionally conflict. These properties have been
found chiefly in old deeds, early wills, and newspaper advertisements, and in
various publications on the early American silversmiths.

It is difficult to know when the homes and shops were together or apart.
It is, however, safe to say that the earliest craftsmen plied their trade in an ell
or out-building connected with their living quarters and that it is probable
that this custom was prevalent through the eighteenth century in many, if not
most, cases.

The late 18th century shops, even those with street names and house
numbers, except in a few instances, cannot be indicated with any degree of
certainty because of inability to identify the numbering of that day with the
system in use today. It will, of course, be understood that public places such
as the Gaol in Philadelphia were removed prior to the establishment of the
shop of certain silversmiths occupying the space as indicated. Those locations
with street names and no numbering are difficult to place because of descrip-
tions such as "On the corner of Maiden Lane and Crown." This puts it entirely
up to the compiler to decide upon which of the four corners the shop was and
in some cases other than corner property, which side of the street. There are
some who advertise as "Maiden Lane and Queen Street" in one year and in the
next year the same silversmith advertised on "Lower End of Maiden Lane."
These two addresses were probably one and the same. In numerous such
instances, it has been assumed that the shop had not been moved. In others,
no such liberty has been taken. This is explained for those readers who may
question the existing difference in checking with published lists. There are
some contemporary craftsmen omitted among the early as well as among the

later. This is due to inability to ascertain their property in some cases and to the fact that later they had become too numerous so that only the best known among the later ones were included.

Changes were made in the names of the streets after the maps were printed which explains a difference in the address given in the index with that on the map. For instance: Prior to and subsequently to the Holland map of New York, Pearl Street began at the Battery and extended only to Whitehall Street. From there to Hanover Square, it was called Dock Street. From Hanover Square the continuation of the early Pearl Street was called Queen Street. Later the entire length of the street was given the name of Pearl Street which curves around opening into Broadway above Chambers Street (Frankford Street on the map). Therefore, silversmiths whose addresses were Pearl Street, after the change, are marked on the map on Queen Street. The same changes occur as well on various streets in Philadelphia and Boston. To complicate matters, in addition to the legitimate changes, several of the streets were called by other than their true names: i.e. Beekman Street was commonly called Chapel Street. This was because St. George's Chapel was on Beekman Street. There was a properly named Chapel Street on the west side of Broadway. In locating the shop of a William Smith, whose address was given as Chapel Street, a place was given him on Chapel Street, but later he was removed to Beekman Street when certain facts, stumbled on accidentally, showed his property was actually on Beekman Street. This incident again occurred in the case of Joseph Pinto whose property was found to have been on Bayard Street. The Bayard farm, then quite far from the center of the active settlement, was marked off in streets: Bayard Street, Judith, Elizabeth, etc. Naturally Joseph Pinto was placed on Bayard Street. As he was one of the active crafstmen of his day, it was perplexing that he should have settled so far out in the country. However, since his property was recorded as such, he was allowed to remain there—a considerable distance from his fellow workers. Later, however, when it was found that Duke Street was commonly called Bayard Street because the estate of the well-known Samuel Bayard, a prominent and prosperous inhabitant and a member of an eminent family of New Amsterdam, was on Duke Street, Joseph Pinto was rescued from his lonely habitation in the distant farm country (not far above where City Hall stands today) and given a place on Duke Street where he rightfully belonged with other craftsmen of his period.

Another well-known silversmith, John Burt Lyng, it appeared, had two addresses, one on Broadway opposite the Lutheran Church, and the other in The Great George Street. Holland's map shows a short street called King George Street and another longer one called George Street. Believing that the longer of the two streets was probably referred to as "The Great George Street" to differentiate between them, John Burt Lyng was placed on George Street. Later, as the research continued, a description of a piece of property was noted thus: "On the corner of Little Queen Street and The Great George Street."

The latter, then could have been none other than Broadway so again a removal was made. Again and again these complications arose making necessary quite a number of changes. Kip Street is another which has caused some uncertainty due to a description in an early deed which differs somewhat from Kip Street as marked on Holland's map. It is generally known that Nassau Street was formerly Kip Street.

When reasonable, though not positive, evidence of certain properties has been found, a few of the silversmiths' shops have been marked on the map in more than one place rather than make a definite choice of the two. This occurs but rarely. The earliest and most important of these were Jesse Kip of New York, and Johannes Nys of Philadelphia. Jesse Kip was given a second location—the first on Kip Street, the second on William—because of convincing evidence. Johannes Nys' shop was on Carpenter's Alley in Philadelphia. Two locations are given him on the map both taken from reliable sources—one giving Carpenter's Alley near the corner of Fourth Street between Chestnut and Walnut—the other giving it on the east side of Front above Walnut—so Johannes Nys will be found in both places.

Gerrit Onckelbag owned several large tracts of land. These are not all indicated on the map because some of them were in outlying districts. The Jacob Boelen property on Queen Street above Burling Slip is questionable. Certain research material revealed such strong facts pointing in that direction as to seem justifiable to place him there. His Broadway property is one of the few very early sites so clearly described in deeds that it has been possible to mark this one of his shops on the map with assurance.

On the other hand, with no assurance, the Cowells of Boston are given their location in the South End of Boston. The research material at hand failed in description of the Cowell property more detailed than "the South End of Boston." Not knowing just where the "South End of Boston" began or just how much of the city was considered the "South End," and also not wanting to omit such early and well-known as well as expert craftsmen as the Cowell family of silversmiths, a spot was selected near some of the other silversmiths of their period and there they will be found on the map although they may be some distance from their true location.

Vast research and close study of all material gathered has been required to establish as accurate locations as possible before making final indication on these maps. It is hoped that the readers will make generous allowance for the decision in the choice as shown.

The maps used were: New York, 1776 by Holland; Boston, by Osgood Carleton, supplied through the courtesy of The Horace Brown Map Collection, Yale University Library; the Philadelphia map, 1762 by Benjamin Eastman after Thomas Holmes, supplied through the courtesy of The Historical Society of Pennsylvania.

Helen Burr Smith

NEW YORK SILVERSMITHS 1660–1750

	Working	*Location*
Bancker, Adrian	1725	Bridge St. near Queen St. (formerly Wynkoop St. —also Brugh St.)
Becker, Fredrick	1725	Beekman St. (commonly called Chapel St., also George St.)
Besley, Thauvet	1727	Golden Hill (John St. from William to Pearl)
Blanck, Jurian, Sr.	1660	South side of Pearl St. between State and Whitehall Sts.
Blanck, Jurian, Jr.	1666	Broadway
Boelen, Henricus	1718	Rotten Row (Hunter's Key) West side of Broadway between Little Queen and Crown Sts. (now Cedar and Liberty)
Boelen, Jacob	1680	Rotten Row (Hunter's Key) West side of Broadway between Little Queen and Crown Sts. (now Cedar and Liberty) Queen St. head of Burling's Slip
Bogardus, Everadus	1698	Corner of Princess and Broad Sts. (sold to Onckelbag)
Bourdet, Stephen	1730	Corner of John and William Sts.
Brevoort, John	1742	Fly Market
Cario, Michael	1728	Crown and Pearl Sts.
DePeyster, William	1730	Queen St. to Fletcher St.
Fielding, George	1731	Broad and Princess Sts.
Goelet, Philip	1731	Narrow St. west side of Broadway Broad St.
Hastier, John	1726	Queen St. in 1735
Hendricks, Ahasuerus	1678	Smith St.
Heurtin, William	1731	Golden Hill (John St. from William to Pearl)
Hutton, John	1720	Smith St.
Kierstede, Cornelius	1696	Queen and Cliff Sts.
Kip, Jesse	1682	Kip St. (Nassau) Smith St. Between Princess and Garden Sts.
LeRoux, Bartholomew	1687	Broadway near Beaver Lane
LeRoux, Bartholomew	1738	Broadway near Beaver Lane

LeRoux, Charles	1710	Beekman St. near Peck's Slip Gold St.
Mariusgroen, Jacob	1701	Pearl St.
Myers, Myer	1745	Water St. Princess St. Greenwich St. Meal Market King St.
Onckelbag, Gerrit	1691	Smith St. between Princess and Garden Sts. Princess and Broad Sts. (bought in 1704 from Everadus Bogardus)
Pelletreau, Elias	1750	Golden Hill (John St. from William to Pearl Sts.)
Quintard, Peter	1731	"Near the New Dutch Church"
Ridout, George	1745	"Near the Ferry Stairs"
Robert, Christopher	1731	Queen St. Broadway at Bowling Green
Roosevelt, Nicholas	1738	Thames Street on the wharf
Schaats, Bartholomew	1695	Near the Meal Market
Soumaine, Simeon	1706	Dock Street
Stoutenburgh, Tobias	1721	Broadway near the Spring Garden
Vanderburgh, Cornelius	1675	High St. (Duke St.) In the Fort
Vanderheul, Hendrick	1733	Queen St. and Smith's Fly (near Burling Slip)
Vander Spiegel, Jacobus	1689	Rotten Row Queen St. near Burling Slip
Van Dyck, Richard	1750	Hanover Square
Vergereau, Peter	1720	"Queen St. commonly called Smith's Valley"
Wynkoop, Benjamin	1698	Smith's Fly and Queen St.
Wynkoop, Cornelius	1726	West side of Smith St.

NEW YORK SILVERSMITHS 1750–1800

Ackley, Francis M.	1797	Warren St. New St.
Alstyne, Jeronimus	1787	Maiden Lane
Andras, William	1795	40 William St.

Archie (Archer), John	1759	Dock St.
Bay, A. S.	1786	William St.
Bayley, Simeon A.	1789	Maiden Lane
		Old Slip
		Queen St.
Bennet, James	1773	Corner of Crown and Queen Sts.
Boelen, Jacob II	1755	Rotten Row (Hunter's Key)
Bowne, Samuel	1780	81 John St.
Brasher, A.	1790	Queen St. north of Crown and Maiden Lane.
Brasher, Ephraim	1766	Cherry St.
Bruff, Charles Oliver	1763	Maiden Lane near Fly Market
	1769	Rotten Row opposite Fly Market
	1772	Upper end of Maiden Lane near Broadway
Buché, Peter	1795	Fly Market
Burger, John	1780	Water St. (southeast of Cherry St.)
		Queen St. north of Cherry St.
		James St. and Rutgers St.
Coen, Daniel Bloom	1787	Maiden Lane
		Gold St.
Coley, Simeon	1767	Near the Merchant's Coffee House by the
		Ferry Stairs
Cook, John	1795	Ann St.
Dally, Phillip	1779	Queen St.
(with Jabez Halsey)	1787	Queen St.
Dawson, John	1769	Rotten Row
DeParisien, Otto Paul	1763	Smith St. at Crown St.
	1769	Near Peck's Slip
April	1774	Smith's Fly; fire
May	1774	removed to Dock St.
DeRiemer, Peter	1763	Cortlandt St.
Dubois, Joseph	1790	81 John St.
		Great Dock St.
Dubois, Tunis	1797	90 John St. (1797)
		Pearl St.
Duche, Benne Roche	1795	Maiden Lane
		Beekman St.
		Nassau St.
Dunn, Cary	1765	Crown St. near New Dutch Church
		Maiden Lane and William St.

Forbes, Abraham G.	1769	Broadway
Forbes, William G.	1773	Broadway
Fournequet, Louis	1795	Ann St.
		William St.
Fueter, Daniel Christian	1754	James St. (St. James St.)
		Back of Hendrick Vanderwater's near Brew House
		of Harmanus Bleecker
		Bayard St. (Duke St. commonly called Bayard)
		Broadway
Fueter, Lewis	1770	Bayard St. (with father)
Gilbert, William W.	1767	Broadway opposite Trinity Church
		Below Peck's Slip on Front St.
Gordon, James	1795	Cliff St. and Ann St.
Gough, James	1769	Beaver St.
Grigg, William	1765	Maiden Lane and William St.
		Broadway and Van Gelder's Alley
Guercy, Dominick	1795	Maiden Lane
		William St.
Halsey, Jabez	1789	Queen St.
(with Phillip Dally)		
Halstead, Benjamin	1764	Maiden Lane and Nassau St. Also Broad St.
Hammersley, Thomas	1756	Near the Exchange in Dock St.
		Hanover Square
Heath, John	1761	Wall St.
Heyer, William B.	1798	Warren St.
Johnson, Samuel	1780	Crown St. (Liberty St.)
Kimberly, William	1790	Crown St. and Fly Market
Lent, John	1787	20 Beekman St.
		61 Beekman St.
		69 Maiden Lane
Lyng, John Burt	1759	Broadway opposite Lutheran Church
Maverick, Peter Rushton	1772	Crown St.
Mears, Samson	1762	Pearl St. (House of Andrew Breasred)
Ogilvie, Gabriel	1791	Beaver St.
Pinto, Joseph	1758	Bayard St. (Duke St.)
Reeves, Stephen	1776	Burling Slip in Queen St.
Richardson, Thomas	1769	Fly Market

Ritter, Michael	1786	Fly Market
Roberts, Michael	1786	Hanover Square
Sayre, Joel	1799	Pearl St. Maiden Lane West side of William St.
Sayre, John	1792	Pearl St.
Schaats, Bartholomew, II	1784	"Near City Hall" Federal Hall Nassau St.
Schanck, Garret	1791	Fair St. (now Fulton)
Schanck, John (with Garret)	1797	Water St. (north of Peck's Slip)
Skinner, Abraham	1756	Near Dock St. between Ferry Stair and Rotten Row
Smith, James	1794	Fair St. Water St.
Smith, William	1770	Chapel St. (Beekman)
Targee, John	1797	Gold St. Water St.
Tingley, Samuel	1754	The Fly Rotten Row
Underhill & Vernon (Thomas) (John)	1787	Water St.
Van Beuren, Peter	1795	Maiden Lane Pearl St.
Van Beuren, William	1790	Cortland St. Maiden Lane
Van Voorhis, Daniel	1782	Hanover Square Queen St. North Pearl St. Broadway
Van Voorhis & Coley	1786	Hanover Square
Vernon, John	1787	Gold St. John St. Water St. with Underhill
Wenman, Barnard	1789	Fly Market "Fournequet's Place on William St."

Wishart, Hugh	1784	Wall St. Market St. William St. Liberty St. (formerly Crown) Maiden Lane Pearl St.
Woods, Freeman	1791	Smith St.
Wood, John	1770	Lower end of Maiden Land and Upper end of Fly Market

BOSTON SILVERSMITHS 1650–1800

Allen, John	1695	Cornhill (with John Edwards)
Belknap, Samuel	1789	30 Cornhill St.
Blowers, John	1738	School St.
Boyer, Daniel	1750	Opposite Governor's House between Marlborough and School Sts.
Brigden, Zachariah	1760	Cornhill
Burt, Benjamin	1750	Fish St.
Burt, John	1712	
Butler, John	1758	Corner of Clark's Ship Yard
Churchill, Jesse	1795	88 Newbury St.
Coburn, John	1750	King St. Head of Town Dock
Coney, John	1676	Court St. near Scollay Square Town Dock near Faneuil Hall Ann St. (now North)
Cowell, John	1728	South End of Boston
Cowell, William, Sr.	1703	South End of Boston
Cowell, William, Jr.	1734	South End of Boston
Dawes, Wm.	1765	Ann St. (with Wm. Homes, Jr.)
Dummer, Jeremiah	1666	Present State and Congress Sts. (where Exchange Bldg. stands)
Eastwick, Thomas	1743	Dock Square William's Court in Cornhill

Edwards, John	1691	Cornhill (with John Allen) 6 Dock Square
Edwards, Joseph, Jr.	1758	Cornhill
Edwards, Thomas	1725	Cornhill
Emery, Stephen	1775	5 Union St.
Farnam, Rufus	1796	42 Cornhill St.
Foster, Joseph	1785	171 Ann St. Fish St.
Gray, John	1713	Near Old State Meeting House
Gray, Samuel	1732	Cornhill — South side of Town House
Griffith, David	1789	26 Newbury St.
Hanners, George, Sr.	1720	Head of Town Dock
Henchman, Daniel	1753	Cornhill opposite Old Brick Meeting House
Homes (Holmes), Wm. Sr.	1739	Near the Draw Bridge
Homes, Wm. Jr.	1783	Ann St. near the Draw Bridge, with Wm. Dawes
Hull, John	1645	Newbury St. north of Mill St. (Summer St.) with Robert Sanderson
Hurd, Jacob	1723	Summer and Bedford St. on Washington South side of Town House Atkinson St.
Hurd, Nathaniel	1755	Exchange Place or corner of State and Congress Sts.
Leach, Charles	1789	Ann St.
Leach, Nathaniel	1789	Kilby St.
Loring, Joseph	1775	Union St.
Minott, Samuel	1764	Ann St. Fish St. Opposite William's Court — Cornhill Northward of Draw Bridge (with Wm. Simpkins)
Mors, (Morse) Obadiah	1733	King St.
Parker, Daniel	1750	Merchant's Row Union St.
Pierpont, Benjamin	1756	Newbury St.
Potwine, John	1721	Newbury St.

Revere, Edward	1796	Back St.
Revere, Paul, Jr.	1757	50 Cornhill St.
		Clark's Wharf
Revere, Paul, Sr.	1725	At Town Dock
		Hutchinson's Wharf
Revere, Joseph	1796	Clark's Wharf (with father, Paul, Jr.)
Revere, Thomas	1789	Newbury St.
Ridgeway, James S.	1789	Friend St.
		Cambridge St.
Sanderson, Robert	1638	Newbury St. north of Mill St. (Summer St.)
		(with Hull)
Simpkins, William	1730	Near Draw Bridge
Simpkins, Thomas		
Barton	1750	Fish St.
Smith, Joseph	1765	Newbury St.
Trott, Jonathan	1758	South End
Turner, James	1744	Near Town House — Cornhill
Webb, Barnabas	1756	Back St. (1761)
		Near the Market (1756)
		Ann St. (1762)

PHILADELPHIA SILVERSMITHS 1695–1800

Alexander, Samuel	1797	17 So. Second St.
		33 So. Second St.
		132 Letitia St.
Alford, Thomas	1762	Front St. between Chestnut and Market Sts.
Allen, James	1720	Market St.
Allen, Robert	1775	215 So. Third St.
Andrews, Abraham	1795	69 Race St.
Andrews, Henry	1800	65 So. Second St.
Andrews, Jeremiah	1776	Second St. Near Market (between Chestnut and
		Walnut Sts.)

Anthony, Joseph, Jr.	1783	Market St., two doors east of the Indian King
		45 Market St.
		74 Market St.
		94 High St.
		Bank St.
		76 South side of Market St. between Second and Third Sts.
Ashmead, William	1797	122 Race St.
Ball, William, Jr.	1785	Market St., also Front St.
Bardon, Stephen	1785	Corner of South and Third Sts.
Bartram, Wm.	1769	Front St. at Golden Cup and Crown
Bayly, John	1755	Lower end of Front St. near Draw Bridge
		Corner of Front and Chestnut Sts.
		Cherry Alley
Beck, Thomas	1774	Chestnut between Second and Third Sts.
Berard, Andrew	1797	Corner of Arch and Eighth Sts.
Best, Joseph	1723	High St.
Black, James	1795	89 So. Second St.
		123 Chestnut St.
Boone, Jeremiah	1791	133 Chestnut St.
		30 So. Second St.
Bordeaux, Augustine	1798	319 So. Second St.
Boudinot, Elias	1730	Next door to Post Office on Market St. (between Third and Fourth Sts.)
		Second St.
Bouvar, Joseph	1797	83 Vine St.
Brooks, Samuel	1793	29 So. Front St.
Brown, John	1785	Third between Spruce and Union Sts.
		36 No. Front St.
Burns, Anthony	1785	Chestnut between Second and Front Sts.
Carman, John	1771	Corner of Second and Chestnut Sts.
Chaudron, Simon	1798	12 So. Third St.
		5 So. Third St.
Cooke, Joseph	1785	Second St. between Market and Chestnut Sts. (corner of Black Horse Alley)
		38 South side of Market St. between Front and Second Sts.

David, John	1763	Chestnut and Second Sts. ("next door to Second St. corner in Chestnut") Fourth door from Draw Bridge
David, Peter	1730	Front St. Second St.
Davy, Adam	1795	Coombs Alley and North Second St.
Dawson, William	1793	55 So. Second St.
Delagrow, Andrew	1795	4 No. Second St.
Descuret, Lewis	1799	55 So. Second St.
Dickerson, Jonathan	1794	73 High St.
Dorsey, Joshua	1793	22 No. Third St.
Dowig, Geo. Christopher	1765	Second between Arch and Race Sts. Front near Coffee House
Douglass, Jeremott William	1790	257 So. Front St.
Doutiemer, Gille	1791	121 No. Front St.
Drewry, George	1763	Walnut St. — four doors below Second St.
Dubois, Abraham	1777	Second St. — four doors below Arch St. 65 No. Second St.
Dumoutet, John Baptiste	1793	17 Elm St. 79 No. Third St. 55–57 So. Second St.
Dupuy, Daniel	1745	A little below the Friends Meeting House on Second St. 114 Sassafras St. (Race St.)
Dupuy, Daniel, Jr.	1785	16 So. Second St.
Dupuy, John	1770	Same as father and brother, Daniel
Dutens, Charles J.	1751	Next to Indian King in Market St.
Eaton, Timothy	1793	9 Cherry St.
Elfreth, Jeremiah	1752	No. Second near Arch St.
Ford, Samuel	1797	39 Arch St.
Frank, Jacob	1793	Front between Market and Arch Sts. 2 No. Front St.
Gee, Joseph	1785	Front between Arch and Race Sts.

Geley, Peter	1793	4 So. Second St. 73 Arch St.
Georgeon, Bernard	1794	74 So. Second St. 74 Elm St.
Germon, John	1782	33 No. Third St. Quarry St.
Gethen, William	1797	14 Coombs Alley 172 So. Front St.
Ghiselin, William	1751	A little below the Church in Second St. (Old Christ Church)
Girreau, Stephen	1785	Chestnut St. between Second and Front Sts.
Grant, William, Jr.	1785	115 No. Third St. Green and Third Sts.
Griscom, George	1791	35 Wood St.
Guerin, Anthony	1791	No. Front St. 52 Race St.
Hall, David	1765	Second St. near Chestnut St.
Halstead, Benjamin	1785	Arch St. between Second and Third Sts.
Harper, David	1755	With Duten on Market St. next to Indian King
Haverstick, William	1781	76 No. Second St. between Arch and Race Sts.
Head, Joseph	1798	Lombard and 7th Sts.
Hollingshead, William	1754	Corner Arch and Second Sts.
Holton, John	1794	39 Race St.
Humphreys, Richard	1772	54 High St. Front St. — 7 doors below Coffee House Front St. Near Draw Bridge
Jenkins, John	1777	16 Green St. Corner Chestnut and Front Sts.
Leacock, John	1748	Sign of the Cup in Water St. Front St. opposite Norris' Alley
Lemar, Mathias	1790	81 Market St. Strawberry St. Front St. corner of Chestnut St.
Lemar, Benjamin	1775	Front St. between Chestnut and Walnut Sts.
Letelier, John	1770	Second St. between Market and Chestnut Sts. Opposite Coffee House 172 No. Front St.

Lownes, Joseph	1780	Front St. between Walnut and Spruce Sts. 130 So. Front St. near Draw Bridge 124 So. Front St. 191 So. Third St.
Lyng, John	1734	Market St. against Market House, next to The Crown
M'Fee, John	1796	22 Coombs' Alley
M'Fee and Reeder	1793	38 No. Front St.
M'Mullin, John	1790	120 So. Front St.
Miles, John	1785	Spruce between 5th and 6th Sts.
Mills, Edmund	1785	Corner Third and Vine Sts.
Mills, John	1793	15 Walnut St.
Milne, Edmund	1757	Next to Indian King in Market St. Market and Second Sts.
Murdock, John	1779	Front between Walnut and Spruce Sts.
Musgrave, James	1795	Chestnut and Third Sts. 42 So. Second St. 74 Spruce St.
Myers, John	1785	13 No. Second St. 71 No. Second St. North side of Market St. between Second and Third Sts.
Nys, Johannis	1695	Front St. and Carpenter's Alley
Olivier, Peter	1790	6 Strawberry St.
Pancoast, Samuel	1785	Front St. between Walnut and Spruce Sts.
Parham, William	1785	Front St. between Walnut and Spruce Sts. 104 Swanson St.
Parker, Richard	1785	36 South side of Chestnut St.
Pascall, William	1695	Second and Walnut Sts.
Perreau, Peter	1797	220 No. Front St.
Pinchin, William	1779	Front St. Opposite Gray's Alley 3 So. Front St. 20 Seventh St. Mulberry St.
Pitt, Richard	1744	Front St.
Poincignon, Francis	1795	55 No. Third St.
Pratt, Henry	1730	Front St. between Walnut and Chestnut Sts., corner of Taylor's Alley

Reeder, Abner	1793	38 No. Front St.
Richards, Samuel R. Jr.	1793	136 So. Front St.
Richardson, Francis	1710	At corner of Letitia Court in Market St.
Richardson, Joseph	1732	50 So. Front St.
Richardson, Joseph, Jr.	1773	50 So. Front St.
Richardson, Joseph & Nathaniel	1771	50 So. Front St.
Richardson, Richard	1793	50 So. Front St.
Robinson, Anthony W.	1798	23 Strawberry St.
Saint Martin, Anthony	1796	85 So. Front St.
Schaffield, Jeremiah	1785	Front St. between Union and Pine Sts.
Sénémand, John B.	1798	79 Elm St.
		37 Union St.
Shields, Thomas	1765	3rd door above the Draw Bridge in Front St.
		7th house above Draw Bridge in Front St.
Shoemaker, Joseph	1793	12 No. Front St.
		24 Pewter Platter Alley
		38 No. Front St.
Smith, Samuel	1785	Front St. between Walnut and Spruce Sts.
Stedman, Alexander	1793	288 So. Second St.
		117 Callow Hill St.
Swan, Robert	1799	77 So. Second St.
Syng, John	1734	Market St. against the Market House
Syng, Philip, Sr.	1715	Near Market Place
Syng, Philip, Jr.	1726	Front St. — seven doors below Coffee House
Van Voorhis, Daniel	1782	West side of Front St. — 6 doors below Coffee House
Walker, William	1793	2 Quarry St.
Walker, William and George	1795	76 No. Second St.
Warner, Samuel	1797	Pewter Platter Alley
Webb, Charles	1738	Front St. with Peter David
Williams, John	1793	91 No. Front St.
Williams, Samuel	1796	70 So. Front St.
Wiltberger, Christian	1793	33 So. Second St.
		Second St. — 3 doors above Arch St.

| Yetton, Randal | 1739 | Front St. opposite Gray's Alley |
| Young, William | 1761 | Three doors above corner of Front and Market Sts. |

SOURCES

American Silversmiths and Their Marks, Stephen G. C. Ensko, 1927
Dom. Selyns Records
Early land deeds and wills
Manuscript Collection of Harrold E. Gillingham
Market Street, Joseph Jackson
Minutes of the Common Council of the City of New York
New York Genealogical and Biographical Society
Pennsylvania Magazine of History and Biography
Scharf & Westcott's *History of Philadelphia*
The Arts and Crafts in New England, 1704–1775, George Francis Dow, 1927
The Arts and Crafts in Philadelphia, Maryland and South Carolina, Series I, 1721–1785 (1929). Series II, 1786–1800 (1932), Alfred Cox Prime
The Arts and Crafts in New York, 1726–1776, Rita Susswein Gottesman
Numerous others and references listed in bibliography with asterisks.

Maps

Showing locations of Silversmiths in New York 1660–1750, New York 1750–1800, Boston 1650–1800, and Philadelphia 1695–1800

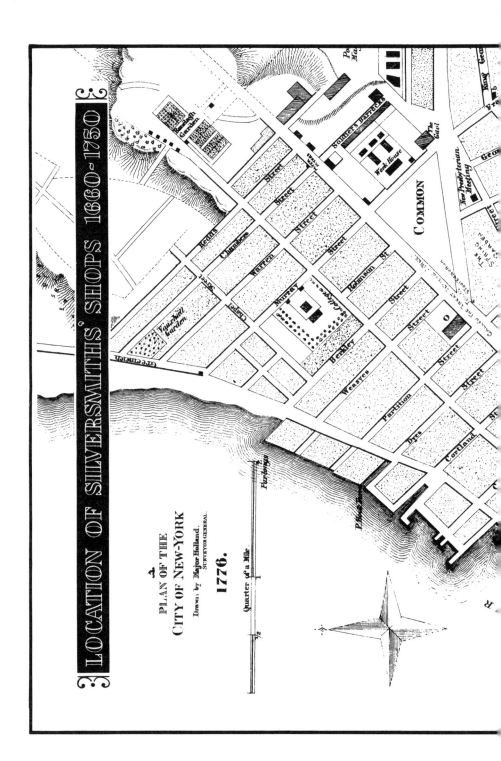

LOCATION OF SILVERSMITHS' SHOPS 1660-1750

PLAN OF THE
CITY OF NEW-YORK

Drawn by Major Holland.
SURVEYOR GENERAL.

1776.

Quarter of a Mile.

COMMON

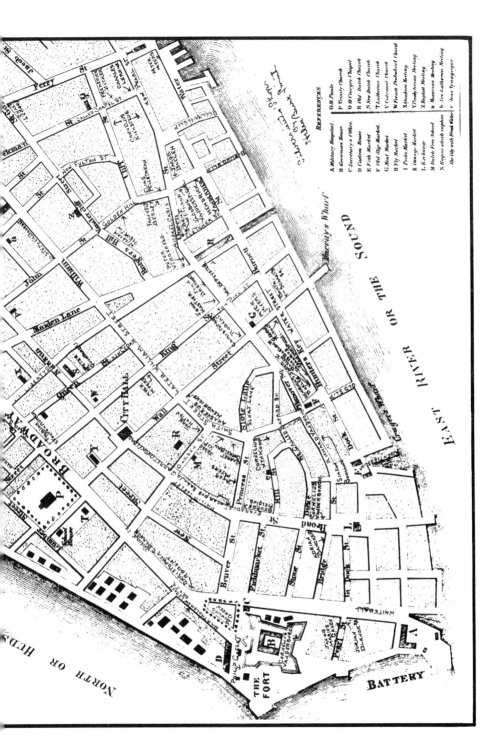

385

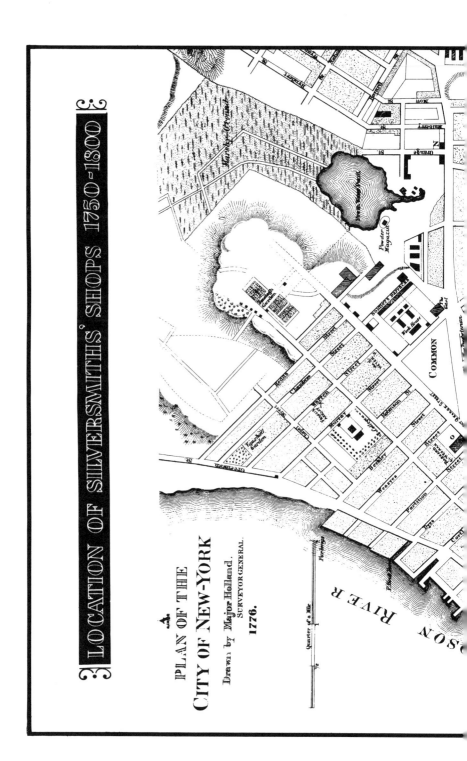

LOCATION OF SILVERSMITHS' SHOPS 1750–1800

PLAN OF THE
CITY OF NEW-YORK
Drawn by Major Holland.
SURVEYOR GENERAL.
1776.

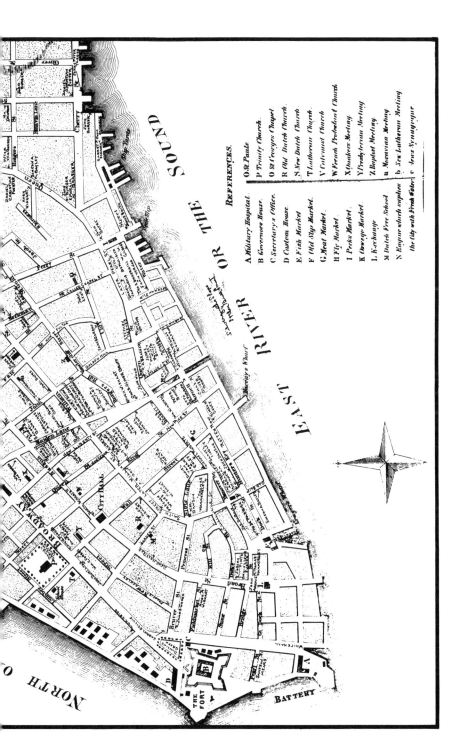

REFERENCES.

A Military Hospital.
B Governors House.
C Secretarys Office.
D Custom House.
E Fish Market
F Old Slip Market.
G Meat Market.
H Fly Market.
I Peeks Market.
K Oswego Market.
L Exchange.
M Dutch Free School
N Engine which supplies
the City with Fresh Water.

O St. Pauls.
P Trinity Church.
Q St Georges Chapel.
R Old Dutch Church.
S New Dutch Church.
T Lutheran Church.
V Calvinist Church.
W French Protestant Church.
X Quakers Meeting.
Y Presbyterian Meeting.
Z Baptist Meeting.
a Moravian Meeting.
b New Lutheran Meeting.
c Jews Synagogue.

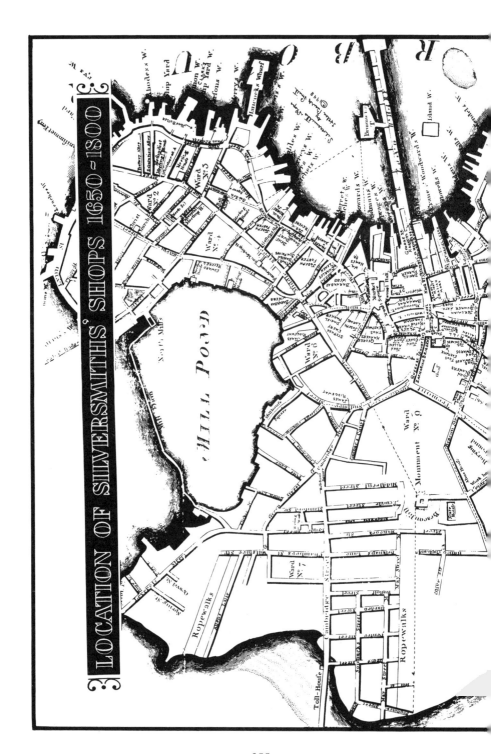

LOCATION OF SILVERSMITHS' SHOPS 1650–1800

MILL POND

A NEW PLAN of BOSTON From Actual Surveys by OSGOOD CARLETON

With Corrections Additions &c. Improvements

BOSTON

Printed and Sold by W. Norman

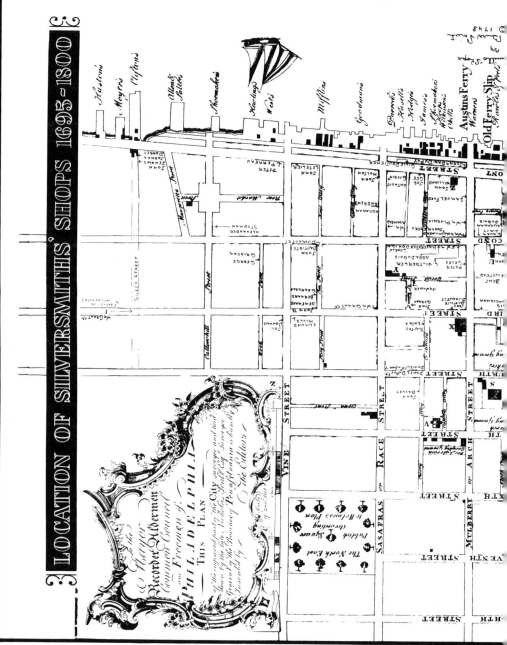

LOCATION OF SILVERSMITHS' SHOPS 1695-1800

390

BIBLIOGRAPHY

This list of publications of early American silver covers the subject from 1886 to 1948 as it appeared in Ensko III, and on until 1969 as continued by Stephen Ensko. Besides books and catalogues, it includes articles that appeared during the same period in the bulletins and journals of museums and historical societies and in a few magazines. Related articles unlisted here also appeared in *The American Collector* and on the antiques pages of *The Boston Transcript*, *The Christian Science Monitor*, and *The New York Sun*. Additional works have been published since 1969, especially studies focused on specific regions or craftsmen. The chronological arrangement of this bibliography emphasizes the ever-increasing interest in the absorbing study of early American silver.

BOOKS AND EXHIBITION CATALOGUES

Catalogue of Albany's Bicentennial Loan Exhibition at Albany Academy. 1886.

Old Plate Ecclesiastical, Decorative, and Domestic. Its Makers and Marks. By J. H. Buck, New York. 1888.

The Life of Colonel Paul Revere. By Elbridge Henry Goss. Two Volumes. 1891.

Paul Revere and His Engraving. By William Loring Andrews. 1901.

Old Plate. Its Makers and Marks. By J. H. Buck, New and Enlarged Edition, New York. 1903.

Catalogue of the Antique Silver. By the Mary Floyd Tallmadge Chapter, Daughters of the American Revolution, Litchfield, Connecticut. 1903.

*American Silver. The Work of 17th and 18th Century Silversmiths. Exhibited at the Museum of Fine Arts, Boston. 1906. Introduction by R. T. Haines Halsey.

The Hudson-Fulton Celebration. Catalogue of an Exhibition held at the Metropolitan Museum of Art. Volume II. New York. 1909.

Catalogue of the Loan Exhibition on the Two Hundred and Fiftieth Anniversary of the Founding of the Town of Norwich, Connecticut, 1659–1909. Faith Trumbull Chapter, D. A. R.

*The Metropolitan Museum of Art. Catalogue of an Exhibition of Silver used in New York, New Jersey and the South, with a Note on Early New York Silversmiths by R. T. Haines Halsey. New York. 1911.

* References, Chapter III.

*American Church Silver, of the Seventeenth and Eighteenth Centuries with a few Pieces of Domestic Plate Exhibited at the Museum of Fine Arts, Boston. 1911. Introduction by George Munson Curtis. Explanation of terms by Florence V. Paull.

Copley Society Retrospective Exhibition of Decorative Arts. Copley Hall, Boston, Mass. 1911.

*The Old Silver of American Churches. By E. Alfred Jones. National Society of Colonial Dames of America. 1913.

*Early Silver of Connecticut and Its Makers. By George Munson Curtis. Meriden. 1913.

Worcester Art Museum Exhibition of Old Silver Owned in Worcester County. Colonial Dames of America. 1913.

The Story of the House of Kirk, the Oldest Silversmiths in the United States, Established 1815. By Samuel Kirk & Son Co. 1914.

Makers of Early American Silver and Their Marks. By Robert Ensko. New York. 1915.

The Spoon From Earliest Times. International Silver Company. 1915.

List of Early American Silversmiths and Their Marks. By Hollis French. Walpole Society, Boston. 1917.

*Historic Silver of the Colonies and Its Makers. By Francis Hill Bigelow. 1917.

Exhibition of Old American and English Silver. Pennsylvania Museum, Philadelphia. 1917.

Wadsworth Athenæum in Hartford. Catalogue of Exhibition of American Silver. Colonial Dames of America. 1919.

*List of Philadelphia Silversmiths and Allied Artificers from 1682 to 1850. By Maurice Brix. Philadelphia. 1920.

*The Metropolitan Museum of Art. American Silver of the XVII and XVIII Centuries. A study based on The Clearwater Collection by C. Louise Avery with a Preface by R. T. Haines Halsey. 1920.

A Collection of Early American Silver. Tiffany & Co. 1920.

*The Pennsylvania Museum Bulletin. Special Silver Catalogue. 1921. Introduction by Dr. Samuel W. Woodhouse, Jr.

Exhibition of Early American Silver. Assembled by the Washington Exhibition Committee of the National Art Museum, Washington, D.C. 1925.

Abel Buell of Connecticut, Silversmith, Type Founder and Engraver. By Lawrence C. Wroth. 1926.

*American Silversmiths and Their Marks I. By Stephen G. C. Ensko. New York. 1927.

Artists and Craftsmen of Essex County. By Henry Wyckoff Belknap. The Essex Institute, Salem, Mass. 1927.

*The Arts and Crafts in New England, 1704–1775. By George Francis Dow. 1927.

*The Silversmiths of Little Rest. By William Davis Miller. Kingston, Rhode Island. 1928.

A Handbook of the American Wing, Metropolitan Museum of Art. By R. T. H. Halsey and Charles O. Cornelius. 1928.

Old Silver of Europe and America. By E. Alfred Jones. 1928.

The Arts and Crafts in Philadelphia, Maryland and South Carolina, 1721–1785, Series I. By Alfred Coxe Prime. The Walpole Society, 1929.

Early American Silver. By C. Louise Avery. New York. 1930.

Maryland Silversmiths, 1715–1830. With Illustrations of Their Silver and Their Marks and with a Facsimile of the Design Book of William Faris, by J. Hall Pleasants and Howard Sill. Baltimore, Maryland. 1930.

Paul Revere. By Emerson Taylor. 1930.

Catalogue of Silver Owned by Nicholas Sever. A.B. 1701, in 1928. By Richard Walden Hale. Fogg Art Museum of Harvard University. 1931.

Early New York Silver. By C. Louise Avery. The Metropolitan Museum of Art. 1932.

John Coney, Silversmith, 1665–1722. By Hermann Frederick Clarke with Introduction by Hollis French. Boston. 1932.

The Arts and Crafts in Philadelphia, Maryland and South Carolina, 1786–1800. Series II. By Alfred Coxe Prime. The Walpole Society, 1932.

Jeremiah Dummer, Colonial Craftsman and Merchant, 1645–1718. By Hermann Frederick Clarke and Henry Wilder Foote, with Foreword by E. Alfred Jones. Boston. 1935.

Connecticut Tercentenary, 1635–1935. Early Connecticut Silver, 1700–1830. The Gallery of Fine Arts, Yale University. Introduction by John Marshall Phillips. 1935.

Catalogue of Silver Exhibition, Held at the Art Museum of the Rhode Island School of Design. Introduction by William Davis Miller. 1936.

Harvard Tercentenary Exhibition. 1936.

The Silversmiths of Utica. By George Barton Cutten. 1936.

Contemporary Industrial and Handwrought Silver. Brooklyn Museum, New York. 1937.

American Silversmiths and Their Marks II. By Stephen G. C. Ensko. New York. 1937.

Silver of New York Makers. V. Isabelle Miller. 1937–8.

Marks of Early American Silversmiths. By Ernest M. Currier. Edited by Kathryn C. Buhler. 1938.

The Arts and Crafts in New York, 1726–1776. By Rita S. Gottesman. New-York Historical Society. 1938.

Early American Silversmiths, Volumes I–II. Articles in *The New York Sun,* Antiques Section; *The Magazine Antiques*; by Helen Burr Smith. 1938–1948.

Three Centuries of Historic Silver. By Mrs. Alfred C. Prime. The Pennsylvania Society of the Colonial Dames of America. 1938.

Three Centuries of European and American Domestic Silver. M. H. de Young Memorial Museum, San Francisco, Calif. 1938.

Hayden & Gregg, Jewelers of Charleston. By E. Milby Burton, Director of the Charleston Museum. April, 1938.

The Silversmiths, Watchmakers and Jewelers of the State of New York, Outside of New York City. By George Barton Cutten. 1939.

Masterpieces of New England Silver, 1650–1800. Introduction by John Marshall Phillips, The Gallery of Fine Arts, Yale University, 1939.

Jacob Hurd and His Sons, Nathaniel and Benjamin, Silversmiths, 1702–1781. By Hollis French, with Foreword by Kathryn C. Buhler. 1939.

Silversmiths of Delaware and Old Church Silver in Delaware, 1700–1850. By Jessie Harrington. 1939.

John Hull, a Builder of the Bay Colony. By Henry Frederick Clarke. 1940.

The M. and M. Karolik Collection of Eighteenth-Century American Arts. Museum of Fine Arts, Boston. By Edwin J. Hipkiss. 1941.

Jacob Boelen, Silversmith of New York. New York Genealogical Society. October 1941.

Paul Revere and the World He Lived In. By Esther Forbes. 1942.

South Carolina Silversmiths, 1690–1860. By E. Milby Burton. 1942.

Kentucky Silversmiths Before 1850. By M. M. Birdwell, published by the Filson Club History Quarterly, Louisville, Kentucky. April 1942.

The Philip Leffingwell Spalding Collection of Early American Silver. By Edwin J. Hipkiss. 1943.

Early Ohio Silversmiths and Pewterers, 1787–1847. By Rhea M. Knittle. 1943.

Silversmiths of Rochester. By Joan Lynn Schild, Rochester Museum of Arts and Science. 1944.

The Silversmiths of Poughkeepsie, New York. By George Barton Cutten. Dutchess County Historical Society. Poughkeepsie, N. Y. 1945.

Wadsworth Atheneum in Hartford. Catalogue of Exhibition of American Silver. Colonial Dames of America. 1945.

Ten Silversmith Families of New York State. By George Barton Cutten. 1946.

The Silversmiths of North Carolina. By George Barton Cutten. 1948.

American Silver. By John Marshall Phillips. 1949.

The Practical Book of American Silver. By Edward Wenham. 1949.

From Colony to Nation, the Art Institute of Chicago, 1949, Exhibition of American Painting, Silver and Architecture, 1650–1812. By Meyric R. Rogers.

The French in America, 1520–1880. The Detroit Institute of Arts. 1951.

Silversmiths of Virginia, Together with Watchmakers and Jewelers from 1694–1850. By George Barton Cutten. 1952.

Myer Myers, Goldsmith, 1723–1795. By Jeanette W. Rosenbaum. 1954.

The Arts and Crafts in New York, 1777–1799. By Rita Gottesman. New-York Historical Society. 1954.

The Arts and Crafts of Newport, R. I., 1640–1820. By Ralph E. Carpenter, Jr. 1954.

The Waldron Phoenix Belknap, Jr. Collection of Portraits and Silver. Edited by John Marshall Phillips, Barbara N. Parker and Kathryn C. Buhler. Exhibition, New-York Historical Society. 1955.

Paul Revere, Goldsmith, 1735–1818. By Katheryn C. Buhler. Museum of Fine Arts. Boston. 1956.

Colonial Silversmiths, Master and Apprentices. By Kathryn C. Buhler. Museum of Fine Arts. Boston. 1956.

Philadelphia Silver, 1682–1800. Catalogue of an exhibition, April 14 to May 27, 1956. Philadelphia Museum of Art. Philadelphia. 1956.

American Silver Collected by Philip H. Hammerslough. By Philip Hammerslough. 1958.

American Silver in the Henry Francis du Pont Winterthur Museum. By Martha Gandy Fales. 1958.

An Exhibition of American Silver and Art Treasures, sponsored by The English-Speaking Union. London. 1960.

New York Silversmiths. Exhibition catalogue, with a Foreword by Kathryn C. Buhler. The Darling Foundation of New York State. 1964.

Albany Silver, 1625–1825. By Norman S. Rice. Catalogue of an exhibition, March 15 to May 1, 1964. Albany Institute of History and Art. Albany, N.Y. 1964.

Checklist of American Silversmiths' Works, 1650–1850, in Museums in the New York Metropolitan Area. Metropolitan Museum of Art. N.Y. 1968.

The Heritage Foundation Collection of Silver, with Biographical Sketches of New England Silversmiths, 1625–1825. By Henry N. Flynt and Martha Gandy Fales. Heritage Foundation. Old Deerfield, Mass. 1968.

ARTICLES IN JOURNALS AND MAGAZINES

American Antiquarian Society: "John Hull, Colonial Merchant, 1642–1683." Hermann J. Clarke. 1937.

Country Life in America: "Old American Silver." 5 Parts, February 1913–January 1915. Luke Vincent Lockwood.

Harper's Magazine: "Old Silver." Theodore S. Woolsey. 1896.

The Filson Club Historical Quarterly: "Kentucky Silversmiths Before 1850." Margaret M. Bridwell 1942.

The Maryland Historical Magazine: "William Faris, 1728–1804." Lockwood Barr. 1941.

The New England Magazine: "Early American Artists and Mechanics. No. I Nathaniel Hurd," July 1932. "No. II Paul Revere," October 1932.

New Jersey Historical Society: "Silversmiths of New Jersey." Julia Sabine. July 1943.

The Pennsylvania Magazine of History and Biography: "The Cost of Old Silver." Harrold E. Gillingham. 1930. "Caesar Ghiselin, Philadelphia's First Gold and Silversmith, 1693–1733." Harrold E. Gillingham. 1933. "Indian Silver Ornaments." Harrold E. Gillingham. 1934.

The Magazine Antiques

"Some Charleston Silversmiths and Their Work." Jennie Haskell Rose. April 1928.

"Two Philadelphia Silversmiths (Anthony Simmons and Samuel Alexander)." Dr. Samuel W. Woodhouse, Jr. April 1930.

"Captain Elias Pelletreau, Long Island Silversmith." Mabel C. Weaks. Part I, May 1931; Part II, June 1931.

"John de Nys, Philadelphia Silversmith." Dr. Samuel W. Woodhouse, Jr. May 1932.

"John Potwine, Silversmith of Massachusetts and Connecticut." Elisabeth B. Potwine. September 1935.

"Cornelius Vanderburgh—Silversmith of New York." Mrs. Russel Hastings. Part I, January 1936; Part II, February 1936.

"A Silversmith of the Genesee Trail (John Cheadell or Chedell, New York State, Nineteenth Century)." M. W. Richardson. June 1936.

"John Nys vs. Jan Nieu Kirke." December 1936.

"Peter van Dyck of New York, Goldsmith, 1684–1750." Mrs. Russel Hastings. Part I, May 1937; Part II, June 1937.

"René Grignon, Silversmith." Ada R. Chase. July 1938.

"John Fitch: Jack of Many Trades." Harold E. Gillingham. February 1939.

"Asa Blanchard, Early Kentucky Silvermith." Margaret M. Birdwell. March 1940.

"The Moulton Silversmiths." Stephen Decatur. January 1941.

"Charles Oliver Bruff, Silversmith." J. Hall Pleasants and Howard Sill. June 1941.

"Daniel Greenough, Early New Hampshire Silversmith." Frank O. Spinney. June 1942.

*"The Ten Eyck Silversmiths." George Barton Cutten. December 1942.

*"Identifying the Mysterious IK: Jesse Kip, New York Goldsmith." John Marshall Phillips. July 1943.

"An Ingenious Yankee Craftsman (Benjamin C. Gilman, New Hampshire)." Frank O. Spinney. September 1943.

"Silversmiths of Lancaster, Pennsylvania." Carl Drepperd. August 1944.

*"Isaac Hutton, Silversmith, Citizen of Albany." John Davis Hatch, Jr. January 1945.

"Silversmiths of Alexandria (Virginia)." February 1945.

"Kentucky Silver and Its Makers." Lockwood Barr. July 1945.

*"An Unrecorded Goldsmith. Jeremiah Elfreth, Jr. of Philadelphia." Carl M. Williams. January 1947.

"Silversmiths of St. Louis." Ruth Hunter Roach. Part I–January 1947; Part II–March 1947.

"Kentucky Silver." Margaret M. Birdwell. November 1947. ·

"Silversmiths of Lynchburg, Virginia." Lucille McWane Watson. January 1951.

"John Conning, Southern Silversmith-Armorer." Francis Rudolph Summers. August 1958.

"New Albany Smith and Further Light on AC and IGL." John D. Kernan, Jr. August 1958.

"Eight Silversmiths of Portsmouth, New Hampshire." Kenneth Scott. August 1958.

"Silversmiths of Barnstable, Massachusetts." Robert McCullock and Alice Beal. July 1963.

"Silver by a New Jersey Smith." July 1963.

"F. Hoffmann, Philadelphia Silversmith." March 1966.

BULLETINS, COLLECTIONS, AND OTHER SOURCES
(Unrevised 1948 List)

Art Institute of Chicago, Illinois
Baltimore Museum of Art, Maryland
Brooklyn Institute of Arts and Sciences, New York
Charleston Museum, South Carolina
Cleveland Museum of Art, Ohio
Detroit Institute of Arts, Michigan
M. H. de Young Memorial Museum, San Francisco, California
Metropolitan Museum of Art, New York
Museum of Art, Philadelphia, Pennsylvania
Museum of Fine Arts, Boston, Massachusetts
Museum of the City of New York
New-York Historical Society, New York
Rhode Island School of Design Museum, Providence
Santa Barbara Museum, California
Wadsworth Atheneum, Hartford, Connecticut
Wilmington Society of Fine Arts, Delaware
Worcester Art Museum, Massachusetts
Yale University Art Gallery, New Haven, Connecticut
Historical Societies, Newspapers, Town Histories, Genealogical and Biographical Societies, Almanacs, City Directories, and other sources.

FACSIMILE PAGES
FROM THE FOUR PREVIOUS ENSKO BOOKS

*T*HE FOLLOWING PAGES contain analogous sections of annotated copies of Robert Ensko's and Stephen G. C. Ensko's books. These books, plus this final volume, encompass the period of American silver collecting from 1915 through 1969. The changes in content, format and style illustrate the evolution of interest and knowledge of American silver during that period.

The 1915 edition, written by Robert Ensko, contained no table of contents or bibliography. Fewer than 800 silversmiths or marks were represented. When available, the town and period in which the silversmith worked was included. A limited number of marks was identified and these by simple typed representation. The period covered concluded with the onset of the nineteenth century, where mass production and electroplating started to replace the silver produced through the old and slower craftsman's art.

As cited in the preface, the primary purpose of the catalogue was to expand the knowledge of the early silversmiths and their marks which might assist in preserving some of "the old plate." In fact forty-three pieces with unidentified marks were included, whereby any reader with knowledge of these might contact Robert Ensko. This method of requesting readers' assistance was to be repeated in the 1937 edition and was only one of the many techniques employed in researching old marks. As can be viewed by the reader, my only copy is highly annotated in Robert Ensko's script, where he noted new information.

The first volume of *American Silversmiths and Their Marks*, published in 1927, established the pattern to be followed in the later editions. Compiled by Stephen G. C. Ensko, this volume contained a greatly expanded list of over twelve hundred silversmiths with available biographical data, locations and dates where they practiced their trade. Further additions were an index, a brief bibliography, photographs and mark representations when known.

The photographs were of some early American silver derived from either private or museum collections. The pieces selected were either of special noteworthy quality to Stephen Ensko, or were representative of a major evolutionary step in silversmiths' pattern or design. Also included were over twenty pages of hand-drawn representations of silversmiths' marks. The tremendous expansion in the information in this edition reflected the expanding

401

wealth and subsequent interest in early American silver. It also represented the increasing commitment to researching and imparting this information on these craftsmen by Stephen Ensko.

The 1937 edition was a compact workbook for the use of collectors and students. It presented the identified marks, names, locations and dates of silversmiths, as well as line drawings of silver design styles evolving from 1650 to 1800. My copies are a maze of added data, drawings of marks, corrections and references noted by Stephen G. C. Ensko and my husband. This version again included a listing of marks requesting the readers' assistance in identifying the silversmith. Assay marks and a clipping of an early "method" (advertisement) were also included.

During this time, however, as public and private collections were expanding, early American silver was becoming increasingly scarce and more expensive.

The 1948 *American Silversmiths and Their Marks III* returned to the style and format of the 1927 version but with amplified biographical detail and over two thousand silversmiths' marks. This expansion in detail was the result of over twenty-five years of continuous research and investigation by Stephen Ensko. His sources included genealogy records, town histories and publications of the period that served to support actual physical verification of marks on plate from public and private collections, as well as those pieces that were acquired in the normal trade of Robert Ensko, Inc.

By this time, exquisite public and private collections had been firmly established, thus securing the preservation of early American silver more than at any previous period. Collectors' interests tended toward the available silver, pieces from the 1800s to the 1850s. The discovery of a pre-nineteenth century authentic piece was a heralded event, as was the determination of a fraudulent copy. The printing of this 1948 edition coincided with early American silver's acquisition of status both as investment and as art.

Dorothea Ensko Wyle
Christopher Charles Wyle

MAKERS OF
EARLY AMERICAN SILVER

ROBERT ENSKO
598 Madison Avenue
NEW YORK CITY

MAKERS OF
EARLY AMERICAN SILVER

SOME early American pieces of silver are worth more to-day than their weight i gold, yet through the want of knowledge as to their real value and scarcity b some dealers, as well as others, many find their way to the melting pot while th collectors are vainly hunting the cities and towns all over the United States in their effort to add to their collections. While I obtain numerous pieces from time to time, I ca supply but very little as compared to the demand. I hope this catalogue will help t save some of the old plate. If we had a man like Mr. George Munson Curtis, of the Inte national Silver Company of Meriden, Connecticut, in every state, it would be but a ver short time before all that could be known about the makers of silver in the differer states would be revealed. He is not only a liberal collector of Connecticut silver bu has published a beautifully illustrated book on early silver of Connecticut and a histor of its makers, well worth reading. In the exhibitions held recently in the New Yor and Boston Museums of Art there was a great display of beautiful and artistic workma ship in the early pieces of American silver.

With all the new methods and our machinery we can produce no better silver th: the old craftsman who knew every branch of his trade thoroughly. While we find th Massachusetts was the home of the earlier silversmiths, New York, Philadelphia, ar Connecticut were also fully supplied with good workmen very shortly after.

On page 27 will be found forty-three pieces of early American plate belonging Hon. Alphonso T. Clearwater, which he has not been able to fully identify to h own satisfaction. Any information in regard to these marks, such as the names makers, time and place where they worked, or the owners' names and addresses of piec bearing the same marks will be gratefully received. I sincerely hope all the marks w soon be fully identified, as it is really too bad to see so many beautiful pieces unidentifie

ROBERT ENSKO

598 Madison Avenue
New York City

3

MAKERS OF EARLY AMERICAN SILVER

IN MANY CASES WHERE THERE IS A RECORD OF BIRTH THE DATE
OF WORKING HAS BEEN GIVEN AS TWENTY-ONE YEARS OF AGE

Connecticut

Ashford

Mark	Name	Article
	Russell, Jonathan	

Berlin

C. B.	Beecher, Clement & Co.	Spoons

Bridgeport

Wardin, Daniel
Young, Levi

Brookfield

Smith, Ebenezer

Brooklyn

Newbery, Edwin C.

Colchester

Breed, John

Coventry

Burnap, Daniel

Danbury

Blackman, Frederick Starr
Blackman, John Starr
Blackman, John Clark
Clark, Joseph
Mygatt, Comfort Starr
Mygatt, David
Mygatt, Eli

Derby

Moss, Isaac Nichols

Durham

Mark	Name	Article
R. Fairchild	Fairchild, Robert	Beaker, Tankard
	Parmele, James	

East Haddam

Foote, William
White, Amos

Enfield

Peabody, John
Terry, Geer

East Hartford

Case, George
Merrow, Nathan
Pitkin, Henry
Pitkin, John O.
Pitkin, James F.
Pitkin, Walter

Essex

	Pratt, Nathan	Masonic Jewels
	Pratt, Nathan, Jr.	
	Spencer, George	

Farmington

	Bull, Martin	
	Curtis, Lewis	
T. N.	Norton, Thomas	Spoons
	Olmstead, Nathaniel	

Goshen

Norton, Andrew

5

ROBERT ENSKO 1915

406

Unidentified makers and marks of American silver in Hon. A. T. Clearwater's Collection. Any information in regard to same will be gratefully received.

ROBERT ENSKO.

A. T. C. Collection	Marks
Tankard	G. F. in Oval twice
Another	I. G. L. in half oval, four times
Mug	L. A. in Cartouche
Another	Phillip Alexander, large block letters
Beaker	L. A. in rectangle, 3 times
Another	S. D. in shaped shield, twice
Bowl	B. E. in rectangle
	R. E. in rectangle
Another	T. T. with Crown above, twice
Sugar Bowl	R. G. in oval
Can with Cover	St. Mars in shaped rectangle
Saucepan	St. Louis in rectangle
Another with Lid	H. P. Head + all in squares
Coffee Pot	J. A. in lobed shield
Tea Pot	I. F. S. in rectangle
Another	C. & N.
Another	I. A. in shaped shield
Porringer	A. W. L. three times
Two Candlesticks	B. M. in square
Tray	J. A. in oval
Pitcher	I. A. in script in oval, twice
	Another J. A. in shaped shield twice
Another	W. L. in shaped rectangle
Another	P. Prie in shaped shield
Creamer	E. D. lion, rampant, twice
Salt Cellar	C. C. K. in rectangle, F. in oval
Another	C. A. in small rectangle
Trencher Salt	J. W. in oval
Two more	I.+P.

A. T. C. Collection	Marks
Ladle	I. N. twice
Another	W. H. in linked letters, small rectangle
Cup	P. J. in heart-shaped shield
Taper Box	D. in script in circle
Box	A. L. in Cartouche
Patch Box	I. W. in oval
Two Knee Buckles	F. B. in shaped shield
Two Shoe Buckles	T. A.
Two more	S. A. in oval
Pepper Caster	J. B. in monogram script in circle
Nutmeg Grater	I. K.
Butter Tester	T. K. twice
Another	T. H.
Wine Funnel Rest	R. K. in square, three times
	L. S. in squares
Brazier	C. lion rampant, in rectangle

Information in regard to the following names will be appreciated by several collectors:

Clarici, J.
Crittenden, N. E., about 1790
Gaither, J.
Gaskins
Ginochio, J. B.
Gouiran, Mel
Greenwood, C. F.
Lynch, J.
Moses, O. H.
I. NR., Phia., 1776
Rae, W. J.
Tenny, 251 Broadway, New York
Tucker, J. W., Pearl St., New York

from ROBERT ENSKO 1915

INDEX

AMERICAN
SILVERSMITHS

AND THEIR MARKS

By

STEPHEN G. C. ENSKO

NEW YORK

PRIVATELY PRINTED

1927

PREFACE

HIS book has been compiled with the paramount object in view of enabling the collector of American silver to come in closer touch and have a better understanding of the silversmiths who, with crude implements but true artistry, wrought the plate. It includes a carefully compiled list of workmen with their dates, records and the marks they struck. This information has been gathered from various sources through assiduous investigation and study; chiefly from town histories, genealogy records, dictionaries, probate court records, early newspapers, directories of all important cities from first issue to 1850; also by tradition subsequently verified by tangible evidence of the silversmith's work.

The American silversmith served an apprenticeship, lasting eight or ten years, to a master craftsman. Later, as freemen, they opened a workshop, advertised for custom and were prepared to carry on their trade. Imported goods were quite fashionable in colonial days and in order to compete with foreign ware these men worked with models and designs popular in the larger European cities.

It is interesting to note the slow evolution and gradual change in church and domestic silver from the simple and yet beautiful vessels of the seventeenth century to the more elaborate forms and greater variety of the eighteenth century. The silversmiths' art kept pace with the times as is self-evident by examining pieces of different periods now extant.

Records show that the silversmiths occupied themselves with other interests than their shop work. They were honored by their fellow citizens by being elected to responsible public offices and were appoint-

[v]

ed to high military commissions, which places the art of the silve worker among the higher classes of craftsmanship.

It is primarily to the business ingenuity of the silversmith that it now possible to identify their handicraft. They marked with a symbo initial, name or combination of the three. In the last two decades di igent research on the subject has made clear the significance of thes various stamps. A comprehensive study of authentic pieces of America silver in churches, museums and private collections has made possib so complete a list recorded in this book.

The illustrations which appear represent objects in the collection of the Metropolitan Museum of Art, Brooklyn Museum of Art, and i private collections. The compiler is indebted to Hon. A. T. Clearwate Mr. Francis P. Garvan, Mr. Luke Vincent Lockwood, Mr. Frederic I Sherman, Mr. Cornelus J. Sullivan, Mr. Walter H. Crittenden, the lat George M. Curtiss and to the publisher, Mr. Frederick W. Anthoense of The Southworth Press, for the interest in the work. To these and a others who have assisted in the preparation of the work my sincer thanks are due.

STEPHEN G. C. ENSKO

New York City, New York
November, 1926

from STEPHEN G. C. ENSKO 1927

CONTENTS

[vii]

STEPHEN G. C. ENSKO 1927

CONNETICUT

DANBURY

BLACKMAN, FREDERICK STARR   1811-98

Born in Danbury. Son of John Starr Blackman; brother of John Clark Blackman.

BLACKMAN, FREDERICK S. & CO.   1840

BLACKMAN, JOHN CLARK   1808-72

Born in Danbury. Son of John Starr Blackman. Moved to Bridgeport after learning his trade.

BLACKMAN, JOHN STARR   1777-1851

Had a shop south of the Court House. His son, Frederick, succeeded him in business.

CLARK, JOSEPH   1791

Served in the Revolution in 1777. Shop located near the Printing Office in 1791. Advertised he made silverware in Newbury, N. Y., 1811. Died in Alabama 1821.

MYGATT, COMFORT STARR   1763-1823

Born in Danbury. Son of Eli. Represented the Town in the General Assembly 1800 and 1802. Worked in partnership with his brother David. Advertised for two apprentices in 1804. In 1807, when his father died, he retired from business and moved to Canfield, O.

MYGATT, DAVID   1777-1822

Born in Danbury. Worked with his father. Partner of brother, Comfort Starr. Moved to South East, N. Y., 1811.

MYGATT, ELI   1742-1807

In partnership with Najah Taylor 1793. Shop on Main Street. Appointed Lieutenant in the Revolutionary War. Colonel in 1778. Represented the Town in the General Assembly many times from 1777 until 1807.

EAST HARTFORD

CASE, GEORGE   1779

Advertised as a working goldsmith and jeweller.

MERROW, NATHAN   1758-1825

Born in Hartford. Mentioned as a goldsmith in town records of East Hartford, 1783.

PITKIN, HENRY   1834

Born in East Hartford. Brother of three silversmiths working there. Taught the different branches of the business to Nelson Pitkin Stratten, who later was one of the organizers of the Waltham Watch Co.

PITKIN, JAMES F.   1834

Brother of Henry. Son of Capt. John. With his brother he set up a shop north of his father's dwelling, and manufactured silverware on a large scale. This business indirectly led to the founding of the present Waltham Watch Co.

[1]

from STEPHEN G. C. ENSKO 1927

HALL MARKS

Allen Armstrong	1806	
Adrian Bancker	1731	
Abel Buel	1763	
A. Beach	1823	
Asa Blanchard	1810	
A. Billings	1780	
Abner Bradley	1774	
A. Brasher	1790	
Alexander Cammon	1813	
Anon Cleveland	1820	
Arnold Collins	1690	
Albert Cole	1844	
Abraham Carlile	1791	
A. Cutler	1820	
A. C. Benedict	1840	
A. C. Burr	1815	
Amos Doolittle	1775	
Abraham Dubois	1777	
Andrew E. Warner	1811	
Andrew E. Warner	1811	
Abraham G. Forbes	1769	
A. G. Storm	1830	
A. & G. Welles	1804	
Ahasuerus Hendricks	1675	
Abraham Hews, Jr.	1823	
Adrian B. Holmes	1801	

Abel Jacobs	1816	
Am Kay	1725	
Aaron Lane	1780	
A. Lockwood	1810	
Adam Logan	1803	
Adam Lynn	1796	
Abel Moulton	1815	
William Andros	1795	
Anthony Rasch	1807	
Abraham Portram	1727	
Anthony Rasch	1807	
Abner Reeder	1797	
Thomas Arnold	1760	
Anthony W. Robinson	1798	
Andras & Richard	1797	
Anthony Simmons	1797	
A. Sanborn	1850	
Anthony Simmons	1797	
Andrew Tyler	1715	
Andrew Tyler	1715	
Andrew Underhill	1780	
Ebenezer Austin	1764	
Nathaniel Austin	1760	
Antipas Woodward	1791	
Amos White	1770	
A. Young	1800	

[177]

STEPHEN G. C. ENSKO 1927

INDEX

from STEPHEN G. C. ENSKO 1927

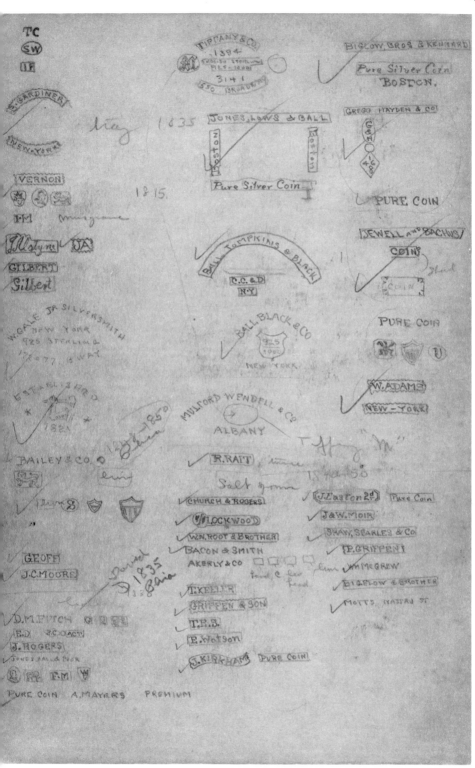

AMERICAN SILVERSMITHS AND THEIR MARKS II

BY

Stephen G. C. Ensko

ROBERT
ENSKO
Incorporated
682 LEXINGTON AVENUE
NEW YORK CITY

1937

ACKNOWLEDGMENT

⁕━━━━⁕

The growing interest in early American Colonial silver is reasonable justification for this book. The reproductions of silversmiths' marks are offered to identify workmanship and the sketches of important examples of their skill to date the age of pieces. We have early wills and inventories which record items not yet found. It is to be hoped that new items of old interest may turn up for study through the information in the following pages.

Important museums have exhibitions of the silver made and used by the early settlers of this country. The Curators in charge of American silver will be pleased to offer you every assistance to an attribution of your unrecorded pieces. Important representative collections may be studied at the Gallery of Fine Arts, Yale University, New Haven, Connecticut; Metropolitan Museum of Art, New York; Museum of Fine Arts, Boston; Museum of the City of New York; Cleveland Museum of Art; Detroit Institute of Art.

For much of our knowledge we are grateful to those who first realized the possibilities of early American silver. We have included a complete list of books issued on this subject. From the first notes of J. H. Buck in 1888, the great work done by R. T. H. Halsey, to the monographs of to-day, we have accomplished much more than would appear to be possible. With all this, as some would say, the surface has just been scratched.

It is my pleasure to thank Mr. John Marshall Phillips, Curator of The Mabel Brady Garvan Collection, Yale University, for his interest in this compilation.

I am grateful to Mrs. John Russell Hastings for notes of New York silversmiths.

For the generous co-operation of Mrs. Stephen G. C. Ensko, I cannot say enough.

5

m STEPHEN G. C. ENSKO 1937

Mr. and Mrs. Charles Messer Stow, of New York, have done much to the success and encouragement of this book with kind advice and interest.

To Mr. Charles E. Ensko, and Lamont N. Ensko, I wish to express my thanks for help accorded to me.

To Miss C. Louise Avery, of the Metropolitan Museum of Art, New York; Dr. J. Hall Pleasants, of Baltimore; Mr. William Davis Miller, of Kingston, R. I.; I wish to express my special thanks for reference material used from their notable books.

For their kind interest and encouragement of this work, I also wish to thank:

Mrs. Harry H. Benkard, of New York; Mrs. Maurice Brix, of Philadelphia; Mrs. Ives Henry Buhler, of the Museum of Fine Arts, Boston; Mr. E. Milby Burton, of the Charleston Museum, Charleston, S. C.; Mr. Hermann Frederick Clarke, of Boston; Dr. George B. Cutten, of Colgate University, Hamilton, New York; Miss Camilla Draper, of St. Louis, Mo.; Mr. George H. Eckhardt, of Philadelphia; Mr. Willoughby Farr, of Edgewater, N. J.; Mr. Hollis French, of Boston; Mr. Richard M. Gipson, of New York; Miss Elizabeth Haines, of the Brooklyn Museum, New York; Mrs. J. Amory Haskell, of New York; Miss Jessie Harrington, of Dover, Delaware; Mr. Stanley Ineson, of New York; Mr. E. Alfred Jones, of London; Mr. Homer Eaton Keyes of New York; Miss V. Isabelle Miller, of the Museum of the City of New York; Mr. Russell A. Plimpton, of the Minneapolis Institute of Arts; Mr. Hardinge Scholle, of the Museum of the City of New York, New York; Mr. Joseph Downs, of the Metropolitan Museum of Art, New York; Mr. Robert H. Tannahill, of the Detroit Institute of Art, Detroit; Mrs. Clifford P. Smith, Waban, Massachusetts; Mr. William G. Snow, of Meriden, Connecticut; Mr. Edward Wenham, of London; Mr. Richard M. Woods, of New York.

New York, 1937, S.G.C.E.

6

from STEPHEN G. C. ENSKO 1937

CONTENTS

m STEPHEN G. C. ENSKO 1937

BIBLIOGRAPHY

Old Plate, Ecclesiastical, Decorative, and Domestic; Its Makers and Marks, by J. H. Buck, with eighty-two illustrations. New York. 1888.

Old Silver. Professor Theodore Woolsey of Yale University. Harper's Magazine. 1896.
Old Plate. Its Makers and Marks by J. H. Buck with numerous illustrations. New and Enlarged Edition. New York. 1903.

Catalogue of the Antique Silver by the Mary Floyd Tallmadge Chapter, Daughters of the American Revolution, Litchfield, Connecticut. 1903.

American Silver. The Work of 17th and 18th Century Silversmiths. Exhibited at the Museum of Fine Arts, Boston. 1906. Introduction by R. T. Haines Halsey.

The Hudson-Fulton Celebration. Catalogue of an Exhibition held in the Metropolitan Museum of Art. Volume II. New York. 1909.

The Metropolitan Museum of Art Catalogue of an Exhibition of Silver used in New York, New Jersey and the South with a Note on Early New York Silversmiths by R. T. Haines Halsey. New York. 1911.

American Church Silver of the Seventeenth and Eighteenth Centuries with a few pieces of Domestic Plate Exhibited at the Museum of Fine Arts, Boston. 1911. Introduction by George Munson Curtis. Explanation of terms by Florence V. Paull.

The Old Silver of American Churches by E. Alfred Jones. National Society of Colonial Dames of America. 1913.

Early Silver of Connecticut and its Makers by George Munson Curtis. Meriden, 1913.
Worcester Art Museum Exhibition of Old Silver owned in Worcester County. Colonial Dames of America. 1913.

Makers of Early American Silver and Their Marks by Robert Ensko. New York. 1915.
List of Early American Silversmiths and Their Marks by Hollis French. Walpole Society, Boston. 1917.

Historic Silver of the Colonies and its Makers by Francis Hill Bigelow. 1917.
Exhibition of Old American and English Silver. Pennsylvania Museum. Philadelphia. 1917.
Wadsworth Athenaeum in Hartford. Catalogue of Exhibition of American Silver. Colonial Dames of America. 1919.

List of Philadelphia Silversmiths and Allied Artificers from 1682 to 1850 by Maurice Brix. Philadelphia. 1920.

The Metropolitan Museum of Art. American Silver of the XVII and XVIII Centuries. A study based on The Clearwater Collection by C. Louise Avery with a Preface by R. T. Haines Halsey.

The Pennsylvania Museum Bulletin. Special Silver Catalogue. 1921. Introduction by Samuel Woodhouse.

Exhibition of American Silver Assembled by the Washington Exhibition Committee of National Art Museum. Washington, D. C. 1925.

American Silversmiths and Their Marks by Stephen G. C. Ensko. New York. 1927.
The Silversmiths of Little Rest by William Davis Miller. Kingston, Rhode Island. 1928.
Early American Silver by C. Louise Avery. Illustrated. New York. 1930.
Maryland Silversmiths. 1715-1830 With Illustrations of Their Silver and Their Marks and with A Facsimile of the Design Book of William Faris by J. Hall Pleasants and Howard Sill. Baltimore, Maryland. 1930.

The Metropolitan Museum of Art. An Exhibition of Early New York Silver by C. Louise Avery. New York. 1932.

John Coney. Silversmith 1665-1722 by Hermann Frederick Clarke with Introduction by Hollis French. Boston. 1932.

Jeremiah Dummer. Colonial Craftsman and Merchant 1645-1718 by Hermann Frederick Clarke and Henry Wilder Foote with foreword by E. Alfred Jones. Boston. 1935.

Connecticut Tercentenary, 1635-1935. Early Connecticut Silver, 1700-1830. The Gallery of Fine Arts. Yale University. Introduction by John Marshall Phillips. 1935.

Catalogue of Silver Exhibition Held at the Art Museum of the Rhode Island School of Design. Introduction by William Davis Miller. 1936.

Utica Silversmiths by George B. Cutten and Minnie Warren Cutten. 1936.

8

AMERICAN SILVER OF THE 17th AND 18th CENTURIES

To enjoy a keen appreciation of silver the collector must first study line and form. The color and the texture of the surface are important to the age of a piece. Details of design used by silversmiths of different localities are of first consideration when identifying silver. The mark should check with all of the above. When in doubt, consult an authority.

The following advertisement appears in the New England Chronicle, June 12, 1773, and it invites you to a better understanding of the present keen appreciation of early American Silver:

"Daniel Henchman takes this method to inform his Customers in Town and Country, that he still continues to carry on the Gold and Silver Smith's Business at his Shop opposite the Old Brick Meeting-House in Cornhill, Boston, where he makes with his own Hands all kinds of large and small Plate Work in the genteelest Taste and newest Fashion and of the Purest Silver. And as his work has hitherto met with the Approbation of the most curious, he flatters himself that he shall have the Preference by those who are Judges of Work, to those Strangers among us who import and sell English Plate to the great Hurt and Prejudice of the Townsmen who have been bred to the Business. Said Henchman will make any kind of Plate they want equal in Goodness and Cheaper than they can import from London and with the greatest Dispatch."

STEPHEN G. C. ENSKO 1937

COVERED CUPS

1700   1725   1790

BOWLS

1690   1725   1770

BEAKERS

1680   1710   1710   1790

CREAMERS

1735   1745   1750   1760   1790

10

from STEPHEN G. C. ENSKO 1937

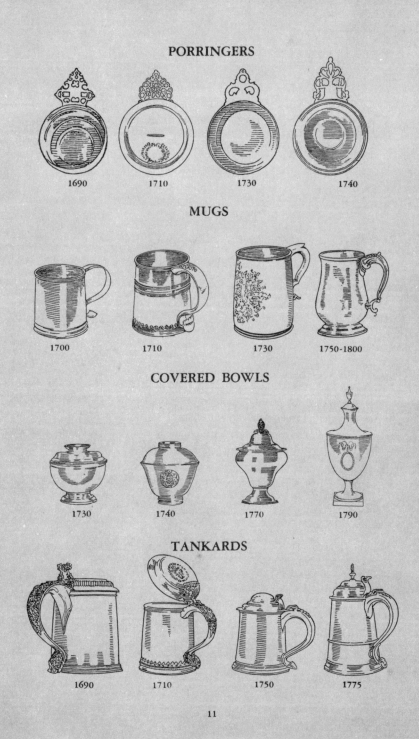

PORRINGERS

1690   1710   1730   1740

MUGS

1700   1710   1730   1750-1800

COVERED BOWLS

1730   1740   1770   1790

TANKARDS

1690   1710   1750   1775

11

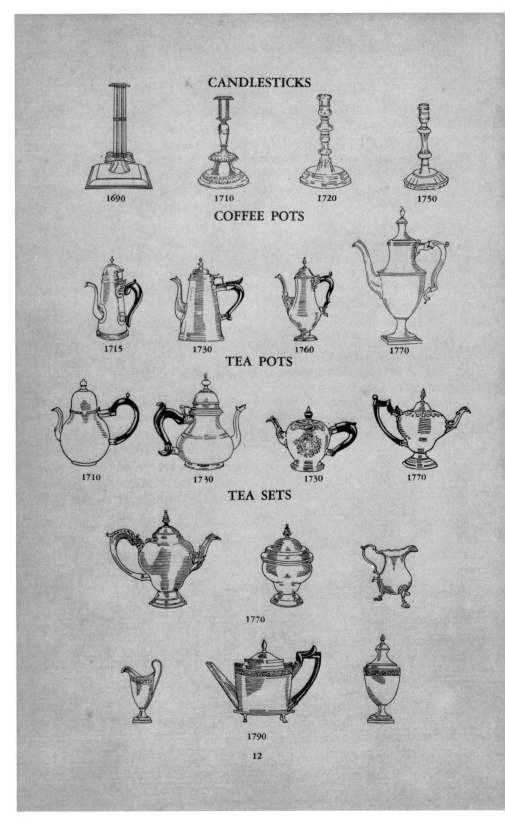

CANDLESTICKS

1690 1710 1720 1750

COFFEE POTS

1715 1730 1760 1770

TEA POTS

1710 1730 1730 1770

TEA SETS

1770

1790

12

from STEPHEN G. C. ENSKO 1937

AMERICAN SILVER SPOONS 1650-1825

The earliest example of an American silver spoon that has been discovered is known as the "Puritan" type, as illustrated, of 1650 date. With variations it was used until 1680 when the "trifid-end" was introduced. The decorations on the handle and the bowl of this spoon were not for long, nor was the "waved-end," as we trace the next development. Spoons of the above designs are of great rarity.

The general acceptance of the "rib-front" continued until about 1760 when we find a plain flat handle with an ovoid bowl. We find this style often engraved with the "feather-edge" and the "bright-cut" work of 1770 to 1790. The "rat-tail" on the back of the bowl changes to the double "drop," the single "drop," variations of the shell, the scroll, the bird, the leaf, and other forms of decoration.

The chart next shows the "pointed-end," sometimes engraved with the "ornamental cartouche," and the pointed bowl of 1790 to 1800. The last of the straight style spoons is known as the "coffin-end" of funeral token. With this end of possibilities the collector has the story of the American spoon. The "fiddle-back" type of spoon is offered rather for record than for interest. With exception of the graceful designs of the "Basket of Flowers" and the "Sheaf of Wheat", these 19th century spoons have little to recommend to any collection.

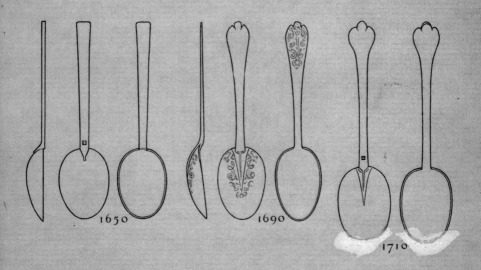

1650   1690   1710

13

STEPHEN G. C. ENSKO 1937

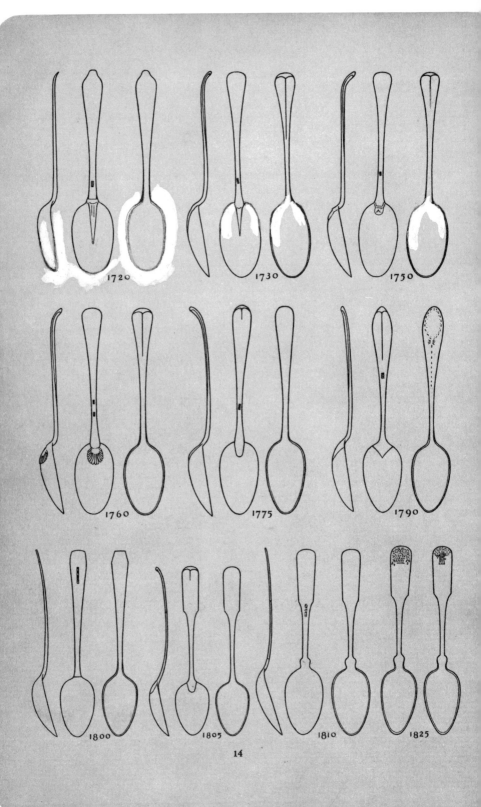

1720 1730 1750

1760 1775 1790

1800 1805 1810 1825

14

from STEPHEN G. C. ENSKO 1937

STANDARD AND ASSAY MARKS

Generally speaking the following marks were used from the end of the eighteenth century to the middle of the nineteenth. Two exceptions are Cesar Ghiselin with his star in 1713 and Philip Syng with his leaf marks. The reason for many of these stamps is not obvious. *Authorities on the history of Baltimore Assay Marks advise that from 1814 to 1830, and later, all assaying and stamping was carefully supervised by specially elected silversmiths.

It seems probable that other cities enjoyed some such organized regulation of standards. In New York the leading silversmiths were members of the Gold and Silversmiths Society after 1786. Boston had its powerful Massachusetts Charitable Mechanic Association. Only with careful research and investigation can we establish the fact that pseudo hall-marks were not a part of our Standard Marks.

*Maryland Silversmiths. Dr. J. Hall Pleasants and Howard Sill. Old Plate. J. H. Buck.

BALTIMORE ASSAY MARKS:

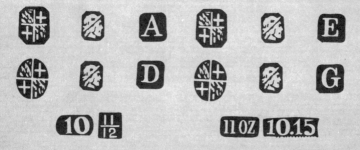

STANDARD MARKS:
1790-1810

16

m STEPHEN G. C. ENSKO 1937

1810 - 1850

PREMIUM   STANDARD

DOLLARS   STANDARD

DOLLAR   PURE COIN

Pure Coin   COIN

17

from STEPHEN G. C. ENSKO 1937

Andrew Billings B. Stonington, Conn. November 25, 1743. Oldest child of John Billings & his wife Elizabeth Page. Prot. apprenticed near his home. Known to have been in Poughkeepsie. 1773-4. Name appears on tax list in 1775. February 6, 1776 Capt. Billings was given orders to enlist another company. In 1774 contracted for making ‥ seals for N. Y. City for £15-10. Shop at main & academy streets until 1799. 1803 elected president of the village. Died 1808.

Children
Elizabeth 1779.
Cornelia 1781
Stonington 1785.
(But in N. Y.) ‥
an. 20. 1785.
Helen 1787
Maria 1789.
Harriet Belphame 1791.
Cadwalader Colden, 1793.

LIST OF ABBREVIATIONS:

Adv.	—	Advertised.
b.	—	Born.
BM.	—	Baltimore Assay Marks.
C.	—	Census of 1790.
d.	—	Died.
D.	—	Directory.
F.	—	Freeman.
M.	—	Married.
SM.	—	Standard Marks.

18

STEPHEN G. C. ENSKO 1937

IDENTIFIED MARKS OF AMERICAN SILVERSMITHS
1650 - 1850

Maker	Name	Place		Date
A ARMSTRONG / A Armstrong	Allen Armstrong	Philadelphia, Pa.	D.	1806
AB / AB / AB	Adrien Bancker	New York, N. Y.		1703-1772
A BEACH	Abel Buel	New Haven, Conn.		1742-1825
A BEACH	A. Beach	Hartford, Conn.		1823
A BILLINGS / A BILLING	A. Billing	Troy, N. Y.		1780
A BLANCHARD	Asa Blanchard	Lexington, Kentucky		1810
A BRADLEY	Abner Bradley	New Haven, Conn.		1753-1824
A BRASIER / A BRASIER	A. Brasier	New York, N. Y.		1790
AC	Alexander Camman	Albany, N. Y.	D.	1813
AC A CLEVELAND	Aaron Cleveland	Norwich, Conn.		1820
AC AC AC	Arnold Collins	Newport, R. I.	M.	1690
	Albert Cole	New York, N. Y.	D.	1844
A Carlile / A Carlile	Abraham Carlisle	Philadelphia, Pa.	D.	1791
A. C. BENEDICT	A. C. Benedict	New York, N. Y.	D.	1840
A C BENEDICT 28 BOWERY	A. C. Benedict	New York, N. Y.	D.	1840
A & C BRANDT	A. & C. Brandt	Philadelphia, Pa.	D.	1800
A C BURR	A. C. Burr	Providence, R. I.	D.	1815
A CUTLER BOSTON	A. Cutler	Boston, Mass.		1820
AD / AD AD AD	Amos Doolittle	New Haven, Conn.		1754-1832
AD AD	Abraham Dubois	Philadelphia, Pa.		1777
A DUBOIS A Dubois	Abraham Dubois	Philadelphia, Pa.		1777
AEW / A DIKEMAN	Andrew E. Warner B M	Baltimore, Md.		1786-1870
AE WARNER	Andrew E. Warner B M	Baltimore, Md.		1786-1870
A E WARNER STERLING	Andrew E. Warner B M	Baltimore, Md.		1786-1870
AF AF NYORK	Abraham G. Forbes	New York, N. Y.		1769
AGF NYORK	Abraham G. Forbes	New York, N. Y.		1769

HOWE & GUION (SM) Basket of Fruit Teaspoons

HS HGS - Hezekiah Silliman - Teaspoon Ca 1790

Howell	James Howell	Philadelphia, Pa.	D.	1802
HP	Henry Pitkin	East Hartford, Conn.		1834
H.PORTER&CO	Henry C. Porter & Co.	New York, N. Y.		1830
H.P.RICE Ⓐ	Henry P. Price	Philadelphia, Pa.		1810
HRT	Henry R. Truax	Albany, N. Y.	D.	1815
HRT	Henry R. Truax	Albany, N. Y.	D.	1815
HS	Hezekiah Silliman	New Haven, Conn.		1739-1804
H.SADD	Harvey Sadd	New Hartford, Conn.		1776-1840
H&S H&S	Hart & Smith	Baltimore, Md.	D.	1815
H ◆ S 🅢	Harris & Stanwood	Boston, Mass.		1835
Huntington	Philip Huntington	Norwich, Conn.		1770-1825
Hurd	Jacob Hurd	Boston, Mass.		1702-1758
HUTCHINS	Jacob Hutchins	New York, N. Y.		1774

- also without albany on cup.

HUTTON 🅐 ALBANY	Isaac Hutton	Albany, N. Y.		1767-1855
HW				
H&W Ⓐ	Hart & Wilcox	Norwich, Conn.		1805-1807

- Sugar Tongs Ca 1790 Hugh Wishart.

H.WALKER PHILA	Hannah Walker	Philadelphia, Pa.	D.	1816
H.WILSON	Hosea Wilson B M	Philadelphia, Pa.	Adv.	1812
H.WILSON&CO	H. Wilson & Co. B M	Philadelphia, Pa.		1815
H.WISHART 🅐	Hugh Wishart S M	New York, N. Y.	D.	1784
HYDE&GOODRICH	Hyde & Goodrich	New Orleans, N. Y.		1810
Hyde&Goodrich	Hyde & Goodrich	New Orleans, N. Y.		1810
Hyde&NEVINS	Hyde & Nevins	New York, N. Y.		1798
IA	Isaac Anthony	Newport, R. I.		1710
IA IA IA	John Allen	Boston, Mass.		1691-1760
IA I.Adam	I. Adam	Alexandria, Va.		1800
IA IAVERY	John Avery	Preston, Conn.		1732-1794

H.SCHOONMAKER - Fiddle Teaspoon Ca 1805

HW Fiddle Teaspoon Ca 1805

41

HUTTON 6 Tablespoons

432

Handwritten annotations at top: I·S·W — tea spoon. 1790. — Baskell. ✓

① J·F — Tea spoon with bird on Bowl ca 1785 ✓

Mark	Date	Mark	Date
A·G·PECK	1825 ✓	COOLEY	1790 ✓
A·LAUDER	1840 ✓	CPB	1800
A·LOWELL	1830 ✓	C·P&U	1830 ✓
A·MUNGER *	1833 ✓	C&W	1820 ✓
A&O	1820 ✓	⊙	1790 ✓
A·PRINCE	1825 ✓	E·ACKLEY	1820 ✓
A·S·DYGERT	1830 ✓	E·B·BOOTH	1850 ✓
A·TIERS	1790 ✓	E·BOWMAN	1810 ✓
A·STOOPS	1825 ✓	E·Braman	1830 ✓
S·Ayres	1790 ✓	E·COOK E·F·W	1820 ✓
BAYEUX S M	1825 ✓	E·CURRIER	1830 1828
B·BEMENT	1815 1805	E·F·Z	1810 ✓
B&C	1815 ✓	E·G	1790 ✓
B·J·R	1780 ✓	E·GUEY	1820 ✓
B·H	1780 ✓	E&I	1820 ✓
B&P N·York	1770 ✓	F·TARBELL	1830 ✓
BRINSMAID'S B&H	1830 ✓	E·B·COOK	1820 ✓
B·R·Jenkins	1835 ✓	FJD	1840 ✓
B·E *	1750 ✓	FLOYD SMITH	1830 ✓
Burke	1790 ✓	FWD	1780 ✓
C&Y	1810 ✓	G·ARNOLD	1820 ✓
C·F·McKINNEY S M	1825 ✓	G&C	1775 ✓
C·J·MONSON	1815 ✓	G·GATTHER	1825 ✓
C·N·S	1810 ✓	G·M	1750 ✓
C&N	1815 ✓	GODDARD	1810 ✓
COCHRANE	1820 ✓	G·W·KING	1790 ✓

Handwritten annotations (right margin): Backe — Clark Pelletreau & N.y. — Edmund M. Laura Jn — Salem mass.

Handwritten (left of BAYEUX): Troy n.y.

*Barent TenEyck,
Albany, New York, 1739-1810

*A. Munger
Auburn, N. Y.; 1833 ✓

Handwritten: 1714 - 1795 — WORKING 1756 FOR SIR WM JOHNSON — (HASTINGS) — 80

from STEPHEN G. C. ENSKO 1937

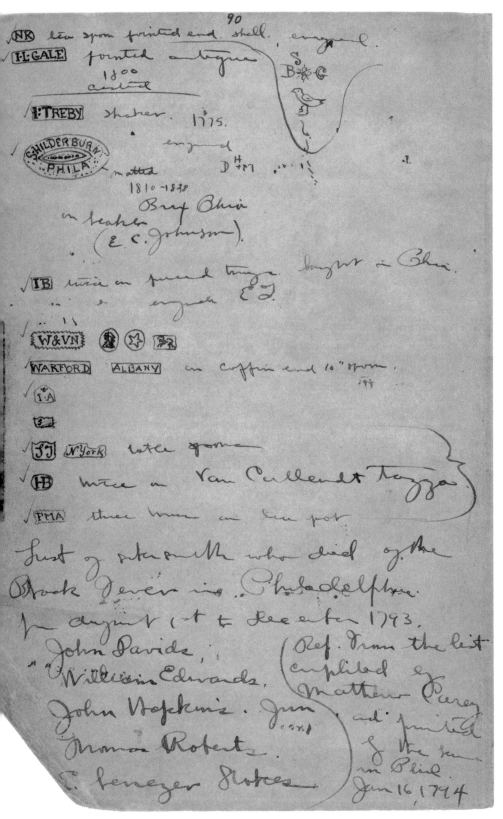

AMERICAN SILVERSMITHS

and

THEIR MARKS III

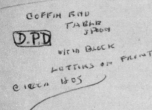

BY

STEPHEN G. C. ENSKO

PRIVATELY PRINTED

ROBERT ENSKO, INC.

Gold and Silversmiths

NEW YORK

1948

from STEPHEN G. C. ENSKO 1948

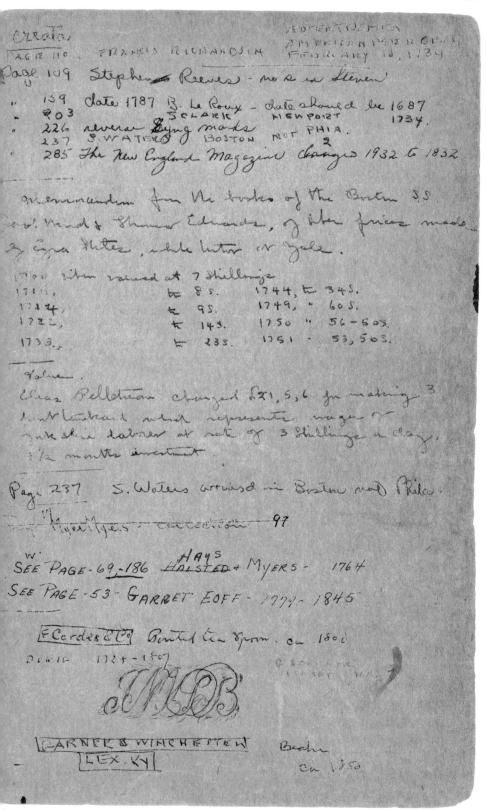

Errata

PAGE 110 FRANCIS RICHARDSON ADVERTISEMEN AMERICAN MERCURY FEBRUARY 18, 1734

Page 109 Stephens Reeves - no s in Steven

" 159 date 1787 B. Le Roux - date should be 1687
" 203 S CLARK NEWPORT 1734
" 226 reverse dying marks NEWPORT PHIA.
237 S. WATERS BOSTON NOT 2
" 285 The New England Magazine changes 1932 to 1832

Memorandum from the books of the Boston S.S. Revd. Nend & Shmus Edwards, of silver prices made by Ezra Stiles, while tutor at Yale.

1700 silver valued at 7 shillings
1713, ℔ 8 s. 1744, ℔ 34 s.
1714, ℔ 9 s. 1749, " 60 s.
1722, ℔ 14 s. 1750 " 56 - 50 s.
1733, ℔ 23 s. 1751 - 53, 50 s.

Value.
Elias Pelletreau charged £1, 5, 6 for making 3 tankard which represents wages of gold skin labourer at rate of 3 shillings a day, 1/2 months investment.

Page 237 S. Waters worked in Boston and Phila.

Myers Myers - correction - 97

W. HAYS
SEE PAGE-69,-186 HALSTED + MYERS - 1764
SEE PAGE -53- GARRET EOFF - 1779 - 1845

F Cordes & Co Printed tea spoon. ca 1800
D (W) 1724 - 1807

GARNER & WINCHESTER
LEX. KY

Beale
ca 1850

STEPHEN G. C. ENSKO 1948

THE ASSOCIATION OATH ROLLS OF THE
BRITISH PLANTATIONS, NEW YORK, VIRGINIA F
AD. 1696.   GANDY   PUB. 1922
                                LONDON

PAGES PAGES.   34 - 47

36 EVERARDUS BOGARDUS.   PA P. AUBIN
38 GERRIT   SNEKELBOGH   CHANNEL ISLANDS
40 JESSE   KIP   1740-50
43 CORNELIUS VANDER BURCH   COFFEE POT
44 JOHANNIS   NISS   FOLGER
                                            COFFEE
44 JACOBUS   VANDER SPIEGEL   COLLECTION
44 ANDRUS   HENDRECUIE   SEE CONNOISSEUR
45 BARTH   LE ROUX   JULY. 1965
44 JACOBM MARIUS GROEN   P. 210
44 SURIJAN   BLANCK

        IW   a spice box $Z \, {}^{P} M$

_____

ANTIQUES, JULY 1963
FREEMAN HINCKLEY, BARNSTABLE. MASS.   finial
B. 1759. MARK. $\boxed{FH}$ SPOONS CIRCA 1790-1800
D. 1808.
EL PALET LORING, BARNSTABLE
B. 1740. D. 1768 M. ABIGAIL, DAU MOODY RUSSELL
APPRAISAL OF ESTATE , "SHOP TOOLS & WROUGHT SILVER 54:19:6
MARK $\boxed{E. LORING}$ AND POSSIBLY USED BY SON. JR.

                ON EITHER
SOLD
P. B. GAL
OCT 3-5, 1940
CAT. 212
#450
6"H. MARKED ON EITHER SIDE
ENGRAVED   OR HANDLE OF
IM UNDER BASE   TEA POT.

from STEPHEN G. C. ENSKO 1948

3

CONTENTS

4

from STEPHEN G. C. ENSKO 1948

ACKNOWLEDGEMENTS

I wish to express my sincere and grateful thanks to Dorothea E. Wyle and Vernon C. Wyle for invaluable help and inspiring cooperation in the preparation and progress of this work.

I appreciate the suggestions and friendly interest extended to me by Prof. John M. Phillips, Director, Yale University Art Gallery; Curator of The Mabel Brady Garvan Collection.

I desire to thank Kathryn C. Buhler, Museum of Fine Arts, Boston, for gracious assistance and constructive criticism.

To Helen Burr Smith I am deeply indebted for the scholarly work of Chapter III, listing silversmiths and showing their locations on the maps of New York, Boston, Philadelphia; and for research work and generous contributions of information and dates.

I am indebted for information to: C. Louise Avery, Metropolitan Museum, N. Y.; Lockwood Barr, Margaret M. Bridwell, E. Milby Burton, Charleston Museum, S. C.; Dr. George B. Cutten, Stephen Decatur, Carl W. Drepperd, Henry F. du Pont, Caroline R. Foulke, Harrold E. Gillingham, Jessie Harrington, Mrs. John Russel Hastings, John D. Hatch, Albany Institute of History and Art, N. Y.; Edwin J. Hipkiss, Museum of Fine Arts, Boston; Stanley Ineson, Walter M. Jeffords, Rhea M. Knittle, Dr. J. Hall Pleasants, Elizabeth B. Potwine, Mrs. Harold I. Pratt, Mrs. Alfred C. Prime, Beverley R. Robinson, Frank O. Spinney, Andrew V. Stout, Mr. and Mrs. Charles Messer Stow, R. W. G. Vail, New-York Historical Society; Mabel C. Weaks, Alice Winchester. To friends and acquaintances who have given me permission to use photographs, and have supplied marks and information, I wish to express my thanks and appreciation.

I am indebted for the use of illustrations to: Mrs. Adelyn B. Breeskin, Baltimore Museum of Art, Md.; Erwin Christiansen, Index of American Design, National Gallery of Art, Washington, D. C.; Downtown Assn., New York; Joseph Downs, Metropolitan Museum of Art, N. Y.; Helen S. Foote, Cleveland Museum of Art, Ohio; V. Isabelle Miller, Museum of the City of New York; Charles Nagel, Brooklyn Institute of Arts and Sciences, N. Y.; Russell A. Plimpton, Minneapolis Institute of Arts, Minn.; Robert H. Tannahill, Detroit Institute of Arts, Mich.; Josephine Setze, Art Gallery, Yale University.

To my wife Dorothea W. Ensko, I owe the greatest debt, for the many years that she has cheerfully given her assistance and generous encouragement.

STEPHEN G. C. ENSKO

New York.

7

INTRODUCTION

STUDY of American silver leads into many fields of interest and profit. One of them is history in general. Another is history in some of its subdivisions — economic, social, esthetic. Best of all, however, it leads to a better understanding and appreciation of the ethos of America.

Now ethos is a word which I believe ought to appear oftener in our thinking. The dictionary definition of it is "the character, sentiment or disposition of a community or people; the spirit which actuates manners and customs." More concretely, I think, the ethos of America is that characteristic inherent in its mentality, its customs and its handiwork which may be comprehended in the phrase the American Way of Life.

So thoroughly is the American ethos embodied in the works of American silversmiths that it has given to their product a typical identity and it never can be mistaken for that of any other country, though other nations may have influenced design and workmanship. Traces of English ostentation, French flourish and Spanish and Italian rococo fussiness may be found, but all these influences have been transmuted into American forthrightness and simplicity.

The same process is seen in the work of American cabinetmakers. Nobody mistakes a Philadelphia Chippendale chair for its English prototype or a Duncan Phyfe Federal period table for its English Regency model. Even the houses our ancestors built, though patterned after those of Georgian England, were so changed by the American ethos that we consider them typically American.

We learn from the earliest silver made in this country that the American spirit is no phenomenon of recent political origin. It started long before America was a nation.

The seventeenth century silversmiths of New England and New York followed English Jacobean and Restoration and Dutch styles, but altered and simplified their copies so that even the earliest known American silver had an individuality of its own — it signified an American ethos already initiated.

One of the contributing causes of the American spirit expressed by our silversmiths was the ingenuity and native skill demanded of them. In the seventeenth century the master silversmiths of London complained to the Guild Hall that their trade had become too specialized. Too many different craftsmen, they grumbled, must contribute to the making of a single piece — the hammerers, the planishers, the handle molders, the engravers. In America one journeyman silversmith accomplished all the kinds of work done in England by shop specialists.

Study of American silver in connection with certain phases of American history shows that it is a record of the economic and esthetic life of the colonies, all and each. At first, cups, tankards, beakers, porringers and other household utensils were made out of the silver acquired by the owner in trade or commerce. They were his equivalent of a savings bank.

from STEPHEN G. C. ENSKO 1948

8

INTRODUCTION

As wealth increased, household silver became an index of the owner's financial status and an indication of his manner of living. Pride of possession led him to have initials or armorial bearings engraved on his silver and these, together with the maker's marks are often an invaluable help to genealogists and other historians.

Study of the variations found in the silver produced in the various colonies is rewarding for the light it throws on local characteristics.

New England silversmiths followed more nearly the designs of England than did the craftsmen of other colonies, perhaps because New England's customs were more like those of Old England than any other colony — except Virginia. There the ties were so close that most of its silver as well as everything else was bought in London. Philadelphia, too, followed English styles (with modifications) but because of Quaker tolerance, design there in every branch of craftsmanship was more or less eclectic.

New York silver is considered to offer the best opportunity for tracing the process of Americanization at work. The city's earliest silversmiths, of course, were Dutch. Then came the English and the French Huguenots. Not one of these alien craftsmen continued the traditions learned in his apprenticeship in Europe. All succeeded in producing something typically American.

When the rococo and chinoiserie fashions flourished in the England of George II, New York silver remained simple, strong, almost stark. When England tired of fussy design toward the end of the eighteenth century and turned to the classics for inspiration, New York silversmiths, and those in the other centers, too, accepted the forms, but made modifications of ornament into a simplicity dictated by the American ethos.

All these suggestions as to the importance of the silversmith, with many others, are to be found in this book, which itself is the most complete study of American silver and its makers yet achieved. Mr. Ensko reckons American silver a manifestation of the American ethos, for he is convinced that it embodies the ingenuity, the spirit and all the other intangible factors that have made America what it is. He believes also that a study of the subject will quicken consciousness to grasp the need for preserving the American ethos, and in this I heartily concur.

CHARLES MESSER STOW.

11

Chapter I

NAMES OF EARLY AMERICAN SILVERSMITHS
1650-1850

HIS LIST of early American silversmiths has been compiled for the convenience of those desiring to know more about the craftsmen who fashioned early American silver. To facilitate reference the names have been listed in alphabetical order. All sources of available information have been used with a considerable amount of critical correction. In keeping with the original intention of this book only silversmiths and allied craftsmen who can be identified with known examples of their workmanship have been included in this list. With the names of silversmiths are earliest working dates; hyphenated double dates indicate births and deaths; and locations of business mentioned are followed by records of marriages, freemanships, apprenticeships, and other pertinent information.

* * * * *

To appreciate and understand the pieces of early American silver illustrated in this chapter it is necessary to know the lines and forms, and the styles of decoration of the various periods represented. This is not difficult if we keep in mind the influence of the early Chinese designs and the evolution into the Grecian shapes. In some instances we find the English and Continental prototypes of slightly later date, especially in the beginning of the eighteenth century, but generally speaking the designs and workmanship are more or less contemporary.

Presenting a simple picture of this development in the eighteenth century we note a globular bowl of 1725 changing into the elongated pear-shape of about 1750, and to the Grecian vase form of 1775. This considerable change in a span of fifty years is also to be found in the square tray conforming to the later fashionable curved outlines; the straight-sided, flat-top tankard acquiring a bulbous body and stepped-domed cover; all reflecting the general tendency to greater height and tapering line. For further study and educative interest the author refers the student to the bibliography included in this book.

from STEPHEN G. C. ENSKO 1948

12

A

JOHN W. ABBOTT [J.ABBOT] 1790-1850
Portsmouth, N. H., 1839, at Market Square.

FRANCIS M. ACKLEY 1797
New York at 95 Warren Street; Bowery Lane; Henry Street; until 1800.

JOHN ADAM, JR. 1780-1843
Alexandria, Va., advertised after 1800. Was also noted Musician and Artist.

PYGAN ADAMS [P.A] 1712-1776
New London, Conn., 1735. Son of Rev. Eliphalet Adams. Married Ann Richards,
May 5, 1744. Capt. Adams held prominent public offices. General Assembly,
1753-1765. Died in New London.

NATHAN ADAMS WISCASSET, ME -1755-1825 [ADAMS] [N·A] N 1755

WILLIAM L. ADAMS 1831
New York at 620 Greenwich Street; 10 Elm Street in 1835. Noted politician.
President of the Board of Alderman, 1842-3. In Troy, 1844-1850.

EDWIN ADRIANCE 1809-1852
St. Louis, Mo., 1835. Born in Hopewell, N. Y. Son of Abraham Adriance and his
Wife Anna Storm. Married Elizabeth O'Connor. Firm of Mead, Adriance & Co.;
Mead & Adriance 1831.

GEORGE AIKEN 1765-1832
Baltimore, Md., in Calvert Street in 1787; 118 Baltimore Street in 1815. Married
Sarah Leret McConnell 1803.

JOHN AITKEN 1785
Philadelphia, Pa., at 607 Second Street, 48 Chestnut Street 1791. No record after
1814. Advertised as, "Gold and Silversmith, Clockmaker, Musical Instrument
Manufacturer and Copper-Plate Engraver".

JOHN B. AKIN 1820-1860
Danville, Ky., 1850.

CHARLES ALDIS 1814
New York at 399 Broadway; 23 Elm Street in 1815.

ISAAC ALEXANDER 1850
New York at 422 Grand Street.

SAMUEL ALEXANDER 1797
Philadelphia at South Second Street until 1808. Firm of Wiltberger & Alexander.

GEORGE HENRY
ALEXANDER & RIKER 1797
New York, at 350 Pearl Street until 1798. *DISSOLVED MARCH 15, 1800*
GEORGE ALEXANDER DIED 89 YEARS OF AGE

ALLCOCK & ALLEN *SILVERSMITH AND JEWELLER* 1820
New York. *NOTICE N.Y. GAZETTE AND*
GENERAL ADVERTISER - APRIL 20 1801

CHARLES ALLEN 1760
Boston, Mass.

ISAAC ALLARD, BELFAST, ME. 1799-1864
[I. ALLARD. JR.]

STEPHEN G. C. ENSKO 1948

[Left margin handwritten:] NEW YORK, AT 303 WATER STREET, (ROSE STREET) IN 1792.

80

NAMES OF EARLY AMERICAN SILVERSMITHS

CORNELIUS KIERSTEDE 1674-1757

New York, 1696. Born December 25, and baptized January 5, 1675, son of Hans and Joanna Loockermans Kierstede. Married (1) Elizabeth ....;(2) Sarah Ellsworth, daughter of Clement and Anna Maria Engelbrecht Ellsworth, in 1708. Appointed Freeman, May 30th, 1702. After 1725 removed to New Haven, Connecticut, where he advertised at Church Street.

LEWIS A. KIMBALL 1837

Buffalo, N. Y.

WILLIAM KIMBERLY 1790

New York at 35 Crown Street; 7 Fly Market in 1792. Advertised, October 5, 1795, *The American Mercury;* "Three journeymen that can work at different branches of the gold and silversmith's trade." Notice of large importation in 1797. Later proprietor of hardware store. Probably in Baltimore, 1804-1821, where he married Elizabeth Webb. Died in 1821.

THOMAS R. KING 181)

Baltimore, Md.

THOMAS KINNEY 1786-1824

Norwich, Conn., 1807, at Shetucket Street. Thomas, Jr. in Cortlandt, N. Y., 1836. Spelled Kinne.

DAVID I. KINSEY 1845

Cincinnati, Ohio, until 1848.

E. & D. KINSEY 1845

Cincinnati, Ohio, at Main and Walnut Streets.

JESSE KIP 1660-1722

New York, 1682. Baptized in Dutch Reformed Church, December 19, 1660, son of Jacob Hendrickson Kip and Maria de la Montague Kip. Married Maria Stevens, September 30, 1695. Held public offices with other silversmiths in the North Ward. Died in Newtown, April, 1722.

GEORGE KIPPEN 1790-1845

Bridgeport, Conn., 1815. Born in Middletown. Apprenticed to Charles Brewer. In partnership with Barzillai Benjamin. In 1824 advertised at corner of Beaver and Broad Streets. Worked with Elias Camp. Last record, with George A. Hoyt.

SAMUEL KIRK 1793-1872

Baltimore, Md., 1815. Born in Doylestown, Pa., of Quaker ancestry. Apprenticed to James Howell, 1810. Opened shop, August 5, 1815 when he advertised for trade. At 212 Market Street in 1816. Partnership with Smith until 1820. Petitioned for modification of Baltimore Assay Law. In 1846 admitted son, Henry Child Kirk into business, founding, S. Kirk, Sons, Co., Inc.

KIRK & SMITH 1817

Baltimore, Md., until 1821.

PETER KIRKWOOD 1790

Chestertown, later Annapolis, Md., 1800.

JOHN KITTS 1838

Louisville, Ky. Associated with Lemon & Kendrick, 1841. In partnership with William D. Scott, 1843. Formed John Kitts & Company, 1859-1878.

CUPS

John Coney
1679

Edward Winslow
1710

John Coney
1718

Jacob Hurd
1725

Jeremiah Dummer
1700

Gerrit Onckelbag
1695

Samuel Vernon
1725

446

STANDING CUPS

Samuel Edwards, 1739

Jeremiah Dummer
1700

Paul Revere
1782

FLAGON

Edward Winslow
1713

TANKARDS

Henry Hurst
1700

Robert Sanderson
1675

Cornelius Vanderburgh
1690

Simeon Soumaine, 1715

Edward Winslow
1700

Samuel Vernon
1710

Peter Van Dyke
1725

TANKARDS

John Coney
1715

John Coddington
1715

Jacob Hurd
1730

Adrian Bancker
1730

Philip Syng
1750

Samuel Minott
1770

Paul Revere
1790

BEAKERS

I. B.
1690

Jeremiah Dummer
1700

Moody Russell
1719

Jacob Hurd
1740

Cornelius Vanderburgh
1685

Myer Myers
1775

John W. Forbes
1833

Garret Eoff
1825

John Kitts
1845

CUPS

| John Coney | Simeon Soumaine | John Coney |
| 1700 | 1710 | 1710 |

| Henricus Boelen | Isaac Anthony | Philip Syng |
| 1730 | 1730 | 1730 |

| Samuel Minott | Paul Revere | William Gale |
| 1770 | 1792 | 1830 |

from STEPHEN G. C. ENSKO 1948

SPOUT CUPS

John Coney
1700

Jacob Boelen
1710

Jeremiah Dummer
1700

Allen & Edwards
1710

John Coburn
1760

John Coney
1715

PITCHERS

Paul Revere
1800

William Thompson
1815

Ebenezer Moulton
1811

Isaac Hutton
1800

John Crawford
1825

William Forbes
1835

from STEPHEN G. C. ENSKO 1948

BOWLS

Cornelius Kierstede
1710

Jacob Hurd
1738

Cornelius Vanderburgh
1690

William Homes
1763

Samuel Bowne
1790

PORRINGERS

Hull & Sanderson
1660

Peter Van Dyke
1715

Benjamin Burt
1760

Jan Van Nieukirke
1715

Johannis Nys
1715

Andrew B
1775

Tobias Stoutenburgh
1740

John B. Jones
1815

from STEPHEN G. C. ENSKO 1948

TEAPOTS

John Coney
1710

Unmarked
1700

Peter Van Dyke
1710

Jacob Hurd
1730

Myer Myers, 1750

Elias Boudinot, 1750

Joseph and Nathaniel Richardson
1775

Daniel Van Voorhis
1790

TEAPOTS

Paul Revere
1785

Philip Dally
1790

William G. Forbes
1800

Paul Revere
1790

William B. Heyer
1815

Thomas Fletcher
1835

COFFEE POTS

Peter Van Dyke
1715

Edward Winslow
1700

John Burt, 1735

David Hall
1760

Philip Syng
1765

Samuel Williamson
1790

HOT WATER KETTLES AND STANDS, CHAFING DISH, DISH CROSS

Cornelius Kierstede
1710

Joseph Richardson
1760

Adrian Bancker
1725

Samuel Tingley
1765

TEA SETS

Abraham Dubois, 1790

Paul Revere, 1799

Jacob G. Lansing, 1765

Daniel Van Voorhis, 1790

TEA SETS

Shepherd & Boyd, 1815

Joel Sayre, 1808

John Sayre, 1825

John Crawford, 1825

from STEPHEN G. C. ENSKO 1948

CREAMERS

Josiah Austin, 1740

Daniel C. Fueter
1755

Bancroft Woodcock
1760

Myer Myers
1775

Freeman Woods
1790

Samuel Richards
1800

Elias Pelletreau
1810

Charles A. Burnett
1825

CANDLESTICKS
SNUFFER STAND

Jeremiah Dummer
1686

Cornelius Kierstede
1710

Cornelius Kierstede
1710

Joseph Lownes
1790

John Coney, 1700

Edward Winslow, 1725

Samuel Tingley
1765

William G. Forbes
1800

Frederick Marquand
1825

from STEPHEN G. C. ENSKO 1948

SUGAR BOWLS

Jacob Hurd
1725

Jacob Hurd
1740

John LeRoux
1750

William Gilbert
1770

Jacob Boelen II
1765

Paul Revere
1775

Daniel Dupuy
1790

John Leacock
1760

Isaac Hutton
1800

TEA CADDIES

Christian Wiltberger
1790

Thauvet Besley
1730

Nathaniel Vernon
1820

PUNCH STRAINERS

Jonathan Clarke
1765

Paul Revere
1765

Bartholomew Le Roux
1740

CASTERS, MUFFINEERS

William Jones
1725

Peter Van Dyke
1725

Jacobus Vander Spiegel
1690

Peter Van Dyke
1710

Philip Goelet
1735

Adrian Bancker
1725

Philip Syng
1750

Daniel Henchman
1760

SALT DISHES

MUSTARD POTS

Simeon Soumaine
1725

Jacob G. Lansing
1700

Jacob Hurd
1730

Peter Van Dyke
1710

Jeremiah Dummer
1690

Joseph Shoemaker
1790

Philip Syng
1750

Daniel Van Voorhis
1790

Lewis Fueter
1775

SUGAR BOXES

Edward Winslow
1702

John Coney
1700

INKSTANDS

John Coney
1700

Philip Syng
1752

TRAYS

Thomas Savage
1700

Henry Pratt
1725

Adrian Bancker
1725

Charles Le Roux
1740

Elias Boudinot
1760

from STEPHEN G. C. ENSKO 1948

SAUCE DISHES

Charles Le Roux
1715

Paul Revere
1745

Gerrit Onckelbag & Jesse Kip
1695

Joseph Richardson
1760

John & Tunis Denise
1800

Joseph Anthony
1785

DISHES AND TUREENS

John Coburn
1764

William Cowell
1716

Joseph Richardson
1775

William Gale
1825

John W. Forbes
1830

Charles L. Boehme
1800

BOXES

William Jones, 1730

Philip Syng
1725

Garret Forbes, 1810

Jacob Hurd
1730

John Ewan
1825

CLASPS AND KNITTING
NEEDLE HOLDERS

Philip Goelet, 1730

Joseph Shoemaker, 1800

FLATWARE

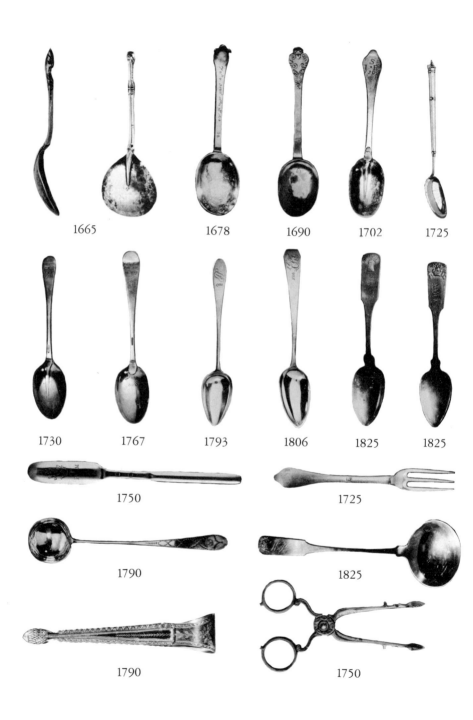

1665   1678   1690   1702   1725

1730   1767   1793   1806   1825   1825

1750   1725

1790   1825

1790   1750

NINETEENTH CENTURY

Wood & Hughes
1845

William Gale
1845

Gale & Hughes
1846

149

Chapter II

MARKS OF EARLY AMERICAN SILVERSMITHS

1650-1850

THE HISTORY of the makers' marks is of broad interest and a matter for special study. A mark essentially is a sign of a merchant or shopkeeper, although its implied significance is to identify an artist-craftsman. Careful attention to the details of a mark is necessary for accurate comparison, identification and attribution. For easy reference and for clarity of presentation the letters of the initials and names of the silversmiths have been listed alphabetically. These early American makers' marks found on various places of pieces of silver fashioned by these skillful craftsmen are as a rule enclosed in rectangles, ovals, shaped shields, and sometimes in the earlier marks, accompanied in combination with symbols such as a cross, crescent, bird, animal, crown, etc.

This system of marking with the silversmith's stamp is not new. In the Old World the master craftsman, when too distant from the Guild-Hall, used his private mark without the hall-marks of the town, city or country. The silversmith of good reputation was responsible for standard of quality of silver and fine workmanship and the patron accepted the pieces of silver in confidence and appreciation. This practice of marking silver in the New World without controls dates from 1650 until the present day, with only one exception.

Later at the close of the eighteenth century and the early part of the nineteenth century we find additional marks of eagles, eagles' heads, sheaves of wheat, stars, and other stamps with pseudo English hall-marks. There were probably used to distinguish silversmiths' work and possibly to compete with English imported silver. In 1814 the State of Maryland passed a law requiring all silver fashioned in Baltimore to be stamped with three marks, Arms of Baltimore, a date-letter, and the Head of Liberty, in addition to the maker's mark. This law was not too popular and was not enforced after 1830 when the practice was discontinued.

In conjunction with marks of similar makers' initials the identification of a piece of early American silver may sometimes be established by tracing the engraved arms or cyphers of the original owner. Genealogical and historical research is very important in proving conclusively the authenticity of a piece of silver.

from STEPHEN G. C. ENSKO 1948

handwritten: ° DUPONT COLLECTION. (170)

150

MARKS OF EARLY AMERICAN SILVERSMITHS

° A·ARMSTRONG	A. Armstrong	Philadelphia	1806
AB AB	Adrian Bancker	New York	1725
AB *(mark)*			
AB *1805 Table spoon*	Andrew Billings	Poughkeepsie, N. Y.	1773
AB *abner Bradley Watertown Conn.*			*1778*
AB (AB)	Abel Buel	New Haven, Conn.	~~1777~~ *1761*
ALSO			
A·BEACH A·BEACH	A. Beach	Hartford, Conn.	1823
ABHALL	Abraham B. Hall	Geneva, N. Y.	1806
[G] *over* WILLIAM *ERASED STAMP ON TWO BRIGHT-CUT* A·BILLING *TABLE SPOONS*			
A·BILLINGS	Andrew Billings	Poughkeepsie, N. Y.	1773
(A·BLANCHARD) *Beaker engraved B.*			
A·BLANCHARD	Asa Blanchard	Lexington, Ky.	1808
* A·BRADLEY *	Abner Bradley	Watertown, Conn.	1778
A·BRASIER	Anable Brasier	New York	1790
EAGLE			
O A·BRINDSMAID O	Abraham Brinsmaid	Burlington, Vt.	~~1815~~ *1809*
AC	Alexander Cameron	Albany, N. Y.	1813
AC AC *Table spoon ca 1765*	Abraham Carlisle *detail*	Philadelphia	1791
AC *design a lock of bowl*	Aaron Cleveland	Norwich, Conn.	1820
(AC) AC AC	Arnold Collins	Newport, R. I.	1690
(marks)	Albert Cole	New York	1844
AC *Albert Cole's A·Coles· MASS.*			
ALEXANDER BROUCKESHANKS BOSTON 1768			
A·Carlisle	Abraham Carlisle	Philadelphia	1791

P.M.—Pseudo English Hall Marks. S.M.—Standard Marks. B.M.—Baltimore Assay Office Marks.

CARD
INDEX
NO &14
RED

BIBLIOGRAPHY

This list of publications of early American silver covers the subject from 1832 to 1948. The chronological arrangement is offered to show the development of everspreading interest in this absorbing study. For original research more information will be found in old public records, newspapers, directories, town histories, and other sources too numerous to mention and include here.

BOOK AND EXHIBITION CATALOGUES

*CATALOGUE OF ALBANY'S BICENTENNIAL LOAN EXHIBITION AT ALBANY ACADEMY. 1886. /

OLD PLATE, ECCLESIASTICAL, DECORATIVE, AND DOMESTIC. Its Makers and Marks by J. H. Buck, New York. 1888. 2

THE LIFE OF COLONEL PAUL REVERE. By Elbridge Henry Goss. Two Volumes. 1891. 3

PAUL REVERE AND HIS ENGRAVING. By William Loring Andrews. 1901. +

OLD PLATE. Its Makers and Marks by J. H. Buck, New and Enlarged Edition, New York. 1903. 5

CATALOGUE OF THE ANTIQUE SILVER. By the Mary Floyd Tallmadge Chapter, Daughters of the American Revolution, Litchfield, Connecticut. 1903. 6

*AMERICAN SILVER. The Work of 17th and 18th Century Silversmiths. Exhibited at the Museum of Fine Arts, Boston. 1906. Introduction by R. T. Haines Halsey.   2 COPIES IN STOCK   7

THE HUDSON-FULTON CELEBRATION. Catalogue of an Exhibition held at the Metropolitan Museum of Art. Volume II. New York. 1909. 8

CATALOGUE OF THE LOAN EXHIBITION ON THE TWO HUNDRED AND FIFTIETH ANNIVERSARY OF THE FOUNDING OF THE TOWN OF NORWICH, CONNECTICUT, 1659-1909. Faith Trimbull Chapter, D.A.R. 9

*THE METROPOLITAN MUSEUM OF ART. Catalogue of an Exhibition of Silver used in New York, New Jersey and The South with a Note on Early New York Silversmiths by R. T. Haines Halsey. New York. 1911. 10

EARLY SILVERSMITHS OF CONNECTICUT. By George Munson Curtis. 1913 1913 11

*AMERICAN CHURCH SILVER, of the Seventeenth and Eighteenth Centuries with a few Pieces of Domestic Plate Exhibited at the Museum of Fine Arts, Boston. 1911. Introduction by George Munson Curtis. Explanation of terms by Florence V. Paull. 12

COPLEY SOCIETY RETROSPECTIVE EXHIBITION OF DECORATIVE ARTS. Copley Hall, Boston, Mass. 1911. 13

COLONIAL SILVERSMITHS, MASTERS AND APPRENTICES
BY KATHRYN BUHLER 1956
BOSTON MUSEUM OF FINE ARTS

AN EXHIBITION OF AMERICAN SILVER AND ART TREASURES
SPONSORED BY THE ENGLISH-SPEAKING UNION, LONDON 1960

SILVERSMITHS OF VIRGINIA, GEORGE BARTON COTTEN
1952

HANDBOOK OF AMERICAN SILVER AND PEWTER MARKS BY
C. JORDON THORN   (NOT AUTHORITATIVE)
1949

FROM COLONY TO NATION, THE ART INSTITUTE OF CHICAGO
1949 EXHIBITION OF AMERICAN PAINTING, SILVER AND
ARCHITECTURE 1650-1812 BY HANS STEYRIC R.ROGERS.

* MYER MYERS, GOLDSMITH   JANETTE W ROSENBAUM
1954

THE ARTS AND CRAFTS IN NEW YORK 1777-1799.
BY RITA GOTTESMAN, PUB, NEW YORK HISTORICAL SOCIETY
1954

THE WALDRON PHOENIX BELKNAP, JR, COLLECTION OF
PORTRAITS AND SILVER, EDITED BY
JOHN MARSHALL PHILLIPS, BARBARA N. PARKER AND
KATHRYN C. BUHLER, EXHIBITED, NEW YORK HISTORICAL
1955   SOCIETY

PAUL REVERE, GOLDSMITH, MUSEUM OF FINE ARTS,
1956, BY KATHRYN C. BUHLER.   BOSTON

AMERICAN SILVER BY PHILIP H. HAMMERSLOUGH
1958   HIS COLLECTION

AMERICAN SILVER IN THE HENRY FRANCIS DU PONT
WINTERTHUR MUSEUM
1958 BY MARTHA GANDY FALES

* THE ARTS AND CRAFTS OF NEWPORT, R.I. BY Ralph E. CARPENTER, JR.
                                              1954

First floor (rear section) of Robert Ensko, Inc.
682 Lexington Avenue, New York (CA 1940)

AMERICAN SILVERSMITHS AND THEIR MARKS
has been set at Meriden-Stinehour Press in Garamond,
an old style typeface derived from French sixteenth-century sources
and one notable for the legibility of its letters,
especially in the smaller sizes, as well as the brilliance of the cutting.
It is loosely based on the *caractères de l'Université*
found in the Imprimerie Nationale in France.

Designed by C. Freeman Keith
and printed at Meriden-Stinehour Press in Lunenburg, Vermont,
on Mohawk Superfine, an entirely acid-free paper.